On the Administrative Law of China in Addressing Climate Change

Shirong Fang · Binglin Tan

On the Administrative Law of China in Addressing Climate Change

華中科技大學出版社
Huazhong University of Science and Technology Press

Springer

Shirong Fang
School of Law
Zhongnan University of Economics and Law
Wuhan, Hubei, China

Binglin Tan
Zhongnan University of Economics and Law
Wuhan, Hubei, China

Translated by
Yahui Jin
School of Foreign Studies
Zhongnan University of Economics and Law
Wuhan, China

Supported by the National Social Science Fund 2011 Key Projects (Project Approval Number: 11AFX011).

ISBN 978-981-19-7704-6 ISBN 978-981-19-7705-3 (eBook)
https://doi.org/10.1007/978-981-19-7705-3

Jointly published with Huazhong University of Science and Technology Press
The print edition is not for sale in China (Mainland). Customers from China (Mainland) please order the print book from: Huazhong University of Science and Technology Press.

Translation from the Chinese Simplified language edition: "回应低碳时代: 行政法的变革与发展" by Shirong Fang and Binglin Tan, © China Social Sciences Press & Huazhong University of Science and Technology Press 2016. Published by China Social Sciences Press. All Rights Reserved.

This Springer imprint is published by the registered company Springer Nature Singapore Pte Ltd.
The registered company address is: 152 Beach Road, #21-01/04 Gateway East, Singapore 189721, Singapore

Brief Introduction of the Content

It is a common concern of the international community in today's world that we should actively respond to the crisis of global climate change. The fundamental way to implement it is to lower dependence on fossil energy, decrease the density of greenhouse gas emissions caused by production and consumption, and finally realize the low-carbonization of global economic development and social life. This will be an epoch-making model of economic development and social life. In this model, we may deal with social aspects like politics, economy, science and technology, culture, lifestyle, and so on, and we need the joint action of all members of society. Also in this model, the government will play an irreplaceable leading and organizing role. It will face the new administrative function of promoting the development of a low-carbon economy and constructing a low-carbon society. Administrative law, as a legal system to regulate government behaviors, thus has a mission of the age to deal with climate change.

This book puts forward new thinking on how the theory and system of China's administrative law can meet the requirements of the low-carbon era, with the basic content and structure of administrative law as the analytical framework. And from the two dimensions of restraining the government's own activities to meet low-carbon requirements and prompting the government to effectively perform the new function of implementing low-carbon regulations, this book systematically studies the due changes and developments of theories and systems like the basic principles of administrative law, administrative entities, administrative actions, administrative processes, and administration liability. This book is the present first legal monograph devoted to low-carbon administration in the field of administrative law, with novel, prospective and pertinent viewpoints, unique analysis, rich content, and detailed information.

The publication of this book can provide a reference for the legal circles to further explore the legal issues of climate change, and also provide a useful reference for the practical circles to make relevant decisions.

Introduction[1]

This is an era of global warming, but also an era for research on global warming.

William D. Nordhaus[2]

Problems and Background

Global climate change has brought about the crisis of the survival of human beings. It is mainly caused by the heavy use of fossil energy in the social and economic development of human activities, especially in developed countries since the industrial revolution. And the activities have created a significant increase in the concentration of greenhouse gases such as carbon dioxide in the atmosphere and an abnormal enhancement in the greenhouse effect. The *Copenhagen Accord*, adopted in December 2009, clearly states: "climate change is one of the greatest challenges of our time ... deep cuts in global emissions are required according to science ... to reduce global emissions so as to hold the increase in global temperature below 2 °C".[3] Thereafter, an international consensus has been reached that the fundamental way to deal with climate change lies in achieving low carbonization of global economic development and social life by reducing dependence on fossil energy, and the density of greenhouse gas emissions caused by production and consumptions.

[1] Part of this section was published in *On Government Functions and Administrative Acts in Promoting Low-carbon Society Construction, Legal Science*, no. 6, 2011.

[2] A US economist, Sterling Professor at Yale University, and the world's leading economist on climate change.

[3] *Copenhagen Accord (2009)*, http://unfccc.int/resource/docs/2009/cop15/eng/l07.pdf. On March 9th, 2010, China wrote to the UNFCCC secretariat and indicated its formal rectification of would formally ratify this accord. See Liu Lu, *China Formally Approve the Copenhagen Accord*, http://www.caijing.com.cn/2010-03-10/110393253.html, *ht Financial*, accessed September 13th, 2010.

In 2003, the UK issued *Energy White Paper "Our energy future—creating a low-carbon economy"*, in which the concept of "low-carbon economy" was first put forward, and the goals of cutting its emissions of greenhouse gases by 60% from 1990 level by around 2050 was set.[4] *Framework Act on low-carbon, Green Growth of South Korea* amended in 2013 set the goal of "low-carbon" as "lowering dependence on fossil fuels, expanding the use and distribution of clean energy, and reducing greenhouse gases (carbon dioxide-based) to an appropriate or lower level by expanding carbon sinks ... and research and development of green technology".[5] In China, Zhou Shengxian, former Minister of Ministry of Ecology and Environment, pointed out that "Low-carbon economy is an economic model based on low energy consumption, low emissions and low pollution, and it is another great progress of human society after primitive civilization, agricultural civilization and industrial civilization. The essence of building this model is to improve energy efficiency and create a clean energy structure. The core is to implement technological and institutional innovation and change the views on development."[6] Zhuangguiyang and other scholars put forward four comprehensive evaluation indicators of low-carbon economy, namely "low-carbon output" (low energy consumption per-unit GDP), "low-carbon consumption" (low per-capita carbon demand and carbon emission level), "low-carbon resources" (high proportion of non-fossil energy in primary energy consumption, high forest coverage, low-carbon dioxide emission factor per-unit energy consumption), and "low-carbon policy" (energy conservation, emission reduction, and cleaner industrial structure should be included into the strategic planning of economic and social development).[7]

Generally speaking, low-carbon development in a broad sense includes at least the following four aspects: first, also the basic requirement of the concept, reducing greenhouse gas emissions, such as carbon dioxide, through various restrictive measures to ensure that the proportion and intensity of carbon emissions in the production and consumption process continue to decline to reduce pollution. Second, optimizing the energy structure by minimizing the use of limited and scarce traditional fossil energy, and developing and utilizing new and renewable energy resources through scientific and technological innovation, institutional innovation, industrial transformation, and other means. This can reduce carbon emissions, on the other hand, can guarantee energy supply and achieve sustainable development. Third, saving energy resources. Implementing a conservation and low-carbon consumption mode through the transformation of social consumption patterns. In the meantime, energy consumption per unit of output should be continuously reduced by

---

[4] Hu Anbing & Wang Yiqian, *Research on Low Carbon Agricultural Development in Sichuan under the Background of Low Carbon Economy, Sichuan Environment*, no. 2, 2015. Department of Trade and Industry, Department for Environment, Food and Rural Affairs, *Energy White Paper: Our Energy Future-Creating a low-carbon Economy*, Norwich: The Stationery Office, 2003, p. 6.

[5] Zheng Tongtong, trans., *Framework Act on low-carbon, Green Growth of South Korea (Rev. 2013), Journal of Nanjing Tech University (Social Science Edition)*, no. 3, 2013.

[6] Zhang Kunmin, Pan Jiahua, and Cui Dapeng, eds., *An Introduction to Low Carbon Economy*, prefaced by Zhou Shengxian, China Environmental Science Press, 2008.

[7] Zhuang Guiyang, Pan Jiahua and Zhu Shouxian, *Connotation of Low Carbon Economy and Building of a Comprehensive Evaluation Index System, Economic Perspectives*, no. 1, 2010.

adopting energy-saving measures to ensure the efficient use of energy resources. Fourth, absorbing, neutralizing, or offsetting carbon emissions that daily activities may produce by expanding carbon sinks in forests, farmlands, grasslands, and oceans and by implementing carbon neutrality.

Obviously, the realization of such an epoch-making economic development and social life mode will be a vast project. Many aspects need to be dealt with such as politics, economy, science and technology, culture, lifestyle, and so on. This requires the government to forcefully promote the mode and the joint efforts of all members of society. In this process, the government plays an irreplaceable leading and organizational role. It should be the leader in building a low-carbon society with its macro-strategy, public resource allocation, and overall regulatory capabilities. While any other social members or market entities cannot be competent in leading because of their individuality, unorganized and profit-seeking nature, and also because of the "Giddens's Paradox"[8] in reality. Therefore, the epochal mission of governments to actively respond to global climate change comes into being. Many scholars at home and abroad have put forward a consistent understanding from different disciplines. German sociologist Beck proposes from a sociological perspective that "climate change constitutes a major challenge to the environmental politics of the risk society in the 21st century", "and dealing with risk must become one of the main tasks of public administration in this era."[9] British political scientist Giddens puts forward the idea of an "Ensuring State" in response to climate change. After a systematic political and economic analysis, American scholar Friedman, argues that "Only the government has the energy to lead all actions pulled together on climate change."[10] Some British economists believe that the externality of greenhouse gas emissions is an important cause of climate problems, pointing out that "greenhouse gas emissions are the biggest market failure in human history"[11] and must be adjusted by the "visible hand" of government intervention. That is to say, only the government has the ability to call, regulate and enforce the low-carbon activities of the whole society through public policies. In the field of law, some American scholars have clearly expressed the same view: "The basic goal of modern government should include the continuous

[8] The "Giddens's Paradox" refers to such a dilemma: since the dangers posed by global warming aren't tangible, immediate or visible in the course of day-to-day life—however, awesome they may appear—many will sit on their hands and do nothing concrete about them. Yet waiting until they become visible and acute before being stirred to serious action will, by definition, be too late. See Anthony Giddens, *The politics of climate change*, trans. Cao Rongxiang, Social Sciences Academic Press, China, 2009, p. 2.

[9] Beck Ulrich. Weltrisikogesellschaft, Frankfurt a. M, 155.

[10] See Thomas L. Friedman. *Hot, Flat and Crowed—Why We Need a Green Revolution and How It Can Renew America*. New York: Farrar, Straus and Giroux, 2008.

[11] Nicholas Stern, *The Global Deal: Climate Change and the Creation of a New Era of Progress and Prosperity*, trans. Wu Xishen, Social Sciences Academic Press, 2011, 14.

reduction of social risks"[12]; while German administrative law scholars have further pointed out from the perspective of administrative law that in modern society, the responsibilities and missions of the state have begun to change, from the previous discipline administration and welfare administration gradually into risk administration.[13] This is different from the task of "survival care" for citizens provided by the welfare state era.[14]

From a practical point of view, in order to deal with climate change, many countries and regions in the world have taken positive actions. At the government level, building a low-carbon society has been promoted as a national strategy in many countries and regions. Following the release of the UK's energy white paper *Our energy future—creating a low-carbon economy* in 2003, Japan began the scientific research project "2050 Japan Low-Carbon Society" in 2004, and successively published a series of research reports, such as *A Dozen of Actions Towards Low-Carbon Societies*,[15] *Japan Scenarios and Actions Towards Low-Carbon Societies*,[16] etc. With these research plans and reports, Japan's low-carbon society strategy has been effectively promoted and developed. The European Commission proposed *Council adopts climate-energy legislative pack* in 2008. The pack includes several institutional measures, such as the Revised EU Emissions Trading System, the EU Member States share the effort to make the carbon emission reductions, A regulatory framework for carbon capture and storage, and the new EU rules promoting the use of energy from the renewable sources.[17] Air pollutants have been declared greenhouse gases by the US Supreme Court in 2007, and then in January 2010, the US Environmental Protection Agency decided to tackle climate change as the top of the agency's seven priorities of regulatory programs.[18] In 2010, South Korea promulgated the *Framework Act on low-carbon, Green Growth of Korea*, which began to bring low-carbon economic development and low-carbon social construction into the legal track.

In order to achieve energy conservation, emission reduction, and low-carbon development, China has actively undertaken the "common but differentiated responsibilities" and set a series of energy-saving and emission reduction targets. In 2009,

---

[12] Cass R. Sunstein, *Risk and Reason: Safety, Law, and the Environment*, trans. Shi Shuai, China University of Political Science and Law Press, 2005, 1.

[13] (Germany) Hans J. Wolff et al., *Administrative Law*, trans. Gao Jiawei, preface, The Commercial Press, 2007, 3:3.

[14] See (Germany) Eberhard Schmidt-Assmann et al., trans. Yu An et al., Higher Education Press, 2006, 53.

[15] "2050 Japan Low-Carbon Society" scenario team, *A Dozen of Actions towards Low-Carbon Societies (LCSs)*, May 2008, http://2050.nies.go.jp/20080522_press/20080522_report_main.pdf/, accessed October 18th, 2010.

[16] "2050 Japan Low-Carbon Society" scenario team, Japan Scenarios and Actions towards Low-Carbon Societies (LCSs), June 2008, http://2050.nies.go.jp/material/2050_LCS_Scenarios_Actions_English_080715.pdf/, accessed October 18th, 2010.

[17] See Council of The Europea Union, *Council adopts climate-energy legislative pack*, Brussels, 6 April 2009, http://www.consilium.europa.eu/uedocs/cms_data/docs/pressdata/en/misc/107136.pdf/, accessed October 18th, 2010.

[18] Lisa P. Jackson, *Seven Priorities for EPA's Future*, http://blog.epa.gov/administrator/2010/01/12/seven-priorities-for-epas-future/ (visited on 09/18/2010).

the Chinese government solemnly announced the objective of "reducing greenhouse gas emissions per-unit GDP by 40–45 percent[19] by 2020 as compared with that in 2005", and "to achieve this goal at the cost of reducing GDP growth rate".[20] Energy conservation has been established as a basic state policy in China's *Constitution, Environmental Protection Law* and *Energy Conservation Law* and other laws and regulations. And building a Beautiful China has become one of the ruling objectives of CPC. In the *Recommendations for the 13th Five-Year Plan for Economic and Social Development*, the CPC Central Committee explicitly called for an overall improvement in the quality of the ecological environment and put forward that "Our modes of production and ways of life should become more eco-friendly and low-carbon. We will extract and use energy and resources with much greater efficiency. Aggregate energy and water consumption, the total amount of land used for construction and aggregate carbon emissions will be effectively controlled" and so on.[21] In the *Guidelines of the CPC Central Committee and the State Council on Accelerating Ecological Civilization*, the government has made special decisions and arrangements on "Promoting Energy Conservation and Emission Reduction" and "Actively Dealing with Climate Change". Chinese President Xi Jinping recently stressed that China should "vigorously promote green development, circular development and low-carbon development", and put forward a clear demand for the "energy consumption revolution": "We should restrain unreasonable energy consumption, resolutely control the total amount of energy consumption, effectively implement the priority policy of energy conservation, and run energy conservation throughout the whole process and all fields of economic and social development. We should firmly promote the industrial restructuring, attach great importance to energy saving in urbanization, establish a thrifty consumption concept, and accelerate the formation of an energy-saving society."[22] In order to achieve the goal of energy-saving and emission reduction, the government has also promulgated a large number of specific policies and regulations, such as *Action Plan for Low-carbon Development of Energy Conservation and Emission Reduction 2014–2015*, making specific arrangements from the aspects of promoting industrial restructuring, building energy-saving and emission reduction projects, paying close attention to energy-saving in key areas, strengthening technical and policy support, etc.

---

[19] Wen Jing and Wang Yun, *China and the United States Arrange Carbon Emission Reduction before the United Nations Climate Change Conference, The Economic Information Daily*, November 27th, 2009, A02.

[20] Xinhua News Agency, *Wen Jiabao: We Do Not Scruple to Lower GDP Growth Rate for Fulfilling the Energy Conservation and Emission Reduction Target, West China City Daily*, September 15th, 2010, 33. Among the main targets set for the five-yea economic and social development in the *12th Five-year Plan Outline*, annual growth rate of GDP is 7%, which is lower than 7.5%, annual average growth rate of GDP set in the 11th Five-year Plan Outline.

[21] *The Recommendations of the Central Committee of the Communist Party of China for Formulating the 13rd Five-Year Plan for Economic and Social Development*, Sina, accessed December 5th, 2015, http://finance.sina.com.cn/china/20151103/160123664965.shtml.

[22] *Xi Jinping: China Actively Promote Energy Production and Consumption Revolution, Xinhua Net*, accessed March 2nd, 2015, http://news.xinhuanet.com/politics/2014-06/13/c_1111139161.htm.

In April 2015, the National Energy Administration issued the *Action Plan for Clean and Efficient Utilization of Coal (2015–2020)*. It proposed that the energy consumption revolution should be promoted through such measures as "developing ultra-low emission coal-fired power generation, speeding up the upgrading and transformation of existing coal-fired units", "promoting the recycling of waste materials and reducing pollutant emissions". The UN Conference on Climate Change in Paris, to be held on November 30, 2015, will conclude the negotiations on the international climate mechanism after 2020 and draw up a new global climate agreement to ensure strong global action to reduce emissions and to limit the temperature rise in this century to less than 2 degrees. In particular, the meeting will change the previous negotiation model: from top-down "showdown" mandatory emission reduction to bottom-up "Nationally Determined Contributions". President Xi Jinping, in his important speech *Making Joint Efforts to Build an Equitable and Reasonable Climate Change Governance Mechanism through Win-win Cooperations*, elaborated on China's latest proposals for global climate governance: "Going forward, ecological endeavors will feature prominently in China's 13th Five-Year Plan. China will work hard to implement the vision of innovative, coordinated, green, open and inclusive development. China will, on the basis of technological and institutional innovation, adopt new policy measures to improve industrial mix, build low-carbon energy system, develop green building and low-carbon transportation, and build a nationwide carbon emission trading market so as to foster a new pattern of modernization featuring harmony between man and nature."[23]

Active response to global climate change has given rise to new administrative functions of governments to comprehensively promote low-carbon development and build a low-carbon society. Therefore, to meet the low-carbon requirements, there is much to be carefully explored and studied in the field of administrative law like new administrative concepts, basic principles, administrative functions and responsibilities, and a large number of administrative actions to implement low-carbon regulations and so on. In a word, the administrative law system that guides and regulates government actions should have appropriate development and improvement, which brings out the important research topics on how administrative law can deal with climate change. This is also a new theoretical and practical issue for administrative law.

In general, the current research on the problem of administrative law is still very weak in China. This is mainly presented in the following aspects: this important issue has not received general concern in the field of administrative law, and only a few scholars are carrying out preliminary research work; the output of the research is very little, so far no special work on administrative law has been seen; the content of the research is still fragmented; and no one has yet systematically explores the development and changes to meet the requirements of the low-carbon era in various important categories such as the basic principles of administrative law, administrative

[23] Xi Jinping: *Making Joint Efforts to Build an Equitable and Reasonable Climate Change Governance Mechanism through Win-win Cooperations*, Sina, accessed December 4th, 2015, http://news.sina.com.cn/o/2015-12-01/doc-ifxmainy1515069.shtml.

entity, administrative process, administrative action, and administration liability. In terms of institutional norms, most of the documents related to low-carbon construction issued by the government are policy documents, and the relevant administrative legislation is to be improved and perfected. Governments at all levels have applied a large number of low-carbon regulatory measures in practice, but these measures still lack sufficient theoretical support in administrative law in the aspects of legal basis, behaviors, legal effects, and so on. All these reflect the absence of the theoretical study in administrative law on tackling climate change.

In the legal system, dealing with climate change is the common task of different branch laws like administrative law, economic law, civil law, and criminal law, among which administrative law plays an important role. This is because the government plays a leading role in the construction of a low-carbon society. Administrative law can urge administrative organs to promote the construction of a low-carbon society from at least two latitudes: on the one hand, as the basis of the authority and responsibilities of administrative organs, it could ensure that the government actively and legally implements low-carbon regulations, and promote the whole society to carry out energy-saving activities. On the other hand, as the norm of behavior of administrative organs, it also requires the government to take the lead in achieving low-carbon administrative activities and to form a demonstration effect in the whole society. Therefore, it is of great theoretical and practical significance to explore the administrative law issues in response to climate change and to urge governments at all levels to effectively perform their functions of building a low-carbon society in accordance with the law.

Research Significance

It is of great theoretical and practical significance to study administrative law issues in response to climate change.

(I) Theoretical Significance

i. The study will develop and innovate the theory of administrative law. The current theory of administrative law in China mainly draws on the theory of German administrative law in civil law system, which was founded in the nineteenth century by Otto Mayer. Although it has gone through and adapted to the development of the era of free rule of law (Liberaler Rechtsstaat) and social rule of law (Sozialer Rechtsstaat), today, when human society enters the era of risk rule of law, this traditional theory has shown its limitations, like many administrative law problems caused by climate change are difficult to be effectively solved under its guide. This book will systematically study the changes and development of traditional administrative law theory in the low-carbon era, and discuss the important issues that should be established by administrative law such as low-carbon administrative principles, entities and processes, various administrative actions and their application of low-carbon regulations, and low-carbon administrative liability and so on. This will undoubtedly help to develop the theory of the existing administrative law, and build system that can embody low-carbon concepts and meet low-carbon requirements.

ii. The study will expand the research contents of administrative law. Traditional administrative law mainly focuses on controlling administrative power and protecting citizens' rights and interests. It emphasizes the legitimacy, rationality, and judicial review of administrative activities, and neglects the running effect of administrative activities and the role of governance tools. This book explores the emergence and application of some new administrative modes to meet the needs of low-carbon regulation, and the social effects of low-carbon administrative regulations as a governance tool for tackling climate change. This should be an extension of the traditional research contents.

iii. The study will enrich the research methods of administrative law. In the past, administrative law laid emphasis on the research methods of conceptualism and legal dogmatics, and centered on law-based administration to interpret and construct a series of rules of administrative law, so as to ensure that administrative activities are legal, reasonable, and subject to judicial review. On this basis, the book emphasizes on the research of legal policymaking, focuses on exploring how the government actively performs the administrative functions of low-carbon regulation and achieves social effects, and proposes the legal system design of low-carbon administration. This study will enrich the research methods of administrative law and break through the limitations of conceptualism research.

(II) Practical Significance

i. The study is conducive to the establishment and improvement of the administrative legal system that promotes the construction of a low-carbon society. As the leader and organizer of low-carbon society construction, the Chinese government is formulating a special climate change response law and related legislation. And its administrative laws and regulations will inevitably become the key content of climate change legislation. With regard to this, the study aims to help with both the establishment and improvement of the administrative legal system for the construction of a low-carbon society. On the one hand, with administrative law being the code of conduct of administrative organs themselves, the study will discuss the low-carbonization of government's own activities such as the setting of administrative entities and the operation of administrative processes from the perspective of administrative self-regulation. This process helps to bring energy conservation and emission reduction into consideration in the administrative organic law and the administrative litigation law, and will urge the government to play an exemplary and leading role in the construction of a low-carbon society. On the other hand, with administrative law being the guide and means of implementation of administrative actions, the study will discuss how administrative guidance, administrative licensing, administrative penalties, administrative enforcement, and other administrative actions can be improved to be effectively applied to implement low-carbon regulation, and explore new administrative activities such as carbon information disclosure management and carbon trading management, and so on, thus urging the government to actively and effectively implement low-carbon regulations, and the entire society to carry out energy-saving activities. In addition, the book will also focus on the low-carbon administrative liability investigation mechanism to help provide rigid institutional constraints for the government to effectively perform its administrative functions in response to climate change. All these have guiding significance for dealing with climate change and for establishing and perfecting the administrative legal system for the construction of a low-carbon society.

ii. Providing theoretical support for the voice from China to be heard in the field of international response to climate change. China has always upheld "common but differentiated responsibilities" in the international joint action to deal with climate change, and voluntarily committed part of the compulsory emission reduction responsibility. When the international commitments are translated into specific systems and measures of domestic law, a considerable part of which may deal with the government functions and administrative activities. Therefore, the study of the response of administrative law to the low-carbon era will help our governments and departments at all levels to effectively stick to and fulfill their solemn commitments to the international community through the construction of corresponding administrative law systems, thus providing theoretical and institutional support for the voice from China to be heard internationally in dealing with climate change in the post-Copenhagen Summit era.

Literature Review

Addressing climate change involves activities in the field of social lifestyle, politics, economy, science and technology, law and so on. At present, in China, it has received extensive attention and is studied in politics, sociology, management, economics, law, and other disciplines, out of which a large number of research results have been achieved. This book mainly studies the response to climate change from the perspective of administrative law, so it focuses on the existing research of administrative law and the existing research of subjects closely related to administrative law.

(I) Review of Overseas Studies

As early as the 1980s, the German political scientist and sociologist Ulrich Beck established the theory of "risk society" from the sociological point of view, and specifically pointed out that "climate change constitutes a major challenge to the environmental politics of the risk society in the 21st century".[24] At the same time, he proposed that dealing with risk must become one of the main tasks of public administration in this era.[25] Later, the relevant political studies further discussed the role and public responsibility of the government in dealing with climate change. For

[24] Beck Ulrich. Weltrisikogesellschaft, Frankfurt a. M, 155.

[25] See (Germany) Beck Ulrich, Weltrisikogesellschaft, trans. He Bowen, The Yilin Press, 2004, 13–15.

example, Giddens, a British political scientist, put forward the model of "Ensuring State" in response to the climate change crisis. He believed that "the state should not only act as a coordinator but also guarantee the exact results, which means, in dealing with energy-saving and emission reductions, the state is responsible for monitoring public goals and for trying to make sure they are realized in a visible and acceptable fashion".[26] On this basis, he put forward "political convergence" and "economic convergence" as the operation scheme of establishing a Ensuring State. "Political convergence" refers to "the degree to which policies relevant to limiting climate change overlap positively with other areas of public policy, such that each can be used to gain traction over the other". While "economic convergence" refers to "the overlap between low-carbon technologies, forms of business practice and lifestyles with economic competitiveness".[27] Australian scholars David Shearman and Joseph Wayne Smith proposed that a Singapore-style elite authoritarian state should be established to deal with climate change and to strengthen the administrative authority of the government. They believed that there exists a problem of "the failure of democracy" in response to climate change in contemporary liberal democracy. Democracy should prevent the majority from suppressing the minority, but "we see that it is in the interests of the individual to break the rules that might be made for the survival of all herdsmen and recourse", thus causing "The Tragedy of the Commons" in the field of climate change.[28] The above studies of sociology and political science provide the basis for administrative law to study the role and function of government in dealing with climate change.

In the field of administrative law, the existing studies abroad are still fragmentary and lack systematicness. The main issues involved include: (i) Coping with climate change and human rights protection. (ii) Administrative legislation to deal with climate change. (iii) Administrative regulation measures to deal with climate change. In the field of human rights research, Schmidt Assmann, a famous German scholar, put forward that the society today has become a risk society, and climate change is the greatest ecological environment risk in the contemporary era. He believes that the legitimate source of national existence is whether the country can effectively complete the task of regulating risk, which is equivalent to the task of providing survival and care for the people in the era of welfare administration. Therefore, this task "has been condensed into the main requirement of a human rights status in the era of risk administration."[29] In terms of legislation research, Heike Schroeder and Harriet Bulkeley took London and Los Angeles as analysis samples to discuss in detail how local legislation can mitigate climate change, and then put forward pertinent suggestions on governance models and the role that laws

[26] Liu Bing, *Anthony Giddens, The politics of climate change, China Public Administrative Review*, no. 10, 2011.

[27] See Anthony Giddens, *The politics of climate change*, trans. Cao Rongxiang Social Sciences Academic Press, China, 2009, 79.

[28] See David J. C. Shearman and Joseph Wayne Smith, *The climate change challenge and the failure of democracy*, trans. Wu Xishen and Li Nan, Social Sciences Academic Press, 2009, 102.

[29] [German] Eberhard Schmidt-Assmann et al., *German Administrative Law*, ed. Hypoxia Battis, trans. Yu An, et al., Higher Education Press, 2006, 53.

should play in dealing with climate change, including self-management of energy-saving and emission reduction in government activities, frugal innovation of resource supply and public services, and regulation and encouragement of energy conservation and emission reduction in society through public-private cooperation.[30] Michael B. Gerrard systematically reviews the current situation of the US federal and state governments in dealing with climate change in the "deletion of statute law" and looks ahead to the future legislation.[31] Ulrich Battis made a special study on architectural planning legislation to deal with climate change. He believed that "urban construction law can make a sustained and planned contribution not only to the local and regional environmental protection, but also to the national climate protection", and that architectural planning "should take into account the responsibility of universal climate protection". From the perspective of local autonomy, the study discussed the cooperative promotion relationship among German federal legislation, legal system, and local architectural planning.[32] In terms of the means of administrative regulation, William R. Blackburn studies integratedly on how the government implements sustainable development and regulates climate change risks. He analyzes the significant impact of government actions on low-carbon and sustainable development, and has constructed the overall framework of government sustainable development from the eight perspectives of "vision, values and policy", "organizational structure", "stakeholder engagement and feedback", "strategic planning for aligned priorities", "indicators and goals", "measuring and reporting progress", "architectural energy conservation regulation", and "green government procurement".[33] Edna Sussman and Jacqueline Peel have discussed the Climate Change Adaption Planning through case analysis, and put forward detailed operation guidelines, including "Build Your Climate Change Preparedness Team", "Identify Your Planning Areas and Sectors Relevant to Climate Change", "Conduct a Climate Change Vulnerability Assessment", "Conduct a Climate Change Risk Assessment", and "Set Preparedness Goals and Develop Your Preparedness Plan". [34] Camden D. Burton makes a special study on the executive guidance of the Securities and Exchange Commission on the disclosure

[30] See Heike Schroeder, Harriet Bulkeley, Global Cities and the Governance of Climate Change: What is the Role of Law in Cities? *Fordham Urban Law Journal*, Vol. 36, 2008.

[31] See Michael B. Gerrard, Climate Regulation without Congressional Action, *New York Law Journal*, Vol. 244, 2011.

[32] See [German] Ulrich Battis, Urban Governance and Climate Protection, in *Renditions Future Climate Crisis: the Social Reality of Climate Change and Ultimate Concern*, eds. [German] Erhan Si Harald Vail et al, trans. Jin Haimin et al, Central Compilation and Translation Press, 2013, 185–196.

[33] William R. Blackburn, *The Sustainability Handbook: The Complete Management Guide to Achieving Social, Economic and Environmental Responsibility*, trans. Jiang He, Shanghai People's Press, 2009, 331–346.

[34] See [German] Ulrich Battista, "Urban Governance and Climate Protection," in *Climate Storm: Social Reality and Ultimate Concern of Climate Change*, eds. [German] Harald Welzer et al, trans. Jin Haimin et al (Central Compilation and Translation Press, 2013), 185–196.

of company climate change risk information.[35] Dennis D. Hirsch, based on Gunther Teubner's Reflexive Law, has studied the government regulation of Green Business. He believes that compared with the rigid "technical standard model" and "outcome output model", the "self-regulation model" is more effective, and he has constructed a set of self-regulation systems consisting of information strategy, communication strategy, and procedure strategy. [36] Othmar Schwank analyses how Swiss administrative management links traffic regulation with climate policy; Rainer Kistler discusses and evaluates the principles and policies of Swedish local governments on energy and greenhouse gas regulations.[37] The above theoretical achievements of foreign administrative law scholars provide references for system building and practical experience for domestic administrative law research.

In addition, economists abroad have also studied the use of market or administrative means to deal with climate change. They generally believe that "greenhouse gas emissions are the biggest market failure in human history"[38] and therefore need to be regulated directly through administrative control measures such as taxation. In general, the relevant studies of the economists mainly focus on the choice of policy tools for energy conservation and emission reduction. In the theoretical analysis of economists, the existing policy tools of energy saving and emission reduction are mainly shown in two ways: one is the market trading method based on total quantity control, and the other is the tax method based on price control. However, different scholars have different opinions on this: for example, Hepburn advocates promoting energy conservation and emission reduction through carbon emissions trading, because carbon trading is less difficult, and greater efforts should be made to coordinate carbon taxes internationally; in the carbon trading mechanism, developing countries can obtain profits by selling carbon emission reduction quotas on the international market, while in the carbon tax mechanism, developing countries cannot do so. In addition, there will be great resistance when implementing the carbon tax. Since the carbon tax cannot set a quantitative emission reduction target, industrial groups under great pressure to reduce emissions will strongly oppose it, and environmental protection groups will also oppose it. Carbon trading goes hand in hand with carbon credit system and can drive the rise of related enterprises. However, carbon tax does not have this effect, and carbon tax lacks economic incentives for energy conservation and emission reduction.[39] Nordhaus argues that "compared to the carbon tax that has long been a mature policy tool, carbon trading is a new thing that has emerged

---

[35] William R. Blackburn, *The Sustainability Handbook: The Complete Management Guide to Achieving Social, Economic and Environmental Responsibility*, trans. Jiang He, Shanghai People's Press, 2009, 331–346.

[36] See Dennis D. Hirsch, Green Business and the Importance of Reflexive Law: What Michael Porter Didn't Say, *Administrative Law Review*, Vol. 62, 2010.

[37] See (Swiss) Walter Meyer, *Sino-Swiss Forum on Climate Change Legislation*, ed. Chang Jiwen, China Environmental Science Press, 2010, 54–60.

[38] Nicholas Stern, *How to Manage Climate Change and Create a New Era of Progress and Prosperity*, trans. Wu xishen, Social Sciences Academic Press, 2011, 14.

[39] See HEPBURN, *Carbon Trading: A Review of the Kyoto Mechanisms, Annual Review of Environment and Resources*, 2007, 32: 375–393.

after the *Kyoto Protocol*, and its future development is uncertain".[40] Nordhaus also pointed out through long-term empirical research on the EU carbon emission trading market and the US sulfur dioxide trading market that "the reason why carbon prices fluctuate dramatically in the market is that there is a lack of balance between supply and demand of carbon emission quotas, and as long as there is a drastic fluctuation in carbon prices, it will lead to the failure of the goal of relying on prices to achieve the allocation of resources".[41] Sir Nicholas Stern pointed out that tax means and market trading means have their own characteristics and advantages and disadvantages. The advantages of tax means lie in fixed prices and convenient implementation, while that of market trading lie in fixed emissions and effective international cooperation.[42] These studies of economics can provide a more scientific analysis tool for administrative law to rationally choose the administrative action mode to deal with climate change, and help the government to weigh the pros and cons to formulate optimal low-carbon regulation policies.

(II) Review of Domestic Relevant Research

Domestic administrative law circles have begun to pay attention to the issue of climate change, but the overall research on the response of administrative law to climate change is still relatively weak. At present, there are only some sporadic studies on low-carbon administrative awareness, organization and actions, and administrative proceedings on climate change. For example, Chen Xiaochun and other scholars have made a preliminary study of low-carbon administrative consciousness in the article *Government's Low-carbon Administrative Consciousness from the Perspective of Ecological Civilization*. They believe that the evaluation indicators of the "consciousness" include the low-carbon awareness, affections, and administrative beliefs of civil servants. They point out that the path to obtain this low-carbon administrative consciousness lies in promoting the co-evolution of low-carbon administrative system, promoting the people-oriented development of low-carbon administrative system, establishing incentive-compatible low-carbon administrative system, and creating a low-carbon administrative atmosphere of caring for the environment.[43] The representative work of administrative organization research is Tian Danyu's *Evaluation and Analysis of China's Current Climate Governance Organizations*. This paper examines the current climate governance organizations and their functions in China from the perspectives of administrative departments (central and local) and management projects (voluntary carbon trading management, clean development project development, external cooperation, and carbon fund management), and

---

[40] Wang Dongfeng & Zhang Li, *Review on the Economics of Climate Change Economist*, no. 11 (2011).

[41] [US] William D. Nordhaus, *Economic Issues in a Designing a Global Agreement on Global Warming, Comparison*, ed. Wu Jinglian, 46, CITIC Press, 2010, 117–124; Wang Dongfeng and Zhang Li, *Review on the Economics of Climate Change, Economist*, no. 11, 2011.

[42] See Stern, N., *The Economics of Climate Change, American Economic Review*, 2008, 98(2): 1–37.

[43] See Chen Xiaochun, Wu Ning, and Shi Zhuohong, *Government" Low-carbon Administrative Consciousness from the Perspective of Ecological Civilization, Huxiang Forum*, no. 4, 2013.

puts forward the direction of improvement of China's climate governance organization system.[44] The related research on administrative actions mainly involves the following three kinds of actions. (i) In terms of administrative collection, Zhang Zitai analyzed the necessity, basic forms, and functional orientation of imposing carbon tax in China.[45] Li Chuanxuan and Chen Hongyan constructed China's carbon tax system from the aspects of tax object, taxpayer, tax rate, tax base, tax links, tax incentives, and tax use.[46] (ii) In terms of administrative licensing, Zhang Peng explored the response of patent licensing system to climate change, and suggested that we should try to speed up the examination system according to application in areas of low-carbon technology, improve the compulsory licensing system for low-carbon technology, strengthen the anti-monopoly regulations in the process of standardization of low-carbon technology, and establish the application subsidy system for low-carbon patents and risk early-warning system, etc.[47] (iii) In terms of administrative contracts, Lin Yaochang demonstrated the feasibility of applying administrative contracts in the construction of low-carbon society, and proposed some modeling administrative contracts, such as carbon emissions trading contracts between administrative entities, industrial restructuring subsidization contracts, low-carbon technology R&D and promotion subsidization contracts, and new energy development and utilization subsidization contracts.[48] There has been concern among scholars in administrative proceedings relating to climate change. At present, domestic-related research mainly focuses on the introduction and analysis of overseas climate change administrative litigation. For example, Chen Dong and Ma Cunli studied the qualification of civil plaintiff in the first case of US climate change lawsuit, *Massachusetts v. EPA*[49]; Wang Hui analyzed the relationship between administrative interpretation and judicial review in *Massachusetts v. EPA*[50]; Shen Yuedong studied the political position and confrontation of the US Federal Court in dealing with climate change,

---

[44] See Tian Danyu, *Evaluation and Analysis of China's Current Climate Governance Organizations, University of Political Science and Law*, no. 1, 2013.

[45] See Zhang Zitai, *Thoughts on Legislation of Carbon Tax in China, China Legal Science*, no. 2 (2010).

[46] See Li Chuanxuan, *Study on Carbo Tax Legislative Framework in Response to Climate Change, China Legal Science*, no. 6, 2010; Chen Hongyan, *Carbon Tax System and State Strategic Interests, China Legal Science*, no. 2, 2012.

[47] See Zhang Peng, On Intellectual Property Right System in Response to Low Carbon Technology Innovation, *Journal of Law and Technology*, no. 3, 2010.

[48] See Lin Yaochang, *On Application of Administrative Deed in Implementation of Low Carbon Policies, Journal of Nanjing Tech University, Social Science Edition*, no. 2, 2010.

[49] Chen Dong, *US Environmental Litigation Against the Background of Climate Change—Take Massachusetts v. EPA as an example, Global Law Review*, no. 5, 2008; Ma Cunli, *Analysis of Plaintiff's Standing in Environmental Litigation against the Background of Global Warming, Peking University Law Journal*, no. 4, 2008.

[50] Wang Hui, *Administrative Interpretation and Judicial Review in Climate Change Litigation,—Take Massachusetts v. EPA as an example, Journal of East China University of Political Science and Law*, no. 2, 2012.

and elaborated on the application of "The Political Question Doctrine" in the US administrative proceedings of climate change.[51]

Compared with administrative law, environmental law is relatively mature and systematic in dealing with climate change, involving research on climate change from different perspectives. The existing achievements are mainly reflected in the following three aspects:

First, the development of environmental law concepts and principles under the background of climate change. For example, Zhang Lu believes that in environmental law, in a low-carbon economy, we should transfer the traditional concept of "controlling" to the legal concept of "cooperation + participation", and update the principles of "respect for the law of nature and ecology", "public participation", "government-led principle" and "Beneficiary-Pays Principle".[52] From the perspective of EU policy and legal practice, Kejian and He Xiangbai discussed the application and function of traditional environmental law principles such as sustainable development principle, public participation principle, precautionary principle, and polluter-pays principle in the field of climate change adaptation.[53]

Second, environmental legislation to deal with climate change. The research under this topic can be divided into two branches. The first is to explore the legislative model and legal framework of climate change at the macro level. For example, Zhang Zitai and Li Yanfang believed that the framework system of China's climate change response law should include comprehensive climate change response law, renewable energy law, climate change mitigation legislation, and climate change adaptation legislation.[54] Sangdongli proposed and demonstrated the concept of "climate law" from the legal principle perspective, and evaluated the two modes of current research of climate change legislation in China: integrated law mode (integrating climate change factors through amending environmental law, resource law, and energy law) and special law mode (formulating comprehensive and specialized climate change law).[55] Professor Yang Jiejun studied low-carbon legislation from the perspective of legal system construction. He pointed out that the existing low-carbon legal system has limitations, such as theoretical limitation, single policy orientation, and unreasonable system structure. The way to improve is to enrich the content of rational basis

[51] See Shen Yaodong, *Judicial Check of Pollical Tug of War in Climate Change, Science of Law*, no. 6 (2014); *Application of Principles of Political Issues in Climate Change Litigation in the United States, Journal of Earth Science*, (Social Science Edition), no. 5 (2014).

[52] Zhang Lu, *Reconstruct Environmental Law in the Process of Low Carbon Economy, China Legal Science*, no. 9, 2011.

[53] Ke Jian, He Xiangbai, *The Application of Environmental Law Principles in the field of Climate Change Adaptation: From the Perspective of European Union Policy and legal Practice, Politics and Law*, no. 11, 2011.

[54] See Zhang Zitai, *Initial Exploration of the Framework System of the Chinese Law on Address Climate Change, Journal of Nanjing University (Philosophy, Humanities and Social Sciences)*, no. 5, 2010; Li Yanfang, *On China's Establishment of a Legal System Addressing Climate Change, Journal of China University of Political Science and Law*, no. 6 (2010).

[55] See Sang Dongli, *Theory Construction and Legislative Interpretation of Climate Law, Tsinghua Discourses on Rule-of-Law*, no. 3, 2013.

of low-carbon legal system, change the orientation of policy foundation and perfect the legal system structure.[56] The second is to study the formulation and improvement of specific climate change-related laws from the micro level. For example, Zhang Yong believes that energy legislation to deal with climate change should adhere to the basic principle of "coordinated development of energy and ecological environment protection", cover social and environmental costs in energy prices, ensure the diversity of price mechanisms, continuously expand the proportion of clean energy in energy mix, and establish greenhouse effect evaluation and ecological compensation system and a low-carbon energy science and technology innovation system.[57] Jinhai believes that in the revision of *Law of the PRC on the Prevention and Control of Atmospheric Pollution*, we should fully implement the "precautionary principle" and "public participation principle", and add carbon emission standard system, carbon accounting system, and other related systems.[58]

Third, environmental litigation in the perspective of ecological protection, mainly on environmental public interest litigation. For example, scholar Yang Chaoxia believes that the current legal system is inadequate for the protection of environmental public interest, which has created real demands for the establishment of the property right to natural resources and the right to environment and for the regime of environmental public interest litigation. As far as China's environmental public interest litigation is concerned, it should include public interest environmental right litigation, natural resource ownership right litigation, and environmental rights litigation trust, and distinguish between natural resources ownership and environmental rights for system construction.[59] Professor Cai Shouqiu systematically demonstrates the legitimacy of the establishment of citizen's environmental rights, national environmental protection obligations, and environmental public interest litigation, taking environmental rights and national environmental protection obligations as clues.[60]

Fourth, the regulatory means and methods of environmental and ecological protection. In this respect, there have been a lot of studies in environmental law. The research topics mainly include three categories: first, to carry out research on the most stringent water resources management system. Liu Chao believes that the current sewage drainage standard system follows a unified control idea and takes the maximum allowable discharge loading of the function of water body in the water function area as the control standard. It is difficult to achieve the anticipated control of the pollutant redline in the above controlling way. The corresponding system construction

[56] See Yang Jiejun & Cheng Yuyan, *Self-examination of the Basis on which China's Low Carbon Legal System is founded, Studies in Law and Business*, no. 2, 2014.

[57] See Zhangyong, *Study on the Issue of Energy Legislation that Addresses Climate Change, Social Sciences in Jiangxi*, no. 8, 2010.

[58] See Jinhai, *Low Carbon City Construction and Revision of the Law on Atmospheric Pollution Prevention and Control, Jianghuai Tribune*, no. 4, 2012.

[59] See Yang Zhaoxia, *On the Rights Foundation of Environmental Public Interest Litigation, — and On the theoretical Key points of Natural Resources Property Rights and Environmental Rights, Legal Forum*, no. 3, 2013.

[60] See Cai Shouqiu, *From Environment Rights to the State's Obligation of Protecting the Environment to Environmental Public Interest Litigation, Modern Law Science*, no. 6, 2013.

should be carried out according to the standard of "the most stringent water resources management" pollutant redline.[61] Zuo Qiting and others analyzed the research framework and core system of the most stringent water resources management system based on the concept of human-water harmony, which should include technical standard system, administrative management system, policy, and regulation system and other components.[62] The second is to carry out a systematic study on the punishment of aggravating environmental violations. The scholar Xiong Zhanglin has systematically demonstrated the nature of the article on "continuous fines calculated on a daily basis" for environmental violations. He holds that in principle, continuous violations can only be regarded as an act of law and multiple punishments can be prohibited. The continuous punishment stipulated in the *Environmental Protection Law* of China for aggravating environmental violations is only an exception to this principle.[63] The third is to study the lifelong investigation of leading cadres responsible for causing ecological environment damage. Gao Guilin and others focused on the path of perfecting the system of life-long accountability for ecological environmental damage: clarifying the subject of responsibility, refining the form of responsibility, distinguishing the time limit of accountability, independent initiated entity, quantitative standards of accountability, and corresponding supporting systems.[64] Wang Yanfang and others have also made a thorough study on the lifelong investigation of environmental damage liability from the perspective of ecological civilization.[65] Some of these research results have become national policies and legal provisions.[66]

Environmental law is a new branch of administrative law. The two have overlap and intersection in the legal system of environmental administration. However, environmental law focuses on the specific management system of environmental protection, while administrative law focuses on the basic theory and system of overall administrative activities. They each have their own emphasis on the issue of environmental administration. These research results of environmental law provide abundant materials and important ideas for forcing research in administrative law, from the basic theory and basic system level, to systematically study general issues such as the

[61] See Liu Chao, *Effluent Discharge Standard Particulization—Making Pollution Controlling Red Line the Center of 'the Most Stringent Water Resource Management, Science of Law*, no. 2, 2013.

[62] See Zuo Qiting, Hu Desheng, Dou Ming, Zhang Xiang, and Ma Junxia, *Research Framework and Core System of the Most Stringent Water Resource Management System that is Based on Harmonious Relationship between Water and People, Resources Science*, no. 5, 2014.

[63] See Xiong Zhanglin, *Determining the Nature of Continuous Imposition of a Penalty —Center on Article 59 of the new Environmental Protection Law, Journal of East China University of Political Science and Law*, no. 5, 2015.

[64] See Gao Guilin and Chen Yunjun, *On the Building of a lifelong Accountability System for Ecological and Environmental Damage, Social Sciences in Guangxi*, no. 5, 2015.

[65] Wang Yanfang&Li Liangguo, *Analyzing the lifelong Accountability System for Ecological and Environmental Damage from the Perspective of Ecological Civilization, Tribune of Study*, no. 7, 2015.

[66] Refer to the *Decision of the Central Committee of CPC and the State Council on Accelerating the Water Conservancy Reform and Development*, Article 59.1 of the *Environmental Protection Law andthe Measures for the Accountability of Party and Government Leaders for Damage to the Ecological Environment (for Trial Implementation)*, etc.

renewal of administrative law concepts in the low-carbon era, the development of basic principles, low-carbon administrative entities, procedures, various administrative acts of implementing low-carbon regulations, administrative accountability and administrative litigation systems related to climate change.

In addition, as a discipline group for studying the public administration organizations and their policy operation mechanisms,[67] public management also involves a lot of research on the government governance in response to climate change. It mainly deal with four aspects: first, the government models for addressing climate change. For example, Huang Aibao put forward a model of "low-carbon government" in response to the shortcomings of traditional government model in dealing with climate change. He pointed out that in the low-carbon era, besides having previous public functions, the government should also fulfill its responsibility of promoting low-carbon economic development and building a low-carbon society. On the one hand, the government should conduct the low-carbon management of social public affairs, on the other hand, it should also implement the low-carbon management of its own internal affairs.[68] According to scholar Li Junpeng, it is the government that should take the lead in building a low-carbon society. The government should make low-carbon administrative planning and development goals, upgrade energy-saving technologies with the help of market means, and establish a corresponding regulatory system.[69] Second, government behavior mechanisms to address climate change. For example, Zhang Huanbo and others made a comprehensive review of the typical measures taken by local governments to cope with climate change (policies and plans, organizational construction, assessment and accountability, legal protection, scientific research, model projects, and clean development projects) and they found that calls from the central government, political promotion motivation, and financial benefits are the main factors that prompt local governments to respond to climate change. On this basis, they suggested that the central government should attach importance to the capacity-building of local governments to deal with climate change and adopt reasonable incentive policies.[70] Third, system construction of government energy conservation and emission reduction. For example, Yin Yanhong and others believe that "requirements for low-carbon government include: first, low-carbon organization, that is, to set up lean institutions and personnel arrangements, scientific and rational distribution of functions and so on, to reduce carbon emissions through saving administrative costs. Second, low-carbon office conditions, which requires as much as possible to control public vehicles and energy consumption with high-carbon emissions, giving priority to the use of low-carbon energy consumption supplies.

---

[67] See Wang Lefu, *On Evolution of the Connotation and Longitudinal Disciplinary System of the Science of Public Administration, Journal Management World*, no. 6, 2005.

[68] See Huang Aibao, *Innovation of Ecological Administration and Construction of Low-Carbon Government, Social Science Research*, 2010.

[69] See Li Junpeng, *Six Hot Issues Concerning Theoretical Study of Low Carbon Government, Study Times*, May 24th, 2010.

[70] See Zhang Huanbo, Ma Li, Li Huimin, and Qi Ye, *Analysis of Chinese Local Governments' Acts and Mechanisms Addressing Climate Change, China Public Administration Review*, 8, 2009.

Third, the low-carbon workflow, that is, to promote the implementation of 'seamless government', should reduce unnecessary levels of government vertically."[71] Fourth, government performance management in response to climate change. Based on the concept of "low-carbon economy", Chen Xiaochun and others constructed a low-carbon government performance evaluation system containing four aspects: the choice of evaluators, the design of evaluation index, the identification of evaluation methods and the management of evaluation results.[72] While with the other four aspects of low-carbon guidance, low-carbon security, low-carbon self-control, and low-carbon management, scholar Guo Wanda, designed the evaluation index of low-carbon government, and evaluated the effectiveness of low-carbon government construction in some areas of China.[73] Public administration and administrative law are both disciplines that study public administration, and are closely related to administrative laws. The above research provides useful research ideas for administrative law research on government functions, administrative actions, organizations, and accountability in response to climate change.

(III) Summary

Facing the severe challenge of global warming, scholars at home and abroad have explored the issue of climate change from different perspectives, such as law, political science, public management and economics, etc., and have achieved rich results. These achievements are of great significance to the research in this book. Sociological and political studies have provided a basis for administrative law to study the government's position and function in dealing with climate change, and help us grasp the administrative mode of low-carbon society construction as a whole. The study of low-carbon regulatory policy tools in economics can provide analytical tools for administrative organs to choose administrative action modes of climate change rationally. The research of environmental law and administrative law have characteristics in common, which provides a theoretical basis for the further study of the development of the principles of administrative law, low-carbon administrative legislation, and low-carbon administrative litigation in this book. However, due to the limitations of research perspectives of different disciplines, the existing research also has some deficiencies, which need to be further explored from the perspective of administrative law.

i. The current studies of political science and sociology mainly illustrate the government's role and basic theory in combating climate change from the perspective of macro principles, but fail to design the specific functions of the government in this regard and the various management systems and measures to achieve the functions. For example, Beck reveals that mankind has entered a

---

[71] See Yin Yanhong& Wang Yong, *Low Carbon Politics from the Perspective of bureaucracy, Journal of Guangdong Institute of Public Administration*, no. 4, 2012.

[72] See Chen Xiaochun and Wang Xiaoyan, *Review of Government Performance Assessment System from Low-Carbon Perspective, Chinese Public Administration*, no. 10, 2012.

[73] See Guo Wanda, Liu Yu, and Liu Yipin, *Construction and Assessment of a Low Carbon Government Index System, China Opening Herald*, no. 4, 2011.

risk society, but does not put forward specific measures to prevent and deal with risks; Giddens put forward the idea of "political convergence" and "economic convergence", but did not provide specific institutional design. In this regard, these measures and designs need to be worked out and concretely implemented by administrative law through the study of the government's administrative functions and actions in response to climate change.

ii. Public Management mainly studies the administrative activities to cope with climate change from the aspects of government's organizational system, management mechanism, administrative decision-making, and implementation; Economics studies the policy tools of energy conservation and emission reduction based on economic analysis such as the relationship between government and market, game theory and cost-benefit analysis. However, Public Administration and Economics have failed to discuss from a legal perspective the government's statutory functions and responsibilities in the construction of a low-carbon society, the administrative acts of setting and applying low-carbon regulations, the rights and obligations of social members to save energy and reduce emissions, legal responsibilities, and their investigation mechanisms, etc., all of which need to be undertaken by the research of administrative law.

iii. Environmental Law is currently the main force in the legal research on dealing with climate change, but it mainly studies specific environmental management systems. These studies cannot replace the study of the basic theories and systems of administrative law on government administrative activities. Generally speaking, environmental law is the specific application of the general principles of administrative law in environmental administration. Therefore, if the basic content of administrative law cannot meet the requirements of low-carbon era, and its research on basic theories and basic systems lags behind that of environmental protection law, it will not be able to guide or even hinder the development of the latter. At the same time, if the research results of environmental law on specific environmental management system are not refined and absorbed through the study of administrative law, the general principles and institutional norms of government administrative actions in the low-carbon era with more universal significance cannot be formed. For example, the *Environmental Protection Law* of 2014 strengthens the administrative enforcement and penalties for environmental violations of enterprises, which brings about the development and changes of China's administrative enforcement and punishment system in the low-carbon era. Those changes and developments are the results of the studies in the basic theoretical level of administrative law.

The research results on climate change abroad can be used for reference in this book, but they are not fully suitable for China's national conditions. Based on the principle of common but differentiated responsibilities and the great differences between China and western countries in terms of economic development level, environmental resources endowment, and degree of climate vulnerability, China cannot copy theories and systems abroad but must study and establish administrative law theories and systems with Chinese characteristics to cope with climate change according to its own political, economic, cultural and ecological environment.

Faced with the challenge of climate change, contemporary administrative law should not be confined to the theory of "power control administration" in the era of free rule of law and the theory of "welfare administration" in the era of social rule of law. It should also develop and form the theory of "low-carbon administration" to deal with the risk of climate change. In this context, the traditional theories and systems of basic principles of administrative law, administrative entities, actions, procedures, and accountabilities are facing adjustments and changes in varying degrees. At present, the study of administrative law has begun to pay attention to climate change, and has been extended on individual topics such as administrative organization and actions in responding to climate change. But overall, the existing results are scattered and lack of systematicness. No one has conducted a comprehensive and systematic theoretical analysis on how the important categories of administrative law such as the basic principles, administrative entities, behaviors, procedures and accountabilities reflect the low-carbon concept and meet the low-carbon requirements from the perspective of the overall system of administrative law. Moreover, the existing achievements mainly focus on the individual countermeasures of specific problems, and have not yet revealed the changes in value orientation and theoretical basis of administrative law under the background of climate change. Administrative law still has a long way to go and needs more in-depth and systematic discussion and research.

This book aims at how contemporary administrative law responds to climate change. Compared with the macro-study of national strategies, basic policies, and micro-study of specific energy-saving and emission reduction methods and technologies, this book mainly studies the development of basic theories and categories of administrative law in the low-carbon era from the perspective of administrative law at the meso-level. The basic technical route is: to achieve the goal of effectively responding to climate change and actively promoting the construction of low-carbon society by administrative law, to carry out thematic discussions on the basic structure of administrative law, to take the legal problems existing in practice as the guide, to comprehensively use the methods of legal philosophy, normative analysis, comparative analysis, legal policy science and interdisciplinary research, to systematically study the development and changes of basic principles of administrative law, administrative entities, actions, procedures, and accountabilities and other items in dealing with climate change, and to carry out a new round of theoretical and institutional construction according to the low-carbon requirements. The main contents include the renewal of the concept of administrative law in response to climate change, the development of the basic principles of administrative law, the low-carbon norms of administrative law for administrative entities and their activities in organizational structure and administrative procedures, various administrative action norms that guarantee administrative organs to effectively implement low-carbon regulations in society, the administration accountabilities that embody low-carbon constraints and the construction of their investigation mechanisms, etc.

Contents

About the Authors

Shirong Fang male, Professor of Zhongnan University of Economics and Law, Chief Expert of Legal Development and Judicial Reform Research Center, Doctor of Law, Doctoral Supervisor. Vice-President of China Administrative Law Society, Vice-President of Hubei Law Society. He has been a senior visiting scholar at Georgetown University, the University of California, Los Angeles, Pace University, and Goethe University. He has presided over more than 20 key programs of the National Social Science Fund, Key Research Projects of Philosophy and Social Science of Chinese Ministry of Education, and Key Projects of Key Bases of Humanity and Social Science of Chinese Ministry of Education. He has written more than 40 books, such as On Specific Administrative Actions, On Administrative Counterparts, Research on Administrative Legal Relations, and Research on Power Restriction Mechanism and Its Legalization. About 200 of his academic papers have been published in important academic journals such as Chinese Journal of Law and China Legal Science. His scientific research achievements have won more than 20 awards at the national, provincial, and ministerial levels.

Binglin Tan male, Doctor of Law, Researcher of Legal Development and Judicial Reform Research Center, Zhongnan University of Economics and Law, Deputy Editor of Studies in Law and Business. He has participated in the research of the key programs of the National Social Science Fund, Key Projects of Key Bases of Humanity and Social Science of Chinese Ministry of Education, Social Science Fund of Hubei Province, and other projects. He has published academic monographs such as The Government and Public Relations in "Participatory Administration", nearly 10 of his papers were published in core academic journals such as Law Science, Dong Yue Tribune, Jiang Huai Tribune, and many papers were reproduced in the full text by RDFY.

Chapter 1
Response of Administrative Law to Climate Change

1 Addressing Climate Change: Contemporary Mission of Administrative Law

1.1 Legal Adjustment to Address Climate Change

In order to meet the tough challenges of climate change, China must actively promote the construction of low-carbon society and achieve low-carbon social and economic development. This will be a complex national governance project, which needs the adjustment, regulation and guarantee from the legal system. First of all, low-carbon development, a new value orientation with the characteristics of the current era, reflecting the construction of ecological civilization and sustainable development, needs to be solidified by law and passed into the idea and behavior-modes of all members of society through institutional arrangements. At each stage of the development of the society, one or several values always play a dominant role, while other values play a secondary or subsidiary role.[1] The dominant value of a society must be confirmed by law to be legitimate, because law is the embodiment of people's will and the greatest common divisor of social opinions. The new value orientation of ecological protection and energy saving and emission reduction put forward in the low-carbon era should be upgraded to the public will and national will through the solidification of law, thus leading and regulating the construction of a low-carbon society as the dominant value of the society. Secondly, the relationships among multiple interests in the construction of a low-carbon society need to be coordinated by law. There are complex interest relationships in the construction of a low-carbon society, which include the intricate relationships formed between various parties such as governments at all levels, different enterprises and citizens, involving different interest demands and claims such as ecological environment interests, economic interests, individual freedom interests, etc. We should comprehensively consider and

[1] Zhang Wenxian, *Philosophical Review of Law (Revised)*, University of Political Science and Law Press, 2003, 189.

S. Fang and B. Tan, *On the Administrative Law of China in Addressing Climate Change*,
https://doi.org/10.1007/978-981-19-7705-3_1

coordinate various interest relationships, balance the relationships with law, so as to promote the benign game between different interest parties, thus prevent and resolve conflicts and disputes. Thirdly, the public policy of low-carbon society construction needs to be implemented by law. At present, the construction of a low-carbon society in China is mainly driven by policies. For example, in 2007, the State Council issued *China's National Climate Change Program*, and in 2009, the Standing Committee of the National People's Congress adopted the *Resolution of the Standing Committee of the National People's Congress on Active Response to Climate Change*. And there is still a lack of special legislation in this area. However, policies tend to be rigid, lack operability and state coercive means, their governance effects are limited. The law can guide all kinds of social entities to take low-carbon actions by allocating rights and obligations and setting behavior patterns, and provide a rigid guarantee for the implementation of low-carbon public policy with civil liability, administrative liability and criminal liability. Therefore, in order to effectively implement the national public policies to deal with climate change and build a low-carbon society, the relevant policies must be transformed into laws in a timely manner.

Climate change has a wide impact on human society. From the perspective of legal relationships, the law to deal with climate change should adjust both international and domestic legal relations. It not only adjusts legal relations of public law such as low-carbon regulation, but also adjusts relations of private law such as carbon finance and environmental tort liability. The above characteristics determine that the construction of low-carbon society needs multi-angle and all-round legal adjustments, including coordinated responses from various departments such as international law, civil law, economic law, environmental law, administrative law, and criminal law.

1.2 Specific Role of Administrative Law in the Construction of Low-Carbon Society

Administrative law plays an indispensable role in the construction of low-carbon society because of its unique legal attributes and adjustment methods, and can not be replaced by other branch laws. This means that the administrative law has a great historic mission for the construction of low-carbon society. It must develop and change with the times in order to respond to the demands of the rule of law in the low-carbon era. The above historic mission is mainly reflected in the following aspects:

(I) Building a Low-Carbon Society is a Task of the Times That Can Only Be Accomplished Under the Leadership of the Government

In the construction of a low-carbon society, the production and operation of corporate enterprises and the living consumption of citizens constitute the most important part of social energy consumption and carbon emissions. According to the *Report of the State Council on the Work of Energy Conservation and Emission Reduction* submitted by the National Development and Reform Commission to the Standing

Committee of the National People's Congress in 2014, energy consumption of only 10,000 key energy-using enterprises accounted for more than 60% of the total energy consumption of the whole society in 2013. And according to *China Energy Statistical Yearbook (1996–2005)*, from 1995 to 2004, the energy consumption of urban residents in China has increased from 2.31 × 108 tons of standard coal to 5.65 × 108 tons of standard coal, increasing from 19 to 30% of the total social primary energy consumption of the year.[2] Therefore, as the main carbon emission entities, enterprises and individual citizens should undoubtedly bear the responsibility of energy saving and emission reduction in the construction of a low-carbon society. However, due to the natural profit-seeking nature of corporate as the main body of the market and the prevailing liberal consumption concept among consumers, as well as the Giddens's paradox widely existing in the field of climate change, it is unrealistic to expect that the actions of the entities will consciously turn to low-carbon in production, operation and living consumption. Energy saving and emission reduction is a long-term work that benefits the present and the future. It can only be achieved at the expense of some immediate interests. But as some scholars have said, "There is but one 'social responsibility' for corporate executives,... they must make as much money as possible for their shareholders. This is a moral imperative. Executives who choose social and environmental goals over profits—who try to act morally—are, in fact, immoral."[3] Due to the inherent profit-seeking nature of corporate entities in market activities and the environmental externalities of climate change, the enterprises only spare minimal cost to bear the consequences of pollution. For most enterprises, it is difficult to expect them to have such a strong sense of social responsibility of public welfare. At the citizen level, from the nature of human evolution, ordinary people are generally more sensitive to immediate or short-term interests, but often lack rational understanding of long-term interests. In addition, the prevailing liberal consumption concept in the consumer society determines that most citizens will not choose to abandon current economic benefits or change existing consumption habits to implement energy conservation and emission reduction in coping with climate change. At the same time, due to the counterfactual characteristics of climate change risks and the "Giddens's Paradox" induced by them, people will not take global warming into account in the short term, let alone take practical actions as although global warming has catastrophic risk consequences, it can not be visualized in daily life. But the problem is that when these problems become tangible and serious, they usually mean that actions are meaningless.[4] In fact, it is precisely because of the states' over-indulgence in the economic activities of corporate and individual citizens in the free market economy that the impending climate crisis today is brought about. Therefore, facing the severe challenges of climate change, among all kinds

---

[2] Department of Energy Statistics of National Bureau of Statistics, *China Energy Statistical Yearbook (1996~2005)*, China Statistics Press, 68–79.

[3] See Joel Balkan. The Corporation, The Pathological Pursuit of Power and Profit, London: Constable & Robinson Ltd, 2004, p. 34.

[4] See Anthony Giddens, *The politics of climate change*, trans. Cao Rongxiang, Social Sciences Academic Press (China), 2009, 2.

of social entities, the government is the most qualified to dominate and guide the construction of a low-carbon society because of its long-term strategic vision and strong support of public resources. "Administrative law is a legal norm concerning the organization, function, procedure and relief of administrative power".[5] The statutory responsibilities, institutional settings, authority foundation, action mode and enforcement of effectiveness of the government in building a low-carbon society can not be separated from the provisions and guarantees of administrative law.

(II) Fulfilling China's International Commitment to Reduce Carbon Emissions Requires the Transformation and Implementation of Domestic Administrative Law

As a responsible power, China has always participated actively in international negotiations in the field of climate change, and has taken the initiative to undertake a series of mandatory emission reduction obligations in accordance with the principle of common but differentiated responsibilities. In 2009, Chinese Premier made a solemn commitment to the world before the United Nations Climate Change Conference.[6] At the UN Conference on Climate Change in Paris held on November 30, 2015, President Xi Jinping made an important speech on *Making Joint Efforts to Build an Equitable and Reasonable Climate Change Governance Mechanism through Win–win Cooperations* and also made a solemn commitment to the world.[7] From then on, China has voluntarily assumed the obligation of mandatory emission reduction in response to climate change. Therefore, how to fulfill and implement the international commitments is an important task for China's domestic law-formulation. This task undoubtedly needs the coordinated response and adjustment of various branch laws, and the administrative law should be in an important position as a leader and flag bearer, because the management system and top-level planning of low-carbon society construction are mainly undertaken by the administrative law. This can be seen in *China's Policies and Actions on Climate Change (2013)*. The first part of the report summarizes the top-level planning of China's response to climate change and building a low-carbon society into the following six aspects: "improving governing bodies", "building a target responsibility system for carbon intensity reduction", "carrying out major strategic studies for addressing climate change", "strengthening plan formulation for addressing climate change", "promoting legislation on climate

---

[5] See Yang Jianshun, *Administrative Law*, ed., China Renmin University Press, 2012, 8.

[6] Premier Wen Jiabao promised to the world on behalf of the Chinse government: the target of cutting carbon dioxide emissions per unit of GDP by 40–45 % from the 2005 level by 2020. At the same time, the Chinese government included this target into the medium- and long-term planning for the national economy and social development as a restraining indicator, and has prepared corresponding statistical, monitoring and assessment methods.

[7] President Xi Jinpin pointed out in a speech, "China's "Intended Nationally Determined Contributions" will make its carbon dioxide emissions reach their maximum by around 2030.Efforts should be made to make this arrive at an earlier time. China will cut its carbon dioxide emissions per unit of gross domestic product, or carbon intensity, by 60–65% from 2005 levels by 2030. China increases the share of non-fossil fuels in primary energy consumption to around 20%. Forest stock volume would increase by around 4.5 billion cubic meters from 2005 levels.".

change" and "improving relevant policy systems". Among them, the improvement of governing bodies needs to be achieved through organization of administrative law. The target responsibility system for carbon intensity reduction depends on the role of internal administrative supervision and administrative performance evaluation. It belongs to the scope of administrative planning to carry out major strategic studies and strengthen plan formulation for addressing climate change. In addition, promoting climate change legislation and improving the relevant policy system are also inseparable from the role of administrative law. Therefore, China's national commitment to carbon emission reduction starts from the step of top-level design by administrative law.

(III) Energy-saving and Emission Reduction Activities of Social Entities Need Comprehensive and Systematic Administrative Laws and Regulations

To cope with climate change, it is necessary to change the current economic production and residents' living modes to a low-carbon behavior mode of energy saving and emission reduction, which will inevitably involve a certain degree of restriction on the rights and freedoms of the entities concerned. In this regard, only with the constraint of public law norms represented by administrative law, the low-carbon behavior mode can be realized. At the same time, mandatory protection can be provided by administrative supervision and law enforcement. Otherwise, without the unified planning and rigid protection of national administrative law, the government cannot continually and steadily from top to bottom implement a low-carbon economy and a low-carbon life of energy conservation and emission reduction in the construction of a low-carbon society. Based on the safeguard effect of administrative supervision on the construction of a low-carbon society, administrative law is of course an indispensable and important supporting law for the construction of a low-carbon society.

(IV) Administrative Activities Themselves are also a Huge Process of Carbon Emissions, Requiring the Restraint of Administrative Law

As we all know, the operation of the state administrative system and administrative activities needs the support of institutions, personnel and corresponding material support factors. From the construction, operation and maintenance of administrative institutions, the financial support of public officials of state organs to the purchase and use of office supplies such as computers, cars and buses, all are accompanied by huge financial costs and energy consumption, and produce direct or indirect greenhouse gas emissions. Therefore, national administrative activities themselves are an important source of carbon emissions, and various public institutions and administrative organizations are the main emission entities of social carbon emissions. According to the official data disclosed in the *Blueprint of Conserving Energy in Public Institutions During the 12th Five-Year Plan Periods* issued by National Government Offices Administration of the State Council, in 2010, the direct energy consumption of public institutions nationwide alone accounted for 6.19% of the total energy consumption in the whole society. In recent years, the ever-expanding expenditure of the three public consumptions directly reflects the huge energy, resources consumption and carbon emissions of the state's administrative activities, and urgently needs to be regulated. In addition, the government, as the representative of the public interest and the flag bearer of the low-carbon society construction, must set an example and take the lead in promoting the low-carbon society construction, so that its administrative activities themselves can meet the low-carbon standards, and it can gain public credibility in the field of energy conservation and emission reduction, and thus plays a pioneering role in the energy conservation and emission reduction for the general public of the society. Therefore, in order to achieve the goal of reasonable control of carbon emissions from administrative activities, the government needs not only streamline institutions and personnel to control the administrative scale, but also simplify and save administrative procedures, including low-carbon operation of material support elements such as office goods used in administrative activities. Controlling administrative power and realizing internal administrative self-control is one of the important functions of administrative law. In order to achieve low-carbon administrative activities, we must rely on administrative law to regulate them. In this regard, China has already issued administrative legislation such as *Energy Conservation Regulation for State-funded Institutions* and the *Regulations on Rigorous Enforcement of Economy and Anti-Waste for the Party and Government Organs* to restrict and control the energy consumption and carbon emission activities of administrative activities.

(V) The Administrative Law has an Irreplaceable Adjustment Function for the Construction of a Low-Carbon Society

In the construction of a low-carbon society, each branch law has a specific adjustment role, and administrative law is no exception. Compared with major branch laws like civil law, criminal law, procedural law and environmental law, administrative law has irreplaceable legal adjustment functions in the construction of a low-carbon society.

i. Civil law mainly regulates the legal relationship between subjects with equal status, mainly restricting the behaviors of the parties through the contractual obligations, tort liability, and creditor's rights and debts of equal subjects. To cope with climate change, the government needs to take necessary measures against citizens, legal persons and social organizations with unequal legal status. This kind of legal relationship obviously has the public law attribute, and it is beyond the adjustment of civil law. Therefore, the relationship must be regulated by administrative actions such as administrative licensing, administrative penalties and even administrative enforcement.
ii. The function of criminal law in the construction of a low-carbon society also has a lot limitations. In the constitution of environmental crime, pollution caused by tangible waste is the object of crime, while the long-lasting intangible pollution (such as carbon emissions) may not be convicted. In addition, there is a contradiction between the unique attribute of the consequences of high carbon emissions(they are difficult to be counted and proved in the short term) and the

requirements for the consequential offense of environmental crimes.[8] Moreover, criminal law mainly deals with illegal acts that seriously endanger social legal interests. But the general minor energy saving and emission reduction and environmental violations are difficult and impossible to be punished at the level of criminal law. For these intermediate illegal zones, the punishment and correction from administrative law are essential.

iii. The function of procedure law is to provide remedies for the infringed legal rights through legal proceedings and judicial trials, such as carbon emission rights and environmental rights in the low-carbon era. However, the adjustment mechanism of the procedure law is mainly post-event adjustment. For environmental hazards with uncertain risks such as climate change, prevention in advance and correction in the process are essential. The procedure law has insurmountable limitations in this respect, which must be avoided by means of administrative law, such as environmental impact assessment and administrative planning in advance, and administrative licensing and inspection system in the process.

iv. Addressing climate change is bound to involve pollution control and market regulation, so environmental law plays an important role in building a low-carbon society. However, both environmental law and economic law are comprehensive branch laws, which include both civil and commercial legal norms of private law nature and administrative legal norms of public law nature, thus overlapping with the adjustment function of administrative law to a certain extent. And in fact they are inseparable from the rule of administrative law. For example, the *2014 Environmental Protection Law* has "teeth" because it contains enforcement penalties (continuous daily penalties for failing to shut down enterprises as scheduled), administrative enforcement (environmental protection departments can enforce closure orders for serious polluting enterprises to rectify) and administrative detention (environmental protection departments can impose administrative detention on the directly responsible executives and other directly responsible personnel of enterprises with serious environmental violations). It can be said that the important function of environmental law and economic law for low-carbon administrative construction itself proves the indispensable adjustment of administrative law.

Compared with the national macro-strategy and basic policies to cope with climate change and the micro-energy-saving and emission reduction methods and technologies, the study of administrative law on this issue is mainly a meso-level study on the principles and basic categories of administrative law. Its role is to implement the national macro-strategy and basic policies from the perspective of administrative law on the one hand, and to provide the government with institutional norms for the development and application of energy conservation and emission reduction methods and technologies on the other.

[8] See Zhang Lei, *Challenges Faced by Establishing Chinese Environmental Criminal Law in a Low Carbon Economy and Countermeasure*, *Journal of Henan University (Social Sciences Edition)*, no. 1, 2011.

Environmental law should study specific environmental management system, but these systems need the support of basic theory and system provided by administrative law. Environmental law should apply the general principles of administrative law to the specific activities of environmental management. Therefore, if the basic categories of administrative law lack systematic development to meet the requirements of the low-carbon era, the basic categories of administrative law can not correctly guide the formulation and implementation of specific systems of environmental law. They overlap and have their own emphasis on dealing with climate change, so the study of environmental law can not replace the study of administrative law. The development of environmental law impels the development and change of the basic theories and systems of administrative law.

2 Two Important Aspects of Administrative Law in Addressing Climate Change[9]

Speeding up the development of low-carbon economy and building a low-carbon society is a clear requirement of *Outline of 12th Five-Year Plan of China*.[10] From the perspective of administrative law research, actively responding to global climate change has become a new administrative function of the government in the current era; therefore, it is necessary to adjust the functions and duties of the government and its administrative actions in order to actively promote the development of low-carbon economy and the construction of a low-carbon society, which inevitably requires administrative law to play a full role.

On the macro level, administrative law has two core functions in dealing with climate change. On the one hand, according to the national strategy and policy objectives of low-carbon development and society construction, we should adjust the allocation of administrative powers and responsibilities and the use of administrative acts, so that the government can effectively play the role of low-carbon regulation of the whole society to achieve the public administration task of building a low-carbon society. On the other hand, the administrative law also has the specific function of regulating and restraining the government's own administrative activities, that is, ensuring those activities to be low-carbon. The implementation is different from the government's low-carbon regulation of the society according to law, and has its specific objects, rules and methods. Therefore, the administrative law can

[9] The content of this section reflects phase-based result of the work done for this topic. The content was published as a paper. See Fang Shirong and Sun Caihua, *On Government Functions and Government Acts that Promote the Building of a Low-Carbon Society*, *Legal Science*, no. 6 (2011).

[10] It is pointed in the *12th Five-Year Plan for Economic and Social Development of the People's Republic of China* that "we will establish green and low carbon development ideas and focus on energy conservation and emission reduction, improve incentives and constraint mechanisms, and stimulate the establishment of resource-saving and environmentally friendly production and consumption to strengthen sustainable development and improve ecological standards.".

deal with climate change from two important dimensions: externally, the administrative law should urge the government to effectively perform the new administrative functions of implementing low-carbon regulations for the whole society. Internally, administrative law must restrict administrative activities to meet low-carbon standards and implement low-carbon administration, which will go beyond the traditional legitimate and reasonable administrative requirements of administrative law and put forward new administrative activity norms with characteristics of the times.

2.1 Administrative Activities Restricting the Government Should Meet the Low-Carbon Requirements

In the construction of a low-carbon society, the government and other public institutions themselves are also important sources of energy conservation and emission reduction control. The cost of financial support and other materials required for the activities of public institutions is also a huge consumption of resources and energy, and will bring a huge amount of greenhouse gas emissions. At present, there are still many energy and resource waste problems in the activities of our government and other public institutions, which will not only increase the financial burden of the country, but also increase carbon emissions and hinder low-carbon development. From a practical perspective, according to the survey report issued by the World Bank, by 2010, there are about 2 million public institutions in China, including 446,200 state organs and other units.[11] In 2010, the largest energy consumption of public institutions in China was coal. The total terminal energy consumption was 192 million tons of standard coal, accounting for 6.2% of the total energy consumption in the country. State organs accounted for 48% of the total energy consumption of public institutions, followed by electricity and gasoline, accounting for 34.3% and 8.54% of the total energy consumption of public institutions respectively. Between 2006 and 2010, energy consumption in public institutions increased by about 15%.[12] These data are not simple numbers or symbols, but they together represent a phenomenon: administrative activities themselves need to comply with low-carbon standards, and they have a great potential in energy conservation and emission reductions. As the representative of public interest and the leader of low-carbon society construction, the government itself must take the lead in energy saving and emission reduction, and give full play to its leading and exemplary role. This must be regulated and controlled by administrative law. Administrative law must restrict administrative activities to meet low-carbon standards by corresponding legal norms, including administrative

[11] In China, public institutions have become a legal concept and refer to state organs, public institutions, groups and organization that entirely or partly use financial fund.

[12] Anonymous author, World Bank Issued a Research Report on Improvement of Energy Efficiency by Public Institutions, website of the Ministry of Finance of the People's Republic of China, http://gjs.mof.gov.cn/pindaoliebiao/diaochayanjiu/201310/t20131029_1004638.html, accessed April 20th, 2015.

organization law norms that guarantee the competence and efficiency of institutions and personnel, scientific, economical and convenient administrative action and procedure law norms, so as to realize low-carbon control of administrative activities themselves. Constraining administrative activities to meet low-carbon standards will require the regulation of many aspects such as administrative entities, ways and procedures of administrative activities, provision of public goods for administrative activities, legal liability and so on by administrative law.

2.2 Urging the Government to Effectively Perform the New Functions of Low-Carbon Regulations

The function of government is the rational design and arrangement of the scope, mode and content of its duties and tasks within a certain space–time range. The purpose of the design and arrangement is to meet the needs of economic and social development. The emergence of the climate change crisis has a significant impact on the global economic and social development. It has put forward more urgent low-carbon emission requirements, and the grand project of building a low-carbon society must be led by the government. The reasons are as follows:

Although the vast majority of manufacturing enterprises and consumer groups are the main targets of energy conservation and emission reduction and have the responsibility to implement low-carbon economic production and consumption, it should also be noted that carrying out energy conservation and emission reduction in response to climate change is a long-term cause conducive to the future survival of mankind and requires a strong sense of public welfare. This process inevitably involves sacrificing some medium-and short-term interests or individual interests, which is in essence in conflict with the profit-seeking nature of various market players. In fact, the material enjoyment which continually breaks the ecological balance mechanism of human beings and the excessive demand of natural energy resources by economic organizations for their own maximum economic interests under the influence of the market are highly related to the environmental and ecological crisis.[13] It's highly relevant. In this sense, it is not feasible for consumers and various economic organizations to spontaneously and consciously build a low-carbon society. The "Giddens's paradox"[14] in reality makes it difficult for any social entity to dominate the construction of a low-carbon society. Only the government has the ability to lead and organize the construction of a low-carbon society. In modern society, the government itself is a huge public policy reserve box, which can regulate, guide and

---

[13] [German]Ulrich Beck, Global Risk Society, trans. Wu Yingzi and Sun Shumin, Nanjing University Press, 2004, 191.

[14] Since the dangers posed by global warming aren't tangible, immediate or visible in the course of day-to-day life—however awesome they may appear—many will sit on their hands and do nothing concrete about them. Yet waiting until they become visible and acute before being stirred to serious action will, by definition, be too late. This is Giddens's Paradox. Giddens, *The politics of climate change*, 2.

even enforce the construction of a low-carbon society through the use of diversified public policies. In addition, carbon emissions exist in almost all kinds of activities of social entities, and the development of national administrative activities will also produce a huge amount of carbon emissions. The low-carbonization of national administrative activities is an important part in the construction of a low-carbon society and it sets an example for the low-carbonization of various activities in civil society. The government must take the lead in energy conservation and emission reduction. And all the above facts require administrative law to play a normative role.

In the low-carbon era, a new and important task of administrative law is to urge the government to effectively perform the administrative functions of low-carbon regulation and actively promote the construction of a low-carbon society. Here, the connotation of low-carbon regulation is broad. It includes not only the administrative regulation of energy saving and emission reduction, but also the administrative supervision of ecological environment protection, which is determined by the coordination and interconnection between energy saving and emission reduction and environmental protection in the construction of a low-carbon society. The administrative law prompts the government to effectively implement the new functions of low-carbon regulation, which should mainly include the following contents:

(I) Establishing and Improving Systematic and Efficient Functional Institutions

As far as performing the new function of building a low-carbon society is concerned, undoubtedly the government should firstly build its own organization. To deal with climate change, China's organized and systematic administrative activities have begun. But there are still some problems that should be paid attention to in the construction of relevant functional institutions and personnel. In the UK, in order to deal with climate change, promote a low-carbon economy and ensure the security of energy supply, the Department of Energy and Climate Change was established specifically as a government agency. This administrative reform in the UK reflects its determination to deal with climate change. Unlike the British model, China implements a complex, multi-headed management organization and management model.[15]

[15] According to the *Notice of the State Council Concerning Establishing a National Leading Group on Climate Change and Energy Conservation and Environmental Protection*, the functional bodies of China that are responsible for low carbon regulation include the national leading group on climate change and energy conservation and environmental protection, the Ministry of Environmental Protection, the National Energy Administration, and the State Forestry Administration, etc. The national leading group on climate change and energy conservation and environmental protection is an advisory and coordinating body of the state that handles work related to climate change and energy conservation and emission reduction. The Office of the Leading Group to Address Climate Change and the Office of the Leading Group for Energy Conservation and Pollutant Discharge Reduction of the State Council are all set up in the National Development and Reform Commission. The work of the Office of the Leading Group for Energy Conservation and Pollutant Discharge Reduction of the State Council that is related to comprehensive coordination and energy conservation is mainly assumed by the National Development and Reform Commission. Work related to

This complex, multi-headed management model takes into account the "compartmentalized" characteristic of the organizational structure of the Chinese government, but whether the system can coordinate internally remains to be observed and tested in practice. In addition, in face of energy saving and emission reduction[16] involving a wide range of contents, how to set up a strong regulatory authority and the corresponding law enforcement team for local governments (especially rank and file) is also an urgent need for further exploration.

(II) **Highlighting the Macro-Control Function for Energy Conservation and Emission Reduction**

The macro-control function for energy saving and emission reduction refers to that energy saving and emission reduction play the role as a dominant tool in building a "resources-conserving and environment-friendly society". As a dominant tool to fully implement the basic state policy of conserving resources and protecting the environment, energy conservation and emission reduction can be brought into play through categorized administrative actions, such as administrative planning, administrative legislation, administrative policies, etc. In addition, we can also find other diversified approaches to bring the macro-control function into play.[17]

(III) **Strengthening the Incentive and Regulatory Functions for Energy Conservation and Emission Reduction**

Actions like administrative guidance, administrative awards, administrative licensing, administrative supervision can be used as ways to achieve the incentive and regulatory functions for energy conservation and emission reduction. Fundamentally speaking, to implement the incentive and regulatory functions means we need to establish a social ecology that is more conducive for energy saving and emission reduction.[18] When implementing the regulatory function, the government should

---

reducing pollutant discharging is mainly assumed by the State Environmental Protection Administration (currently called the Ministry of Environmental Protection). Such functions as the development of new energy resources and carbon sink management are respectively assumed by such bodies that are directly under the State Council as the National Energy Administration and the State Forestry Administration.

[16] The content of energy conservation and emission reduction is quite wide and mainly includes protection and governance of the environment, management of natural resources and energy, finance and tax adjustment, low carbon technology innovation, carbon sink and carbon market management protection and governance, product carbon footprint management and providing publicity and guidance about low carbon consumption, and all other aspects of the work.

[17] This mainly includes organizing the preparation and implementation of special medium and long-term energy conservation plans and annual energy conservation plans; establishing industrial policies that are conducive to energy conservation and environmental protection, changing growth model, and adjusting energy structure and energy consumption structure; comprehensively stipulating the rights and obligations of all sides related to energy conservation and emission reduction such as the government, economic and social organizations and citizens.

[18] Social ecology that is conducive to energy conservation and emission reduction at least includes encouraging and supporting the development of low energy-consuming low emitting and high value-added industries; and limiting the development of high energy-consuming and heavily polluting

pay specific attention to establish the target responsibility and evaluation systems, and build restrictive mechanisms like administrative enforcement and administrative penalties for energy saving and emission reduction.

(IV) Giving Full Play to the Publicity and Education Functions on Energy Conservation and Emission Reduction in the Whole Society

General risks are immediately perceived, but the ecological risks assocbiated with climate change are a slow accumulation process that is difficult to perceive by us in a short period of time. This characteristic of ecological risks determines that the government must give full pllay to the publicity and education function on energy saving and emission reduction in the whole society, so that people can pay attention to its danger and consciously carry out energy saving and emission reduction actions.

(V) Innovating Administrative Management Methods in Low-carbon Developments

Carbon trading, carbon sink management, carbon tax collection and carbon fund management are new administrative methods that have been established and adopted in many countries to deal with climate change and promote low-carbon development. These methods involve new developments and changes in government administrative actions, which are worthy of our study and reference, and also need to be further explored theoretically in administrative law. In order to give full play to the guiding and regulatory function in the construction of a low-carbon society, the government must also notice the deficiencies in the implementations and modes of traditional administrative actions in coping with climate change, and according to these deficiencies, constantly explore and innovate the low-carbon regulatory administrative management methods that are more in line with China's national conditions.

3 Responding to the Low-Carbon Era: Reflections on the Basic Contents of Administrative Law

In order to give full play to the role of promoting the government to effectively perform the low-carbon regulatory function and restrain the low-carbon administrative activities, the present administrative law should update its contents to adapt to the development and changes of the low-carbon era, which should be perceived in all major aspects of the framework of administrative law.

---

industries; encouraging and supporting the development and utilization of biomass energy, wind energy, solar energy, water energy, geothermal energy and nuclear power and other renewable resources and new energy; accelerating the development and spreading of energy conservation and environmental protection technologies, developing energy conservation and environmentally-friendly industries, circular economy, constructing key energy conservation and emission reduction projects.

3.1 Basic Contents of Administrative Law

There are systematic theoretical summaries about the framework of administrative law both at home and abroad, which could be found in the classic textbooks of administrative law in various countries.

According to the contents elaborated in *Administrative Law*[19] by French scholars Jean Rivero and Jean Waline and *French Administrative Law*[20] by Professor Wang Mingyang, a famous scholar of law in China, the French administrative law mainly includes the following contents: basic principles of administrative law, the executive organs of administrative actions (or administrative organizations), the civil service system, the behaviors of administrative organs, the supervision of the government, administrative litigation, remedies other than litigation, and the compensation liability of administrative entities and civil servants. In addition, the property, public expropriation, public requisition and public works of administrative entities are also discussed.

In the works on German administrative law like Schmidt Assmann's *Insights into German Administrative Law*,[21] Hartmut Maurer's *Introduction to Administrative Law*[22] and Hans J. Wolff's *Administrative Law (3 volumes)*,[23] all of the authors have focused on the contents like the principles of administrative law, administrative organizations, activities, behaviors and procedures, supervision over administration, and state compensation, etc.

Japanese administrative law is deeply influenced by the German one and inherits the framework of German administrative law to a certain extent. From the contents discussed in *Administrative Law*[24] written by Japanese scholar Hiromasa Minami and "Trilogy" of Japanese Administrative Law written by Shiono Hiroshi, including *General Introduction to Administrative Law*, *Administrative Remedies*, and *Administrative Organization Law*,[25] and *The General Theory of Japan Administrative Law*

---

[19] [French] Jean Rivero and Jean Waline, *French Administrative Law*, trans. Lu Ren, The Commercial Press, 2007, Table of Contents, *French Administrative Law*, trans. Lu Ren, The Commercial Press, 2007, Table of Contents.

[20] Wang Mingyang, *French Administrative Law*, Peking University Press, 2007, Table of Contents.

[21] [German] Eberhard Schmidt-Assmann, *Insights into German Administrative Law*, trans. Yu An, Higher Education Press, 2006, Table of Contents.

[22] [German] Hartmut Maurer, *Introduction to Administrative Law*, trans, Gao Jiawei, Law Press, 2000, Table of Contents.

[23] [German] Hans J. Wolff, Otto Bachof, Rolf Stober, *Administrative Law*, trans. Gao Jiawei, Commercial Press, 2003, Table of Contents, 1; [German] Hans J. Wolff, Otto Bachof, Rolf Stober, *Administrative Law*, trans. Gao Jiawei, Commercial Press, 2014, 2; [German] Hans J. Wolff, Otto Bachof, Rolf Stober, *Administrative Law*, trans. Gao Jiawei, Commercial Press, 2006, Table of Contents, 3.

[24] [Japan] Hiromasa Minami, *Administrative Law*, trans, Yang Jianshun, 6th ed., China Renmin University Press, 2009, Table of Contents.

[25] [Japan] Shiono Hiroshi, *The General Theory of Japan Administrative Law*, trans., Yang Jianshun, Peking University Press, 2008, Table of Contents; [Japan] Shiono Hiroshi, *Administrative Remedies*, trans, Yang Jianshun, Peking University Press, 2009; [Japan] Shiono Hiroshi, *Admirative Organization Law*, trans, Yang Jianshun, Peking University Press, 2008, Table of Contents.

written by Chinese scholar Yang Jianshun, Japanese administrative law also involves the main parts like administrative organization, administrative functions, administrative actions, administrative procedures, compensation for administrative losses and damages, litigation of administrative cases, etc. Yang Jianshun refined these contents into five parts in *The General Theory of Japan Administrative Law*,[26] including "Overview of Administrative Law", "Administrative Organization Law", "Administrative Function Law", "Administrative Litigation Law" and "Administrative Remedy Law".

Compared with the administrative laws of civil law countries such as France and Germany, the administrative laws of common law countries such as the United Kingdom and the United States lay particular emphasis on the control of administrative power in both content and structure, thus mainly highlighting the parts of delegated legislation, administrative procedures and judicial review. However, apart from this, a large number of English and American administrative law textbooks also have special chapters to study administrative organizations (administrative organs), administrative actions, liability of illegal administration, etc. For example, in Wang Mingyang's *British Administrative Law* (Peking University Press, 2007) and Zhang Yue's *British Administrative Law* (China University of Political Science and Law Press, 2004), which are influential in China, both of the authors elaborated on the contents like central government and local government, public corporations or administrative organization law, administrative action law and administrative remedy in Britain. Peter Leyland's Textbook on *Administrative Law* (translated by Yang Weidong, Peking University Press, 2007) specifically discusses administrative violations and tort liability of public organs. Textbooks of American administrative law, such as Schwartz's *Administrative Law* (translated by Xu Bing, Qunzhong Press, 1986), Gellhorn and Lewin's *Administrative Law and Process* (English version, Law Press, 2001) and Wang Mingyang's *American Administrative Law* (China Legal Publishing House, 1999), all involve a great deal of contents about U.S. federal and local governments (administrative organs), rule-making (administrative legislative acts), etc.

Drawing lessons from the theories of foreign administrative law, Chinese scholars systematically summarize the theories about the content and structure of China's administrative law in line with China's national conditions. At present, the most authoritative and influential textbooks of administrative law are *Administrative law* by Professor Luo Haochai (Peking University Press, 2012), *Administrative Law and Administrative Litigation Law* by Professor Ying Songnian (Law Press, 2009), and *Administrative Law and Administrative Litigation Law* by Professor Jiang Ming'an (Peking University Press, Higher Education Press, 2015). In addition, there is *Administrative Law* by Mr. Weng Yuesheng, known as the "Classic Work of Administrative Law" in Taiwan (China Legal Publishing House, 2009). Although these classic works of administrative law have some differences in the content arrangements, almost all

[26] Yang Jianshun, *The General Theory of Japan Administrative Law*, China Legal Publishing House, 1998, Table of Contents.

of them summarize the basic contents of administrative law into several main components such as basic principles of administrative law, administrative entities (including administrative organs and public servants), administrative actions, administrative procedures, administrative remedies (including administrative review, administrative litigation or judicial review, administrative compensation and reparation), etc.

Accordingly, whether in the administrative law of civil law countries, the administrative law of common law countries or the administrative law of our country, there is basically a consensus that administrative law mainly consists of the above contents, and they are all regarded as several core categories of administrative law.

i. Basic principles of administrative law. Legal principle is the "basic truth or principle of law".[27] For any branch law, the basic principle is the cornerstone of its framework. It is the highest standard and essence guiding the development and application of other supporting structures. It is at the "top" of the whole pyramid of legal construction, and its function in administrative law is no exception. The basic principles of administrative law have four functions: one is to control and multiply the specific norms of administrative law. The second is to act as a guideline for the implementation of administrative acts. The third is to act as a guideline for courts to conduct judicial review of administrative acts. The fourth is to supplement the gaps or deficiencies in the positive law and improve the rigidity of its application.

Throughout the structure arrangements of administrative law textbooks at home and abroad, the basic principles of administrative law are generally reflected in the introduction or summary part, except that in English and American textbooks they are are not listed separately, but are included in the judicial review part. Apart from the concepts, characteristics, legal sources and historical development of administrative law, the basic principles of administrative law are generally the first to be presented or discussed, so they should be the primary factor in the category system of the basic structures of administrative law.

ii. Administrative entity. In terms of concept, when administrative entity is used as the subject of administrative legal relationship relative to the administrative counterpart, it is called "administrative entity"; when it is used as the administrative organ or administrative body that assumes the administrative power, it is called "administrative organization". In the actual process of administrative management activities, the existence of administrative entity is the premise of the operation of administrative law. Because all administrative activities must be implemented by administrative organs, requiring them to have corresponding personnel, entity qualifications and legal status. From the perspective of the content arrangement of administrative law textbooks, almost all of the textbooks have special chapters on "administrative entity" or "administrative organization" despite the many differences between domestic and foreign ones. We could say that "administrative entity" is one part the framework of administrative law, which is a remarkable consensus in the circle of administrative law in the world. For example, the first chapter of *Administrative Law* written by Jean Rivero after "the Basic Principles of Administrative Law" is the "Executive Agency

[27] *Black's Law Dictionary*, West Publishing Co. 1983, p. 1074.

of administrative actions". About German administrative law, whether in Schmidt Assmann's *Insights into German Administrative Law* or Hartmut Maurer's *Introduction to Administrative Law*, both authors have written special chapters on "Administrative Organization". Professor Shiono Hiroshi of Japan has even written a special textbook on administrative organization law. Although the concepts of "administrative entity" or "administrative organization" are seldom mentioned directly in the textbooks of British and American administrative law, contents about the terms like "central government", "local government", "public corporations", "authorization of administrative organs", and "federal government and civil service system" are all undoubtedly discussions on the power allocation and institutional settings of administrative entities. In the domestic administrative law textbooks, administrative entity or administrative organization has also been generally recognized as the basic category of administrative law by scholars. It is elaborated in a single chapter in most of the books, which highlights the importance of administrative entity as part of the framework of administrative law. Another question to be discussed is whether the administrative counterpart corresponding to the administrative entity is also a basic category of administrative law. There is no doubt that administrative counterpart is one of the basic categories of administrative law and plays an important role in the whole theoretical system of administrative law. However, according to the contents of administrative law textbooks in developed countries ruled by law, the administrative counterpart does not belong to the fundamental construction of administrative law, but is analyzed in various theoretical categories integratedly. The reason is that being regulated and protected by administrative law, the administrative counterparts can not form an independent institutional mechanism and play an influential role in the administrative legal relationship, compared with the administrative entity, they should rely on the support of other administrative law categories and thus lack independent theoretical significance. For example, in modern administrative law, although the administrative counterparts enjoy a wide range of rights of participation, the rights must be realized through the administrative entities' performance of corresponding safeguarding obligations. Moreover, administrative law mainly adjusts the use of administrative power. In this sense, the administrative counterparts do not belong to the ontological category of administrative law.

iii. Administrative action. Administrative action plays a important fundamental role in the construction of administrative law. It was once referred to as the "core concept" of administrative law by Otto Mayer, the founder of administrative law in civil law system.[28] We can say that the whole theoretical system of administrative law is built on the "Archimedes fulcrum" of administrative actions.[29] In the administrative law textbooks of the civil law system, administrative actions are discussed as a special category with detailed elaborations. For example, in German administrative law textbooks, "administrative activities" usually form a separate chapter and an important part; in Japanese administrative law textbooks, all specific administrative

[28] Yu Lingyun, *Administrative Law*, 2th ed., Tsinghua University Press, 2014, 214.

[29] Lu Pengyu, *On Archimedean Point in Administrative Law—Examination with German Administrative Legal Relation as the Core*, *Contemporary Law Review*, no. 5, 2009.

acts are collectively referred to as "administrative roles". Although some scholars in China occasionally advocate "administrative treatment" or "administrative sanction" to replace administrative actions, at present no one can shake the monopoly position of the term of administrative action. Although there is no singular terms of directly appeared and recognized in the textbooks of Anglo-American law system, the important contents such as "delegated legislation", "investigation" and "administrative adjudication" can undoubtedly be classified into the category of administrative action virtually. From the perspective of the overall structure of administrative law, the category of administrative actions is the logic guidance and functional targets of other theoretical categories. Specifically, the purpose of setting the basic principles of administrative law is to provide general rules of activities and standards of judicial review for administrative actions. The role administrative entities play is ensuring the entity qualifications and delegations of administrative actions. The administrative procedure is the step, order, mode and time limit that the administrative entity should follow in carrying out the administrative actions. It is the design of the due process of the administrative actions. Therefore, some textbooks even directly name it "the administrative action procedure".[30] Administrative remedy is also highly administrative- action-oriented, because different relief methods like administrative supervision, administrative review, administrative litigation and administrative reparation are all pointing to the legitimacy, rationality and damage remedy of administrative actions. Based on the above analysis, administrative actions should be regarded as the core category in the basic structure of administrative law.

iv. Administrative process. Administrative process is also an important category in the basic structure of administrative law. Administrative process has been abstracted separately as a theoretical category and legal system of administrative law, which is mainly the theoretical contribution of administrative law of modern Anglo-American law system. Due to the principle of natural justice in Anglo-American law system, the administrative law of the system emphasizes the legitimacy of administrative procedures. Full attention has been given to this in both practice and theory in the field of law.[31] From the perspective of textbook content arrangement, the textbooks of Anglo-American administrative law generally have a chapter on administrative procedure or due process. For a long time, the administrative law of the civil law system lays more emphasis on the administrative substantive law and tends to ignore the procedural law. Its emphasis on administrative procedures is closely related to the codification of administrative law procedures after World War II. But up to now, the

[30] Yang Haikun and Zhang Zhiyuan, *On Administrative Law of China*, China Renmin University Press, 2007, 289.

[31] William Douglas, a Chief justice of the Supreme Court of the United States, thinks It is not without significance that most of the provisions of the *Bill of Rights* are procedural. It is procedure that spells much of the difference between rule by law and rule by whim or caprice. See Ren Donglai et al., *Constitutional History of the United States: 25 Major Judicial Cases Affecting the United States*, China Legal Publishing House, 2004, 427; the US scholar Bernard Schwartz thinks that "administrative law is a law that is more about procedure and remedies and is not a substantive law." See Bernard Schwartz, *Administrative Law*, trans. Xu Bing, Qunzhong Publishing House, 1986, 3.

independent theoretical significance of administrative process in the construction of administrative law has been generally recognized in civil law countries. In the above-mentioned textbooks of administrative law written by German and Japanese scholars, almost all the authors specifically elaborate on "administrative process".

It should be pointed out that a few administrative law writers introduce administrative process as part of administrative actions. In their books, they only reveal the simple relationship between administrative process and administrative actions in form and content, and fail to see the value of administrative process independent of administrative actions. In modern administrative law, administrative process is not only a form of administrative action, but also a due process with independent value of justice. As a kind of due administrative process, it not only shows the shape and process of administrative actions and guarantees administrative efficiency, but also has independent values such as safeguarding the dignity of administrative counterparts, and guaranteeing the democracy, legitimacy and scientific rationality of administrative actions. Accordingly, administrative process, as a part of the framework of administrative law independent from administrative actions, is more in line with the trend of the development of modern administrative law.

v. Administrative liability mechanism. There must be relief for rights, and there must be liability for power. The purpose of administrative law is not only to protect citizens' rights and interests, but also to restrain administrative power, and to restrain it through rigid system. If the administrative actions of the administrative entities violate the provisions of administrative legal norms or cause damage or loss to the administrative counterparts, the state has the obligation to set up the corresponding administrative legal system to investigate their liability, so as to achieve corrective justice. This is not only the logical extension of administration according to law, but also the prerequisite of constitutional principles of popular sovereignty and human rights protection for administrative law. Therefore, the basic structure of administrative law should also include the category of administrative liability.

It is a strong common understanding among Chinese and foreign scholars of administrative law that the implementation mechanism of administrative liability is part of the basic structure of administrative law. In the Anglo-American law system, the scholar Roger once said, "British administrative law is built around the core of giving formal relief to the infringement caused by the acts of public institutions".[32] From a stylistic point of view, the above-mentioned textbooks of administrative law in Anglo-American law countries all emphasize the implementation of administrative liability, such as "administrative tribunal", "the availability of judicial review", "administrative adjudication" and "administrative ombudsmen". In the textbooks of civil law system, administrative liability is introduced separately, as in *Administrative Remedies* written by Professor Shiono Hiroshi. Or it is composed of scattered forms of liability such as administrative supervision, administrative review(appeal), administrative litigation and damage actions against the government, which are

[32] Roger Warren Evans, *French and German Administrative Law: with Some English Comparisons, International and Comparative Law*, Quarterly 1965, no. 14.

typical in French and German administrative law. Both ways of content arrangements can be found in administrative law textbooks in China in recent years. Generally speaking, administrative liability and its implementation mechanism are considered as an independent category in administrative law, which is a common understanding in the academic circles. In China's administrative legal system in a broad sense, the implementation mechanism of administrative liability should include administrative performance evaluation, administrative letters and visits, administrative accountability, administrative review, administrative litigation, and administrative compensation and reparation.

3.2 The Basic Contents of Administrative Law Have Not Yet Fully Addressed Low-Carbon Related Problems

The response of administrative law to the low-carbon era means the concept and requirements of low-carbon development are fully embodied and systematically implemented in the basic content of administrative law. This requires not only the theoretical development of administrative law, but also the construction and improvement of relevant low-carbon administrative legal system. Specifically, the basic principles of administrative law, administrative entities, administrative actions, administrative processes and administrative remedies should reflect the requirements of administrative law with the characteristics of the low-carbon era. However, if we recall the above-mentioned basic contents of the present administrative law, we can find that they have not fully responded to the changes brought about by the low-carbon era. The reasons are as follows:

Firstly, in terms of the basic principles of administrative law, the two traditional basic principles of legitimate administration and reasonable administration could no more regulate the low-carbon administrative activities that administrative organs must carry out in the present and future. Due to the differences in guiding concepts and adjustment methods, the contents of these basic principles have limitations in adapting to the requirements of the low-carbon era, which need to be supplemented by the establishment of new low-carbon administrative principles. Low-carbon administration not only requires legal and reasonable administrative actions, but also requires that administrative activities take ecological protection as a new administrative goal and value orientation with the characteristics of the times. It requires the establishment of low-carbon standards of administrative actions, and the strengthening of the administrative management mode of ecological risk prevention. And it as well requires that low-carbon environmental protection should be treated as part of the work performance of administrative entities and their civil servants.

Secondly, in terms of administrative entities, the traditional administrative law requires the acts of administrative entities to be legal and efficient. On the basis of that, it is also necessary to emphasize the low-carbon requirements for the establishment and operation of organizational structure of agencies.

As an important consuming body of material resources in the society, the administrative entities will also produce a huge amount of carbon emissions. The larger the scale, the more levels, and the more redundant personnel of administrative entities, the greater the demand for public administrative resources, and the higher the consumption of energy resources and carbon emissions. It should be noted that administrative costs can be converted into carbon emissions according to a certain quantitative relation. The country that started the practice is Britain.[33] The practice in Britain has shown us that more reasonable government functions, scientific institution settings and the control of personnel are important ways to reduce administrative expenditure and save energy and reduce emissions. These ways should be reflected in the norms of administrative organization law.

Without the low-carbonization of the administrative entities themselves, a low-carbon society can not be built. Therefore, it is extremely necessary to regulate the entities based on low-carbon standards. The regulations can be implemented in the basic elements of the rules of organization of administrative entities. In the regulation of the element of agencies, we must focus on streamlining the current over-staffed deliberation and coordination bodies and provisional institutions, controlling the hidden expansion of derivative administrative bodies, abolishing the mechanical point-to-point settings of superior and subordinate institutions, and appropriately removing or merging the working departments with the same or similar functions. In the regulation of the element of personnel, we should deal with the problem of over-staffing and its accompanying structural redundancy, and establish a normal mechanism for the removal of redundant civil servants. In the regulation of the element of material support, firstly, we should establish relevant low-carbon national standards to restrict the allocation of administrative buildings and office goods; secondly, we should formulate corresponding energy-saving and emission reduction guidelines to guide the operation and use of administrative guarantee elements; finally, we should establish necessary internal and external regulatory mechanisms to ensure the

---

[33] According to the *UK 2005 Hampton Report*, administrative burden could be achieved through streamlining independent regulators (by reducing them from 73 regulators to seven thematic bodies) and emphatically regulating high risk projects based on risk assessment. According to the data provided in the investigation report issued by UK regulation optimization work team in 2005, if the rules of "what you see is what you get" and "one in, one out" were observed and such methods as simplifying regulatory programs and reasonably determining the order of regulatory precedence (base on occurring possibility and severity level of risks) were used to reduce administrative costs, the potential economic value of the methods would reach 1% of UK's GDP. Since UK's GDP was 1.565 trillion in 2002, while the amount of carbon dioxide generated was equivalent to 655.8 million tons. Therefore, when this kind of measures such as improving the establishment of the administrative bodies and allocation of functions, were used, it was equivalent to saving admirative costs of 15.6 billion US dollars, and was also equivalent to reducing carbon emission 6.558 million tons. See Philip Hampton, Reducing Administrative Burdens: Effective Inspection and Enforcement, London: Her Majesty's Stationery Office, March 2005, pp. 115–120; Better Regulation Task Force, Regulation–Less is More: Reducing Burdens, Improving Outcomes, London: Cabinet Office Publications and Publicity Team, March 2005, p. 3; UK Department of Energy and Climate Change, UK Climate Change Sustainable Development Indicator: 2008 Greenhouse Gas Emissions, Final Figures, London: UK Department of Energy and Climate Change, February 2010.

low-carbonization of the allocation and use of the administrative entities' material guarantee elements.

Thirdly, speaking of administrative procedures, they are the specific processes of the administrative actions carried out by administrative entities. Through eliminating red tape in links and procedures, we could build more simple and convenient procedure models, thus effectively reducing unreasonable carbon emissions. At the same time, it can also facilitate the work of the counterparts, reduce unnecessary social cost consumption, and reduce energy consumption and carbon emissions in the overall sense of low-carbon life. Therefore, putting forward low-carbon requirements for administrative procedures and standardizing them accordingly should also be a development of administrative law in adapting to low-carbon requirements. However, due process and procedural rationality have been the focus of our attention on the concept of administrative process until now, and the low-carbonization of the procedures has not aroused much concern. The "due process" discussed in academic circles mainly emphasizes the concepts like "administrative openness", "administrative hearing", "safeguarding the right to know, the rights of participation and relief of administrative counterparts and interested parties" and "avoidance" and so on. Its purpose is to control (power) and protect (rights), which does not reflect the "the justice of climate change" of low-carbon development today.

The promotion of low-carbon development requires the establishment of low-carbon administrative procedures. In the present specific system, we fail to consider about energy saving and emission reduction of the ecological environment in the current administrative processes. This not only reveals the waste of resources and high carbon emissions in the operation of the processes themselves, but also shows that the existing procedure mechanism can not effectively bring into play the functions of law enforcement and decision-making to promote energy conservation and emission reduction in the society. Therefore, constructing and improving the low-carbon administrative processes for energy conservation and environmental protection is another important task in administrative law in responding to the low-carbon era. In the low-carbonization of the major components of administrative processes, we should eliminate unnecessary procedural matters (such as abolishing various unnecessary proofs) and relatively centralize the powers of administrative entities, thus reducing unnecessary procedural parties and reducing carbon emission sources. Speaking of the time elements, the longer the administrative procedure lasts, the longer the carbon footprint will be. Because the carbon footprint of administrative process is the total amount of carbon dioxide emissions caused by all activities of the participants in the process in a certain period of time. Therefore, the low-carbonization of the time elements requires the improvement of the prescription system of administrative processes and the shrinking of the cost of time of the participants in administrative procedures. In the low-carbonization of the space elements, we could establish flexible close proximity jurisdiction rules, remove or merge cumbersome and redundant procedures, and use extensively of low-carbon, convenient and economical methods (like online office) in the procedures. Therefore, in order to improve the administrative procedures in China, we should take low-carbonization into consideration and optimize the administrative processes. We could reduce the excessive formalized and tedious procedures in administrative activities, and properly expand the scope of application of administrative summary procedures in administrative activities. At present, summary procedures can only be applied to a very small number of areas, such as administrative penalties, which needs to be improved. In order to fully realize the low-carbonization of procedure, we can consider expanding the scope of application of summary procedures in administrative activities in the future.

Fourthly, the administrative law has put forward new requirements for administrative actions in response to climate change, which are mainly manifested in two aspects: on the one hand, the administrative organs should effectively perform the new function of implementing low-carbon regulations in their actions in the whole society. They need to be adjusted, developed and innovated, because the traditional administrative actions were mainly formed in the free and social rule of law periods, and they have some limitations in concepts, types and modes to fully meet the requirements of the new functions in the risk rule of law era represented by environmental risks like climate change. For example, we need to highlight the risk control and preventive functions of administrative actions. And we must adjust the ways according to new problems and new situations, when applying traditional administrative actions such as administrative licensing, administrative awards, administrative guidance, administrative penalties and administrative enforcement to the field of energy conservation and emission reduction management. In addition, facing the new management issue of low-carbon regulation, we must innovate the types and ways of administrative actions, explore and establish new administrative actions such as carbon information management, carbon trading management, carbon sink management and so on. On the other hand, the organs need to standardize and realize the low-carbon operation of the administrative actions themselves. In fact, there is room for low-carbon improvement in all kinds of administrative actions, and there is also great potential for energy conservation and emission reduction in them.[34] At the same time, the material support for administrative activities, i.e., the office goods, office space and vehicles, need low-carbon control and must meet the low-carbon standards. The materials needed for administrative activities are huge energy and resource consumption, and can produce huge carbon emissions.[35] The low-carbonization of material resources

[34] For example, online examination and approval of permits, administrative guidance, electronic law enforcement and video teleconference, etc. are all behaviors that save energy and reduce carbon emission.

[35] Take the US Federal Government as an example, it is because the federal government consumes significant amount of energy and resources and emits huge volume of carbon emission, the President of the United State required that all agencies of the federal government play a leading role in establishing clean energy economy, and has provided a detailed implementation plan to the Chairman of the Council of Environmental Quality and Office of Management and Budget (OMB). The plan involves greenhouse gas emissions that are directly generated by the resources owned or controlled by bodies of the federal government, greenhouse gases emissions directly caused by the power, heat, gas, etc. purchased by bodies of the federal government, and greenhouse gases caused by activities of or controlled by or related to the activities of the bodies of the federal grommet (for example, postal services, the supply chain of automatic vending machines and transport of civil servants.). According to the targets of energy conservation and emission reduction

used in administrative activities embodies at least the following aspects: building and using energy-saving office buildings; saving the use of coal, gas, water, electricity and other energy sources; using energy-saving and environmental-friendly lighting equipments, office supplies, vehicles and other public facilities; strengthening the greening construction of the office area; implementing the recycling of office supplies and so on.

Fifthly, the low-carbonization of administrative liability means: the administrative law should endow the government with legal obligations to implement low-carbon regulations and comply with low-carbon standards. If the government neglects to fulfill its duties or related obligations, it should assume corresponding political and legal responsibilities. This means the government should establish a legal liability system with low-carbon requirements in administrative law. This system must be a very strict and rigid one, because protecting the environment accords with the major long-term interest of human beings and the damage of the environment is irreversible once made. The measures we could use including the implementation of life-long accountability for ecological environment decision-making, strict performance evaluation and internal administrative accountability, and corresponding administrative review and litigation systems as well. In the construction of this liability system, the current administrative law regulations indeed need to be improved.

---

set by the bodies of the federal government, the federal government of the United States will directly reduce carbon emissions by 28% on the basis of the carbon emissions in 2020 and 2008 (for example, raw oil and energy efficient buildings), and will indirectly reduce carbon emission by 13% (for example, commuting of employees of the federal government and disposal of office wastes). According to such a target, the federal government can reduce energy consumption that is equivalent to 646 trillion J, which is equivalent to conserving 235 million barrels of raw oil or reducing the number of cars by 17 million. By 2020, This will be equivalent to accumulatively reducing energy expenditure by 8 billion to 11 billion by 2020. The White House Office of the Press Secretary, President Obama Sets Greenhouse Gas Emissions Reduction Target for Federal Operations, January 29, 2010, http://www.whitehouse.gov/the-press-office/president-obama-sets-greenhouse-gas-emissions-reduction-target-federal-operations, last visited on September 18th, 2010.

Chapter 2
Study on Low-Carbon Administrative Principle

1 Basic Principles of Traditional Administrative Law and Their Era Limitations

1.1 Main Contents of Basic Principles of Traditional Administrative Law

The basic principles of administrative law highly embody the spirit, purpose and value orientation of administrative law, and guide the formulation, implementation and compliance of administrative law. They are the foundation of specific rules of the administrative law. Therefore, the administrative law should guide and standardize the corresponding administrative activities to deal with the climate change in the present era. This should first be embodied in the basic principles. Thus, it is a must to discuss and study the basic principles of the administrative law first.

The basic principles of administrative law are highly refined in many countries, among which, France and Germany in the civil law system and Britain and America in the common law system are the representatives.

France, as the home country of modern administrative law, first established and developed an independent administrative law system, and then summarized two basic principles, i.e., principle of legally prescribed administration and principle of proportionality. As for the "principle of legally prescribed administration", most French scholars believe that it means administrative activities shall comply with laws, and those who violate laws shall undertake the corresponding legal liability, such as invalidity, revocation or administrative compensation. Specifically, this principle includes three aspects: the administration shall be legally authorized; administrative actions shall comply with legal form, standard, purpose and requirement; and the administrative organs shall guarantee the implementation of the administrative law by means of

Part of this chapter was published in the 8th issue of Dong Yue Lun Cong in 2013 under the title of Establishment and Development of Low-carbon Administration Principle.

S. Fang and B. Tan, *On the Administrative Law of China in Addressing Climate Change*,
https://doi.org/10.1007/978-981-19-7705-3_2

all kinds of administrative actions.[1] With regard to the "principle of proportionality", Gustave Peiser, a French administrative jurist, put forward its three core requirements from the perspective of judicial review: the results of administrative decisions cannot "be seemly offensive to conscience, discreditable and shameful, or defy logic"; means shall be commensurate to the purpose; and losses and interests shall be balanced.[2]

The basic principles of German administrative law are well-known for their systematization and refinement, and have a profound impact on the administrative law of various countries. They mainly include the principle of law-based administration, the principle of proportionality and the principle of reliance protection. Otto Mayer, the founder of German administrative law, believed that the principles of law-based administration consist of three sub-principles: creativity of law on regulations, priority of law, and law reservation.[3] In a broad sense, the principle of proportionality includes three sub-principles: appropriateness (administrative means should help to achieve the goal it seeks), necessity (the principle of least infringement), and proportionality of legal interests (the intervention of the administration in citizens' personal interests must be basically proportional to the public interests achieved).[4] The principle of reliance protection came into being after "World War II". Scholars have a consensus view on it: when the members of society trust that some factors in the behavioral process of the administrative entity will remain unchanged, and such trust should be protected according to laws, the administrative entity shall not change these factors arbitrarily, or must make reasonable compensation to the members of society for their loss of trust if it changes these factors in order to protect public interests.[5]

British administrative law mainly adopts the rules and forms of common law. The law-based principle and natural justice principle in the common law tradition played a vital role in the formation and development of British administrative law. Thus, three basic principles of British administrative law come into being, i.e., the principle of ultra vires invalidity, rationality and procedural justice.[6] As the core principle of British administrative law, the principle of ultra vires invalidity prohibits the ultra vires of public authorities, but its specific content has not been clearly stipulated in the statute law. According to jurisprudence of British courts, violation of the principle of natural justice, ultra vires in procedure or ultra vires in essence

[1] See Maurice Hauriou, *Essentials of Administrative Law and Public Law* (First Edition), France, Trans. Gong Mi, et al., Liao Hai Publishing House, Chunfeng Art and Literature Press, 1999, pp. 45–67. Leon Duguit, *Public Law Changes · Law and State*, France, Trans. Zheng Ge, Leng Jing, Liao Hai Publishing House, Chunfeng Art and Literature Press, 1999, pp. 56–62.

[2] See Gustave Peiser, *French Administrative Law*, France, Trans. Liao Mingkun, et al., National School of Administration Press, 2002, pp. 45–51.

[3] See Otto Mayer, *German Administrative Law*, Germany, Trans. Liu Fei, The Commercial Press, 2002, p. 68.

[4] See Chen Xinmin, *Theory of Public Law of Germany*, Shandong University Press, 2001, p. 369.

[5] See Georg Nolte, *General Principles of German and European Administrative Law-A Comparison in Historical Perspective*", Germany, Trans. Yu'An, Issue 2, *Administrative Law Review*, 1994.

[6] See William Wade, *Administrative Law*, the UK, Trans. Xu Bing, et al., Encyclopedia of China Publishing House, 1997, p. 95.

will constitute the ultra vires in administrative law, and will lead to the invalidity of the decisions made by public authorities. The principle of rationality, mainly set up for administrative discretion, is the standard to measure whether the exercise of administrative discretion is reasonable and whether it is abused. This principle also derives from the jurisprudence of British courts. The criteria to judge rationality mainly include whether the legal purpose is violated, and whether there is false motivation, irrelevant consideration or obvious injustice.[7] The principle of procedural justice requires the exercise of administrative power should ensure a minimum level of fairness, justice and rationality, and to be specific, it includes the rule against bias and the rule of fair hearing.[8]

Influenced by the concept of "natural justice" in British common law tradition, American administrative law pays special attention to two basic principles: administrative due process and administrative openness. The principle of administrative due process is the specific application of the principle of due legal process in American Constitution in the field of administrative law. Its core idea is if the decision of the administration will infringe or have other adverse effects on the life, property or freedom of the administrative counterpart, the administration should listen to the opinions of the administrative counterpart. The administration should also eliminate prejudice or avoid bias during the administrative activities. The principle of administrative openness is gradually established based on statute law. The *Freedom of Information Act* and *Government in the Sunshine Act* promulgated in 1967, and the *Privacy Act* promulgated in 1974 stipulate clearly the obligations of the administration in disclosing government documents, meeting minutes and personal records respectively,[9] thus the basic principle of administrative openness in American administrative law is established. This principle requires the administration must issue the administrative information to the public in a timely manner, and actively accept the real-time supervision of the public on its working attitude and working efficiency, thus the deficiencies of other supervision methods can be made up.

China's administrative law started late, but China also refined a series of basic principles by studying and referring to the theoretical achievements and institutional experiences of administrative laws of other countries based on the reality of own administrative law. Among them, the two most commonly viewed and highly generalized basic principles are "legal administration" and "reasonable administration".[10] The principle of legal administration requires the administration must implement administrative management according to laws. The principle of legal administration requires the administrative organs must implement administration according to law. Without clear legal basis, the administrative organs shall not make decisions

[7] See Zhou Youyong, *Study on the Basic Principle of Administrative Law*, Wuhan University Press, 2005, pp. 74–76.

[8] See Zhou Youyong, *Study on the Basic Principles of Administrative Law*, Wuhan University Press, 2005, p. 77.

[9] William F. Funk, Richard H. Seamon, *Cases and Analysis of Administrative Law*, the U.S., China Citic Press, 2003, p. 331.

[10] See Luo Haocai, *Administrative Law*, ed., China University of Political Science and Law Press, 1999, pp. 56–65.

that affect the rights or obligations of the administrative counterparts. According to different functions and contents, this principle specifically includes three sub-principles: authority ruled by law, law priority and law reservation. The principle of reasonable administration requires the administrative organs to implement administration in accordance with legal rationality, for example, fairness and justice, including equal treatment, due process, principle of proportionality and principle of reliance protection. In addition, some scholars believe that the basic principles of administrative law should also include the principles of law-based administration, rationality, administrative responsibility, good faith and due process.[11] Some scholars also expressed their viewpoints from the perspectives of substantive principle and procedural principle. They think the former includes the sub-principles of law-based administration, respecting for and protecting human rights, ultra vires invalidity, reliance protection, proportionality, etc., and the latter includes the sub-principles of due legal process, administrative openness, administrative justice, administrative fairness, etc.[12] Some scholars, on the basis of rethinking the above-mentioned basic principles of administrative law, and taking "the fundamental values and basic contradictions of administrative law" as the internal basis, divide the basic principles of administrative law into three parts: administrative legality, administrative balance and administrative justice. The principle of legally prescribed administration is equivalent to the principle of legal administration in the general sense. Specifically, it includes three sub-principles: authority ruled by law, law priority and law reservation. The principle of administrative proportionality includes the sub-principles of equal treatment, prohibition of excesses and reliance protection. The principle of administrative legitimacy includes such sub-principles as avoiding bias, administrative participation and administrative openness.[13]

These above-mentioned basic principles refined and formed from Chinese and foreign administrative law schools have some differences in terms of cognitive perspectives, required standards or ways of expression, but they all share a common core point in terms of their substantive connotations: basically speaking, they require that all administrative activities of the government must conform to laws and be fair and reasonable, and that the administrative power shall not be imperious or arbitrary, thus constructing a harmonious relationship between the government and citizens. In response to climate change, the administrative law highlights the low-carbon requirements of energy conservation and emission reduction, aiming at adjusting the harmony between people (including government and citizens) and nature. This obviously adds new constraint standards to administrative activities, that is, administration is subject to not only legal and reasonable constraints, but also low-carbon constraint. This low-carbon constraint includes saving resources and energy, reducing carbon

[11] See Ying Songnian, *Administrative Law in Contemporary China*, ed., Founder of China Publishing House, 2005, pp. 80–119.

[12] Jiang Mingan, *Administrative Law and Administrative Litigation Law*, ed., Peking University Press, 2005, pp. 64–79.

[13] See Zhou Youyong, *Study on the Basic Principle of Administrative Law*, Wuhan University Press, 2005, pp. 158, 200, 238.

emission and protecting ecological environment. On the one hand, it requires administrative activities to be low-carbon, and on the other hand, it requires administrative activities to actively promote the low-carbon development of the whole society as its new objectives. This connotation is obviously beyond the content and orientation of the basic principles of legal administration and reasonable administration, thus the basic principles of traditional administrative law have historical limitations to some extent.

1.2 Era Limitations of Basic Principles of Traditional Administrative Law

Generally speaking, administrative law has gone through three different eras: free rule of law (Liberaler Rechtsstaat), social rule of law (sozialer Rechtsstaat) and risk rule of law. Administrative law in different eras has different tasks, thus the basic principles in different eras have different connotations and functions.

(I) **Basic Principles of Administrative Law in the Era of Free Rule of Law**

With the victory of bourgeois revolution and the establishment of constitutional system in European and American countries, modern administrative law came into being and developed gradually. Politically, it aims to restrict the autocracy of the government and protect the legal rights and interests of citizens from illegal infringement by the government. In the period of free capitalism, the capitalist relations of production, which got rid of the shackles of feudal autocracy, required that the principles of free competition, automatic regulation and laissez faire should be followed in economy, and the state should be opposed to intervene in economy in any form, so that the capitalist economy can develop completely according to the law of the market itself. To this end, the administrative law of this period requires the government to act only as a "night watchman" and take "order administration" as its main function, i.e., "the function of the government is to act as a police and guard, but not to provide food, clothing or shelter."[14]

Based on this, the administrative laws of different countries have established different principles to restrict administrative power, for example the principles of law priority and proportionality in France, Germany and other countries of civil law system. These principles aim to control the administrative power in terms of entity and require the administration to be absolutely restricted by laws. Meanwhile, the principles of ultra vires invalidity and due process established by Britain, America and other countries of common law system mainly restrict administrative power in procedure. These principles differ in content expression and control mode, but their core idea is to ensure the administration exercises the administrative power within the

[14] As Louis Henkin said, quoted from Yang Xiaojun, The *Expansion of Western Administrative Power in the 20th Century*, Issue 2, *Journal of Northwest University of Political Science and Law*, 1986.

scope of law, so as to avoid ultra vires and power abuse. Therefore, the administrative law in the period of free rule of law could be regarded as negative administrative law, and the essence of the basic principles of administrative law throughout this period is "power control".

(II) Development of Basic Principles of Administrative Law in the Era of Social Rule of Law

The basic principles of administrative law with power control as their essence satisfied the needs of administrative power control in the era of free rule of law. However, in the period of monopoly capitalism of the capitalist society in the late nineteenth century and early twentieth century, the inherent defects[15] of the laissez-faire market economy began to appear continuously and brought about many social problems. This urgently required the government to make comprehensive and regular adjustments to the economy and undertake the task of intervening in the market economy and providing survival care for citizens. For this reason, the administration has begun to intervene in all aspects of social life. Besides economic affairs, the government covers a mass of administrative services in the fields of science and technology, education, medical treatment, transportation and other social undertakings. Thus, administrative functions were improved, especially the role of administrative supply in realizing public welfare has been given into full play. The administrative laws in the era of social rule of law helped to generally construct "countries substantially ruled by laws" and "comprehensive systems of country supply", that is, the administrative organs should become the supply entity and give full care to the people.[16]

In order to ensure the government can effectively assume the important task of social welfare supply, the basic principles of administrative law in the period of social rule of law helped not only continue to emphasize the supervision and restriction of administrative power, but also focus on promoting the active and effective exercise of administrative power to respond to the needs of people's livelihood. Therefore, the basic principles of administrative law were extended on the basis of the principle of the era of free rule of law guided by "power control". Under the principle of reliance protection and the principle of convenience and high efficiency, the government was urged to actively perform its administrative duties of ensuring people's livelihood, in which "people's livelihood" was highlighted.

These two principles aim at active administration. The principle of reliance protection was first put forward by scholars from Germany and other countries of civil law system after the substantive rule of administrative law replaced the formal one. In a welfare state, citizens expect to arrange their present and future life according to decisions of the administration, so the relationship between country and citizens should be trustworthy. If an administrative action of the administrative agency brings predictable and trustworthy benefits to citizens, the administrative agency shall not

[15] There are some inherent defects for laissez-faire market economy, such as spontaneity, blindness and lag.

[16] Cheng Zhongmo, *New Trends in the Development of Modern Administrative Law*, Taiwan, Issue 6, *Personnel Monthly*, 1988.

revoke that administrative action arbitrarily. If the administrative action must be revoked due to the protection of public interests or in case of emergency, the administration shall make reasonable compensation to the counterpart according to laws. Conflicts will occur between the principle of reliance protection and the principle of administrative legitimacy, which has already reflected in the case of "widow's allowance" of Higher Administrative Court of Berlin, Germany in 1956. Therefore, the relationship between the principle of reliance protection and the principle of administrative legitimacy must be well balanced in each individual case.[17] The principle of convenience and high efficiency means that administrative agency must strictly abide by the legal limit of time and continuously improve its work efficiency when exercising its administrative power or performing its administrative duties, thus provide conveniences for citizens, legal persons and other organizations. The principle of reliance protection and the principle of convenience and high efficiency formed gradually in the development from free rule of law to social rule of law. They mean no abandoning of the basic principles of administrative law in the era of free rule of law, but the expanding and deepening of the same. They can ensure that administrative actions are lawful and reasonable, and at the same time can effectively control administrative power and protect social welfare of the public.

(III) Limitations of Basic Principles of Traditional Administrative Law in the Era of Risk Rule of Law

In the twentieth century, the huge consumption of traditional fossil energy and massive emission of carbon dioxide have brought about the continuous enhancing global greenhouse effect: increasing temperature, frequent occurrence of extreme climate, rapid environment deterioration, etc. Therefore, the exercise of administrative power should include an important task, i.e., regulating environmental risks, besides the requirements of legitimacy and meeting the needs of people's livelihood. Administrative management is also expanding to a wider range of social welfare and environmental fields.[18] Different from the restriction of administrative power in the era of free rule of law and the emphasis on people's livelihood in the era of social rule of law, the administrative law in the era of risk rule of law pays more attention to the protection of ecological environment and the pursuit of ecological civilization, with "ecological protection" as its essence. Therefore, the thoughts of power control

[17] In this case, there is a contradiction between the public interest guaranteed by the principle of law-based administration and the private interest protected by the principle of trust protection, both of which represent the principle of constitutional value. After the case was confirmed by the German Constitutional Court, it was believed that this was the manifestation of the principle of legal stability in protecting the legitimate rights and interests of citizens. To infringe upon the trust of citizens would constitute a violation of the principle of legal stability, applying the principle of trust protection to protect the private interests of citizens. For the specific contents of the case, see Wu Kuncheng: *Preliminary Study on Trust Protection Principle in Public Law*, contained in Cheng Zhongmo, ed., *General Legal Principles of Administrative Law* (II), Taiwan San Min Book Co., Ltd, 1997, p. 241.

[18] See *Administrative Law* written by Bernard Schwartz and translated by Xu Bing, Qunzhong Press, 1986, p. 55.

and ensuring people's livelihood in the basic principles of traditional administrative law can not fully satisfy the requirements of the era of risk rule of law, and gradually exposed its era limitations.

i. Limitations of basic concepts

The basic principles of traditional administrative law focus on the control of administrative power. The principle of legitimate administration formed during the free rule of law period adheres to the strict "power control" concept to ensure the administrative power is exercised within the legal scope and[19] it abides by the rule that "no law, no administration". The principle of reasonable administration is the development of and supplement to the principle of administrative legitimacy. It requires that the administrative power and its exercise should not only conform to laws, but also be properly applied within the limit prescribed by laws. In the following era of social rule of law, this principle played an especially important role. The economic crisis brought about by the failure of market regulation and the social livelihood problems left over from the First World War put forward new requirements for the government to exercise its administrative functions, that is, to actively utilize the wide range of discretion to meet citizens' requirements for survival and development. However, administrative discretion also brought about the problems of abusing administrative power and arbitrary administration. Therefore, the administrative law must attach importance to the restriction on the rational use of administrative discretion, thus deriving such specific contents of reasonable administration as "appropriateness", "necessity", "proportionality of legal interests" and "reliance protection". This shows that the principle of legitimate administration and the principle of reasonable administration aim at restricting administrative violation and maladministration. This idea, limited by the specific era, can not effectively respond to the requirements of the contemporary administrative services of dealing with climate change and promoting low-carbon development. It does not embody the new globally recognized concept: saving resources and energy and protecting ecological environment. After going through the development from the era of free rule of law to the era of social rule of law, now the development of administrative law has entered the era of risk rule of law. Facing the risks of energy, climate and environment crises, the power control concept of traditional administrative law and the principles of legitimate and reasonable administration formed therefrom cannot adapt to the government's tasks in promoting the construction of a low-carbon society or its new functions. Therefore, it is required to establish new basic principles as an important supplement.

ii. Limitations of value objectives

For the principle of legitimate administration and the principle of reasonable administration (including derived sub-principles) in the period of "free rule of law", they play the important role of strictly restricting the ultra vires and abuse of administrative power. The main value objective pursued is to protect citizens' personal dignity,

[19] [English] *Administrative Law* written by William Wade and translated by Xu Bing et al., Encyclopedia of China Publishing House, 1997, p. 5.

freedom and property rights from being infringed by administrative power and to ensure fair treatment. This is mainly reflected in realizing the "harmony between government and citizens" at the political level.

In the era of social rule of law, the principle of reliance protection and the principle of convenience and high efficiency were added on the principle of legitimate administration and the principle of reasonable administration, which played an important role in urging the government to actively perform its service duties. The main value objective pursued is to protect social and economic rights, such as citizens' survival and welfare, social equity and equal development. This is mainly reflected in the "harmonious relations among social members" at the social level.

In the present era of "risk rule of law", dealing with energy and resources security, ecological environment risks and sustainable development bearing intergenerational justice has become a new value objective. This is reflected in the "harmony between people and nature" at the ecological level. It requires the government to perform new functions and take active measures to ensure the realization of the objectives. Therefore, the administrative law needs to clarify the rules for government's actions. However, this new value objective is not mentioned neither in the principles of legitimate and reasonable administration in the era of free rule of law, nor in the principles of reliance protection, and convenience and high efficiency in the era of social rule of law in traditional administrative law.

iii. Limitations of regulatory standards

The differences on basic concept and value orientation determine that administrative law in the present era should follow different requirements in regulatory standards. The legitimacy standard of administrative law requires that the administrative organs must strictly abide by laws when performing administrative actions, and can not conduct any action that is not expressly stipulated in laws. The administration should ensure administrative activities comply with formal rule of law through the rules of law priority and law reservation. It means that the administration must obey and follow the will of the people. The rationality standard of administrative law requires that any administrative action must be performed in a fair, just and open manner. This means the administrative organs should not only ensure legitimate administration, but also realize substantive rule of law in accordance with the principles of reasonable administration, such as the principles of equal treatment, proportionality and due process. Thus, the requirement that the administration should conform to social ethics is put forward. In the eras of free rule of law and social rule of law, the legitimacy and rationality standards can meet the requirements of the society on regulating of administrative actions. However, when human society enters the era of risk rule of law, high carbon emission, extreme climate, environment deterioration and other risks have seriously threatened the survival and development of human beings. Energy conservation and emission reduction and low-carbon development are urgent. The standards of legitimacy and rationality are two major standards to regulate administrative actions. They can ensure the legitimacy and rationality of administrative actions, but they both belong to the standards for social ethics. In the important tasks of promoting energy conservation and emission reduction and building a low-carbon society, more emphasis should be placed on the application of science and technology, and administrative actions should also be regulated through rational technical means, for example, quantitative carbon emission data calculation and environmental risk assessment. This shows that low-carbon standard should obey science and technology ethics, and low-carbon administrative actions should be carried out in strict accordance with scientific standards.

The legitimacy and rationality of social ethic standards alone cannot guarantee the administrative actions to be low-carbon and green. Thus a new standard, i.e., low-carbon standard, for regulating administrative actions in the era of risk rule of law is put forward. Putting forward low-carbon standard does not deny the legitimacy standard or rationality standard. Any administrative action must strictly follow the two standards first. However, with the change of the era background, the connotation of government functions and its administrative actions have changed. Energy conservation and emission reduction and the realization of ecological civilization have become the objectives of administrative actions. Therefore, the essence of low-carbon standard is that administrative actions must conform to the laws of ecology. According to this standard, the administrative organs should, on the one hand, achieve the low-carbonization of administrative activities by optimizing administrative procedures and reducing carbon emission, and on the other hand, promote the whole society to achieve energy conservation and environmental protection through its own demonstration and leading effect, thus assuming the important task of promoting the construction of a low-carbon society. The standards regulating administrative actions are extended from legitimacy standard and rationality standard to low-carbon standard, which can meet the new requirements for administrative actions in the low-carbon era.

iv. Limitations of adjustment methods

In the low-carbon era, the traditional administrative law with certainty and administration as its essence is increasingly influenced by the theory of risk society. The administrative action regulated by the traditional administrative law are basically guided by the definite decision-making basis, i.e., definite legal and regulatory basis and definite scientific evidences are required. Therefore, the administrative actions based on this concept require definite fact finding, sufficient evidence, reasonable administrative discretion, etc. In the era of free rule of law and social rule of law, in order to effectively regulate the growing administrative power, ensure the administration can provide stable order and good social welfare for the public, and reasonably balance the relationship between limiting public power and protecting civil rights, the mode of post-event certainty is adopted to adjust the administrative power. Administrative organs must conduct an administrative action based on facts and legal provisions determined by laws. Only after it has fully judged the scale, degree and possible damages of that action can it use its administrative power for intervention according to laws. The adjustment methods generally adopted are post-event punishment and post-event enforcement. The traditional adjustment methods of administrative actions show the characteristics of certainty and responsiveness. However, the arrival of the era of risk rule of law makes the objects of the exercise of administrative power more and more uncertain. In view of the problems in the low-carbon field, how to identify potential environmental risks and effectively prevent and avoid them to ensure safety for the public and guarantee the public interests, have become the focus of administrative actions. "The focus of government duties has obviously changed, that is, from paying attention to order and protecting the public's freedom and rights from illegal interference, to comprehensively shaping society through future goals."[20] The environmental risks in the low-carbon era have the characteristics of higher uncertainty, complexity and disastrous. In particular, the probability of some environmental risks is very low, but the risks can easily bring about disastrous consequences. In addition, the public holds limited understanding of the risks, it is difficult for them to analyze and recognize the risks objectively and rationally, thus, they are extremely prone to panic. All these factors make it impossible for the risk to be rationally recognized in advance, and it is difficult to intervene in advance with effective preventive adjustment through the existing administrative law concepts and principles. The basic requirement for administration in a country ruled by law is to administer according to law. Any administrative action should be under the rule of law. However, this *ex post facto* adjustment method is no longer suitable for the requirements of the low-carbon era. The administration cannot guarantee a safe life for the public if balking in the face of uncertain environmental risks. Therefore, guided by the preventive concept, administrative organs should advance the timeline of administrative actions, prevent potential adverse effects through careful advance planning, and ensure that the administrative actions taken are preventive and proactive.

The existence of the above-mentioned limitations requires that the basic principles of administrative law in the era of risk rule of law be deepened and expanded on the basis of the principles of traditional administrative law, so as to guide the government to actively perform its administrative duties of ecological protection, and to ensure that administrative actions are legal and reasonable as well as low-carbon and environmentally friendly, and that government activities can not only save energy resources, but also alleviate the environmental crisis. Therefore, it is necessary to establish new basic principles of administrative law in order to effectively respond to the above new requirements of administrative law in the low-carbon era.

---

[20] [Germany] *German Administrative Law Reader* edited by Eberhard Schmidt Assmann et al., compiled by Ulrich Bbattis and translated by Yu An et al., Higher Education Press, 2006, p. 53.

2 Proposal of Low-Carbon Administrative Principle

2.1 The Need to Establish Low-Carbon Administrative Principle

The multi-level measures taken and complexity in addressing climate change determine that the low-carbon administrative principle is an principle with novel connotation and rich contents. According to the presupposition of the theoretical basis of this article, the connotation of low-carbon administrative principle can be defined as follows: the government, as the principal part to realize public interests and the standard bearer to build a low-carbon society, has the legal responsibility to address climate change, which requires the government and the public to save energy resources and continuously reduce energy consumption, encourage and support the development and use of new energy through technological transformation, and regulate the use of traditional fossil energy, carry out carbon neutrality by increasing carbon sinks etc., so as to achieve energy conservation and emission reduction targets in various specific fields and effectively cope with the challenges of climate change. It is urgent, practical and necessary to establish low-carbon administrative principle for the following reasons:

(I) The Need to Implement the Strategy of Sustainable Development

The concept of sustainable development was first put forward by Brundtland, Chairman of the World Commission on Environment and Development (WCED), in her report *Our Common Future* released in 1987, which summarized the basic connotation of the sustainable development principle as "development that meets the needs of the present without compromising the ability of future generations to meet their own needs". The WCED has thus put forward the *Legal Principles on Environmental Protection and Sustainable Development*, which sets "protection and sustainable utilization" as the general principle of environmental protection and requires all countries to maintain the ecosystems and ecological processes necessary for the biosphere to function in order to protect biodiversity. The Principles also emphasize that when utilizing biological resources and ecosystems, the principle of optimal sustainable yield should be observed. Some scholars have summed up the specific connotation of the sustainable development principle as follows: the principle of coordinated development of environment, economy and society; the principle of comprehensive development, utilization, protection and control of environmental resources; the principle of combining prevention with control; the principle of environmental responsibility; and the principle of public participation.[21] Other scholars believe that the sustainable development principle consists of four basic

[21] Shen Muzhu, *Sustainable Development Principle and Theoretical Analysis of Answering Global Climate Change, Shandong Social Sciences*, 2013, Vol. 1.

elements: intragenerational equity, intergenerational equity, coordination of environmental, economic and social development, and sustainable utilization of resources.[22] In 1991, China initiated the Ministerial Conference of Developing Countries on Environment and Development and issued the *Beijing Declaration*. In 1992, the Chinese government signed the Declaration on Environment and Development at the Rio de Janeiro World Summit and made a solemn commitment to implement *Agenda 21*. In 1994, the State Council compiled and adopted *China's Agenda 21*. In 1997, the 15th National Congress of the CPC explicitly took sustainable development strategy as the basic strategy for China's economic development.

In the context of climate change, the proposal of low-carbon administrative principle is an important way to implement sustainable development strategy. Firstly, energy conservation and emission reduction as well as low-carbon development, have become requisites and prerequisites for sustainable development in addressing global climate change. They complement each other and promote each other. Sustainable development requires that contemporary utilization of resources cannot endanger the viability of the next generation, and relies on government regulation to promote all social entities to save resources, energy and protect the ecological environment. Secondly, the government itself as an administrative organization consumes huge amount of resources, and the implementation of sustainable development strategy is inseparable from the economization and green development of the administrative organization. Therefore, it is necessary to make requirements for the sustainable development of the government itself through low-carbon administrative principle. Thirdly, as a development strategy of the international community and sovereign states, the sustainable development strategy involves social, political, economic, technological and other issues. It requires overall planning and coordination based on the overall development capacity of the country and society, which by no means can be achieved by any private entity, other than by the country and government that is with strong capacity to allocate public resources and capacity for long-term strategic planning. Therefore, it is necessary to establish and implement corresponding legal principles in the administrative law, which is regarded as the "government management law".

(II) **The Need to Implement Common but Differentiated Responsibilities**

Common but differentiated responsibilities is a national responsibility in the field of climate change. It was first proposed by Principle 7 of the 1992 *Rio Declaration on Environment and Development*.[23] *The United Nations Framework Convention on Climate Change* once again emphasized and reaffirmed this responsibility in 1998:

[22] Zhang Ping, Liu Xiaohong and Yang Ping, *Analysis of Environmental Sustainable Development Principles*, *Western Law Review*, 2008, Vol. 5.

[23] Specifically, the principle states that "All the countries shall cooperate with a spirit of global partnership for the preservation, protection and restoration of the health and integrity of the earth'bs ecosystems. Given the different factors leading to global environmental degradation, all the countries shall undertake a common but differentiated responsibility. Developed countries recognize that they should be responsible in international efforts to pursue sustainable development considering the pressures they exert on the global environment and their technological and financial resources.".

"Each Party shall protect the climate system for present and future generations of mankind on the basis of fairness and in accordance with their common but differentiated responsibilities and respective capabilities." In terms of normative connotation, the principle of common but differentiated responsibilities includes two elements: "common responsibilities" and "differentiated responsibilities". "Common responsibilities" require the international community to treat climate change as a holistic issue for the whole world. All countries should carry out extensive international cooperation and participate in comprehensive and effective international actions to deal with climate change in accordance with their common but differentiated responsibilities, respective capabilities and their social and economic conditions. The "differentiated responsibilities" originate from the huge amount of carbon emissions (including past and present emissions) and the advantages of emission reduction capability (technical and financial resources) of developed countries. Based on "differentiated responsibilities", developed countries should take the lead in undertaking mandatory emission reduction obligations, while developing countries will not undertake quantitative and mandatory emission reduction obligations until they reach the socio-economic level of developed countries due to "development priorities", but are encouraged to take the initiative to undertake emission reduction obligations. As for the relationship between the two, "common responsibilities" should be the fundamental and dominant principle. Whether in the international political negotiations on climate change or in the domestic actions of various countries to save energy and reduce emissions, "common responsibilities" as the bottom line should be unconditionally observed. Different from the universal application of "common responsibilities", "differentiated responsibilities" mean that each country should bear different responsibilities according to its own economic and social situations. However, some scholars have proposed that the application of "differentiated responsibilities" should be subject to necessary restrictions—first, it should not deviate from the fundamental purpose of the Convention[24]; second, the principle should be suspended when the application of "differentiated responsibilities" does not exist. Therefore, theoretically, the two aspects of the principle of common but differentiated responsibilities should take "common" as the principle and "difference" as the exception, and they complement and restrict each other.[25]

Based on common but differentiated responsibilities, China has promised to reduce the carbon dioxide emission rate per unit of GDP by 40%-45% by 2020 compared with 2005, and to include this rate in the binding indicators of the national economy. In order to implement this national responsibility, the government need to rely on domestic legislative, administrative and judicial activities to transform and put it into practice. This puts forward new requirements for legislation, administration and judicature—to scientifically formulate climate change legislation, actively use

[24] See Kerry Tetzlaff. Differentiated Treatment in International Environmental Law. International& Comparative Law Quarterly, 2007, Vol. 56.

[25] See *Breaking the Deadlock: A New Interpretation of "Common but Differentiated Responsibilities"* written by Li Yanfang and Cao Wei, *Journal of Renmin University of China*, 2013, Vol. 2.

administrative actions to promote energy conservation and emission reduction, and to implement judicial review on serious non-low-carbon acts and climate infringement acts according to the national share of or commitment to emission reduction. In particular, administration is needed to play a role. Because legislation is only the premise and standard of administration and judicature, and judicature can only provide relief and punishment afterwards, which has its inherent lag, while administrative organs can perform regulatory actions to restrict the energy conservation and emission reduction activities of administrative counterparts. We can say that the low-carbon administrative principle in the field of administrative law should be the front line for fulfilling common but differentiated responsibilities.

(III) **The Need to Prevent Ecological Risks**

In the long run, climate change holds serious irreversible effects, but the effects are seriously "counterfactual"—that is to say, the direct harm in real life is inversely proportional to the degree of risk. Although it leads to disastrous consequences, such adverse consequences often take decades or even longer to emerge. To some extent, this shows the "Giddens's paradox" in the field of climate change, that is, because climate change is not obvious and visible in daily life, people are often indifferent to the dangerous consequences it brings before they occur, but once the dangerous consequences become obvious and visible, all actions are too late, thus irreversible risk consequences may appear. Compared with previous environmental damages, the environmental risks of climate change to a certain are for beyond the cognitive scope of ordinary people. In this regard, we could make use of the principle of low-carbon administration to promote the government to strengthen the low-carbon awareness and actively adopt policies and countermeasures in the face of climate change risks.

2.2 *Legal Basis of Low-Carbon Administrative Principles*

From the perspective of practical needs, it is urgent to put forward the principle of low-carbon administration. However, its possible legal basis from the normative level still needs to be analyzed before it is included in the theoretical system of administrative law as a legal principle. The following analysis is mainly carried out from two perspectives of legal philosophy and constitutional norms.

(I) **The Legal Philosophical Basis of Low-Carbon Administrative Principle**

Justice is an eternal topic in legal philosophy and the ultimate tool for evaluating the legitimacy of legal phenomena. As Rawls pointed out, justice is the primary value of the social system.[26] From the perspective of legal justice, the low-carbon administrative principle conforms to the horizontal justice and vertical justice of legal philosophy.

---

[26] [US] *A Theory of Justice* written by John Rawls and translated by He Huaihong et al., China Social Sciences Press, 1988, p. 1.

i. Horizontal justice: protection of climate-vulnerable groups. In dealing with climate change, horizontal justice mainly refers to the protection of climate-vulnerable groups. Groups vulnerable to climate change are mainly those who are most likely to be first threatened by the consequences of climate change due to geographical locations, resource endowment, economic and social status and other conditions. For example, residents of some small island states are typical groups vulnerable to climate change, because they may lose territory of the nation on which they live and the corresponding survival and development opportunities as global warming and sea level rise intensify. As General Secretary Xi Jinping stressed during his visit to Hainan in 2013, "a good ecological environment is the fairest public product and the most inclusive welfare for the people."[27] The groups vulnerable to climate change can bear the lowest risk of climate change. The basic survival security of these subjects is the minimum standard that the international community and governments should follow when setting targets to deal with climate change. It is also the bottom line ethics that the legal governance of climate change must abide by. The aim of setting low-carbon administrative principle is to guarantee and realize the ecological welfare of the whole society and even the whole world through the construction of low-carbon society. By urging the government to actively provide the inclusive public goods of "addressing climate change", the low-carbon administrative principle fully takes into account the interests of climate-vulnerable groups and covers the ecological security of all subjects in climate change, fully reflecting the horizontal justice of climate change.

ii. Vertical justice: intergenerational equity in climate change. The vertical justice of climate change mainly requires that the survival and development of the present generation should not damage the ecological security and development resources on which future generations depend for their survival and development, that is, the fairness of the survival and development conditions enjoyed by different generations. Rawls put forward the theory of intergenerational justice in resources and environment as early as 1972, which believed that the next generation should at least enjoy the same resources and environmental foundation as the previous generation. Climate change not only affects the survival and development of the present generation, but also threatens the interests of future generations. Therefore, based on intergenerational justice, the carbon emission of one generation should not reduce the carbon emission amount of the next generation. However, based on the human behavior mechanism of short-term thinking (which can only respond to immediate benefits or risks),[28] it is difficult for the present generation to consider the needs of future generations when developing economy and society. In this regard, the low-carbon administrative principle can help to promote the government to control the total amount of social carbon emissions in a proactive and systematic way through its administrative activities. Complying to the principle, the government can guide and regulate the energy consumption and carbon emissions of the whole society through

[27] Commentator of *Guangming Daily: A Good Ecological Environment, the Most Inclusive Well-Being of the People, Guangming Daily*, November 7, 2014.

[28] See E.O. Wilson, *The Future of Life*, London: Little Brown, 2002.

long-term policy considerations that fully take into account the amount of carbon emission and survival and development ability of future generations, thus realizing intergenerational equity of climate change.

(II) The Constitutional Normative Basis of Low-Carbon Administrative Principle

As a detailed explanation of constitution, administrative law derives its principles from the basic spirit and value of the constitution. Judging from the relevant provisions of China's *Constitution*, the low-carbon administrative principle is based on the following constitutional norms:

i. "Human Rights". China's *Constitution* clearly stipulates that "the state respects and guarantees human rights." Air and water quality problems, snow disasters, floods and other extreme weather caused by climate change have seriously affected citizens' environmental rights. Moreover, sea level rise also caused by climate change may lead to the inundation of coastal cities and regions, thus threatening people's right to subsistence. A report from the International Council on Human Rights Policy (ICHRP) points out that climate change will directly or indirectly threaten almost all human rights, including the right to health and even the right to life, the right to food, water and housing, the right to culture, and the right to personal livelihood and security.[29] Among them, the right to health, the right to life and the right to housing all belong to the most basic category of human rights. Of course, citizens cannot request the state to pay or indemnify or compensate for threats that do not directly come from the state's power. However, according to the theory of objective order of value in basic rights, the state has the obligation to provide "institutional guarantee" for the realization of basic human rights such as environmental rights and the right to life,[30] that is, the state should respond to climate change by establishing corresponding legal systems and actively taking actions. This is also included in the basic connotation of low-carbon administrative principle.

ii. "Unification of Citizens' Rights and Duties". Climate change is the result of the "organised irresponsibility"[31] of human beings to the ecological environment and the utilization of resources in economic and social development. As Professor Christian pointed out, the massive carbon emissions of some social members put human beings and the entire ecological system in general danger, which means that individuals "hurt others at will but are not responsible for their own actions."[32] Therefore, the government holds constitutional legitimacy to regulate the carbon emission activities of social members through administrative activities abiding by the low-carbon administrative principle. Paragraph 4 of Article 33 of China's *Constitution*

---

[29] ICHRP, Climate Change and Human Rights: A Rough Guide, at http://www.ohchr.org/Documents/Issues/ClimateChange/Submissions/136_summary.pdf, p. 3.

[30] See *The Dual Nature of Fundamental Rights*, Zhang Xiang, *Chinese Journal of Law*, Vol. 3, 2005.

[31] [Germany] *World Risk Society* written by Ulrich Beck and translated by Wu Yingzi and Sun Shumin, Nanjing University Press, 2004, p. 191.

[32] [Sweden] *Solving the Climate Challenge* written by Christian Azar and translated by Du Heng and Du Ke, Social Sciences Academic Press, 2012, Preface.

stipulates that every citizen is entitled to the rights and at the same time must perform the duties prescribed by the Constitution and the law.[33] Article 51 of the *Constitution* stipulates that there is a boundary for citizens to exercise their rights, that is, they shall not harm public interests and the legal rights of other citizens.[34] These are two restrictive clauses in citizens' constitutional rights, and they are two closely related legal principles. First, citizens have the obligation not to damage the legal rights and freedoms of the state, society, the collective and others while exercising the rights and freedoms stipulated in the constitution and laws. Second, in order to safeguard the public interests of the state, society, the collective and others, the rights and freedoms of citizens can be reduced to a certain extent. In the present age, any citizen, legal person or other organization undoubtedly enjoys legitimate carbon emission rights and environmental rights. But at the same time, it should be noted that it is the common excessive carbon emissions of social individuals that put human beings and ecosystems in great danger, thus threatening the common survival and development rights of social members. Therefore, based on the "Unification of Citizens' Rights and Duties" in the *Constitution*, the government can impose the obligation of energy conservation and emission reduction on serious high-carbon emission subjects through the legal system, and restrict their unreasonable carbon emission activities through administrative regulation, so as to protect the common and long-term interests of the society and maintain the survival and development of the community.

iii. "Economization" and "Environmental Protection and Pollution Prevention". Article 14, paragraph 2, and article 26 of China's *Constitution* clearly set forth the national goals of "practise strict economy" and "protects and improves the environment in which people live and the ecological environment". As for the provision of "practices strict economy and combats waste", "practices strict economy" not only includes the saving of administrative costs, but also necessarily covers the low-carbon requirements of saving resources and energy, under the background that the Party and the state propose to build a resource-saving and environment-friendly society, strengthen ecological civilization and build a beautiful China. In the "Control Pollution and Other Public Hazards" provision, although the current environmental standards of China have not yet explicitly listed greenhouse gases,[35] listing greenhouse gases as air pollutants has become the development trend in today's world environmental law.[36] Under this background, there is nothing wrong to include reducing

---

[33] Article 33 (iv) of China's *Constitution* stipulates that "Any citizen shall enjoy the rights stipulated in the *Constitution* and the law, and must fulfill the obligations stipulated".

[34] Article 51 of the *Constitution* stipulates that "citizens shall not harm the interests of the state, society and the collective and the lawful freedoms and rights of other citizens when freely exercising rights".

[35] See *Integrated Emission Standard of Air Pollutants of the People's Republic of China* (GB16297-1996).

[36] For example, in Massachusetts v. EPA, the Supreme Court of the United States has ruled that greenhouse gases are air pollutants.

greenhouse gases into the scope of pollution control through expansionary constitutional interpretation. According to the above analysis, in the low-carbon era, through the two national purpose clauses of "Economization" and "Environmental Protection and Pollution Prevention", the constitutional obligations that the government should actively promote the "energy conservation" and "emission reduction" in the whole society can be explained, thus the constitutional normative basis of the low-carbon administrative principle is formed.

3 Basic Parts of Low-Carbon Administrative Principle

From the perspective of the rule of law and practical needs in the low-carbon era, the low-carbon administrative principle should include the following specific parts.

3.1 Administrative Value Goal of Ecological Protection Priority

Facing the risk of climate change with disastrous consequences, the concepts of power control administration and supply administration in traditional administrative law have become very feeble in helping prevent the land from sinking into the sea due to climate warming. Therefore, the administrative law in the low-carbon era cannot but take ecological security as the preferential value goal. The value goal of ecological protection requires administrative activities to correctly handle the relationship between economic development and ecological civilization and to realize the harmonious and sustainable development between human beings and nature. However, due to the inherent tension between the infinity of human desires and the finiteness of ecological capacity, economic development and ecological protection are sometimes not completely consistent or even contradictory.[37] In this regard, the government should give priority to ecological protection so that the acquiring of economic benefits are within the scope permitted by ecological security. This is first determined by the supremacy of the right to subsistence. The trade-offs between different values are fundamentally in the service of human rights and interests. An ICHRP report pointed out that the aggravation of climate change will directly or indirectly threaten the basic living rights of human beings, such as the right to health, food, drinking water and housing.[38] In other words, ecological protection is a necessary measure to protect human beings' right to subsistence, and economic development mainly corresponds to the right to development and welfare. The right to subsistence, as the

[37] See *On the Construction of Legal Guarantee System of Ecological Civilization Construction*, Wang Canfa, *China Legal Science*, Vol. 3, 2014.

[38] See ICHRP, Climate Change and Human Rights: A Rough Guide, at http://www.ohchr.org/Documents/Issues/ClimateChange/Submissions/136_summary.pdf, p. 3.

"primary" and the "first" human right,[39] occupies the highest position in the value order of human rights. Therefore, in balancing the interests of the above two, the protection of the support system for life on earth should be given top priority. This value must prevail over economic interests.[40] At the same time, the consequences of climate change are irreversible. In order to avoid missing the precious time to deal with the change and the permanent loss of environmental benefits, it is undoubtedly the most rational choice to temporarily slow down economic development and give way to ecological environment protection. In addition, the limited capacity of climate and environmental resources also calls for the principle of ecological priority in law, that is, human development, construction and utilization of resources must be within the limits of the environmental capacity of the ecosystem.[41] At present, this point of view has been acknowledged in the *Opinions of the CPC Central Committee and the State Council on Accelerating the Construction of Ecological Civilization*, which emphasizes that "In environmental protection and development, priority should be given to protection, that is, protect in development and develop in protection." Therefore, the priority of ecological environment protection is clearly defined in relation to social and economic development.

In view of the basic impact of ecological environment on human survival and development rights, and the specific activities of all administrative departments will directly or indirectly affect the environmental behavior of the counterpart, the principle of ecological priority should not only be taken as the low-carbon requirement for environmental protection administrative departments, but also be further established as the overall and universal principle of administrative law in all departments.

3.2 Administrative Actions Requirements for Energy Conservation and Emission Reduction

Administrative action is a basic tool to achieve the purpose of administrative management. For this reason, the implementation of low-carbon administrative principle will inevitably require administrative action to save energy and reduce emissions. The energy conservation and emission reduction requirements of administrative actions specifically include two aspects:

(I) The Low-Carbonization of Administrative Entities in Administrative Actions

As the agent to exercise the administrative power, the government itself is a source of huge carbon emissions. A large amount of energy consumption and waste generated

---

[39] *On the Right to Live*, Li Long, *Law Review*, Vol. 2, 1992.

[40] [Australia] *The Climate Change Challenge and the Failure of Democracy* written by David Hillman and Joseph John Smith and translated by Wu Xishen and Li Nan, Social Sciences Academic Press, 2009, p. 212.

[41] *On the Construction of Legal Guarantee System of Ecological Civilization Construction*, Wang Canfa, China Legal Science, Vol. 3, 2014.

by the government's public consumption increases carbon emissions and affect the realization of low-carbon administrative goals.[42] The government is required to set an example to build a low-carbon society. This requires that administrative action should not only be constrained by the requirements of legitimacy and rationality, but also meet the low-carbon standards. From the perspective of the components of administrative power, the low-carbon standard of the administrative entity in conducting administrative action can be divided into three aspects: low-carbonization of the administrative entity, low-carbonization of the material support for official activities and low-carbonization of the administrative procedure. (i) The low-carbonization of the administrative entity, i.e., the setting up of administrative institutions and personnel organization should meet the low-carbon requirements. A streamlined and scientific organization and staffing will help reduce administrative costs and carbon emissions. (ii) The low-carbonization of the material support for official activities means that the administrative entity should carry out self-restraint with strict low-carbon standards in the selection and use of public property and office items. This mainly includes two aspects—the first is the low-carbonization of the administrative entity in the selection of public property. This requires mandatory or prioritized government procurement of energy-saving and environmental-friendly public goods, strict control of procurement costs, and reduction of carbon emissions from the source. The low-carbonization in the selection of government property should be established as a basic principle in the *Government Procurement Law*. The second is the low-carbonization of administrative entities in the use of public property. low-carbon and economy should also be emphasized even if the government uses public property. This requirement is clearly reflected in China's *Energy Conservation Regulation for State-funded Institutions*, Article 29 of which stipulates that "public institutions shall reduce standby energy consumption of electrical equipment such as air conditioners, computers and photocopiers and shut down electrical equipment in time", for example. (iii) The low-carbonization of the administrative procedure. The administrative procedure means the process of the implementation of the administrative action. Whether the administrative procedure is low-carbon or not directly determines whether the process of the administrative action is low-carbon or not. The low-carbonization of the administrative procedure requires that the procedure design, operation and responsibility of administrative actions must conform to the low-carbon standard, minimize unnecessary links and steps, merge correlated links, and shorten the time limit of the procedures. Such as vigorously promoting e-government, streamlining administrative approval, reducing the administrative cost of the counterpart and the energy and resource consumption of administrative activities.

(II) Administrative Actions Take the Implementation of Low-Carbon Regulation as a New Important Goal

In order to cope with climate change, the present administrative actions must take the implementation of low-carbon guidance and regulation in the whole society as new

[42] See *Ecological Administration Innovation and Low-Carbon Government Construction*, Huang Aibao, *Social Science Research*, Vol. 5, 2010.

important goals and tasks, and employ administrative power to vigorously promote the construction of a low-carbon society. This is a necessary change of strategic focus of administrative activities in the current era. For the total amount of carbon emissions of the society, enterprises are one of the main sources, accounting for more than 1/3 of the world's energy consumption.[43] The amount from individual citizens also account for a significant proportion. Statistics show that in Britain, carbon emissions from households (including residents' travel) account for about 40%,[44] while in China, 21% of the total carbon emissions of the whole society come from household energy consumption, with the average annual carbon emissions of households reaching 2.7 tons/person.[45] Basically, in responding of administrative law to climate change, we need to mobilize enterprises and individual citizens to implement common low-carbon actions. The principle of low-carbon administration should be established to adjust the activities of enterprises, citizens and other administrative counterparts. From the perspective of action mechanism, this is mainly achieved through effective administrative regulation of the government's low-carbon administrative activities.

Administrative actions, with the new important goal of implementing low-carbon regulation, should meet the following requirements:

(i) The active implementation of low-carbon regulation should become the legal responsibility and obligation to restrict the administrative actions of administrative entities. Although all members of society have the responsibility to conserve energy and reduce emissions as there are resource consumption and high carbon emissions in the process of production or consumption, it is very difficult to expect people to take conscious actions. For individuals, consumption belongs to individual freedom. As long as citizens can afford and are willing to bear the corresponding consumption cost, they can choose their own consumption patterns and types. For an enterprise, the pursuit of profit is the fundamental reason for its establishment and operation. Thus, "it is immoral to replace profit with environmental goals".[46] The costs of personal consumption and corporate profits can only reflect a very small part of the negative effects of their actions, due to the natural "externality" of climate change, the ecological effects of climate change are actually shared by all members of society. This may lead to the "tragedy of the commons" of global climate change, which refers to what Garrett Hardin, the father of the commons theory, pointed out: "Freedom in a commons brings ruin to all."[47] Moreover, the conscious actions of individual citizens or enterprises is difficult to be infiltrated by the concept of low-carbon value. When the external effects and risks of carbon emissions are obvious, all actions will be too late. Based on this, the administrative entity must implement

---

[43] [English] *The Politics of Climate Change* written by Anthony Giddens and translated by Cao Rongxiang, Social Sciences Academic Press, 2009, p. 134.

[44] [English] *The Politics of Climate Change* written by Anthony Giddens and translated by Cao Rongxiang, Social Sciences Academic Press, 2009, p. 119.

[45] Chen Xuehui, *How Much Carbon Did You Emit Today?*, *Xiamen Business*, December 19, 2009.

[46] Joel Balkan. *The Corporation, The Pathological Pursuit of Power and Profit*, London: Constable & Robinson Ltd, 2004, p. 34.

[47] G. Hardin, The Tragedy of the Commons, *Science*, vol. 112, 1968, p. 1244.

strong administrative intervention on the production and consumption activities of social members (including individual citizens and business entities) to restrict them to vigorously carry out energy conservation and emission reduction. This is the social responsibility of administrative power exercised as public power. Therefore, the administrative entity should actively use administrative actions to implement low-carbon regulation to fulfil its legal duty and obligation.

(ii) The main part of low-carbon regulation includes efforts to promote ecological protection, energy conservation and reasonable consumption. In terms of ecological protection, the harmony between man and nature is the core value goal of low-carbon administrative principle, which is different from the goal of "harmony between government and citizens" and "freedom and equality between people" of traditional administrative principles. Therefore, low-carbon regulation should first be used to restrict and guide administrative counterparts to consciously protect the ecological environment, so as to reduce and prevent the human survival crisis caused by the deterioration of the ecological environment. In addition, the situation of resources and energy conservation is becoming more and more severe in dealing with climate change. China's *Constitution* and *Energy Conservation Law* have already established the conservation of resources and energy as the basic state policy. And this state policy must be implemented through strong low-carbon regulation. In terms of equitable consumption, "the final solution to environmental problems may be found in the consumption field itself."[48] Most of the carbon emissions of the society are generated by consumption, at the same time consumption concept and mode have an important impact on the construction of a low-carbon society, so we need to strengthen the guidance to promote equitable consumption. Equitable consumption includes two aspects, i.e., moderate consumption and green consumption: on the one hand, moderate consumption means the control of consumption quantity within an equitable range and decreasing luxury consumption, as excessive consumption and luxury consumption do not derive from "the real needs of people", but from "a false need"[49] only, and the carbon emissions generated thereby must be strictly limited; on the other hand, green consumption requires that priority be given to the quality of low-carbon or even zero-carbon goods or services, so as to minimize or eliminate one-off consumption and high-energy consumption. Among them, green consumption holds great potential for Energy Conservation and Emission Reduction. According to relevant calculation data, if energy-saving electric lamps are widely used in households nationally, more than 70 billion kWh of electricity can be saved a year. For another example, if all the existing 100 million refrigerators are replaced with energy-saving ones across the country, more than 40 billion kWh of electricity can be saved in a year, and the two together can save the energy equal to power generated from more than one Three Gorges Power Station.

---

[48] Chief editor Xu Xiangmin, *Environmental Law Research in the Climate Change*, Intellectual Property Publishing House, 2012, Preface, p. 5.

[49] [US] *One-Dimensional Man* written by Marcuse and translated by Zhang Feng and Lü Shiping, Chongqing Publishing House, 1988, p. 6.

(iii) Using and innovating administrative actions actively to achieve low-carbon regulation. Administrative entity is required to actively use and innovate targeted administrative actions in low-carbon administration according to the functions and characteristics of different administrative actions, in order to achieve the goal of low-carbon regulation. Administrative actions under low-carbon regulation mostly include guiding and mandatory acts. Effective use of various administrative actions requires improving and perfecting "flexible" ways such as administrative award, administrative contracts and administrative guidance, giving full play to its role in guiding and advocating low-carbon economy and low-carbon life, and improving and perfecting administrative licensing, administrative penalties and administrative enforcement to effectively control energy resources consumption and greenhouse gas emissions. In addition, the administrative entity must actively explore and research the effective behavior of new administrative affairs management, such as carbon trading management, carbon information disclosure management, carbon fund management, etc.

3.3 Strengthening the Administrative Mode of Ecological Environment Risk Management

Climate change will pose a catastrophic risk to ecological environment in the future. It will cause multiple irreversible negative impacts on the ecological environment system and social and economic sectors, and the cannot be replaced by other environmental goods.[50] In response, the Risk Assessment report released by the Intergovernmental Panel on Climate Change (IPCC) clearly put forward that "addressing climate change is a repeated risk management course, which includes adaptation and mitigation, and takes into account the losses, symbiotic benefits, sustainability, fairness and attitude towards risks caused by climate change."[51] Therefore, according to low-carbon administrative principle, administrative activities are required to strengthen the new administrative mode of environmental risk management. According to Jurgen Habermas, the needs of restricting the threat of nation power to freedom, overcoming the poverty caused by capitalism, and preventing the ecological risks arise from industrial civilization, have provided the administrative laws of different eras with their respective agendas and institutional goals: freedom safeguard, social

[50] For irreversibility of the consequences of climate change, see [U.S.] *Worst-Case Scenarios* written by Cass R. Sunstein and translated by Liu Kunlun, China Renmin University Press, 2010, pp. 170–179. *The National Assessment Report of Climate Change* in China also clearly points out that if we do not take effective measures to reduce the greenhouse effect, glacier area of western China will be 27% less by 2050 than that of the middle of the twentieth century. The river flow of southern region will increase by 24% averagely, causing the regulation capacity of river flow by seasons is greatly reduced so as to lead to much worse flooding. See *National Assessment Report of Climate Change* (Abstract), Drafting Committee for *National Assessment Report of Climate Change, World Environment*, Vol. 2, 2007.

[51] IPCC, Climate Change 2007: Synthesis Report, IPCC, 64(2007).

welfare and risk prevention.[52] The administrative mode of risk management has set forth challenges for the traditional administrative means and decision-making mode: The traditional Administrative Law basically regulates decision-making oriented to certainty, requiring administrative activities to have clear facts, conclusive evidence support and definite legal basis, and even making more accurate proportional judgment between means and purposes. However, faced with the uncertainty of climate change risks, the decisions in administrative activities are forced to be made in the unknown situation, and the prevention and treatment of various risks, such as risks of climate, ecology and energy, shall be deemed as a core task. During this course, In this process, there may be a lot of uncertain information about the existence and probability of risks as well as the degree of risk control, and how to impute damages. Therefore, in order to rationally respond to the ecological risks of climate change, institutional mechanisms that can be scientifically used to deal with risks must be established, such as environmental monitoring and early warning systems, zoology planning systems, environmental impact evaluation and environmental risk assessment systems, information disclosure and risk communication systems, in different kinds of administrative activities such as administrative legislation, administrative decision-making and administrative law enforcement.

3.4 Building a New Low-Carbon Administrative Performance Management System

Performance management is the "baton" of the administrative activities of governments and their officials at all levels. From the perspective of political incentives, different types of performance evaluation indicators lead to different kinds of government actions. Since the reform and opening up, China has long applied a GDP-oriented administrative performance management system. Under this system, it is very commonly seen that local government officials pursue short-term economic development at the cost of ecological environment, resources and energy for sake of promotion, or even cooperate with pollution-discharging enterprises as the patron for the purpose of attracting investment. As a result, it has not only done great damage to the ecological environment on which the economy depends for development, but also provoked a series of social contradictions. Relevant data show that during the "11th Five-Year Plan" period, there were over 300,000 letters and visits relevant to environmental claims.[53] This shows that the traditional performance evaluation system can hardly address the ecological crisis of industrial civilization, and even to some extent intensifies the crisis. Therefore, the administrative performance management

---

[52] See [Germany] *Between Facts and Norms-A Negotiation Theory on Law and Democratic and Ruling Countries* written by Habermas and translated by Tong Shijun, Joint Publishing, 2003, p. 537.

[53] Anonymous, *Warning of Series of Environmental Mass Events and Government's Response*, *Xinhua Yu Qing*, October 27, 2013.

system oriented to low-carbon environmental protection needs to be established to achieve the realization of the low-carbon administrative principle.

Fortunately, the Party and the country have started to reform the traditional performance assessment system from the top-level planning in recent years, and strive to change the previous political incentive mode of merely focusing on economic development and ignoring the ecological environment, so as to solve the problems of high energy consumption, high pollution and high emission caused by GDP-oriented assessment. The report of the 18th National Congress of the Communist Party of China clearly included resource consumption, environmental damage and ecological benefits into the evaluation system of economic and social development. The *Decision of the Central Committee of the Communist Party of China on Some Major Issues Concerning Comprehensively Deepening the Reform* emphasizes that the weight of indicators such as resource consumption, environmental damage and ecological benefits should be increased in the evaluation system of development results. On this basis, *Communiqué of the Fifth Plenary Session of the 18th CPC Central Committee* further clearly regards "green development" as one of the development goals of the "13th Five-Year Plan" period. The above-mentioned policies and regulations fully show the firm determination of the central government to pay attention to environmental performance and build ecological civilization. However, it only draws the general outline of low-carbon performance management macroscopically, while in practice, how to truly transform low-carbon environmental performance management into a political incentive for promotion of officials depends on the concrete implementation of the following two dimensions:

(I) **Design of Assessment Indicators**

Considering the systematic and complex work required to address climate change, a three-dimensional and diversified evaluation index system shall be built in low-carbon performance management, where three aspects shall be focused on as follows:

i. Low-carbon development and environmental protection shall be taken into consideration in assessment indicators, to realize the coordinated control of greenhouse gases and environmental pollution. Low-carbon development is closely related to environmental protection, and they cannot be separated as they are linked, promoted and developed with each other. The experiences of developed countries show that most of them have undergone a development course from mere control of environmental pollution to a comprehensive management of low-carbon development and environmental protection. The U.S. Environmental Protection Agency has included greenhouse gases as air pollutants, while the European Union has prepared a package of policies to address climate change, save energy and protect the environment, thus setting mitigating and adapting to climate change as the goal of preventing and controlling environmental pollution.[54] Therefore, the assessment indicators of low-carbon performance management should include not only pollution control indicators, but

[54] See Tian Chunxiu, Feng Xiangzhao and Zhang Xi, *Establish a Unified Supervision System for Emission Reduction of Air Pollutants and Greenhouse Gases*, *China Environment News*, December 10, 2013.

also energy conservation and emission reduction indicators, such as total greenhouse gas load control indicators and total pollution load control indicators, energy consumption intensity indicators and carbon intensity indicators, PM2.5 improvement indicators and greenhouse gas concentration indicators, etc.

ii. Evaluation indicators should include both the positive and negative indicators. Performance evaluation is to comprehensively evaluate both advantages and shortcomings, rather than merely "reward" without "punishment". In this case, both positive and negative indicators should be included in the low-carbon assessment indicator system. Positive indicators, such as air improvement and pollution control results, should be given extra points and rewards; while negative indicators, such as the number of environmental accidents and the number of days of severe smog, will be deducted certain points or will be given punitive evaluation.

iii. Long-term consideration of evaluation indicators. Due to the high technical requirements for the goal of low-carbon economy and low-carbon life promoted by low-carbon administration at present, it may take half a century to fully realize the low-carbon transformation of the whole society with great costs, with long cost recovery cycle; it is of low or negative value in terms of short-term economic benefits. The analysis by Chatham House in the UK shows that the city of Jilin needs an additional investment of RMB 2.6 billion per year to achieve the 65% building energy efficiency target, and needs 33 years to recover the cost.[55] Therefore, there is a "secular inequality",[56] as proposed by Cass Robert Sunstein, between costs and benefits. This determines that the efficiency evaluation criteria for low-carbon administration must be long-term ones and for public welfare, covering a time span exceeding the term of one or more governments generally. Therefore, the low-carbon performance evaluation indicators must be designed to exceed immediate and partial economic benefits, and to cover the long-term and overall benefits in the law.[57]

iv. Scientific allocation of the weight of evaluation indicators. The weight of the assessment indicators must be scientific as it determines the impact of different indicators on the evaluation results (points), otherwise it will affect the fairness and incentive effect of the assessment. The indicator weight includes two aspects for low-carbon evaluation: (i) The weight of low-carbon indicator relevant to GDP indicator. To include the indicators in low-carbon environmental protection, we should not go through the motions, but should actually give full play to the role of constraint and inspiration of the indicators. Therefore, the principle of giving weight to low-carbon indicators is to play a balancing role on GDP indicators. For example, the 2011 *Opinions of the State Council on Strengthening Major Environmental Protection Work* included "a veto system

[55] London: Chatham House, 2010, Appendix D.

[56] [U.S.] *Worst-Case Scenarios* written by Cass R. Sunstein and translated by Liu Kunlun, China Renmin University Press, 2010, P 140.

[57] See Lü Zhongmei, *Roadmap for Law Construction of China's Ecological Rule, Social Sciences in China*, Vol. 5, 2013.

for environmental protection" for the selection, appointment and management supervision of cadres, which fully reflects the rigid binding force of low-carbon indicators on GDP and other evaluation indicators. What's more, the proposal of low-carbon performance evaluation does not mean that GDP is no longer important; instead, GDP will remain as an important factor in the future evaluation system (but its importance should be appropriately diluted) as environmental problems will ultimately be solved through social and economic development. (ii) Weight of different indicators within the low-carbon indicator system. Low-carbon development and environmental protection are a common task for the world, though, the specific objectives and methods to address climate change and control environmental pollution are not the same due to the different social and economic development conditions and environmental resource endowments in different regions. It should be reflected in the weight difference of different low-carbon indicators in the assessment indicators. For example, the indicator weight of energy conservation and air cleaning may be greater in industrial functional areas; and the indicator weight shall lean towards cultivated land protection in agricultural functional areas; while more attention may be paid to biodiversity, soil and water conservation, vegetation coverage and other indicators in ecological functional areas.

(II) **Application of Assessment Results**

The authority and restraint of performance management are demonstrated by the application of evaluation results, in this case, we should leverage evaluation results to motivate the government and its officials to implement corresponding administrative actions. As for general principles of government performance management, the evaluation results can be mostly applied in these ways:

i. Application in the appointment and supervision of officials. The results of low-carbon performance assessment should be taken as the basis and obligatory premises for the appointment and promotion of the Party and government cadres, to solve the problem of lack of low-carbon and environmental incentives for officials; including both positive and negative assessment results. For example, for positive results, it can be stipulated that officials who have been assessed as excellent in low-carbon environmental protection work for two consecutive years during their term of office will be given priority in promotion or exceptional promotion; that is to say, when an official is competent for a certain level of leadership position, it may be stipulated that he must have passed examinations excellent or above in low-carbon and environmental protection. As for negative results, it can be stipulated that officials who have ecological environmental liability during their term of office and are assessed as basically qualified should not be promoted; while if the assessment result is unqualified, those holding leadership positions shall be demoted. Cadres, who are discovered to cause major damages to ecological environment due to their decision-making mistakes during their term of office or after leaving office, shall be investigated for lifelong responsibility, regardless of their current position, or whether they are retired, he shall be investigated for corresponding legal and political responsibilities according to national laws and party regulations.

ii. Application in governmental/departmental benefit distribution. The results of performance evaluation cannot only apply to government officials, but also to the administrative regions to be assessed as an entity similar to "public corporations" while bearing the corresponding legal consequences. And the results should also affect the regional benefit distribution. That is because the actual targets of the ecological environment performance (including excellent performance and bad performance) assessments, in terms of environmental resource capacity, is the specific government jurisdiction area or specific administration, and the individual official is only the personality representative of the jurisdiction area or unit. Specifically, the results of low-carbon performance evaluation can be applied in the following governmental/departmental benefit distribution: (i) Budget rewards and punishments. According to the evaluation results, the superior financial department should reward or punish the regions and departments whose low-carbon environmental performance has been obviously improved or deteriorated through increasing or decreasing financial transfer payments. (ii) Limited approval on regional new projects. The legal basis for the limited approval on regional new projects is the *Decision of the State Council on Implementing the Scientific Development View and Strengthening the Environmental Protection*[58] issued at the end of 2005; and the Clause 2 of Article 44 of the *2014 Environmental Protection Law* has similar provisions.[59] Limited approval on regional new projects has a good effect on the bad environmental performance of local government. In 2007, the Ministry of Ecology and Environment of the People's Republic of China carried out a centralized rectification of environmental impact assessments, suspending the approval of environmental impact assessment for newly building, rebuilding and expanding projects of coal-fired units in the following administrative regions that violated the "simultaneous design, construction and going into operation" system of environmental impact assessment, including Tangshan in Hebei Province, Luliang in Shanxi Province, Laiwu in Shandong Province and Liupanshui in Guizhou Province. It was estimated that the emission of sulfur dioxide would be reduced by more than 190,000 tons per year.[60] The limited approval on regional new projects can also be absorbed and applied in the low-carbon performance evaluation. For administrative regions that fail the low-carbon environmental performance evaluation,

[58] See Article 5 (21) of the *Decision of the State Council on Implementing the Scientific View of Development and Strengthening Environmental Protection.*

[59] See Article 44 (ii) in the *Environmental Protection Law.*

[60] Pan Yue, the deputy director of the State Environmental Protection Administration, concluded, "The effect of the three-month regional approval limit is more obvious than that of any previous enforcement of EIA, which has not only solved some serious environmental violations, but also transformed some local governments' thinking of treatment after pollution, and development after accumulation. They have gradually got rid of the dependence on the scale and quantity of high energy consuming industries and stepped into developing new industries." Ministry of Environmental Protection of the People's Republic of China: *Lüliang, Liupanshui and China Huadian*

the superior government (mostly the development and reform department) shall suspend the approval of construction projects with high pollution, high energy consumption and high-carbon emissions, and correspondingly reduce the total load control quota indicators of pollutants and greenhouse gas emissions. (iii) Application in striving for excellence. The activity of striving for excellence refers to a top-down evaluation system that grants advanced honorary titles to local governments or administrative departments that have been evaluated as excellent; such as the evaluations of "national civilized unit", the "national advanced unit", the "national civilized city", the "national health city" and so on. It is relevant to the corresponding local and administrative departments' preferential policies and civil servants' salary incentives at present, thus it plays a great role in motivating departments and local governments. Therefore, it is essential to take into consideration of the low-carbon performance evaluation results into the competitions among activities of striving for excellence, in order to ensure the effectiveness of low-carbon performance evaluation and strengthen the incentive effect of low-carbon evaluation. At present, as strongly advocated by national policies, some national standards for striving for excellence have included low-carbon evaluation results to a certain extent. For example, the *2014 National Civilized City Assessment System (Prefecture-level Cities)* has specially set up an assessment section for "ecological environment for sustainable development", taking the assessment results of indicators, such as urban air quality, energy conservation and emission reduction, as secondary indicators. However, on the whole, the application of the results of low-carbon performance assessment has not been totally involved in many regional standards. For example, an evaluation project of "harmonious and beautiful internal and external environment" is set up in the *Evaluation Method for Provincial Civilized Units in Hubei Province*, though, it shall be improved in the future as it mostly assesses the sanitation and greening of the unit but not includes assessment results of energy conservation and emission reduction and recycling of resources.

Corporation were the last to be relieved of the "approval limit". The State Environmental Protection Administration will sum up the experience of the approval limit and seek greater achievements http://www.zhb.gov.cn/gkml/hbb/qt/200910/t20091023_180066.htm, January 11, 2015.

Chapter 3
Research on Low-Carbon Administrative Entity

As has been noted, administrative law can address climate change from the following two aspects: first, urging administrative entity to actively and effectively perform the function of low-carbon regulation for the whole society; second, restricting administrative entity, so as to realize low-carbonization. Among them, the low-carbonization of the administrative entity itself involves, at least, the low-carbonization of the internal organizational structure of the administrative entity and that of administrative activities. The organizations, staffing, various financial expenditures and material resources in need, etc. of administrative entities can be converted into corresponding carbon emissions. The low-carbonization level of the entities is determined based on the following factors: whether administrative entities have scientific and equitable organizational design; scientific division of functions; lean staffing; simplified use of funds; and green and environmentally friendly office facilities. While the administrative activities will show its low-carbonization level from whether administrative courses, i.e., administrative processes, are simplified, smooth and efficient. Administrative process is the way, step, time limit and sequence that administrative activities should follow.[1] The intensity of carbon emissions from administrative activities is highly correlated with the efficiency of administrative courses. The administrative costs and resources consumed by red tape and inefficient administrative courses are definitely greater, thus the carbon emission intensity are also greater, and vice versa. Not only can the administrative processes determine the low-carbonization level of the administrative entity's own administrative activities, but also can directly or indirectly affect the carbon emission level of the administrative counterpart when participating in the relevant activities of the administrative processes, that is to say, it has external radiation effect. This is because, except for pure internal administrative procedures, all external administrative processes are not only the processes

[1] See *Administrative Law and Administrative Litigation Law*, editor Jiang Mingan, Peking University Press, Higher Education Press, 2002, p. 260.

S. Fang and B. Tan, *On the Administrative Law of China in Addressing Climate Change*,
https://doi.org/10.1007/978-981-19-7705-3_3

of administrative activities, but also the processes of activities when the administrative counterparts participate in the administrative courses, and should be repeatedly applied to the unspecified administrative counterparts. Therefore, redundant and inconvenient administrative process design will cause administrative counterparts to bear unnecessary costs or resource consumption. For instance, if matters that could have been completed at one administration but are required to be completed after going through procedures at multiple administrations, carbon emissions from such activities will be even greater with no doubt. In this case, the low-carbonization of the organizational structure of the administrative entity and the low-carbonization of the administrative activity courses should both rely on the scientific, efficient, simple and economical design of relevant systems of the administrative organization law and the Administrative Litigation Law. We will first discuss the administrative entity in this chapter.

In dealing with climate change, the administrative entity itself is a huge carbon emission entity. In 2011, China's "three public consumptions" (Overseas trip expenses, vehicle purchase and operation expenses, and official reception fees) reached RMB 300 billion, accounting for 18.6% of the fiscal expenditure, far beyond that of other countries such as Japan, Britain, Canada and the U.S. (that of the four countries accounted for 2.38%, 4.19%, 7.1% and 9.9% of their budgets respectively).[2] And these "three public consumptions" reflect the generation of mass carbon emissions in administrative entity activities. As it were, without the low-carbonization of the administration itself, the government will lose its exemplary effect in practicing the low-carbon administrative principle, and the low-carbon society would not be built.

However, due to "Parkinson's Law" and the public burden of administrative entity's expenditure, carbon emission activities of administrative entity are often in an "organised irresponsibility"[3] state without external constraints. Under the impact of "Parkinson's Law", the institutions and personnel of the administrative entities have an impulse of self-expansion, so it is difficult to get out of the vicious circle of "simplification → expansion → re-simplification → re-expansion" in both the institution setting and the staffing. Meanwhile, it is the taxpayers and the national treasury that pay for the expenses and daily operation of the administrative entities, making the administrative entities and their staffs lack the motivation to reduce costs and save resources and energy in the process of services. For example, in 2005, a report showed that the average daily power consumption of public institutions in China was 19 times as much as that of the general public.[4] Under the influence of the joint actions of the continuous expansion of personnel in the organization and the extravagant and wasteful use of public property by personnel in the organization,

---

[2] Jiang Yanxin, *Government expense of RMB 300 Billion on Food Per Year; The Jiusan Society Suggesting to the Central Committee that "Three Public Wastes Should be Punished"*, *The Beijing News*, March 2, 2012.

[3] [Germany] *World Risk Society* written by Ulrich Beck and translated by Wu Yingzi and Sun Shumin, Nanjing University Press, 2004, p. 191.

[4] Wang Wentao and Yu Lihong: *The Power Consumption of Civil Servants in One Day is Equivalent to that of Ordinary People in 19 Days*, *Morning Herald*, July 5, 2005.

the waste of resources and high carbon emission in the operation of the administrative subject will inevitably appear. Therefore, it is extremely essential to regulate the administrative entity's use of resources and energy and their carbon emission activities based on the requirements of energy conservation and emission reduction.

1 Organization Law Elements of Administrative Entity

In administrative organization law, the administrative entity consists of institutional element, personnel element and material element.[5] First, the institutional element, also known as the administrative organization in the narrowest sense, includes the setting, authority, legal status and mutual relations of administrative organizations. The second is the personnel element. The institutions are only the form and nominal carrier of administrative organizations, and the administrative tasks must actually be conducted through the actions of public servants. Third is the material element. It includes financial funds, buildings and other office supplies necessary for administrative organizations to exercise their functions and powers.

The three organization law elements of the administrative entity promote and supplement each other to jointly determine the carbon footprint of the administrative organization. Among the three, institutional elements provide the source and admittance of administrative organizations' carbon emissions, which belong to indirect emissions. Generally speaking, the more institutions set in the government, the more potential carbon emitting entities there will be. Personnel elements are organized based on institutional elements and affect the carbon emissions of administrative organizations from the following two aspects. On the one hand, the payments and duty activities of public officials need to be guaranteed by certain financial costs and material resources, which can be converted into carbon emission equivalent finally; on the other hand, whether the public officials use the material elements equitably and economically also affects the level of carbon emissions. Material elements is the material basis for administrative organizations to produce carbon emissions, including these important elements that restrict carbon emissions: whether the scale of public property is appropriate, whether public property procurement is green, whether public property use is low-carbon and economical, etc. In this case, the task of low-carbon regulation of administrative organizations is to maintain the energy consumption and carbon emissions of various elements within administrative organizations at a scientific and equitable low level through optimization of system and equitable arrangement.

[5] See *General Introduction to Administrative Law*, Chief Editor Yang Jianshun, China Renmin University Press, 2012, p. 60.

2 Low-Carbon Regulation of Institutional Elements of Administrative Entity

2.1 Non-Low-Carbonization of Institutional Elements

In practice, the expansion and overstaffing of institutions represent the non-low-carbonization of the institutional and personnel elements of administrative entities. And dealing with these phenomena has undoubtedly become the key task in streamlining institutions and increasing administrative efficiency. However, in terms of addressing climate change, the harm of overstaffing of institutional elements and personnel elements is far more than hindering administrative efficiency, which should be interpreted from a new perspective. Firstly, the expansion of institutional and personnel elements undoubtedly does harm to the ecological civilization and the construction of a beautiful China for it has greatly increased the consumption of resources and financial costs in the administrative course, and has brought about a huge amount of corresponding carbon emissions. Secondly, the institutional waste and overstaffing of administrative entity have, to a large extent, has damaged the image of the government as exemplar in the construction of a low-carbon society; and in the long run, it will foster a bad model for the citizens' low-carbon actions. Specifically, the non-low-carbonization of the institutional elements of the administrative entity is mostly manifested in the aspects as follows.

(I) **Too Many Deliberation and Coordination Bodies and Provisional Institutions**

As statistics shows, in 2012, 38 work leading groups were set up in Suojie Township, Shimen County, Hunan Province at one time. In 2007, the Hangzhou Xiaoshan district office found that there were 235 deliberation and coordination bodies of the district Party committee and district government.[6] Since the mass line campaign was started in 2013, a total of more than 130,000 deliberation and coordination bodies have been collectively cleared across the country. These bodies have various names, including leading groups, coordination groups, committees, headquarters, offices and so on; and involve diverse business areas: "Office of Prohibiting Drinking at Noon", "Leading Group for Promoting Foot Therapy and Health Care", "Watermelon Office", "Steamed Bread Office" and "Live Pig Office". What's more, the "Provincial SARS Prevention and Control Headquarters" is still retained in some places even after ten years ...[7] Thus, we can see the overstaffing of China's deliberation and coordination bodies. According to Article 11 of the *Regulation on the Organization Establishment and Staffing Administration of Local People's Governments*

---

[6] See *Experts Talking about the Phenomenon of "Steamed Bread Management Office": Similar Local Organizations are Common*, Cheng Guochang, *Henan Business Daily*, June 18, 2014.

[7] See Zhou Lin and Zhu Hong: *Is there helplessness or incompetence behind the abolishing of 130,000 "coordinating bodies" across the country and frequent "leadership in command"?* Xinhua: http://news.xinhuanet.com/politics/2014-10/22/c_1112929815.htm, November 19, 2014.

at All Levels, no other deliberation and coordination bodies shall be established if existing bodies can assume functions to solve problems. However, numerous local-level deliberation and coordination bodies have independent permanent agencies, approved budgets and staffing. Meanwhile, provisional institutions also are widely distributed at the local level. They have entity offices and huge expenditures without legal evidence, with a scale several times larger than that of government functional departments. As media reports, there are 162 provisional institutions in Lishui City, Zhejiang Province alone; more than 200 provisional institutions in the Lengshuitan District of Yongzhou City in Hunan Province, with annual financial expenditure of more than RMB 50 million.[8] The numerous deliberation and coordination bodies and provisional institutions have not only resulted in overstaffing of agencies and more personnel than work available, causing a huge amount of unnecessary carbon emissions; but also brought about tons of unnecessary work in the daily operation of administrative organizations, indirectly causing secondary waste of resources and carbon emissions.

(II) **Hidden Expansion of Derivative Institutions**

Government derivative institutions refer to non-internal subordinate institutions derived from administrations, including affiliated public welfare organizations, government-owned intermediary service institutions, trade associations and various enterprises and institutions. Generally speaking, they can be divided into administrative institutions, professional institutions, operating institutions and public welfare institutions. In practice, they exist everywhere, in multiple administrative institutions at different levels and departments, from central institutions to local institutions, from Party committee working institutions to government functional institutions, from service institutions to law enforcement institutions. Derivative institutions, whose establishment is more flexible, fall within the gray area stipulated by law. This has resulted in the number of derivative institutions of many administrations being equal to or even more than their internal institutions. Take the Ministry of Finance, Ministry of Commerce and National Development and Reform Commission for instance, the number ratios of derivative institutions and internal institutions are 31: 23, 35: 31 and 30: 31 respectively.[9] Among them, the Ministry of Commerce has over 30 derivative institutions of different natures and types, including China International Center for Economic and Technical Exchanges, China Commerce and Trade Press, China Association of Enterprises with Foreign Investment, and China Association of International Trade, in addition to its official internal and resident agencies. Meanwhile, the number of their staff is often more than that of their superior administrative institutions as the staffing of derivative institutions is not limited by the staffing of civil servants. Many of the sources of funding for derivative institutions, which are truly "quasi-administrative institutions", are full financial allocations or balance

---

[8] See Shen Liang and Wei Juan: *Leaders are Tired of So Many Temporary Organizations*, *Southern Weekly*, May 6, 2010.

[9] See Zhang Xiaojin and Ji Mingming, *Recessive Expansion: Grey Zone of Government Institution Reform*, *People's Tribune*, Vol. 12, 2014.

allocation. The exercise of their duties links closely to and even to some degree overlaps with their parent institutions. Therefore, such derivative institutions are called "hidden expansion"[10] of government scale by some scholars. Compared with the expansion of formal administrative institutions, that of derivative institutions is more invisible, with difficulties in regulation of the use of staff, property and materials, thus fostering numerous carbon emission sources that go out of the control of organic law.

(III) Setting of Counterpart Government Institutions

Regulations on Administration of the Establishment and Staffing of the administrative institutions of the State Council and the *Local Regulations* have clearly stipulated that higher-level governments shall not require lower-level people's governments to set administrative institutions corresponding to their businesses, though, in practice, the problem of governments at all levels being "generally overstaffing both at higher and lower levels" is still very common.[11] Many grass-roots governments have arranged administrative institutions with complete categories but superficial and unoccupied cores. For instance, a county has set up a counterpart Taiwan Affairs Office with seven staffs, while there is only one resident from Taiwan registered in the county.[12] Obviously, it is unnecessary to set such a "counterpart" mechanism.

(IV) Overlap of Administrative Institutions and Party Committee Departments

Having both Party system and government system in China, Party committees at all levels have established many work departments with similar or identical functions to government institutions at present, such as the rural work committee corresponding to agricultural administrative institutions, the university work committee corresponding to educational administrative institutions, and the enterprise work committee corresponding to industrial and commercial administrative institutions. Some Party and government institutions are overlapping in responsibilities but in possession of independent office buildings, public property allocation, financial expenditure and staffing, which is not beneficial to the overall saving of administrative costs and the reduction of carbon emission.

---

[10] See Zhang Xiaojin and Ji Mingming, *Recessive Expansion: Grey Zone of Government Institution Reform, People's Tribune*, Vol. 12, 2014.

[11] Li Junpeng: *Nine Hot Issues in Theory and Practice of Administrative System Reform, Study Times*, November 5, 2007.

[12] See Ma Shanji: *A Discussion on" The Superior Department Corresponding to the Subordinate Department", China State Finance*, Vol. 4, 1992.

2.2 Path Selection of Low-Carbonization of Institutional Elements

The following improvements should be made on the basis of the low-carbon requirements against the problems existing in the current administrative entity setting:

i. The problem of excessive deliberation and coordination bodies and provisional institutions should be solved at three levels as follows: Firstly, the deliberation and coordination bodies play an important role in communicating the relationship between different departments so as to achieve cross-departmental administrative tasks. And they should be retained, if necessary, but the total amount of actual institutions should be limited to prevent unlimited expansion. According to the *Notice of the State Council on the Establishment of Advisory and Coordinating Organs* (GF [2008] No. 13), at present, the State Council has 29 deliberation and coordination bodies. The quota of deliberation and coordination bodies of local governments shall be based on it and shall not exceed the number of those of the State Council at least. In the next place, the deliberation and coordination bodies of the people's governments at all levels, in principle, shall not set separate substantive offices. The established substantive ones shall be abolished and the specific work shall be transferred to the existing functional departments. If it is really necessary to set a separate office to handle a specific administrative task, it shall be canceled when the task is completed or the deadline expires. Secondly, the concept of "provisional institutions" originated from the *1998 Notice of the State Council on the Establishment of Provisional Organs and Organs in Charge of Deliberation and Coordination* (GF [1998] No. 7). However, the *Local Regulations* issued in 2007 and the *Opinion Concerning Deepening Reforms of Administrative and Management Systems* adopted at the Second Plenary Session of the 17th CPC Central Committee in 2008 clearly abolished the concept of "provisional institutions" and only retained the "deliberation and coordination bodies". That is to say, as a legacy of the administrative system reform, numerous provisional institutions are no longer valid according to organic law and become hotbeds of resource waste and high carbon emissions, thus they should be promptly cleaned up and abolished. Thirdly, the governance of the excessive establishment of deliberation and coordination bodies and provisional institutions must ultimately be guaranteed by supervision and inspection. According to the provisions of the existing *Local Regulations*, the supervision and inspection of the establishment of institutions shall be carried out by the establishment and management authorities at the same level. In case of illegal establishment found, opinions and suggestions shall be given to the government at the corresponding level. However, in practice, the deliberation and coordination bodies and provisional institutions are generally led by the Party and government leaders; and it is just like asking a tiger for its hide to expect that institutions and management agencies in the government at the corresponding level may propose supervision suggestions and make rectification by themselves. Therefore, it is necessary to change the current supervision and inspection mechanism of the *Local Regulations* from peer supervision to superior supervision. For instance, it is stipulated that the provincial people's government staffing management agencies shall supervise and inspect the establishment of institutions of the people's government at or above the county level; the State Commission for Public Sector Reform and the State Commission Office for Public Sector Reform shall supervise and inspect the institutional stipulation of the people's governments of provinces and municipalities directly under the Central Government. Meanwhile, in case of illegal establishment of institutions, it is not only required to investigate the legal responsibility of the competent leaders, but also required to revoke the institution itself in accordance with the law, so as to eliminate carbon emission entities without legal basis.

ii. In order to control the expansion of derivative institutions, we must first limit the institutional setting right of administrative institutions in a strict manner according to organization law, and legalize the institutional forms that the administration has the right to set, such as internal institutions, deliberation and coordination institutions, etc.; and any other derivative institutions must not be set up in any sense. Secondly, the existing derivative institutions can be dealt with through a classification reform according to the *Guiding Opinions of CPC Central Committee and State Council on Classified Promotion of Institution Reform*. Administrative derivative institutions that undertake certain supervisory functions or internal service functions should be merged with formal administrative institutions, with a equitable total limit of staffing. Operating derivatives should be gradually transformed into self-supporting enterprises. Public welfare derivative institutions that undertake certain types of public service tasks can be kept remained in the list of public institutions, with unified management of institutional setting and staffing. Specialized derivative institutions such as trade associations and research institutes should be timely transformed into self-funded and internally autonomous non-governmental social organizations.

iii. To solve the problem of unnecessary counterpart government institutions, it is required to change the existing institutional mode and adopt the responsibility adjustment model instead in arranging the counterpart institutions. That is to say, under the premise of equitable allocation of government responsibilities at all levels, their respective functional agencies shall be established according to the different responsibilities of different levels of government, except for institutions under the direct leadership of the central government and the provincial government.[13] Generally, in principle, the grass-roots government shall undertake specific management responsibilities closely relevant to residents' lives, such as social security, household registration management, resource supply, environmental protection, social safeguard, town and city planning and urban construction; while governments above the provincial level are suitable to undertake macro management responsibilities such as major administrative decisions, financial transfer payments, economic and social development

[13] See Xu Jimin, *Local Administrative System Reform and Service-oriented Government Construction*, Journal of Zhejiang Party School of C.P.C, Vol. 2, 2009.

planning and ethnic and religious affairs.[14] On the basis of the duty adjustment model, governments at all levels can set administrative institutions according to their duties, rather than setting institutions according to the institutional structure, thus to effectively avoid duplicate or similar administrative institutions at different levels, and achieve the goals of streamlining agencies and saving resources.

iv. With regard to the overlapping of Party and government organs, the Fourth Plenary Session of the 16th CPC Central Committee has put forward the principle of "canceling and merging work departments with the same or similar functions of the Party committee and the government". "To cancel" means to nullify departments assuming similar responsibility to the existing government agencies by Party committees; those that have already been set should be canceled in batches step by step. The so-called "to merge" means that the form of joint office should be implemented as much as possible for missions to be jointly undertaken by the administrative departments of the government and the working departments of the Party committee, and the institutional setting of "joint institution" should be implemented, such as the combination of Commission for Discipline Inspection and Supervision, the Party school and the school of administration, the working committee of colleges and universities and the educational administrative institutions. At present, China has carried out fruitful work in the aspect of "merging", but there is still a lack of effective measures in the aspect of "cancelling", which needs to be further explored in the reform of administrative system.

3 Low-Carbon Regulation of Personnel Elements of Administrative Entity

3.1 Non-Low-Carbonization of Personnel Elements

The low-carbon organizational standard of personnel elements requires the government to keep the staffing of administrative organizations at a proper scale required for the performance of their duties, and to have a reasonable and clear division of responsibilities, so as to avoid unnecessary redundant officials. However, there are serious overstaffing problems in China's administrative organizations, which does not meet the requirements of low-carbon standard.

(I) **There are Various Degrees of Overstaffing**

Overstaffing has always been a long-standing problem in China's administrative organizations. The actual investigation on the staffing of a provincial administration by a scholar shows that the lower the level of government, the more serious the

[14] See Zhu Guanglei and Zhang Zhihong: *Critique of "Isomorphic Responsibility"*, *Journal of Peking University (Philosophy and Social Sciences)*, Vol. 1, 2005.

problem of overstaffing. According to the research results of the scholar, the size of provincial government staffing is 6.5% above the required in H Province, the size of municipal government staffing in XF city is 36.9% above the required, and the sizes of FC district and NZ county governments are 90% and 72.5% above the required ones, respectively.[15] According to another report, the number of official staff of the Environmental Inspection Team of Lingbi County Environmental Protection Agency of Anhui Province is 73, while the stipulated number of the staff of the Environmental Inspection Team is only 21 according to the formation documents approved by the organization formulation committee of the county, which means the team has 200% too many staff members.[16] The financial funds, resources and energy used to support these overstaffed personnel, undoubtedly, are unreasonable carbon emissions.

(II) The Overstaffing of Deputy Personnel and Structural Redundancy of Personnel

In addition to the overstaffing of the total number of personnel, the overstaffing of leadership positions such as deputy positions is also obvious. Regarding the central level, the Organic Law of the State Council specifically stipulates that the number of deputies in ministries and commissions should be 2–4, but in practice, there are far more than 4 deputy ministers in some ministries and commissions, which obviously violates the provisions of the Organic Law.[17] Regarding the local level, a media found that the number of deputy positions of local governments is generally 7–9, while the number of deputy secretaries of some local governments reaches 15–16, far higher than the number of deputy leaders, according to the responses of information disclosure applications and official websites information of 42 provinces and cities.[18] From the perspective of resource consumption and carbon emission, the consumption of administrative leaders is much larger than that of ordinary civil servants, as they are generally equipped with secretaries, assistants, drivers and other auxiliary personnel, enjoying larger office space and better welfare treatment, etc. All these factors will greatly increase the average carbon emission intensity of the whole administrative organization. At the same time, influenced by the excessive number of deputies and other leaders, the administrative organization has a structural redundancy of "more officers and less soldiers", that is, the proportion of administrative leaders and general public servants is obviously unbalanced, and the number of people who command is more while that who handle affairs is less. Some scholars pointed out that the ratio of "responsible person" to "administrative staff and other personnel" is 1:0.84 in China's administrative system, which is much higher than that of the United States (1:2.7) and

---

[15] See Zeng Jun: *Problems in the Establishment and Formulation of Local Party and Government Organizations and The "Fundamental Solutions"*, *Journal of Shanghai Administration Institute*, Vol. 4, 2008.

[16] See Wang Limin: *"Diagnose" the Overstaffing of Government Departments and Public Institutions*, *Shaanxi Daily*, February 25, 2008.

[17] See Ying Songnian, *Exploration of Perfecting Administrative Organization Legal System*, *China Legal Science*, Vol. 2, 2013.

[18] Anonymous: The Reduction of Deputy Secretaries-General of the Government Announced across the Country, *Southern Metropolis Daily*, August 18, 2014.

Japan (1:3.6).[19] The institutional redundancy of personnel means that the completion of the same amount of administrative tasks needs more human and material resources, leading to the unreasonable increase of the average resource consumption and carbon emission of administrative personnel, which further increases the carbon emission intensity of administrative organizations.

3.2 The Path Selection of Low-Carbonization of Personnel Elements

Regarding how to simplify the overall overstaffed personnel, the current practice of governments at all levels is to "digest" in the system, such as diverting the overstaffed personnel to other public institutions, etc.[20] Although the number of regular employees has been reduced apparently, in fact, the number of people supported by the government's finance has not been reduced. These people have only been transferred to other nonadministrative public institutions,[21] which is a way, as the saying goes, of "robbing Peter to pay Paul", which can not really achieve the low-carbon effect of saving administrative costs and reducing resource consumption. To this end, the fundamental solution should be to establish a normal exit mechanism for civil servants, to clear up and dismiss redundant and overstaffed personnel, and to guide them to reemployment in society, rather than to arrange them to other public institutions in disguised form. This should be made clear in the *Civil Servants Law* and *Regulation on the Organization Establishment and Staffing Administration of Local People's Governments at All Levels.*

The problem of overstaffing of deputies and the accompanying structural redundancy should be alleviated from the two aspects of "head end control" and "end control". In terms of head end control, the number of Deputies of governments at all levels and their functional departments should be clearly limited in the administrative organization legislation. There are some quantitative provisions in the *Organic Law of the State Council*, but there are still some deficiencies in the *Organic Law of Local People's Congresses at All Levels and Local People's Governments at Different Levels*, which need to be improved in the amendment. At the same time, certain scientific standard must be followed for specification of the proportion of leaders and clerks in principle. Considering the practice, the "leaders" here include not only the actual leading positions, but also the non-leadership positions such as examiners,

---

[19] Xu Gang: *Reflection on the Mechanism of Deputy Government Officials under Structural Redundancy and Future Choice*, *Study and Exploration*, Vol. 2, 2013.

[20] See Zhang Guifeng: *How to "digest" the over 4000 overstaffed officials in Wuhan City*, *China Youth Daily*, September 8, 2009; The Report on the Overstaffed Party and Government Organs in Huanggang City, http://www.hbcz.gov.cn/421101/lm2/lm4/2011-11-22-1197171.shtml, November 19, 2014.

[21] According to the definition in *Energy Conservation Regulation for State-funded Institutions*, the so-called "public institutions" refer to state organs, institutions and organizations wholly or partially funded by public funds.

investigators and inspectors who actually enjoy leadership treatment, to achieve a reasonable personnel structure. In terms of end control, first, the legal responsibility of overstaffing by setting deputy positions in violation of law should be specified clearly in the Organic Law; second, for overstaffed deputy personnel, they should be demoted and dismissed according to the organizational principle of cadres' promotion and demotion and the original treatment should not be retained, to achieve the low-carbon effect of financial support cost and resource and energy consumption.

4 Low-Carbon Regulation of Material Support Elements of Administrative Entity

For a long time, due to the principle of organization legality, administrative organization law usually focuses on the legal authority, organization structuring and staffing of administrative entities, while material support elements are rarely dealt with in the administrative organization law. In the low-carbon era, the use of material support elements of administrative entities has become an important source of social energy consumption and greenhouse gas emissions. Under the practical constraints of energy conservation and emission reduction, it is an inevitable trend for administrative entities to reconsider the normative structure of material support elements within the low-carbon framework in order to respond to low-carbon administrative tasks. From the perspective of life cycle of carbon emission activities, the low-carbon regulation of material support elements can be analyzed in the aspects of the configuration, use and supervision of public goods.

4.1 Non-Low-Carbonization of Material Support Elements

In terms of institutional and personnel elements, China has preliminarily established the constraint and supervision systems regulated by the laws for organization structuring and staffing management. However, the supervision of material elements is rarely found in the current organization law systems. This brings about many non-low-carbonization problems in the use of material support elements of the administrative entities in China. The problems are mainly reflected in the non-low-carbonization of the allocation and use of material elements. In terms of the configuration of material elements, official activities in China involve the use of huge amount of public goods and facilities. For example, currently, the total number of official vehicles used by Party and government organs and administrative institutions is more than 2 million, the annual consumption expenditure on these official vehicles is nearly RMB 200 billion (excluding those of hospitals, schools, state-owned enterprises, military forces, and overstaffed vehicle configuration), and the annual growth rate of the acquisition expenses on official vehicles is more than 20%.[22] In terms of the use of material support elements, the administrative activities in China involve the consumption of huge amount of resources and energy. According to statistics in 2010, the total energy consumption of public institutions in China is 192 million tons of standard coal,[23] accounting for about 6.2% of the total energy consumption in China. The above-mentioned information all show that China's administrative entities are far from meeting the low-carbon standards in terms of material support elements, indicating a great potential for energy conservation and emission reduction.

4.2 Path Selection of Low-Carbonization of Material Support Elements

(I) **Low-Carbon Configuration of Material Support Elements**

The low-carbon configuration of material support elements is a "static" low-carbon organization norm. In a specific administrative organization, the total carbon emission of material elements can be regarded as the product of the carbon intensity per unit substance and the total amount of substances possessed. Therefore, the low-carbon configuration of material support elements can be addressed from two aspects: technology and scale. The former requires that the material elements configured by administrative organizations should be green and energy-saving low-carbon products. The latter requires the quantity and scale of the material elements configured by administrative organizations must be economical and controlled at the minimum level required to perform their duties in order to avoid waste of financial funds and social resources. The former refers to low-carbon in "quality" and the latter in "quantity". The two aspects complement each other and jointly constrain the low-carbon configuration of material elements. Neither of them can be omitted. The configuration of material elements of administrative organizations can be divided into two types: office building and office supply. The specific requirements for the low-carbon configuration of the two are:

i. Low-carbonization of office building configuration. In terms of technical specifications, the construction, maintenance and renovation of office buildings and their equipment systems should meet the scientific standards for energy conservation and emission reduction. To be specific, building standards for energy conservation and emission reduction are divided into two levels, i.e., "energy-saving building standard" and "zero carbon building standard" according to their carbon reduction capability. "Energy-saving building standard" requires that the design of a building in its whole life cycle from planning, engineering, construction, operation, demolition and recycling must be conducive to reducing energy consumption, maintaining energy and

[22] Li Xinxin: *Open the Gray Consumption Box of Official Vehicles*, Outlook Weekly, Issue 1, 2010.

[23] One ton of standard coal is approximately equal to 1.9 tons of carbon emissions.

improving energy utilization efficiency, thus, optimizing carbon emission performance of the building in its life cycle.[24] Specifically, it includes the following technical specifications of the building: shape coefficient, window-wall ratio, heat transfer coefficient or heat transfer resistance of each part of building envelope, shading coefficient of glass window, and seasonal energy efficiency ratio, heating seasonal performance factor, and integrated part load value of refrigerating unit of air conditioning system.[25] The prevailing *Design Standard for Energy Efficiency of Public Buildings* (GB 50189-2005) belongs to this level. "Zero carbon building standard", also known as "carbon neutral building standard", requires that all energy consumed by the building should be supplied by renewable energy resources, all the water required should be provided by rainwater and reclaimed water, and all the waste generated should be sorted and then destroyed locally or reused, or carbon neutrality should be realized by increasing the means of carbon sinks through greening and vegetation planting.[26] Among them, the energy-saving building standard is the basic and initial requirement for the buildings of administrative organizations to achieve low-carbonization. After the energy-saving building standard is gradually achieved within a certain period of time, the administrative organization law should further upgrade the standard to zero-carbon building standard in order to cope with the increasingly fierce climate change. For example, the *Energy Independence and Security Act of 2007* promulgated by the United States specifies that, new and renovated federal buildings must reduce fossil fuel use by 55% (from 2003 levels) by 2010, and 80% by 2020. All new federal buildings must be carbon–neutral by 2030.[27] In addition, for old buildings with high energy consumption and high pollution, their building envelopes and energy-consuming systems should be subject to energy-saving transformation as required. In terms of scale, the construction scale of new buildings of administrative organizations shall be reasonably determined in strict accordance with the *Notice of the General Office of the CPC Central Committee and the General Office of the State Council on Further Strict Control of the Construction of Office Buildings of Party and Government Organizations* (ZBF [2007] No. 11), *Construction Standards for the Office Premises of Party and Government Organs* (JTZ [1999] No. 2250) and other regulatory documents, considering the organization's building level, number of staffing, and approved floor area per capita. No luxurious decoration is allowed. The office area of leading cadres at all levels shall be within the standard stipulated in the *Construction Standards for the Office Premises of Party and Government Organs*, and those above the standard shall be timely evacuated and adjusted in a concentrated manner among departments. If the existing buildings and their equipment systems can be used normally, they shall still be used. In this case,

---

[24] See Li Haibing: *Analysis on the Similarities and Differences between "Ecological Buildings" and "Energy-saving Buildings"*, *Building Energy Efficiency*, Issue 1, 2010.

[25] Ye Ling, et al.: *Elementary Study on Evaluating Index System of Energy-efficient Buildings*, *Building Science*, Issue 6, 2006.

[26] See Chen Shuo: *Technical Guide of Zero Carbon Building*, *Architecture Technique*, Issue Z5, 2011.

[27] See Energy Independence and Security Act of 2007, SEC.432.

it is not allowed to construct or purchase new office buildings, or expand or relocate the existing office buildings.

ii. Low-carbonization of office supply configuration. The technical specifications for the low-carbon configuration of office supplies require administrative organizations to purchase energy-saving and environmental-friendly office supplies. In this regard, China has clearly stipulated in Article 18 of the *Energy Conservation Regulation for State-funded Institutions*,[28] and authorized the Ministry of Finance and the Ministry of Ecology and Environment to jointly formulate and adjust the Government Procurement List for Energy-saving Products and the Government Procurement List for Environmental Labeled Products through the *Notice of the General Office of the State Council on Establishing the System of Compulsory Government Procurement of Energy-saving Products* and has clearly defined a list of compulsory procurement and limited procurement of office supplies. This initially constitutes the technical specifications for the configuration of office supplies of administrative organizations, and should be strictly implemented by all administrative organizations for the implementation of green procurement. The specifications for the scale of low-carbon configuration of office supplies include three aspects: First, except that some administrative organizations with special needs for office supplies can implement the centralized procurement system by departments, the office supplies of all other administrative organizations should be purchased by government procurement units or procurement centers at the same level in a centralized manner, and their quantities should be strictly controlled to avoid frequent and repeated procurement of office supplies by administrative organizations. Secondly, a mechanism for coordination of office supplies among administrative organizations should be established to revitalize the stock of office supplies on the whole. If the requirements for office supplies of administrative organizations can be satisfied through inter-department coordination, these office supplies will not be purchased by the government again. Finally, the office supplies provided should be made best of. It is not allowed to organize government procurement for new office supplies to replace the ones reaching service life span but can still be used normally (except for official vehicles which have come to the end of their service life).

(II) Low-Carbon Use of Material Support Elements

After the low-carbon configuration of material support elements, carbon emissions in the subsequent operation of administrative organizations depend on whether the use of material elements meets the low-carbon and environmental protection standards. This is the "dynamic" low-carbon organization norm. Specifically, the low-carbon use of material elements can be divided into total carbon emission control from the macro level and the energy conservation and emission reduction behavior at the micro level.

i. Total amount control of low-carbon use of material support elements. The energy and resources consumed by the use of material elements by administrative

[28] See the provisions of Article 18 *Energy Conservation Regulation for State-funded Institutions*.

organizations are paid by the state treasury, so they are likely to be wasted and it is required to constrain their use by the total amount control of carbon emissions. The total amount control for low-carbon use of material elements requires the central government to formulate a unified control plan for the total amount of carbon emissions or energy conservation and emission reduction of all administrative organizations nationwide. For example, on January 29, 2010, President Obama set the federal government's overall goal of reducing greenhouse gas emissions by Executive Order 13,514, i.e., the federal government's total carbon emissions will be reduced by 28% on the basis of 2008 till 2020, equivalent to reducing 646 trillion BTUs, 205 million barrels of oil or 17 million road vehicles per year.[29] On August 6, 2012, the State Council of China issued the *12th Five-Year Plan for Energy Conservation and Emission Reduction* (GF [2012] No. 40), which requires that by 2015, the unit area energy consumption and per capita energy consumption of public organizations should be reduced by 12% and 15% on the basis of 2010 respectively. On this basis, each region should decompose and implement the overall target for energy conservation and emission reduction set by the nation to the government of the next level and its functional departments. The lower-level administrative organizations should set their own energy conservation and emission reduction targets and implementation schemes according to the indicator allocation. In addition, considering the intensifying trend of global climate change, the goal of total carbon emission control should be higher accordingly.

ii. Operation rules for low-carbon use of material support elements. When the total amount of carbon emissions in the use of material elements in administrative organizations are under control, specific operation rules are still needed to constrain and guide the daily low-carbon use of material elements. According to different methods of energy conservation and emission reduction, the operation rules for low-carbon use of material support elements can be roughly divided into the following categories: (i). energy saving rules for equipment systems, for example, rationally setting the number and time of elevator opening, reasonably controlling indoor temperature, reducing standby energy consumption of computers, photocopiers and other electrical equipment, making full use of natural lighting, reducing lighting duration, turning off electrical equipment in time, and implementing time-sharing power supply in office areas; (ii). green consumption rules, for example, using environmental-friendly renewable paper, reducing the use of disposables, and saving water; (iii). resource recycling rules, for example, recycling major waste products according to their classifications, including non-classified waste paper, waste electronic products and kitchen waste; (iv). energy-saving rules for official vehicles, for example, strictly controlling the use of official vehicles, strictly enforcing the energy-saving driving standards, and implementing the motor vehicle energy consumption

---

[29] The White House Office of the Press Secretary, *President Obama Sets Greenhouse Gas Emissions Reduction Target for Federal Operations*, January 29, 2010, at http://www.whitehouse.gov/the-press-office/president-obama-sets-greenhouse-gas-emissions-reduction-target-federal-operations, visited on November 15, 2014.

accounting system.[30] In addition, administrative organizations should be encouraged to adopt the contract-based management method, that is, on the premise of clarifying the responsibility targets for energy conservation and emission reduction, delegating own department's energy conservation and emission reduction work to a third-party service institution for the diagnosis and management of own department's low-carbon work.

(III) **Low-Carbon Supervision of Material Elements**

In order to guarantee the low-carbon configuration and use of material elements of administrative organizations, corresponding supervision system should be established. According to different methods, the low-carbon supervision system of material elements can be divided into internal supervision and external supervision.

i. Internal supervision means supervising the energy conservation and emission reduction of material elements of an administrative organization by its internal organs. Article 25 of *Energy Conservation Regulation for State-funded Institutions* stipulates that a public institution should have energy management positions and should implement the responsibility system for energy management positions. The internal supervision system for low-carbonization of material elements of administrative organizations has been preliminarily established. However, this is only a rough rule. Many issues need to be further clarified, for example, how to create supervisory positions and what are the position responsibilities. The supervision of energy conservation and emission reduction is a highly technical task that requires professional competence. Therefore, national registered energy managers can be hired from the society or talents with professional skills in energy management or environmental engineering can be selected through civil service examination. The number of supervisory positions should be reasonably determined according to the scale and energy and resource consumption of own unit. Depending on the actual needs, the responsibilities of these supervision personnel should include at least: assisting the unit in formulating rules and regulations for energy conservation and emission reduction; purchasing office supplies for the unit according to the catalog for product procurement in energy conservation and emission reduction and environmental protection formulated by the government and the regulations on mandatory purchase and priority purchase; preparing and organizing the implementation of the energy conservation and emission reduction target plans of the unit based on the indicators set by the superior; checking and adjusting the operation of key energy-consuming and water-using equipment of the unit; regularly evaluating the energy conservation and emission reduction status of the unit and proposing suggestions for improvements; and training the staff of the unit on the knowledge about energy conservation and emission reduction.
ii. External supervision means the government supervises and evaluates the low-carbon use of material elements of each administrative organization through

[30] See the provisions of paragraph 2 of Article 24 of *Energy Conservation Regulation for State-funded Institutions*.

specific government organizations, and makes disposal and rectification decisions on this basis. In 2010, China set a public agency energy-saving management office in government office administrations of all levels, which is specifically responsible for organizing the energy-saving assessment and evaluation, supervision and inspection and energy auditing of administrative agencies, and also clarifies the legal liability of administrative agencies for violation of regulations in the *Energy Conservation Regulation for State-funded Institutions*. The current supervision systems are equitable basically, and generated good supervision results. However, as far as the goal of comprehensively guaranteeing the low-carbonization of material elements of administrative organizations is concerned, they still need to be improved. First, the current supervision responsibilities fully rely on the public agency energy-saving management offices under the government office administrations, and there is a risk of unbalance of power and responsibilities. From a professional point of view, the management office has long been positioned as service function within the government, and it lacks capacity in the professional and technical energy conservation and emission reduction work to some extent. From the perspective of power in law enforcement, manage office administration is a relatively small organization within the government. When facing the tasks of supervising a large number of administrative agencies' energy conservation and emission reduction work, it will inevitably lack power in law enforcement. In order to make up for the deficiencies of supervision by single administration in terms of professionalism and power in law enforcement, it is necessary to consider establishing a diversified and coordinated supervision system with clear work division, where the government office administration leads and the development and reform, finance, audit, statistics and environmental protection departments participate in the supervision work, and then forming a comprehensive external supervision system. In this aspect, the experience of the United States is worthy of reference. The Office of the Federal Environmental Executive (OFEE) set under the Council on Environmental Quality (CEQ), supervises the implementation of each administrative agency in the federal government's performance target for energy conservation and emission reduction together with the President's Office of Management and Budget (OMB) and the Environmental Protection Agency (EPA).[31] Second, the current legal liability against violation of energy conservation and emission reduction regulations only focus on punitive liability, but lack corrective and restorative legal liability. For example, the legal liability in the *Energy Conservation Regulation for State-funded Institutions* are almost punishment against responsible person of the law-breaking organizations, rather than the remedies or neutralization of excessive energy consumption or excessive carbon emissions. Thus, on the basis of total carbon emission control and energy-saving targets, it is necessary to further emphasize restorative and corrective legal responsibilities while setting punitive responsibilities. For example, if the energy consumption or carbon emission of an administrative organization exceeds the specified

[31] *About the Office of the Federal Environmental Executive*, at http://www.ofee.gov/about.asp#ofee.

values, the first step should be considering the transfer payment from the energy consumption and carbon emission balance of other organizations at the same level. If the balance is not enough for transfer payment, that organization should be ordered to purchase the same amount of carbon emission right or carbon sink (CCER) from the carbon trading market for carbon neutrality.

5 Improvement of Organization Law for Low-Carbonization of Administrative Entity

According to the above analysis, administrative entities should realize the low-carbon transformation in the aspects of institution setting, staffing and material support. In this regard, the organization law of China should be improved and revised, and administrative entities should be constrained by legislations to follow the low-carbon requirements. To be specific, regulations should be made from the following aspects.

5.1 Establishing the Principles of Low-Carbon Organization Law

At present, the administrative organization laws and regulations at the central government level mainly include the *Organic Law of the State Council of the People's Republic of China, Organization Law of the People's Republic of China for Local People's Congresses at All Levels and Local People's Governments at All Levels, Regulations on Administration of the Establishment and Staffing of the Administrative Agencies of the State Council*, etc. The principles of organization law established by the above administrative organization laws and regulations are mainly "simplification", "unification" and "efficiency". It is true that these principles are consistent with low-carbon development to some extent. In many cases, the simplification and efficiency of administrative entities can help to reduce the carbon emissions of administrative activities. However, the traditional principles of organization law mainly aim at the scale and efficiency of administrative organizations, have not yet clearly embodied the low-carbon concepts, and in some cases, even contradict with low-carbon concepts. For example, the simplification principle requires administrative entities to maintain their agencies and staff on a reasonable scale, but does not require administrative entities to use low-carbon, energy-saving and environmental protection office supplies, and also demands no total amount control over the energy consumption and carbon emissions in the process of administrative activities. The efficiency principle emphasizes the work efficiency of administrative entities, but does not take into account the carbon emission intensity and energy utilization efficiency. This may lead to such a situation that administrative activities may be highly efficient, but consume huge environmental and financial resources, which is not low-carbon.

Therefore, the administrative organization laws of governments at all levels should include new principles of low-carbon organization law on the basis of the three principles of "simplification", "unification" and "efficiency". In this regard, the following contents can be stipulated in the general part: "In terms of institution setting, staffing and authority activities, people's governments at all levels should strictly abide by the requirements for comprehensive, coordinated and sustainable economic and social development, and abide by the principles of simplification, efficiency, unification of power and responsibility, low-carbon development and environmental protection."

5.2 Setting Low-Carbon Behavior Modes

If the administrative entity is regarded as the behavior subject in the sense of organization law, it is necessary to set low-carbon behavior modes in organization laws to restrict and guide the non-low-carbonization performance of administrative entity in institution setting, staffing and material support.

(I) **Institution Setting**

i. It is strictly prohibited to set any provisional or derivative institution

For a long time, provisional institutions and derivative institutions are out of control of organization law and become the gray zone in the ruling of administrative law. In fact, according to the principle of organization legality, the two institutions do not fall into any type of administrative organizations set according to the current organization law, and have no legitimacy granted by organization law. Thus, they should be explicitly prohibited in the legislation in order to completely eliminate such illegitimate and unreasonably set carbon emission entities. In this regard, the following provisions may be made in the legislation: "People's governments at all levels and their functional departments are not allowed to set any provisional or derivative institutions other than internal institutions and deliberation and coordination bodies."

ii. Reasonably controlling the scale of deliberation and coordination bodies

Due to the current administrative management mode of compartmentalization in China, the existence of deliberation and coordination bodies is reasonable in order to deal with cross-department or even cross-regional administrative affairs, but the scale of the bodies should be reasonably controlled. In this regard, *Regulations on Administration of the Establishment and Staffing of the Administrative Agencies of the State Council* and *Regulation on the Organization Establishment and Staffing Administration of Local People's Governments at All Levels* have stipulated in principle that the establishment of deliberation and coordination bodies by the government should be strictly controlled, but this lacks operability. Therefore, it should be stipulated that the number of deliberation and coordination bodies established by the governments at all levels should not exceed a specific value or a certain proportion in the number of internal bodies, so as to effectively restrict the unreasonable establishment of deliberation and coordination bodies.

iii. Establishing counterpart organizations for governments at higher and lower levels according to administrative functions

For the establishment of counterpart organizations for governments at higher and lower levels, Article 7 of the *Regulation on the Organization Establishment and Staffing Administration of Local People's Governments at All Levels* has made provision for the principles.[32] However, that provision only forbids the governments at higher level to intervene in or force the establishment of counterpart organizations by the governments at lower level, but does not restrict the governments at lower level from actively establishing counterpart organizations to cater to the needs of the governments at higher level, nor gives the governments at lower level any specific guidance on how to establish counterpart organizations, so this provision is not complete. Therefore, relevant organization laws should adopt the responsibility adjustment mode, and further stipulate that: "In addition to the institutions under the vertical leadership of the central and provincial governments, governments at all levels should establish their organizations according to their administrative functions, and without authorization, shall not establish any counterpart organization to cater to the governments at higher level".

iv. Canceling and merging work departments with the same or similar functions of the Party committee and the government

With regard to the overlapping of Party and government organs, the Fourth Plenary Session of the 16th CPC Central Committee has put forward the principle of "canceling and merging work departments with the same or similar functions of the Party committee and the government". In this regard, relevant organization laws should stipulate and implement this provision in a timely manner. In terms of "canceling", it can be stipulated that the Party committee should not establish similar work departments in principle if there is existing government agency that assumes the same or similar functions, and those that have already been established should be canceled gradually. In terms of "merging", government administrative agencies and Party committee work departments assuming the same or similar functions should implement the form of joint office to avoid waste of resources due to overlapping of agencies.

(II) **Staffing**

First, the organization law must control the total number of staff, and prohibit overstaffing by governments of all levels. Second, it is required to strictly control the number of deputy leaders and eliminate the structural redundancy in the staffing of administrative entities, so as to reduce the carbon intensity. At present, the *Organic Law of the State Council of the People's Republic of China* has clearly stipulated

[32] See the provisions of Article 7 of *Regulation on the Organization Establishment and Staffing Administration of Local People's Governments at All Levels.*

that: "Each ministry should have only one minister and two to four vice ministers. Each committee should have one director, two to four vice directors and five to ten members". However, at the local level, *Organization Law of the People's Republic of China for Local People's Congresses at All Levels and Local People's Governments at All Levels* and *Regulation on the Organization Establishment and Staffing Administration of Local People's Governments at All Levels* have no clear restriction on the configuration number of leadership positions. The future revision of the organization laws should scientifically set the upper limit of the number of deputy leaders of governments at different levels, and should clearly stipulate that the deputy leaders should include not only the actual leading positions, but also non-leadership positions which enjoy leadership treatment, such as examiners, investigators and inspectors, so as to effectively reduce the structural redundancy of staffing.

(III) **Material Support**

In recent years, China has issued some laws and policies on the waste of resources by administrative entities in material support elements, for example, *Notice of the General Office of the CPC Central Committee and the General Office of the State Council on Further Strict Control of the Construction of Office Buildings of Party and Government Organizations* issued in 2007, *Energy Conservation Regulation for State-funded Institutions* implemented from October 1, 2008 and *Regulations on Rigorous Enforcement of Economy and Anti-Waste for the Party and Government Organs* promulgated and implemented from November 25, 2013. These regulations play an important role in promoting the low-carbonization of material support elements of administrative entities. However, the existing regulations are still fragmented, and some of them fall into the category of policies and are not rigidly legally binding. Therefore, future organization laws should make systematic provisions on the low-carbon requirements for material support elements of the administrative entities from the following three aspects:

i. Total amount control of material support elements

The material support elements configured and used by administrative entities are paid by the state treasury, so they are likely to be wasted. And we should restrain their configuration and use through the total amount control system, which is a basic system for energy conservation and emission reduction. Therefore, the legislation should authorize the central government (specific affairs should be undertaken by the government affairs work department) to formulate a unified control plan for the total amount of carbon emissions or energy consumption of all government agencies in China, which shall be decomposed to and implemented by the governments at the next levels and their functional departments level by level according to certain standards.

ii. Low-carbon configuration of material support elements

The organization laws should stipulate the low-carbon configuration of material support elements from two aspects, i.e., "quality" and "quantity". In terms of "quality", the legislations should stipulate that office buildings built by and office supplies purchased by administrative entities must meet the specific low-carbon or environmental protection standards, and should advocate the use of green, energy-saving and low-carbon products. For example, it is required that the office buildings of administrative entities must meet energy-saving standards for public buildings, and office supplies purchased by administrative entities should be low-carbon and environmental-friendly. It is strictly prohibited to purchase office supplies with high carbon emission or high energy consumption. In terms of "quantity", the legislations should specify that the material support elements configured by administrative entities should be maintained at a low quantity required for the performance of duties, the scale and area of office buildings and the quantity of office supplies of administrative entities should be strictly controlled, and repeated purchase of office supplies should be prohibited.

iii. Low-carbon use of material support elements

At present, *Energy Conservation Regulation for State-funded Institutions*, *Regulations on Rigorous Enforcement of Economy and Anti-Waste for the Party and Government Organs*, and other laws and regulations have preliminarily stipulated the low-carbon use of material support elements by administrative entities, but such provisions are not comprehensive and complete. According to different ways and means of energy conservation and emission reduction, the legislations can stipulate the behavior modes of low-carbon use of material support elements in a systematic manner from three aspects: (i) energy-saving management rules. These rules may require administrative entities to minimize the energy consumption during the operation of the equipment in office buildings and the use of office supplies, and should provide for specific energy-saving measures, for example, properly setting the number and time of elevator opening, reasonably controlling the temperature of air conditioner, strictly complying with energy-saving driving regulations in vehicle operation, and implementing quota management over fuel consumption of official vehicles. (ii) Green consumption rules. For example, these rules may stipulate that administrative entities should use environmental-friendly and renewable paper, reduce the use of disposables, and save water during work. (iii) Resources recycling rules. For example, these rules may stipulate that administrative entities should classify and recycle the non-classified waste paper, waste electronic products, kitchen waste and other major waste. In addition, the legislation may also advocate administrative entities to explore the contract-based management mode, i.e., engaging qualified third-party hinstitutions to provide professional energy conservation and emission reduction services.

5.3 Adding Legal Liability Clauses

The behavior modes set by legislation will ultimately be guaranteed by legal liability, without which the behavior modes will not be rigidly binding. In order to ensure that the principles of low-carbon organization laws and all kinds of low-carbon behavior modes will be effectively observed by administrative entities, the legislation should also stipulate the corresponding consequences of legal liability. The legislation should especially stipulate, based on objective needs, two types of legal liability: corrective liability and punitive liability.

(I) **Punitive Liability**

Punitive liability aim at punishing the administrative entities and their civil servants who have violated the low-carbon behavior modes for the purposes of education and deterrence. The specific liability forms can include circulating a notice of criticism against or having an admonitory talk with the responsible personnel, transferring his/her post, ordering him/her to resign, removing him/her from his/her post, demoting or implementing other administrative sanctions on him/her, and disqualifying administrative entities from the excellent unit evaluation, depending on the seriousness of the case.

(II) **Corrective Liability**

The main function of corrective liability is to stop and remedy the illegal non-low-carbon behaviors of administrative entities, thus making them low-carbon again according to law. The liability clauses of the current organization laws pay much attention to the punishment against illegal behaviors, and corrective liability are rarely found. For example, for the administrative entities that illegally establish internal institutions or are overstaffed, the *Regulation on the Organization Establishment and Staffing Administration of Local People's Governments at All Levels* stipulate no liability consequences accordingly. This is obviously not conducive to the remedy of non-low-carbon behavior of these administrative entities. Therefore, it is necessary to add corresponding corrective liability against the non-low-carbon behavior of administrative entities. For example: (i) For those who violate the provisions of organization laws and excessively establish institutions, the legislation should stipulate that the staffing administration should declare such institutions are invalid and cancel them. (ii) For those who allocate finance supported overstaffing personnel or overstaffing leaders, the legislation should establish necessary systems for them to clear and cancel these allocations. The overstaffing personnel should be dismissed and should not be arranged to other public institutions in disguised form. If they fulfilled their duty in work, they should be appropriately compensated and guided for reemployment. The overstaffing leaders should be demoted, or removed or transferred to non-leading positions, without retaining their original treatment. (iii) For those who configure or use material resources beyond the legal standards or quotas, the legislation should order them to make correction and reduce the allocation of material resources according to the total amount control plan. For example, if any administrative entity purchases official vehicles in violation of the regulations, standards or establishment, these vehicles may be dealt with by means of recovery, auction, return, etc. If any administrative entity fails to perform the energy-saving target responsibilities and causes energy waste, it should be required to make rectification in time, and be ordered to purchase equivalent carbon emission rights to offset its excessive energy consumption. The expense for purchase should be deducted from the financial appropriation of the next year.

Chapter 4
Research on Low-Carbon Administrative Procedures

Normativity and legitimacy of administrative process are the traditional research focuses of administrative law on administrative procedure, which do not involve low-carbon value judgement as they basically do not involve analysis from a low-carbon perspective. This is actually a limitation on research perspective, and is not conducive to the construction of low-carbon administrative procedures. The goal and structure of administrative procedures are closely related to carbon emissions, and this can be analyzed through a case.

On October 11, 2013, CCTV *Focus Report* exposed a case about administrative procedures: a citizen in Hebei Province repeatedly went through 11 times of passport procedures because of administrative procedures, making 6 trips to and from his hometown, travelling an unnecessary distance of 3,000 km.[1] In this case, the public, media, academic circles and the administrations all just blamed the bureaucratic inaction of the handlers or the problems of increasing burdens on the citizen and causing inconvenience, but they all completely ignored the low-carbon problem involved in the case. The case can be analyzed from the perspective of carbon emissions: that citizen travels an unnecessary distance of 3000 km because of the complicated passport handling procedures. As far as the vehicle alone is concerned, the carbon emissions would be increased by 25.8 kg if by train, 417 kg by airplane, and 735.9 kg by a medium fuel-efficient car. If 100 million Chinese citizens travel unnecessary distance of 3,000 km each year due to unreasonable administrative procedures, for example, administrative licensing approval procedures, the total carbon emissions will be about 73.6 billion kilograms (by car), 41.7 billion kilograms (by airplane), 2.6 billion kilograms (by train). Take the year 2013 as an example, the total amount of social carbon emissions in China is about 10 billion tons (10 trillion kilograms).[2]

[1] Zhong Xin and Shao Guodong: *A Beijing Drifter Returned Hometown 6 Times for Applying for A Passport and A Jiangsu Citizen Went Through 11 Times of License Procedures, Beijing Youth Daily*, October 13, 2013.

[2] See The Paper.cn: *China's Carbon Emissions in 2013 Ranks the First in the World, Which May Promote the Acceleration of Energy Structure Adjustment* at http://j.news.163.com/docs/99/201409 2320/A6RVCDOK9001CDOL.html, visited on October 23, 2014.

S. Fang and B. Tan, *On the Administrative Law of China in Addressing Climate Change*,
https://doi.org/10.1007/978-981-19-7705-3_4

The carbon emissions caused by this administrative procedure problem alone would account for 0.736% if by car. This is a huge amount, but such carbon emissions should have been completely avoided. Therefore, the influence of administrative procedures on low-carbon construction is evident.

Under the ecological risk of climate change, these carbon emission data are undoubtedly "an inconvenient truth" in administrative procedures.[3] The causes for this certainly include the bureaucratism of civil servants, however, the root cause lies probably in the defects in the concepts and systems of administrative procedures. Why a non-local citizen must "apply to the exit and entry administration department of the public security bureau of the city/county where his/her registered residence is located" for passport[4] instead of applying nearby? This reflects that the current administrative procedures lack ecological considerations in energy conservation and emission reduction. However, this is only the tip of the iceberg in the whole Administrative Litigation Law. The weakness of the existing administrative procedures in dealing with climate change is not only presented through the waste of resources and high carbon emissions within the procedures, but also refers to that the procedures cannot effectively assume the law enforcement and decision-making functions of promoting social energy conservation and emission reduction. For example, the whole set of current law enforcement procedures provide a relatively complete procedural guarantee for the rights of the counterpart, but in environmental law enforcement, due to the long cycle of enforcement procedures, "a polluting enterprise cannot be shut down in ten years". Instead, administrative procedures became the patron for companies to evade law enforcement[5]; A public participation mechanism aiming at widely listening to the opinions of the public has been introduced into the administrative decision-making procedures, but some public projects that benefit low-carbon development and environmental protection are frequently suspended or canceled due to the "Not In My Back Yard" effect of the public.[6]

The Decision of the Central Committee of the Communist Party of China on Some Major Issues Concerning Comprehensively Deepening the Reform adopted at the Third Plenary Session of the 18th CPC Central Committee regards "optimizing the setting, functional configuration and work flow of government agencies" as a clear requirement for transforming government functions, among which the work flow problem of government is also a problem of administrative procedures. Facing the

---

[3] Quoted from *An Inconvenient Truth*, a documentary film starred by the former United States Vice President Al Gore.

[4] See the provisions of Article 3 of *Rules for the Implementation of the Law of the People's Republic of China on the Control of the Exit and Entry of Citizens*.

[5] Liang Siqi: *Why A Polluting Enterprise Can Not Be Closed in Ten Years*, *Shenyang Evening News*, November 4, 2006.

[6] For example, in recent years, it is common that nuclear power projects and waste incineration projects are not approved or forced to be suspended due to fierce opposition by the public during the administrative decision-making process. See Suo Hanxue: *CNNC Encountered Attack from Both Left and Right and Lost Its Core Power*, *China Business Journal*, July 19, 2013; Liu Qian: *Waste Incineration Site Selection Ran into the "Not In My Back Yard" Effect*, *Nanfang Daily*, April 29, 2011.

"most urgent environmental challenge in this era" of global warming,[7] constructing and improving low-carbon administrative procedures of energy conservation and environmental protection is undoubtedly an urgent task for administrative law in the low-carbon era, and also a major concern in this chapter. Optimizing administrative procedures from a low-carbon perspective is not only an important way to save energy and reduce emissions, but also an effective measure for the Chinese government to actively perform its administrative functions in response to climate change and to fulfill its commitment to reduce emissions, which is of great strategic value. Therefore, the research on low-carbon administrative procedures is of fundamental significance for the development and reform of the whole administrative legal system in the low-carbon era, and can be used as a theoretical support for the establishment of a low-carbon administrative law system.

1 Types of Traditional Administrative Procedures and Their Defects in Low-Carbon Era

1.1 Basic Types of Administrative Procedures

With the development of the society and public administration, the contents and fields involved in administrative procedures are continuously expanding, and professionalism is also increasing. Procedures in different fields often have different characteristics and functions, thus develop into different categories and pedigrees. It is difficult to describe them with a uniform pattern. According to value goal and adjustment mechanism, existing administrative procedures can be roughly divided into three ideal types: managed administrative procedures, judged administrative procedures, and participatory administrative procedures.[8] These types of procedures played important roles in different fields, however in the context of the new low-carbon era, their structures and functions can no longer effectively bear the historic mission of addressing climate change.

(I) **Managed Procedures**

Managed procedures were mainly formed in the twentieth century, and their core goal is to improve the management efficiency and economic benefits of the administration. Their typical forms were mainly found in the former Soviet Union and China.

---

[7] See *Massachusetts v. EPA*, 127 S. Ct. 1438 (2007).

[8] The "ideal type" method is a social science research method created by Max Weber. In practice, each type has connections with other types more or less, and may contain each other's elements. No type can appear in a pure form in reality. See [Germany] Max Weber: *The Methodology of Social Sciences*, translated by Han Shuifa, et. al., Central Compilation and Translation Press, 2002 edition, p.19.

In the early stage of socialism in the Soviet Union, in order to resume production and develop the national economy as soon as possible, maintain and consolidate the revolutionary order, strengthening government management became the focus of the systems and regulations of administrative law. A representative academic point of view for this is the "management theory" put forward by Manoshin et al. in the *Soviet Administrative Law:* "Administrative law, as a concept, is a management law, and to be more precisely, a national management law."[9] Just as Duncan, an American administrative law scholar, said, the word most closely related to management is efficiency.[10] Under the control of management theory, the construction of the entire Soviet administrative law system focused on the efficient operation of administrative power, while administrative procedures, as the work process and subject behavior of the administration, naturally took the efficiency of administrative management as a criterion. Later, this procedural concept was adopted and further developed by China. In the early days of the founding of the people's Republic of China, for political and ideological reasons, China established a planned economy and administrative-led management system based on the experience of the Soviet Union. In theory, the Soviet administrative management theory also occupied a dominant position. At that time, scholars and legislators regarded administrative law as the management law to ensure the implementation of national policies, and naturally, the efficiency of administrative management became the most important and even the only goal of administrative procedures. The Third Plenary Session of the 11th CPC Central Committee initiated reform and opening up, the Party and the nation began to focus on economic construction, and accordingly the economic benefit was regarded as the basic goal of administrative procedures.[11] The *Provisions on Capital Construction Procedure* jointly issued by the former State Development Planning Commission, Construction Commission and Ministry of Finance clarified the goal of the administrative procedures in the construction field at the beginning: "developing national economy at high speed, and building socialism with greater, faster, better and more economic results."[12] On this basis, China's managed administrative procedures aiming at administrative efficiency and economic benefits formed. In addition, this mode was also adopted by many other countries in their administrative procedures, and even explicitly stipulated in their legislations. For example, *The Administrative Litigation Law* of Spain in 1958 expresses the general principle of administrative procedure as: "administrative acts shall be carried out according to the rules of economy, speed and efficiency."[13]

---

[9] [Soviet] B.M. Manoshin et. al.: *Soviet Administrative Law,* Qunzhong Press, 1983 edition, p. 29.

[10] W. Jack Duncan, Great Ideas in Management: Lessons from the Founders and Foundations of Managerial Practice. Oxford: Jossey Bass Publishers, 1990, p. 27.

[11] See Wang Xixin: *The Concept and System of the Administrative Litigation Law: Development, Current Status and Evaluation–Concurrently Comments on the Official Promulgation of the Hunan Provincial Administrative Procedure Provisions, Social Sciences in Hunan,* Issue 5, 2008.

[12] See Li Zongxing: *Humble Opinions on Strengthening Administrative Procedure Legislation, China Legal Science,* Issue 4, 1985.

[13] *Compendium of Foreign Administrative Litigation Laws,* edited by Ying Songnian, China Legal Publishing House, 1999 edition, p. 259–260.

(II) Judged Procedures

The judged procedures originated in the mid-nineteenth century. It is a classic procedural mode involving the imitation of the role of judges and adjudicative procedures to protect individual rights and ensure administrative legitimacy. It mainly exists in the administrative law enforcement behaviors against specific counterpart, for example, the statement, defense and hearing procedures in administrative licensing, administrative penalties and administrative enforcement. The "judge according to law" mode can be traced back to Otto Mayer's theory of administrative action. Mayer's idea on the ruling by administrative law is that administrative activities should be restricted by laws, and specific contents should also be included to guarantee individual rights and individual's predictability on administrative activities.[14] For this purpose, he advocated that "Administration should be judicialized as much as possible",[15] and administrative institutions should, like judges, follow legal procedures of investigation, inquiry, cross-examination and explanation, and on this basis, make decisions. He regarded the administrative actions as "government decisions subordinate to administration" or "counterpart of judicial judgments in administrative procedures".[16] Because in his view, the judicial process was a "model of rational public law activities". With a set of systematic and strict legal procedures, the judicial law cannot only realize self-restraint, but also help to protect the rights of the parties.[17] Another important origin of this mode is the due process principle in British and American administrative law. The due process principle originated from the Great Charter of the United Kingdom in 1215 and was carried forward in the Fifth Amendment to the U.S. Constitution. According to the Fifth Amendment, the Federal Supreme Court settled more than 40,000 due process lawsuits against civil rights in the 1970s. The most representative one is the Goldberg V. Kelly case, which requires the administration to give a relatively complete trial-style hearing procedure before canceling the welfare payment of the party.[18] Thus, a judicial administrative procedure with distinctive American characteristics is formed, that is, it emphasizes the procedural defense of the counterpart more, and provides protection for the rights of the counterpart through the quasi-judicial procedural process. At present, this mode can be found in the administrative procedures and Administrative Litigation Laws of many countries, such as Germany and the United States. The typical one is the *Administrative Litigation Law* of Japan, which divides the administrative procedures into general identification procedure, hearing procedure for non-interest disposition and public hearing procedure for disposition applications involving the interests of

---

[14] [Germany] Otto Mayer, *German Administrative Law*, translated by Liu Fei, The Commercial Press, 2013 edition, p. 99.

[15] [Germany] Otto Mayer, *German Administrative Law*, translated by Liu Fei, The Commercial Press, 2013 edition, p. 66.

[16] [Germany] Otto Mayer, *German Administrative Law*, translated by Liu Fei, The Commercial Press, 2013 edition, p. 99–107.

[17] See Zhao Hong: *Systematic Construction and Balance of Administrative Law*, *The Jurist*, Issue 5, 2013.

[18] Goldberg v. Kelly, 397 U.S. 254, 262 (1970).

third parties. Some separate rules even specifically establish the administrative adjudication procedure where the collegial administration makes decisions according to the administrative procedures similar to judicial litigation.[19] Undoubtedly, these procedures have the obvious characteristics of adjudication.

(III) **Participatory Procedures**

With the rapid development of the postwar economy and the emergence of the welfare state, it was required that the governments should continuously expand their functions. Due to the diversity and complexity of the administrative affairs, public opinion organs have to authorize the administrations to carry out necessary administrative legislation and administrative decision-making, and give them extremely broad discretion, thus the participatory procedure formed. For example, the French Constitution of 1791 stipulates that the legislative power belongs to the parliament, while the French Constitution of 1958 clearly specifies that the Cabinet has the legislative power on administrative affairs. These facts leads to the bankruptcy of the classical model of administrative legitimacy, i.e. "the transmission-belt theory".[20] Because the exercise of the above power was no longer the enforcement of the laws made by the public opinion organs to a large extent, thus generating "democratic deficit" with thin public opinion foundation.[21] The solution given by theorists and legislators is to introduce the democratic participation of the counterpart in the design of administrative procedures, and to overcome the democratic deficit of modern administration by reproducing the democratic deliberation process of parliamentary legislation, so as to guarantee the legitimacy of administration. This constitutes the basic idea of participatory procedures. At present, many countries have established and introduced this procedural mode, and widely apply it in administrative legislation, administrative decision-making and other public policy fields. One of the most representative countries is the United States. The U.S. Administrative Procedure Act of 1946 stipulates that the formulation of all informal administrative rules must go through three steps, i.e. announcing the content of the proposed regulations and the issues involved, being commented by interested parties in writing or orally, and explaining the basis and purpose of formulating these rules, and the interested parties are allowed to apply for the formulation, modification or abolishment of administrative rules.[22] The U.S. Negotiated Rulemaking Act of 1990 further stipulates that when the administrations make rules, they can convene representatives of different interests to form a consultative committee, and then develop the draft of the administrative rules on the

[19] See Zhu Mang: *Basic Composition of Legitimate Devices in Administrative Procedures–An Investigation of the Opinion Statement Procedure in the Japanese Administrative Litigation Law*, *Journal of Comparative Law*, Issue 1, 2007.

[20] For the analysis of conveyor belt theory, see [United States] Richard B. Stewart, *The Reformation of American Administrative Law*, translated by Shen Kui, The Commercial Press, 2011 edition, p. 5–11.

[21] Wang Xixin: *Democratic Deficit of Contemporary Administration and Its Overcoming*, Studies in Law and Business, Issue 1, 2009.

[22] Administrative Procedure Act 5 U.S.C. §§ 551–559 (2000).

basis of the consensus and majority decision procedures.[23] In recent years, China also stipulates many institutional provisions to guarantee the public participation in administrative legislation and administrative decision-making process legislation. For example, it is required to provide opportunities and ways for public participation through administrative legislation or decision-making in the process of project establishment, announcement, drafting, deliberation and evaluation, and listen to their opinions and suggestions.[24]

1.2 Defects of Managed Procedures

In many cases, the managed procedures are of positive significance to achieving the goal of low-carbon administration. For example, in order to improve the efficiency, the administrations will simplify the work process and shorten the affairs handling period. This is conducive to energy conservation and emission reduction, but the disadvantages are also quite obvious: (i) The efficiency orientation of this administrative procedure mainly refers to the efficiency of the administrations, and the procedure design only focuses on saving administrative cost and the convenience of duty performance, but the efficiency of administrative counterpart in the procedure is rarely taken into consideration. The counterpart will also consume some human, material and financial resources and its time in the procedure, and it is easy to get the following results: Although the administrative efficiency is improved and the administrative cost is saved, the procedural burden of the counterpart is greatly increased and the procedural efficiency of the counterpart is decreased. Therefore, for the whole society, this will bring about low efficiency and high cost of the administrative procedure and fall into non-low-carbon procedure. Such cases are common in practice. The *Law of the People's Republic of China on Administrative Penalty* specifies that administrative punishment shall be governed by the administration of the place where the illegal behavior takes place. This provision makes some counterparts pay much more money on travel than on the fine for their cross-regional tickets of traffic administration,[25] and travel here means unnecessary carbon emission and

[23] Negotiated Rulemaking Act 5 U.S.C. §§ 561–570(1994).

[24] In terms of administrative legislation, for example, Article 58 of the *Legislation Law of the People's Republic of China* and Article 15 of *Ordinance concerning the Procedures for the Formulation of Administrative Regulations* stipulate that: "During the drafting of administrative regulations, the opinions of relevant agencies, organizations and citizens should be widely heard". At present, there is no unified national legislation on administrative decision-making, but many local procedure legislations have included the provisions on public participation, for example *Provisions of Guangzhou Municipality on Major Administrative Decision-making Processes* and *Provisions of Guizhou Provincial People's Government on Major Decision-making Processes* clearly require that: "Decision-making process drafting department should fully consider and adopt the reasonable opinions of the representatives attending the hearing" or "should absorb and adopt the reasonable opinions and suggestions put forward by the public".

[25] Cao Shulin, Yinyan and Gao Xiang: *Trans-provincial Tickets No Longer Toss People*, People's Daily, July 22, 2013.

energy consumption. (ii) Another defect of this kind of administrative procedure is to measure its efficiency with economic benefit alone. This is essentially a kind of instrumental rationality "deprived of religious and ethical significance".[26] Under the efficiency mode, the administration is likely to ignore the social and environmental costs in order to pursue economic interests without the guidance of value rationalities of low-carbon development and environmental protection when the short-term and local economic interests contradict the long-term and overall environmental interests. In fact, Weber had realized the danger of bureaucratic system under the efficiency mode in the last century, that is, using resources without restraint in order to achieve the efficiency goal until the one last ton of oil is burned out. In today's China, such danger is widely reflected in reality. For example, many administrations, especially local governments, simplify or even omit necessary procedures at will in order to attract investment. In 2007, the Ministry of Ecology and Environment found in law enforcement inspection that many industrial parks in China had the problem of establishing pollution projects first and then performing environmental impact assessment (EIA) procedures or even loosing EIA procedures, which led to serious environmental consequences.[27]

1.3 Defects of Judged Procedures

Undoubtedly, judged procedures have played an irreplaceable role in restricting administrative power and protecting the rights of the counterparts, and now still have a strong application value in China where administrative power is extremely strong. However, when addressing the climate change in a modern risk society, such a procedure mode of a past administrative state also shows obvious inadaptability, and sometimes even generates negative effects. This is reflected in: (i) Influenced by the idea of Mayer's governing the nation by law, this administrative procedure is designed as a method only applicable to the positive law, and only requires administrative procedures to conform to the legal provisions in form. Therefore, it is in essence a procedure of formal rule of law, and lacks a low-carbon transcendental value scale to reflect, guide and even shape the positive law. The hazards resulted therefrom are: When the existing Administrative Litigation Laws do not meet the low-carbon standards, the mechanical application of procedural rules may produce high-carbon results. This can be proved by the case in the introduction that a merchant ran 11 times to change business license registration. When the Administrative Litigation Laws have no provision or obscure provisions on some matters, the judged procedure cannot guide the administrations to adopt procedural methods that are conducive to energy conservation and

---

[26] See [Germany] Max Weber: The Methodology of Social Sciences, translated by Han Shuifa, et. al., Central Compilation and Translation Press, 2002 edition, p.182.

[27] See Ge Xinzhong: *Environmental Violation by Ninety Percent of Industrial Parks in Eleven Provinces Reflects Local Governments' Flattering Behaviors Towards Merchants*, *China Reform News*, August 6, 2007.

emission reduction, that is to say, it cannot provide guidance of low-carbon value for the discretion and administrative interpretation. (ii) This administrative procedure regards the private rights and freedom as the highest pursuit of value, and provides maximum support for them through strict and quasi-judicial procedures. However, as scholars have pointed out: "In specific cases, the value of individual justice usually coexists with the overall value, but they conflict each other fundamentally."[28] When individual freedom conflicts with the social low-carbon development and environmental protection value, the procedure setting that excessively emphasizes on rights protection may hinder the proceeding of low-carbon administrative tasks. A typical example is that a lot of statutory punishment procedures, including investigation and evidence collection, statement and defense, warning and rectification order, should be followed for smoking control punishment. This has a positive significance for the protection of the legal rights and interests of individual smokers, but these excessively tedious procedures have made the smoking control in some places difficult to be enforced.[29] This is not conducive to overall interests of the society such as low-carbonization and environmental protection, and residents' health.

1.4 Defects of Participatory Procedures

The participatory procedures effectively make up for the lack of administrative legitimacy in the post-transmission belt era, especially with the rise of public participation in the contemporary era,[30] its function as a carrier of the administrative democratization system has been further highlighted. However, it is precisely because of its path dependence on public participation that the procedure has encountered a waterloo-like dilemma in low-carbon administration. Prominent problems of the procedure in practice are: (i) At present, citizens can participate in administrative procedures mainly through hearings, symposiums, demonstration meetings, and public solicitation of opinions. However, these methods are not convenient and economic enough to some extent in practice. Meetings such as hearings, symposiums and demonstration meetings, are a relatively formal form of procedural participation, but their operating cost is high and efficiency is low, they often require a large number of participants to travel long distances to arrive at the meeting site. This will cost much on transportation and paper for meeting recording, and it generally takes a long period of time

[28] Orly Lobel, The Renew Deal:The Fall of Regulation and the Rise of Governance in Contemporary Legal Thought. pp. 34–46.

[29] For example, Guangzhou government only gave six tickets in one year because the punishment procedures for smoking control stipulated by laws are too many and too complicated. Although some counterparts were successfully punished, repeatedly warnings and ordering for rectification as required by procedures costed law enforcement personnel a large amount of time, causing serious load on law enforcement cost. See Zheng Xusen: *Only 6 Tickets for Guangzhou Smoking Control in One Year*, *Yangcheng Evening News*, October 11, 2011.

[30] See Wang Xixin: *Public Participation and China's New Public Movement*, China Legal Publishing House, 2008 edition, Preface.

to make decisions. The carbon emissions in administrative procedures are produced by the participants of the procedures. The more the participants are, the greater the carbon emissions of the unit subject and the entire administrative procedure will be. Undoubtedly, participatory procedure has more subjects than other types of procedures. The inconvenient and non-economic design of the modes of participation, will generally lead to non-low-carbon consequences. (ii) In some cases, this kind of administrative procedure sets too many democratic requirements for some new low-carbon and environmental protection regulation fields, which impedes the effective performance of duties by administrations. This is especially the case in the process of formulating technical standards of environmental regulations. Some American scholars, based on case study, pointed out that currently, the too strict technical standard formulation procedures and judicial review make the Environmental Protection Agency (EPA) exercise undue caution in formulating air pollution act and implementing the Clean Air Act.[31] For example, in the "Shell Oil Company v. Environmental Protection Agency case", the court believed that EPA didn't seriously perform the announcement obligation of fully explaining the rule contents because the list of new pollutants finally released by EPA was inconsistent with the list of proposed new pollutants at the time of announcement, and then overturned the air pollution identification rule involved in the case.[32] In fact, in low-carbon and environmental protection regulation fields, it is often the case that the contents of the rules finally published by administrations are inconsistent with the announced rules due to the rapid changes in the subjects and environment targeted by the rules. If the administrations are under control by the mechanical application of the "announced" procedure, it is undoubtedly an inappropriate restriction, and this is also where the case is criticized later on. (iii) The reliance on democratic procedures in administrative procedures involving climate change may lead to deviations in agenda setting or even make the regulatory policies "abort" completely. We may analyze first from the agenda setting. Because climate change risks have a "counterfactual" characteristic without obvious harmful consequences, they are often placed in a position which is extremely disproportionate to their dangers in the public's sequencing of risk regulations. Many studies or surveys have shown that in the public's sequencing of the main problems faced by humans, the importance of addressing climate change lags far behind wars, terrorism, traffic safety, diseases and unemployment, and has not even entered the top ten.[33] In this case, if the procedural model of democratic participation is used to set the agenda, the regulatory policies for climate change will be difficult to be implemented properly and timely. Secondly, energy conservation and emission reduction, as a long-term public welfare undertaking, needs to

---

31 R. Shep Melnick, *Regulation and the Courts: The Case of the Clean Air Act*, The Brookings Institution, 1983.

32 *New Perspectives on Administrative Law*, edited by Luo Haocai and Bi Honghai, The Commercial Press, 2013 edition, p. 314.

33 See Paul Slovic, Perception of Risk, 236 Science p. 280, 1987; Cabecinhas, R., Lazaro, A., & Carvalho, A. Lay representations on Climate Change. In Proceedings of LAMCR's 25 Conference:504–508. Retrived March 23, 2010, from http://repositorium.sdum.uminho.pt/bitstream/1822/5335/1/Cabecinhas_Lazaro_Carvalho_IAMCR_2006.pdf.

sacrifice economic benefit or freedom of life to some extent, and this is in conflict with the profit-seeking and autonomy of individuals as rational economic people. When a climate policy adds citizens' obligations or reduces their acquired rights, it is almost impossible for it to be supported in the democratic deliberation from the very beginning. For example, Australia tried to levy the carbon tax in 2012, but due to the fierce opposition of the public, the Senate of the Australian Federal Parliament had to abolish the carbon tax act in 2014.[34] In Germany, a number of land-based wind power projects planned to be launched by the German government in recent years also had to be suspended in the evaluation process due to the widespread "Not In My Back Yard" effect among the public.[35]

The above defects of current administrative procedures in dealing with climate change calls for the construction of new low-carbon administrative procedures.

2 Elements and Requirements of Low-Carbon Administrative Procedures[36]

2.1 Importance of Constructing Low-Carbon Administrative Procedures

According to the research purpose and theoretical assumption of this article, the low-carbon administrative procedure should refer to a procedural model where all elements within the administrative procedures meet the low-carbon and economic requirements, so that the procedural costs, energy and resource consumption and carbon emissions of each participant involved in the whole administrative procedure are kept at a reasonably low level. The low-carbonization of administrative procedures is an important response of the administrative law to the low-carbon era. The low-carbon era requires not only the corresponding administrative law principles, administrative entities and administrative actions, but also the construction of low-carbon administrative procedures. The reasons are:

First, administrative procedures are the procedures and ways of administrative entities to implement administrative actions. Without the low-carbonization of administrative procedures, even if all elements of the organization law of the administrative entities meet low-carbon standards, or when low-carbon administrative actions are implemented, high-carbon results will also be obtained. Imagine that no matter how streamlined the agencies and personnel of an administrative organ are, and how low-carbon and energy-efficient the configuration and use of office buildings and

---

[34] See Bao Jie: *Australia Abolished Carbon Taxes in Dispute*, *People's Daily*, July 21, 2014.

[35] See Guan Kejiang: *"Not In My Back Yard" Effect and Energy Transition*, *People's Daily*, August 13, 2013.

[36] Some contents in this section was used as phased achievements on this topic. A thesis written by the research team members Fang Shirong and Tan Binglin titled *Optimizing the Counterparts of Administrative Procedures* was published in Issue 1 of *Jiang Huai Tribune* in 2015.

office supplies are, if the administrative procedure of a matter need to go through tedious steps or a long cycle, the low-carbon emissions of the administrative entity will be offset by the high-carbon emissions of the administrative procedure. Take the environmental law enforcement mentioned at the beginning of this chapter as an example. The administrative punishment of ordering polluting enterprises to stop production and wind up business is undoubtedly beneficial to low-carbon development and environmental protection, but a polluting enterprise cannot be closed in ten years due to the long cycle of the administrative procedures. This result is undoubtedly contrary to the original intention of conducting low-carbon and environmental protection administrative actions.

Second, administrative procedures have a wide radiation effect, not only for administrative entities, but also for the specific or non-specific administrative counterpart participating in the administrative procedures. Moreover, administrative procedures are repeatedly applied in the process where corresponding administrative actions are conducted. Therefore, even if an insignificant redundancy or waste in the administrative procedure design, after being amplified by the radiation effect in practice, will produce astronomical resource waste and huge carbon emissions. Thus, administrative procedures play a role of leverage in the whole administrative activity, especially in the carbon emission of the administrative counterparts.

Third, materials and resources are needed to guarantee the compliance and implementation of administrative procedure system, but the use of materials and resources in the process of the administrative procedure will cause corresponding energy consumption and greenhouse gas emission. In this regard, the administrative procedure itself is also a source of carbon emissions, and should be regulated according to low-carbon requirements.

2.2 Basic Elements of Administrative Procedures

Addressing climate change involves many aspects of administrative activities. This determines that the construction of low-carbon administrative procedures must be a complex systematic project, and making only random or fragmented alteration may cause a dilemma of "taking stopgap measures only" or "selecting one but omitting ten thousand". In this regard, the constructionism methods can be used to deconstruct the internal elements of administrative procedures, in order to build the theoretical framework for the construction of low-carbon administrative procedures. Because the constructionism advocates the "vertical, three-dimensional and organic analysis"[37] of all elements of legal procedures, it can help us to design the low-carbon administrative procedure system in a relatively systematic and comprehensive manner.

From the viewpoint of the connotation of administrative procedures, the construction of administrative procedures mainly deals with the general elements and basic devices that support the operation of administrative procedures. According to the

[37] Long Zongzhi and Du Jiang: *Comment on "Evidence Constructionism"*, *Chinese Criminal Science*, Issue 10, 2010.

definition of jurisprudence, the connotation of legal procedures is "the legal steps and methods that must be followed or performed during legal behaviors in terms of time and space".[38] Therefore, the internal structure of legal procedures should be a three-dimensional structure composed of behavior subject, legal time and legal space. In the administrative procedure, time element means the sequence and time limit of performing administrative procedures, while the space element includes the jurisdiction rules, links and procedures and working mode of the administrative procedure. As for the subject element, the academic circles generally think that the subject of administrative procedure is only the administrative entity, not including the administrative counterpart.[39] This is a misunderstandings, which is not conducive to the scientific design of low-carbon administrative procedure system. The reasons are: First, without counterpart, administrative procedures cannot be initiated. According to different initiation ways, administrative procedures can be divided into application-based procedure and authority-based procedure. Undoubtedly, the application-based procedure is initiated by the application of the counterpart. The authority-based procedure is superficially initiated by the administrative entity unilaterally according to its authority, but the cause and effect analysis shows its cause is the behavior of the administrative counterpart or the legal events related to the counterpart. For example, the administrative penalty procedure is initiated by the behavior of the counterpart in violation of the administrative laws or regulations, while the administrative rescue procedure may be initiated by the personal injury or property damage of the counterpart due to natural disasters or other legal events. Second, it is impossible to form the decision or result of the administrative procedure without the behavior or intention of the counterpart. The decision of the administrative punishment procedure cannot be made without listening to the statements and defense of the counterpart. Third, without the exercise of rights or performance of obligations by the counterpart, the unilateral behaviors of the administrative entity only cannot implement the result of the administrative procedure. Analyzing from the perspective of addressing climate change, the procedural activities of counterparts will also produce carbon emissions. If only the administrative entity is concerned while the counterpart is not treated as an important subject, the system design of low-carbon administrative procedures must be imbalanced. There are even some cases that the carbon emissions reduced by the administrative entities are offset or even exceeded by the carbon dioxide equivalent of the procedural activities of the counterparts. This is also a theoretical crux that brings about the non-low-carbon procedural consequences similar to the example that the counterpart made 11 round trips for handling administrative procedures. Therefore, the administrative counterpart should also be an indispensable subject

---

[38] Sun Xiaoxia: *Analysis of Legal Procedures, Science of Law*, Issue 6, 1993.

[39] For example, classic administrative law textbooks at home and abroad almost define the administrative procedures as: "the ways, steps, time limit and sequence that administrative entities should follow when performing administrative actions" or "all the activities carried out by administrations in order to make decisions, take other measures or sign contracts". See *Administrative Law and Administrative Litigation Law*, edited by Jiang Ming'an, Peking University Press, Higher Education Press, 2002 edition, p. 260; [Germany] Hartmut Maurer:*A General Introduction to Administrative Law*, translated by Gao Jiawei, Law Press, 2000 edition, p. 451.

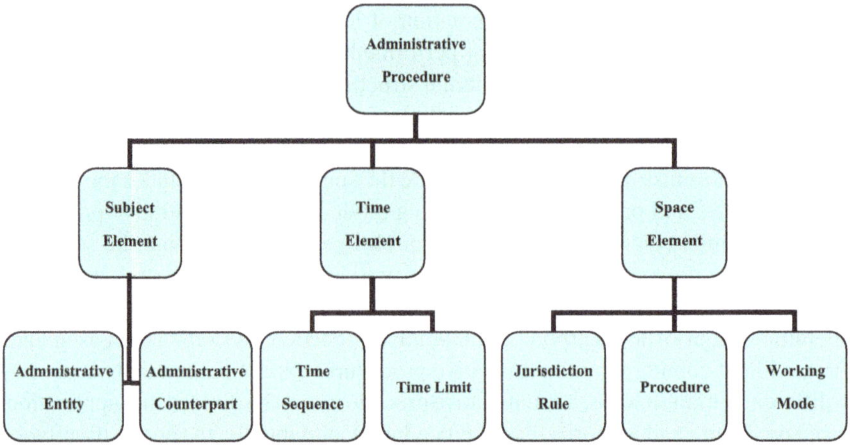

Fig. 1 The Carbon Emission Process of Administrative Procedure

element in the administrative procedures as the administrative entity. The interactions among behavior subject, legal time and legal space form the carbon emission process of the whole administrative procedure: the behavior subjects generate the sum of greenhouse gases directly or indirectly, while participating in the administrative procedures through specific spatial relations and methods within a certain procedure time period (Fig. 1).

According to the analysis of the basic construction of administrative procedures, the main requirement for the construction of low-carbon administrative procedures is to reduce or avoid unnecessary resource consumption and carbon emissions in the operation process of the subject, time, space and other procedural elements. The administrative procedures, as a whole, are a process of introducing low-carbon procedural devices and stripping high-carbon procedural devices.

2.3 Requirements for Low-Carbon Procedures in Terms of Subject

According to the analysis from the perspective of carbon footprint,[40] the carbon emissions of administrative procedures are actually the sum of carbon dioxide equivalent

[40] The concept of carbon footprint, derived from the concept of ecological footprint, mainly refers to the total amount of greenhouse gases emitted in the production and consumption activities of humans. Compared with other carbon emissions, carbon footprint, from the perspective of life cycle, breaks the so-called "pollution only comes from chimneys" concept, and analyzes the product life cycle or the carbon emission process directly and indirectly related to activities. See Wang W, Lin J Y, Cui S H, Lin T. An overview of carbon footprint analysis. Environmental Science and Technology, 2010, (7): 71–78. Wu Yan, Wang Xiaoke, Lu Fei: *Carbon Footprint in Food Consumption of Beijing Residents*", *Journal of Ecology*, Issue 5, 2012.

directly or indirectly generated by all procedural subjects when they carry out procedure activities. In other words, whether the administrative procedures are low-carbon is closely related to the number of subjects being involved in administrative procedures. The more subjects involved in the administrative procedures are, the greater the carbon dioxide equivalent generated by the administrative procedures will be. If less subjects are involved in the administrative procedures, the administrative procedures will be relatively low-carbon and economical. Therefore, reducing the number of subjects being involved in the administrative procedures is a source control method of low-carbon administrative procedures. This includes not only reducing the number of administrative entities, but also reducing the number of administrative counterparts.

(I) **Overall Level**

Generally speaking, if there is no need to go through administrative procedures to handle a matter, we will undoubtedly eliminate the possibility of generating carbon footprints by all subjects. Therefore, reducing unnecessary administrative procedures is an effective method to promote the low-carbonization of administrative procedures. Although this method does not directly reduce the number of subjects in the administrative procedures, it filters some potential subjects that may be involved in the administrative procedures, and this filtering function will make a great contribution to energy conservation and emission reduction. For example, to obtain a Birth Approval Certificate in Guangzhou, 8 departments will be involved, 13 seals and 16 procedures are needed and 19 working days will be spent. A local CPPCC member made out a bill. If the Birth Approval Certificate handling procedures are optimized, the handling duration can be reduced to 4 working days, and RMB 81.5 billion can be saved annually (without calculating travel cost and other intermediary costs).[41] The saved money can be used to purchase 1.43 billion tons of carbon emission allowance according to the latest average carbon trading price in August 2014 in China (about RMB 57/ton).[42] If the birth approval procedures can be canceled just like the practice in Heilongjiang, Jilin, Jiangsu, etc., the low-carbon benefits of energy conservation and emission reduction may be higher.

Of course, different methods should be used to reduce different administrative procedures in different fields and for different matters. It is difficult to form a uniform scheme. Here, we only take the administrative licensing procedures as an example. Generally, the administrative licensing procedures are set according to two modes. One is the "positive list" mode, i.e. authorizing the legislations at all levels to stipulate the matters that must go through the administrative licensing procedures. For example, the *Law of the PRC on Administrative Permission* stipulates that the administrative licenses of 6 types of matters may be established by means of law. Where there is no governing law, administrative licenses may be established by means of

[41] Niu Richeng: *Only Elimination of "Administrative Redundancy" Can Avoid "Long March of Approval"*, *Yangcheng Evening News*, August 8, 2013.

[42] China's Carbon Emission Trading Website: http://www.tanpaifang.com/tanshichang/201408/2036998.html, visited on September 13, 2014.

administrative regulations. Licenses other than qualifications, legal person levels and their pre-licenses may be established by local regulations and rules. The other one is the "negative list" mode, i.e. establishing "exclusion" provisions for the matters that need to be approved by means of a unified legal norm. For other matters, there is no need to establish licensing procedures. This mode is adopted by China (Shanghai) Pilot Free Trade Zone for licensing the foreign investment access.[43] By contrast, the "negative list" mode is obviously more advisable. The reasons are: First, the "positive list" mode grants the licensing procedure setting rights to the administrative entities at different levels in different places, and this may cause great randomness and power abuse in making decisions. For local and departmental interests protection, governments and their functional departments with licensing procedure setting rights at all levels often make a variety of "lists of licenses", and some of them even create ingenious licensing titles by means of "review and approval", "filing", "registration" or other hidden forms, resulting in a large expansion of the licensing procedure. Take the city of Wuhan as an example. The number of administrative review and approval items canceled and adjusted by Wuhan in the sixth batch in 2004 alone is up to 1,268.[44] This indirectly reflects the numerous licensing procedures in the "positive list" mode. While, in the "negative list" mode, the exclusionary rule of "Absence of Legal Prohibition Means Freedom" can occasionally solve this problem fundamentally. Second, "negative list" mode does not directly reduce the number of administrative procedures superficially, but it allows a lot of matters and activities to access without going through the licensing procedures. This in fact greatly reduces administrative procedures. Third, from the perspective of administrative counterpart, "negative list" mode also has obvious advantages. The "negative list" mode clearly informs the counterparts of the fields or matters that have access restrictions, so that they can carry out self-check against the list and avoid those requiring licenses, thus preventing some procedures in the application stage.[45] In view of this, we should actively promote the "negative list" mode and gradually replace the "positive list" mode. Of course, the listing of "negative list" is not once and for all, but a process of dynamic adjustment and continuous simplifying according to economic and social development. For example, 2014 "negative list" of Shanghai is significantly simplified compared with 2013 "negative list", to further reduce the start of unnecessary administrative procedures and their carbon footprints.

(II) **Administrative Entity Level**

Generally speaking, which administrative entities are involved in the administrative procedures depends on whether the administrative entities have the management

---

[43] The *Special Administrative Measures for Access of Foreign Investment to China (shanghai) Pilot Free Trade Zone* (2014 revision) stipulates 139 foreign investment access prohibited fields, and all the rest industries, fields and economic activities can be assessed by foreign investment.

[44] See *Wuhan Municipal People's Government Decision on the Sixth Batch of Administrative Approval Items Canceled and Adjusted (WZ [2004] No. 54).*

[45] See Yang Haikun: *Interpretation and Promotion of the Special Administrative Measures (Negative List) on Foreign Investment Access to the China (Shanghai) Pilot Free Trade Zone*, *Jiang Huai Tribune*, Issue 3, 2014.

authority over the matters involved in the administrative procedures. For a procedural matter, the more administrative entities with management authority are, the more entities will be involved, and the more carbon emissions will be generated accordingly. Thus, relatively centralizing administrative authorities can be an effective way to reduce the entities being involved in the administrative procedures. The so-called "relatively centralized administrative authorities" means combining those administrative authorities with similar business nature, similar jurisdiction scope and same or closely related administrative functions, and then allocating the combined administrative authorities to one administrative department for unified exercise.[46] In China, due to legislative gaps and the ambiguity and conflicts in legal norms, authority overlapping among departments exists in many administrative fields, thus resulting in a series of repeated law enforcement in practice. This not only wastes precious law enforcement resources, but also increases the burden of the counterparts under management, thus increasing the carbon emissions of the whole administrative procedures. For example, the original *Regulations on Fire Management of Transport Ships* issued by the Ministry of Transport authorizes both shipping administration and maritime administrative agencies to carry out fire safety inspection against ships. As a result, the two departments carried out administrative inspections against ships according to different standards, causing the counterparts tired of dealing with the situation.[47] Similar phenomena also exist in audio–video product management and other fields.[48] In order to solve this problem, it is necessary to invest the overlapped administrative authorities to one department based on actual situations, and try to reduce the involving of unnecessary administrative entities into the administrative procedures to reduce carbon emissions. In legislation and in practice, the system of relatively centralized administrative authorities in China only applies to administrative punishment and administrative licensing, and its application field is mainly the urban comprehensive management field.[49] This is undoubtedly one-sided. In fact, besides the urban comprehensive management field and administrative punishment and licensing, the system of relatively centralized administrative authorities can still be widely used in other fields. For example, in the field of agricultural management, 14 departments are involved in the management before, during, and

[46] See Shi Youqi and Yang Zhikun: *Demonstration and Analysis on the Relative Centralization of Departmental Administrative Authorities*, *Journal of Jinan University (Philosophy & Social Science Edition)*, Issue 3, 2010.

[47] See the research groups of Zhongnan University of Economics and Law and Changjiang Maritime Safety Administration: *Research Report on Risk Prevention and Control in Maritime Administrative Law Enforcement* (internal publication).

[48] For example, according to the *Regulations on Administration of Audio-visual Products*, the press and publication departments, audio-visual products administrative departments, cultural administrative departments, industrial and commercial administrative departments, and public security departments all have the power to impose administrative penalties.

[49] See Shi Youqi and Huang Xuejun: *A Preliminary Discussion on the Relative Concentration of Departmental Administrative Authorities in China*, *Journal of Jiangsu Administration Institute*, Issue 1, 2008.

after agricultural production, and authority overlapping is inevitable.[50] For another example, according to the PRC *Urban and Rural Planning Law* and *Land Administration Law*, both the urban and rural planning management department and the land and resources management department have certain administrative planning authorities for the land use in some areas (the former has the urban construction planning authority and the latter has the land use planning authority). Due to the differences in guiding ideology and statistical caliber, conflicts between land use planning and urban planning take place from time to time in practice, resulting in repeated construction and serious waste of land resources. In the future, these fields and functions can be expanded and improved in the system design of the relatively centralized administrative authorities. However, this should not include the administrative functions exclusive to a department, such as the punishment of enforcement of restricting personal freedom, which should still be subject to the legal reservation principle.

(III) **Administrative Counterpart Level**

The purpose of administrative counterparts to participate in administrative procedures is to exercise certain administrative law rights or perform certain administrative law obligations. Then, if a reasonable system can be designed to ensure such right exercise and obligation performance only through the unilateral legal behaviors of the administrative entities or the counterparts without the entering of the counterparts into the formal legal procedures, not only the counterparts' procedural purpose can be achieved, but also the number of counterparts being involved in the administrative procedures can be reduced, thus reducing or even avoiding the carbon emissions from the activities of unnecessary counterparts during the administrative procedures. In this article, this system will be temporarily called "automatic formation procedure system" by reference to the formation right theory of the civil law, i.e. "the right to produce legal effect based on one party's expression of intention"[51] Its key feature is the rights can be exercised without any behavior of the counterparts (counterparts to the rights)",[52] so that "the rights or legal relationships can be quickly determined, making the complicated legal relationships simple and clear".[53] In administrative procedures, the automatic formation procedure system can be designed and divided into two types. The first type is the automatic formation procedure of the beneficial administration, which is mainly realized by the unilateral legal behaviors of the counterparts. At present, the automatic formation procedure has been locally applied

---

[50] See Shi Youqi and Huang Xuejun: *On the System Construction of Relative Concentration of Departmental Administrative Authorities*, *Journal of South-Central University for Nationalities (Humanities and Social Sciences)*, Issue 3, 2010.

[51] Han Zhongmo: *An Introduction to Legal Theory*, China University of Political Science and Law Press, 2002 edition, p. 181.

[52] Wang Yuanzhi: *Preliminary Research on the Right of Formation Theory*, *China Legal Science*, Issue 3, 2003. The original text is: "realize the behavior without the involvement of counterparts". The contents in brackets are added by the author to distinguish it from the concept of administrative counterpart in administrative law.

[53] Chen Huabin, Chen Junyong: *On the Right of Formation*, *Guangxi Social Sciences*, Issue 4, 2006.

in the administrative licensing field in China. For example, in the customs administrative licensing for the import of mechanical and electrical products and the export of textiles, for all products that are clearly listed in relevant lists and catalogues, the counterparts can automatically obtain import and export permits as long as they make applications.[54] In this procedure, counterparts can obtain permits as long as they make applications, thus eliminating the tedious steps after the counterparts enter the formal licensing procedures. According to the actual conditions, such automatic formation procedures can be copied and promoted in the fields of administrative payment, administrative rewards, etc. in the future. The second type is the benefit-damaged administration, which is mainly realized by the unilateral legal behaviors of the administrative entities. The benefit-damaged administration involves restrictions on the rights of the counterparts, and the due process principle generally requires the participation of the counterparts, so the automatic formation procedure in the benefit-damaged administration should be applied only when the counterparts fail to perform their obligations in the administrative procedures or the cost for obligation performance is too high. In the current legislation, the automatic formation procedure of benefit-damaged administration mainly exists in a few areas such as acting- performance in the area of administrative enforcement and tax withholding in the area of administrative collection. However, this does not mean that there is no room for expansion in its scope of application. Based on the requirements for energy conservation and emission reduction, when the cost for the counterpart to perform the obligations in the administrative procedures is too high, in principle, the automatic formation procedure can be applied upon the application or consent of the counterpart.

2.4 *Requirements for Low-Carbon Procedures in Terms of Time*

The time element includes the sequence and prescription of administrative procedures. The low-carbonization of administrative procedures mainly depends on the improvement of the time sequence system and the time limit system. The key elements that affect the operation of the administrative procedures are mainly the time limit of administrative procedures and the legal consequences of violating the time limit.

(I) **Time Limit of Behaviour**

Time limit has an important impact on low-carbon administrative procedures. "Time is money". From the perspective of carbon footprint, time is also a kind of carbon emissions. Because carbon footprint is the total carbon dioxide emissions generated

---

[54] See the provisions in *Measures for the Implementation of Automatic License for Import of Electromechanical Products* and *Interim Measures for Automatic Export Licensing for Textile Products*.

by all activities of the behavior subject within a certain period of time, the longer the administrative procedure lasts, the longer the carbon footprint will be. In this regard, the requirement for constructing low-carbon administrative procedures in terms of timeliness is to minimize the operating period of administrative procedures by rationally setting the time limit and legal consequences of the procedures. In China, the current time limit system of administrative procedures cannot fully adapt to the requirements of low-carbon administration and needs to be improved urgently. This is mainly reflected in the fact that the legal regulations of many administrative procedures have no clear provisions on the time limit for the administrative entities to complete the procedure, so that they can arbitrarily delay the progress of the procedure, causing the endless consumption of manpower, material resources, time and energy to the counterpart, and the extension of the entire carbon footprint of administrative procedure. For example, Article 9 of *Regulation on the Handling of Medical Accidents* stipulates that local health administrative department shall organize the investigation and handling of medical accidents or incidents, but it has no clear provisions on the time limit for such investigation, handling of medical accidents and incidents, or the investigation of the liability of responsible persons. The *Measures for the Administration of Pure Cultures of Edible Fungi, Measures for the Administration of Grass Seeds* also have no provisions on the statutory time limits of a considerable part of the administrative procedures. In addition, the abuse of time limit of procedures by administrative entities still exists in practice, for example, intentional delay of time limit to its deadline. Some scholars found in the investigation on the government information disclosure that some administrations, for the purpose of maximizing the extension of the response period, inform the counterparts that they need to postpone the handling period or the counterparts are required to provide supplementary application materials only when the statutory time limit is about to expire.[55] This is contrary to the low-carbon goal no matter from the perspective of the application handling by administrative entities or from the perspective of the re-application by the counterparts. In view of the above problems, in addition to clearly specifying the minimum statutory time limit of administrative procedures, administrative entities should also be further vigorously advocated to timely handle or complete the procedures ahead of time as soon as possible within the prescribed time limit if the conditions permit, and shall not intentionally delay the procedures to the deadline, in order to avoid unnecessary carbon footprints caused by human factors in the administrative procedures. At the same time, for some counterparts who seriously violate laws by emitting pollutants or greenhouse gases, a law enforcement procedure accelerating system can be established, that is, establishing special provisions to shorten the reconsideration and litigation period of low-carbon and environmental protection administrative law enforcement decisions, in order to realize rapid case filing, rapid trial and rapid execution, thus avoiding the irreversible harm to the ecological environment caused by the delay of law enforcement time limit.

[55] See Lv Yanbin: *Implementation Status and Improvement Path of Disclosure upon Application System - Analysis Based on Empirical Research of Government Information Disclosure*, *Administrative Law Review*, Issue 3, 2014.

(II) Legal Consequences

Legal consequences, as the core mechanism of the administrative time limit system, specifically include two forms of consequences: legal responsibility and legal effect. From the perspective of low-carbon procedures, the current administrative time limit system has two deficiencies in the design of legal consequences: First, many legal norms do not clearly stipulate the legal responsibilities of administrative entities for violating the provisions on time limit, causing administrative entities to arbitrarily violate the provisions on time limit. This will lead to the ineffectiveness of the legal time limit, which is not conducive to urging the administrative subject to complete the procedure in time, so as to reduce the carbon footprint of the procedure process. For example, Article 24 of the *Regulation of the People's Republic of China on the Disclosure of Government Information* stipulates the maximum response period of information disclosure upon application shall not exceed 30 days, however, its articles related to "monitoring and safeguarding" only stipulate the legal responsibilities of "not performing the obligation of government information disclosure according to laws", but not stipulate any legal responsibility of "not performing the obligation of government information disclosure in a timely manner". This needs to be improved in the system design of low-carbon administrative procedures urgently. Second, although some legal regulations stipulate the legal responsibilities of administrative entities for violating the provisions on time limit of administrative procedures, they match no legal effect of shortening or terminating the procedure period. Although this single legal consequence setting has the power of deterring and urging the administrative subject to abide by the time limit, it could not promote the proceeding or completion of the procedures by relying on its own power. In other words, it can only control high-carbon by negatively preventing the delay of administrative procedures, but cannot help to actively promote low-carbon administrative procedures in a more positive manner. Here, take the time limit system of the *Administrative Coercion Law of the People's Republic of China* as an example for analysis. Article 25 thereof stipulates the maximum period of seizure shall not exceed 60 days, and Article 62 stipulates the legal responsibilities (administrative sanctions) for not making any decision within the legal period of seizure or failing to rescind the seizure in a timely manner according to laws. When an administrative entity violates the provisions on time limit of administrative procedures, the investigation of legal responsibilities cannot directly eliminate the legal relationship of the administrative procedures (rescinding the seizure), which can only be realized by means of external procedures such as applying for relief by the counterpart and ordering correction by higher authorities. Undoubtedly, this process will generate a large number of new carbon footprints. As some scholars in the field of procedure law have pointed out: "The most fundamental law enforcement guarantee of the procedure law lies in the self-guarantee ability of the procedure law itself".[56] Similar logic also exists in the operation of low-carbon administrative procedures, i.e. "low-carbon administrative procedure with responsibilities only cannot operate

[56] Wang Junmin: *Legal Responsibilities for Witnesses' Refusal to Testify in Court Should Be Equally Important as Legal Consequences*, *Oriental Law*, Issue 3, 2012.

by itself, but together with legal effect can". Based on this, the system design of low-carbon administrative procedures should make full use of the legal effect of the administrative time limit system, that is, to shorten or terminate the procedure period directly through the reasonable setting of legal effect, in order not to increase new carbon footprint. For the design, some time limit rules in the administrative licensing procedures provide useful institutional resources. As stated in Article 32 of *the Law of the PRC on Administrative Permission*, if the applicant is not informed of the need for material supplement or correction within the time limit, the day when the application materials are accepted shall be considered as the acceptance day. Article 9 of the *Law of the People's Republic of China on Assemblies, Processions and Demonstrations* stipulates that if the competent authority, after receiving the application for an assembly or a procession, fails to notify whether or not the permission is granted and explain the reasons within the time limit, the permission shall be deemed to be granted. Their common characteristic is that the behaviors that exceed the time limit of administrative procedures will have a presumed legal effect of approval (presumed to be accepted or approved) to directly change or eliminate the legal relationship of administrative procedures, thus cutting off the carbon footprint chain in subsequent procedures.

2.5 Requirements for Low-Carbon Procedures in Terms of Space

The space element mainly deals with and regulates the "certainty of the behavior subject and their behavior and the relevance between the two"[57] in the process of the procedure, and is the procedural rule that directly regulates the legal behavior of all procedural subjects. Once the specific administrative entities and the administrative counterparts enter the procedural process as the procedural subject, their carbon emissions per unit of time are determined by the orchestration of various space elements. It can be said that the space element is the terminal link of the construction of low-carbon administrative processes, which has the most direct and obvious influence on the low-carbonization of the whole administrative processes, and belongs to the "visible and tangible" low-carbon administrative processes system. Specifically, the low-carbon requirements on space elements can be illustrated from three perspectives, i.e. jurisdiction rules, procedures and working mode.

(I) **Establish Flexible Close Proximity Jurisdiction Rules**

Jurisdiction directly manifests the spatial relationship between the administrative entities and the administrative counterparts in the procedural process, and largely determines the travel distance of the procedural subject in the procedural process. Transportation is the main source of carbon emissions of residents and society. It is estimated that in 2010, the emission from transportation and travel of Shanghai

[57] Sun Xiaoxia: *Analysis of Legal Procedure*, *Science of Law*, Issue 6, 1993.

residents was 6.358 million tons, accounting for 35.5% of the total direct carbon emissions of residents' life in this city, becoming the second largest source of carbon emissions.[58] Therefore, it is not hard to see that jurisdiction rules play a pivotal role in the low-carbon administrative processes system. However, many of the current jurisdiction rules have not fully met low-carbon requirements yet and need to be improved.

In terms of level of jurisdiction, some existing legal norms have vague provisions on how to determine the level of jurisdiction, only providing general principle of jurisdiction falling under administrative entities above the county level, for example, Article 3 of the *Law of the People's Republic of China Against Unfair Competition* provides that the industrial and commercial administration of the government above the county level shall supervise and inspect acts of unfair competition, and Article 8 of the *Product Quality Law* provides that the government departments for supervision of product quality above the county level shall supervise and manage the quality of products in the administrative region within their jurisdictions. Some scholars have pointed out that, according to such rules, administrative entities at the central, provincial, city and county levels have jurisdiction over a certain administrative procedure in principle, as long as it falls within the scope of competence.[59] In practice, this may lead to the higher administrative entities, driven by departmental interests and other factors, arbitrarily having jurisdiction over administrative affairs which are not within its jurisdiction, leading to non-low-carbon consequences: on the one hand, the higher administrative organs and their staff participate in the administrative processes of counterparts crossing boundary of administrative division; on the other hand, the counterparts may also participate in the administrative processes of higher level of administrative entities crossing the boundary of administrative division. From the perspective of both spatial relationship and travel distance, this is undoubtedly a double waste of the carbon footprint of administrative processes. In fact, the administrative entities at the city and county level are usually closer to the place where the administrative affairs take place in terms of spatial distance, and it is more economical for them to handle the administrative affairs in the first place to reduce the cost and carbon footprint of both the administrative entities and the administrative counterparts to participate in the administrative processes. To this end, it should be clearly defined that the general administrative affairs be governed by the county and municipal administrative entities for the first time, the provincial administrative entities can only take over the complex affairs or affairs with significant social impact, affairs crossing the administrative division or involving significant public interest, etc.

The main problem of territorial jurisdiction is that it is designed only to facilitate management for the administrative entities, without fully taking into account the spatial distance of administrative counterparts to participate in administrative

[58] See Zhang Gangfeng et al., *Study on Shanghai Residents' Domestic Carbon Emissions Based on Urban-RAM Model*, *Acta Scientiae Circumstantiae*, Issue 2, 2014.

[59] See Zhang Jiansheng, *Exploration of Administrative Jurisdiction System*, *Law Science*, Issue 7, 2002.

processes. Especially, many jurisdiction rules require the counterparts to go to a region other than where they live to handle matters, traveling back and forth to participate in administrative processes, causing the endless consumption of manpower, material, financial resources and time and to the counterpart, and a huge carbon footprint in transportation. This is very common in administrative licensing, administrative confirmation, administrative punishment, etc. For example, Article 18 of the *Regulations of the People's Republic of China for Controlling the Registration of Enterprises as Legal Persons* stipulates that an enterprise legal person can only apply for change registration to the original registration authority, which is the root cause that led to "a merchant in Jiangsu traveled 11 times[60] to change his license registration"; the *Law of the People's Republic of China on Administrative Penalty* stipulates that administrative penalties are under the jurisdiction of the administrative authority where the violation occurred, which has also led to some counterparts being accused of the cross-region violation "paying round-trip fare many times higher than the fine".[61] To address such drawbacks, the jurisdiction rules should be established to facilitate the travel of the counterparts to minimize the carbon footprint caused by the long distance travel. Such as the implementation of close proximity jurisdiction, allowing counterparts to choose the nearest authority to handle the matters without being restricted by the jurisdiction area.[62] In 2012, the Ministry of Public Security of China piloted the "processing of traffic violations and payment of fines in a place other than the place where the violation occurs" and "jurisdiction of motor vehicle license inspection and annual examination",[63] a useful attempt in this regard, which is worth promoting nationwide.

In addition, in order to reduce the carbon footprint caused by inconvenient jurisdiction, the administrative entities should also actively implement the transfer of jurisdiction, and take the initiative to transfer the administrative procedures they have accepted but have no jurisdiction over to the competent authorities. This plays a positive role to low-carbon processes in two ways: one, generally, within the administrative system, there are dedicated mechanisms for the transmission of official documents and administrative coordination, which ensures more efficient administrative processes comparing to returning to the counterparts for re-apply to the authority with jurisdiction, with much lower travel costs. Second, transfer of jurisdiction can bring together the procedural requests of different counterparts for a single transfer, reducing the carbon footprint caused by counterparts' long distance traveling.

---

[60] See *Focus Interview*, October 11, 2013: "Difficulties in Certificate Handling and Communicating with the Staff", http://news.cntv.cn/2013/10/11/VIDE1381493160336435.shtml, March 20, 2014.

[61] Cao Shulin, Yin Yan, and Gao Xiang: *"Inter-provincial Traffic Ticket" is No Longer a Problem*, People's Daily, July 22, 2013.

[62] Of course, the innovation of such jurisdiction rules mainly depends on the national or inter-regional networking technology of relevant management information (such as household registration and vehicle registration).

[63] See Jiang Hao, *Ministry of Public Security Launches 14 Convenience Measures*, *Legal Daily*, September 9, 2012.

(II) Streamline Cumbersome and Redundant Procedures

A link or a procedure is the basic unit that makes up the chain of administrative processes. In a certain sense, each link or procedure is equivalent to a small administrative procedural unit, encompassing all the elements like subject, time and space. In some cases, the handling of links or procedures in the same administrative process may also involve new procedural subjects, further increasing the carbon footprint of the process. If we compare the carbon emission of the whole administrative process with the flow of the main stream of a river, then the procedures and links are like its tributaries, and the more tributaries there are, the higher the flow of the main stream; meanwhile, some tributaries may also generate secondary tributaries, thus increasing the flow of the main stream. Therefore, streamlining the procedures and links of administrative processes according to reasonable standards is a "cost-saving" measure to reduce the carbon footprint of the processes. Specifically, this can be done in two ways: "abolish" and "merge". To "abolish" means to abolish formalities or links not essential; to "merge" means to merge duplicate or similar procedures. The following methods could be used to build corresponding systems of administrative procedures.

i. Simplify the procedures. There are a large number of lengthy formalities in rule of law practice in China, and simplifying them according to the above criteria is the prerequisite for the establishment of low-carbon administrative processes. For example, the *Interim Regulations on the Management of Public Rental Housing Leases in Wuhan* has been criticized by society and the media less than a month after the introduction for their overly complicated application procedures.[64] For low-carbon and convenience purpose, many of these procedures and links can be abolished and merged, which is not difficult technically. For example, one provision in the Interim Regulations requires applicants to go to the community to apply for the lease record to prove that it is currently renting a room to live before the formal submission of applications. It is a redundant link that is not only dispensable, but also may unnecessarily generate carbon emissions from new administrative procedures, and should be promptly deleted. For one thing, this can be fully proved by the applicant's rental contract, and asking the applicant go to the community for the record would be like painting the lily. For another, to complete the filing, the landlord (copies of ID card and property ownership certificate of landlord are required for the filing), a third procedural subject in addition to the Housing Authority and the applicant, needs to be involved, resulting in needless resource costs and carbon emissions. Another example, the Interim Regulations require applicants to provide housing certificate issued by the Wuhan Housing Security and Management Bureau, in fact, the city and district housing authorities share one set of information system, during the qualification process, the district housing authority only need to consult information on the computer to determine whether the applicant has a property. That is to say, the

[64] See Anonymous: *Thinking about the Complicated Data and Torturous Procedures for Residents Applying for Public Rental Housing*, *Changjiang Daily*, June 5, 2013.

procedure of "providing a housing certificate issued by the Wuhan Housing Security and Management Bureau" can be merged into the audit of the housing authority.

ii. Procedure selection system. Under the shadow of adjudicative administrative procedures, some low-carbon administrative enforcement procedures are cumbersome, hindering the timely implementation of administrative enforcement decisions, thus discouraging the achievement of low-carbon administrative goals. According to the general procedure, if the party is not satisfied with the decision made by the law enforcement agency, theoretically, it will be 13 months from the application for administrative review to the filing of administrative litigation against the reconsideration decision (without considering the non-working days and the extension of the litigation period),[65] on the other hand, during the whole litigation period, the administrative enforcement decision is in fact in suspension of execution, which provides an excuse for the counterpart to delay the fulfillment of obligations. However, in order to protect the legal rights of the counterpart, no procedure shall be arbitrarily omitted (reconsideration and litigation). In this regard, certain procedure selection system can be established based on the existing system provisions. For example, to establish certain final system allowing optional reconsideration in some low-carbon enforcement decision relief procedures for the choice of the counterparts, the counterparts who choose administrative review may not then file administrative litigation, and the ones choosing administrative litigation may not apply for administrative review. On the one hand, this reduces the number of relief procedures involved in the entire enforcement process and improves the timeliness of the implementation of low-carbon administrative enforcement decisions; on the other hand, it also provides administrative counterparts with appropriate procedure support, thus striking a balance between achieving the freedom of individual rights and the goal of low-carbon management.

(III) **Adopt a Convenient and Economical Working Mode**

If the carbon footprint of the administrative procedure comes from the carbon emissions of the procedure subject per unit of time, then whether the way of procedural subject acts is low-carbon or not is directly related to how convenient and saving the working mode of the procedure is. Therefore, designing working mode for energy conservation and emission reduction is an important aspect of the institutional design of low-carbon administrative procedures. Just as there are various ways to save energy and reduce emissions, there is also a lot of room for improvement and innovation of low-carbonization of working mode. For the time being, there are at least the following optimized working modes that are worth applying.

---

[65] Among them, the prescription and duration of administrative review are 2 months and 30 days respectively; If an administrative lawsuit is filed against the reconsideration decision, the prescription and duration of the first instance are 15 days and 6 months respectively; the prescription and duration of the second instance are 15 days and 3 months respectively. See Article 26 of the *administrative review Law*, and Articles 81 and 88 of the *Administrative Litigation Law*.

i. Fully implement the one-time notification system. One-time notification means that the administrative entities inform the counterparts of the steps, deadline, conditions and requirements, supporting materials and other information involved in handling the affairs at one time. Its significance for low-carbon administrative procedures is that by informing the information on the procedures involved in handling administrative affairs at one time, it avoids the carbon footprint generated by long distance travel by the counterparts due to multiple submissions or supplementation of materials. From the perspective of legislative provisions, the current one-time notification method is only used in the administrative licensing process, and is not a statutory requirement in administrative penalties, administrative supply, administrative publicity and other fields, which may make the counterparts run unnecessary long way, resulting in additional energy consumption and high carbon emissions. In practice, especially in supply administration, it is frequently reported in the press that the counterparts have not figure out the materials required until traveling back and forth many times,[66] an important reason is that the administrative entity fails to provide the information comprehensively. To this end, the one-time notification should be fully implemented in all future procedures involving the rights and obligations of the counterparts and be all-roundly promoted as an universal statutory requirement to shape a low-carbon working mode.

ii. Improve the joint processing system. Joint processing in China is currently mainly found in the field of administrative licensing, the legal basis is the provisions of Article 26 of the *Law of the PRC on Administrative Permission*. Joint processing plays a positive spatial integration role in administrative procedures, which on the one hand reduces the carbon footprint generated by the counterparts traveling back and forth between different departments, and on the other hand reduces the carbon footprint of the resources generated by the counterparts for repeated submission of materials to different departments and exchange and transmission of materials between departments, thus greatly reducing the greenhouse gas emissions in the process. For example, in Jinan, Shandong Province, after the post-approval of enterprise establishment was jointly handled, the forms to be filled for approval decreased from 5 to 1; the time required decreased from the original 14 days to 6 days; the applicants' number of round trips for the procedure was decreased from the original 8 to 2.[67] Here, the reduction in quantity of materials, travel mileages and time can be converted to CO_2 equivalent. In the construction of low-carbon administrative procedures, joint processing should be promoted as a general working mode and be commonly applied in a wide range of administrative fields such as administrative charge, administrative registration and administrative investigation (inspection). For

[66] See Lin Yanzhen and Li Fang: *There's no notice that conditions for applying for subsistence allowances are not in conformity, causing the disabled to spent two months in vain*, http://news.xmnn.cn/xmxw/200808/t20080814_673975.htm; *It's Torturous for Poor College Students to Apply for Student Loan*, *Chongqing Times*, August 5, 2013.

[67] See Chao Mingchun: *Jinan Administrative Examination and Approval Optimization Process Speeds Up, Saving more Time for Enterprises*, *Dazhong Daily*, April 10, 2013.

example, in the field of administrative confirmation, Yiwu in Zhejiang province and other places have begun to implement the joint registration in commercial housing, i.e. the registration procedures involving any of the three departments (finance and taxation, housing and construction, land and resources) are accepted and handled in single one service window, so that the time required of the processing reduced from the original 11 working days to 6 working days, and the average annual number of round trips required for the procedure reduced about 6,000.[68] In some countries, joint processing is even a statutory requirement, for example, Article 14 of the *Basic Law of Administrative Investigation* of Korea clearly stipulates that joint investigation shall be implemented when different internal agencies of the same administrative organ "conduct an administrative investigation on the same subject in the same or similar field" or when different administrative organs "carry out administrative investigations on the same subject".[69] This not only reduces the waste of administrative costs caused by repeated enforcement of laws, but also save the time and energy for the counterparts to respond to frequent inspections.

In China, under the central government's strong support and policy promotion,[70] the policy of joint approval for licensing has been initially established and run nationwide, becoming a typical system of joint processing. However, in practice, the operation of the joint approval for licensing still faces some challenges. To some extent, these challenges also reflect the difficulties that the whole joint processing system is facing or may face, which should be seriously reflected and treated. The rather prominent challenges are: First, because the *Law of the PRC on Administrative Permission* only authorizes the "people's governments at same level" to unite its subordinate functional departments for administrative licensing, coupled with the absence of rigid binding law supporting for the provision of "determining a single department to handle", some municipal administrative approval departments directly under central or provincial governments refuse to cooperate with the local government and violates the provision of "the local government has the rights to handle the local affairs", ignoring the "one window acceptance". Second, some cities and

[68] See Yiwu Construction Bureau: *Joint Handling of Commodity House Registration in Yiwu City*, website of Ministry of Housing and Urban-Rural Development of the People's Republic of China (MOHURD): http://www.mohurd.gov.cn/dfxx/201210/t20121012_211611.html, September 25, 2014.

[69] Jin Xuanmo, *Basic Law of Administrative Investigation in Korea*, *Administrative Law Review*, Issue 2, 2009.

[70] For example, in 2004, the *Notice of the General Office of the State Council on Implementing the Work Arrangement of the Administrative Licensing Law* (GBF [2003] No. 99) required that "local people's governments should actively explore the establishment of a relatively centralized administrative licensing system and a unified, joint and centralized system for administrative licensing"; In 2011, the *Opinions of the General Office of the CPC Central Committee and the General Office of the State Council on Deepening the Openness of Government Affairs and Strengthening Government Affairs Services (ZBF [2011] No. 22)* further emphasized the need to "standardize the operation of service centers and gradually implement the operation mode of' one-window acceptance, one-stop approval, one-stop service and one-window charge'. For any administrative examination and approval items involving more than two departments, the joint handling or parallel examination and approval shall be gradually implemented."

counties, although with joint processing agencies established, fail to establish a clear leadership relationship between the upper and lower levels. Even there is no link between the two in joint processing, resulting in some cross-level and cross-regional licenses that cannot be implemented or are extremely inefficient.[71] To deal with the above challenges, first of all, legislation system shall be improved to remove legal restriction of "joint processing is limited to local government departments, the organizer can only be the government at the same level", and the non-compulsory provision of "may carry out joint processing" shall be changed to compulsory provision of "shall carry out joint processing". Second, joint processing agencies at all levels should establish unified standards and processes for the licensing of the same matter or area, and establish business leadership relation and information interoperability mechanism between departments at the upper and lower levels for joint processing agencies.

From the functional point of view, the joint processing system and the system of relatively centralized administrative powers of departments complement each other. The administrative functions and powers of departments are relatively centralized, and the powers originally belonging to different departments are combined and allocated to one department according to certain standards, so as to fundamentally eliminate the source of unnecessary carbon footprint. However, due to the nature of business and factors in the field of management, many administrative powers cannot be centralized or are not suitable for centralization in terms of norms; also some administrative powers, although can be and need to be centralized theoretically due to their co-related and overlapped scope, are difficult to be centralized due to institutional barriers, immature practical conditions and other reasons. For this kind of decentralized administrative powers, using joint processing to achieve "end control" can help to realize a certain "centralized" state for the powers, shorten the travel distance of procedural subjects (including distance between the administrative entity and the administrative counterpart and different administrative entities), reduce the resource consumption, and thus play the same function as the relative centralization of administrative powers to reduce emissions. To draw a more imaginative analogy to express the relationship between the two, the relative concentration of administrative powers of departments is like "chemical cooling" to reduce the procedural carbon footprint from the internal source, while the joint processing is "physical cooling" to reduce the carbon footprint of the procedure from the perspective of the external spatial relationship. The two complement each other in functions.

iii. Flexibly use summary procedure system. Administrative summary procedure refers to the "administrative rules of conduct for the rapid, simple, and unconventional handling of the administrative affairs",[72] which aims to minimize the procedural costs and shorten the administrative process in a simplified manner in accordance with the statutory conditions and without compromising procedural justice. This is consistent with the requirements for construction of low-carbon administrative

---

[71] See Ren Jingtao: *Problems and Countermeasures in Administrative Examination and Approval*, http://law.china.cn/features/2013-10/15/content_6373419.htm, September 23, 2014.

[72] Zhang Shufen: *On Administrative Summary Procedure*, *ECUPL Journal*, Issue 2, 2010.

procedures. Unfortunately, the application of summary procedures is still limited to the domain of administrative penalties, and accounts for a very low proportion in the overall administrative procedures system. This results from the traditional thinking of one-sided emphasis on power control. According to the requirements for low-carbon development, efficiency and convenience for people, on the basis of maintaining procedural justice, the application scope of the summary procedures should be expanded in all administration management domains, especially in the domain of beneficial administration. In principle, all matters with clear case facts and minor legal disputes may be subject to summary procedure without excessive restrictions if this will not violate the provision of prohibitive procedures at law.

For example, in terms of the administrative licensing procedures, the *Law of the PRC on Administrative Permission* has very detailed regulations on the application and acceptance procedures, but does not establish any summary procedure. This should be a defect. In practice, administrative licensing can be involved in a wide range of domains, and the summary procedure can be completely applicable to some matters that need administrative licensing. For example, simple matters that can be reviewed against clear standards or applications for renewal of licenses of which the applicants performed well in the previous supervision and inspection can be quickly handled in accordance with the summary procedure, to reduce the carbon footprint of both licensing authorities and applicants in the process. In fact, this kind of summary procedure for renewal of license has been partially tested in some administrative fields in China. For example, Article 26 of the *Provisions of the China Securities Regulatory Commission on the Procedures for the Implementation of Administrative Licensing* provides that summary procedure can be applied to administrative licensing where the review standard is clear, the matter involved is clear, and the application is prepared in the text format specified, and acceptance department, after a formal review on the spot, shall decide whether to accept the application or to require for supplementary materials.

In payment administration, the summary procedure is also very useful. The implementation of summary procedure enables the administrative counterpart to obtain payment more quickly. On the contrary, the mechanical and inflexible application of general procedures may lead to dangerous consequences such as survival difficulties and intensification of contradictions because the counterpart cannot obtain material help in time. Meanwhile, the administrative entities will not bear any legal responsibility for the application of the summary procedure in the favorable administrative act, and the counterparts will not doubt this.[73] For example, with respect to the review of the minimum living security and low-rent housing, persons who are granted support of the especially poor (persons having no labor capacity, no source of income, and no persons with statutory obligations to support, raise or foster them) specified in the *Interim Measures for Social Assistance* may be directly included in the scope of the minimum living security and low-rent housing support by applying the summary procedure. The reason is the information on the economic status of these counterparts have already been reviewed in other types of social assistance,

[73] See Zhang Shufen: *On Administrative Summary Procedure*, *ECUPL Journal*, Issue 2, 2010.

and their conditions are clear. When they apply for new types of social assistance, it is no need to go through the general procedures to repeat the review.

In addition, even in the domain of administrative penalties, it is difficult to give full play to the summary procedure currently because the conditions for its application are too strict. According to the *Law of The People's Republic of China on Administrative Penalty*, the summary procedure is only applicable to illegal acts where the fact is clear and the amount is small.[74] However, with the development of society and the economy, the legislative provisions on the penalty limits of the summary procedure have significantly lagged behind the practice. For example, a practitioner, according to law enforcement records, pointed out that penalties or warnings of less than RMB 500 against individual business in the fire administrative penalties in a region accounted for 70–90% in the penalty decisions, but the administrative entities had to apply the general procedures because the strict application standard of the summary procedure for administrative penalties cannot be satisfied. According to the general procedures, a minor illegal act fined RMB 200 involves 3 times of approval by leaders, 3 legal documents served by law enforcement officers, and 3 round trips of counterparts. The law enforcement case file has more than 20 pages.[75] This greatly reduces the actual effectiveness of the summary procedure and causes unnecessary consumption of law enforcement resources and carbon footprint. In this regard, it is recommended to relax the applicable conditions of the summary procedure for administrative penalties. In addition to the requirement of meeting the conditions that the fact of malfeasance is confirmative and legal basis is available, it should also be allowed to apply the summary procedure that applies to penalties or warnings to minor illegal acts where the counterparts actively eliminate or mitigate the harmful consequences. Meanwhile, it is recommended to appropriately increase the penalty limits of the summary procedure according to the social and economic development and the law enforcement practice of each department, or not to provide specific restrictions in the *Law of The People's Republic of China on Administrative Penalty* but decentrally authorize each department to flexibly prepare their own administrative penalty laws and regulations based on actual conditions to expand the coverage against minor illegal acts.

iv. **Establish and improve the electronic administrative procedure system**. The electronic administrative procedure, as a type of E-government, can optimize and reorganize the organizational structure and work flow of administrative procedures by utilizing digital equipment and communication technology, and realize the functions of administrative procedures, such as online information (e.g. illegal acts, penalties, etc.) query, online application and handling, online progress feedback and result notification. The electronic administrative procedure is a technical means to promote procedural low-carbonization. It goes beyond the restrictions of materials, time and

---

[74] See Article 33 and Articles 46-48, *Law of The People's Republic of China on Administrative Penalty*.

[75] See Mi Qiyan and Zhao Yifeng: *On Reconstruction of Summary Procedures of Fire Administration*, Journal of the Armed Police Academy, Issue 7, 2012.

space, and can minimize the carbon footprint during the procedural process. Therefore, some people point out that "E-government is low-carbon".[76] Specifically, once the initial infrastructure is established, the operation of the electronic administrative procedure almost no longer consumes new physical resources but only needs to exchange virtual data. This means "zero-carbon" is expected to be achieved in the communication between the procedural subjects during the procedural process. Furthermore, the electronic administrative procedure allows procedural subjects to freely access the procedure system at any time and place. On the one hand, it saves the traffic carbon footprint of each procedural subject for participating in the administrative procedure on site. On the other hand, compared with the "five-days and eight-hours" working system of the manual administrative procedures, the "all-weather" working system of the electronic administrative procedure is obviously much more efficient. This is equivalent to indirectly reducing the carbon intensity in unit time and unit procedure. In addition, the electronic administrative procedure also provides an excellent technical platform for the application of other low-carbon program devices. With the help of electronic administrative procedure, the above-mentioned flexible jurisdiction, one-time notification and joint handling systems can function better. For example, through the electronic administrative procedure, a department, after obtaining remote authorization and information sharing, can flexibly govern procedures nearby online no matter how far the distance is. For one-time notification, online notification and instruction provided through the electronic administrative procedure can even achieve better effect compared with in-person notification. The information provided is clear, intuitive, and can be repeatedly viewed by counterparts at any time. Joint handling of matters based on the application of the electronic administrative procedure is also a development trend of the future administration. Using electronic administrative procedure to realize information sharing can greatly reduce the information cost for coordination among departments.

The electronic administrative procedure system can be especially applied to the following domains of administrative procedures: (i) electronic administrative procedures for administrative licensing and administrative approval. The electronic licensing and approval procedures not only use computer technology to transfer traditional administrative licensing and administrative approval procedures to an electronic network platform, but more significantly, to optimize and restructure the organizational structure and procedural flow of administrative licensing and administrative approval through certain software designs, break down departmental divisions and implement inter-departmental business collaboration and other systems and mechanisms to achieve resource sharing. This reduces the time and material costs of transmitting permit and approval information between departments, as well as reduce the transportation and information acquisition costs of the counterparts participating in the administrative procedures, thus improving the overall efficiency of the entire administrative procedures and reducing the energy and resource consumption of all parties involved in the administrative procedures and their corresponding carbon emissions. (ii) Electronic administrative procedures for the implementation

---

[76] Zheng Yi: *low-carbon and E-government*, *Information Construction*, Issue 6, 2010.

of administrative decisions. The implementation of an administrative decision by the counterpart and the enforcement of an administrative decision by the administrative entities both entail significant costs. If some administrative law obligations are performed and enforced on the basis of electronic administrative procedures, saving the costs for both the administrative entities and the administrative counterparts can be achieved. For example, administrative fines can be discharged by online payment. (iii) Electronic administrative procedures for public participation. As the electronic administrative procedure improves the way of public participation in the form of the network platform, the cost of public participation is reduced. Compared to the traditional administrative procedures, participation of citizens in electronic administrative procedures provides a completely new means. With the help of the Internet, the public can participate in administrative procedures at home by using e-mails, electronic bulletin boards, online forums, etc. (iv) Electronic administrative procedures for administrative inspections. The application of electronic administrative procedures enables online submission and verification of administrative inspection materials, thus significantly reducing paper consumption, transport carbon emissions and human and material resources in the administrative inspection process. For instance, a joint online annual inspection system for foreign-invested enterprises has been set up by the Department of Foreign Investment Administration of the Ministry of Commerce of the People's Republic of China, in conjunction with various departments such as Industry and Commerce, Finance, Taxation, Statistics and Foreign Exchange, which allows enterprises to go through most of the annual inspection procedures online by simply logging in to the joint annual inspection website.[77]

Driven by the National Informatization Development Strategy and the Government Online Project, the construction of electronic administrative procedures in China has made considerable progress. Nevertheless, in terms of achieving the low-carbon goal, the following problems remain to be solved: (i) Repeated construction. Due to the lack of sufficient demonstration and unified standards, various administrations at all levels and in all places, often rush into their own R & D and construction, and the phenomenon of repeated construction or abandonment due to incompatible software are more prominent, which leads to serious waste of resources. And this is a deviation from the original intention of low-carbon and environmental protection. In response, a standardized and intensive construction of electronic administrative procedures needs to be implemented on the basis of integrated planning. (ii) Low utilization rate. According to the evaluation of the Chinese Academy of Social Sciences in consecutive years, the number of people conducting affairs through electric procedures on government websites is still at a low level. On average, only 25.4% of people have visited the government website, indicating that the number of utilization is much smaller than that of construction.[78] The idle resources offsets to some extent the low-carbon performance of electronic administrative procedures.

---

[77] "Online Joint Declaration System for Annual Operation of Foreign-invested Enterprises in China": http://www.lhnj.gov.cn, visited on September 26, 2014.

[78] Wang Xiangdong, *Progress, Present Situation and Development Trend of E-government in China*, E-government, Issue 7, 2009.

To relieve this problem, more efforts are needed to improve the content and operation of electronic administrative processes from the position of the counterpart, as well as to increase publicity efforts to attract people to choose electronic administrative procedures when conducting their affairs. (iii) Focus on external procedures but underestimate internal procedures. At present, many matters involved in the electronic administrative procedures are not those related to the counterpart, but the information release and handling of matters in the government, thus the public-oriented online business and service items are obviously lagging behind.[79] This of course has limitations. (iv) Unsound functions. The ability of the electronic administrative procedures to truly achieve the goal of energy conservation and emission reduction depends to a large extent on the degree of completeness of their functions. Any gap in functions implies that the corresponding steps need to be performed on site, thus resulting in additional carbon footprints. At present, many electronic administrative procedures are functionally deficient and cannot fully undertake the work of online business. Take the government websites of 10 provincial capitals or municipalities as an example, 6 of them are not equipped with online application and handling functions for their electronic administrative procedures; 7 of them are not equipped with online progress feedback and result notification functions; besides, 4 websites are actually paralyzed in some of their procedure functions.[80] (v) Contradictions with current legislation. An important feature of electronic administrative procedures is that they are paperless, thereby achieving a low-carbon objective of saving resources. However, this contradicts with much current legislation at the normative level. Examples include the *Law of the People's Republic of China on Administrative Penalty*, which specifies that a written penalty notice must be issued to impose administrative penalties; the *Law of the PRC on Administrative Permission*, which stipulates written evidence is required for both the acceptance and decision of a permit; and the *Customs Law of the People's Republic of China*, which also requires the use of written customs declaration documents. Although the *Electronic Signature Law of the People's Republic of China* implemented in 2005 confirms the legal status of data messages and electronic signatures, it does not involve the specification of electronic signature for administrative activities, and consequently cannot solve the current problem of the legality of the signature in the use of electronic administrative procedures. Therefore, the legislation on electronic administrative procedures should also take into account the issue of convergence and coordination with the relevant legal norms on administrative procedures.

v. **Improve the system of evidence collection for administrative procedures**. Evidence collection is an important system and working mode of administrative procedures. The current administrative law enforcement procedure adopts absolute authority principle for evidence collection and investigation, with the responsibility

---

[79] See Chen Hongwei and Wang Feng: *Ten-Year Online Development of Government*, Legal Daily, June 18, 2009.

[80] Including: www.whhome.gov.cn, www.gzonline.gov.cn, www.changsha.gov.cn, www.changsha.gov.cn, www.cdzw.gov.cn, www.xzfw.nc.gov.cn, www.beijing.gov.cn, www.shanghai.gov.cn, www.tj.gov.cn, www.cq.gov.cn.

of evidence investigation and collection fallen entirely on the administrative entities, who are required to "investigate and collect relevant evidence in a comprehensive, objective and impartial manner".[81] Nevertheless, in the practice of low-carbon and environmental protection administrative law enforcement procedures, evidence collection is often difficult, which on the one side comes from administrative counterparts suppressing evidence or failing to cooperate with investigations. Some polluting enterprises, for example, often hide or transfer evidence by means of discharging without permission, burying or even discharging underground; in order to save costs, many companies normally turn off their pollution treatment facilities and only turn them on temporarily when they are inspected by law enforcement departments; some even refuse to accept questioning or refuse to sign on or seal questioning or inspection transcripts, for the fact that the environmental law enforcement departments do not have the power of administrative compulsory measures. On the other side, evidence collection also faces the practical bottleneck of a lack of law enforcement forces. China is now in a period of intense environmental problems that is typical of a transitional society, and the tasks of environmental monitoring and law enforcement are becoming increasingly challenging. Meanwhile, law enforcement resources of all kinds, from staff to evidence collection equipment, are quite limited. Based on the data currently obtained, more than 3,000 environmental law enforcement institutions nationwide, each with only 2.7 evidence collection tools and 1.4 vehicles on average, are responsible for supervising tens of thousands of construction sites, more than 700,000 "tertiary industries" enterprises and investigating and handling more than 60,000 pollution incidents each year.[82] The situation of "investigating waste water by watching, waste gas by smelling and noise by listening" is still widespread.[83] However, constraints like financial budget and personnel allotment make this situation difficult to rectify in the short term.

For the difficulty in evidence collection for low-carbon and environmental protection law enforcement, a self-monitoring and reporting procedural working mode of administrative counterparts can be established to share and transfer the investigation and evidence collection obligations that were originally fully attributable to the administrations to the counterparts to some degree. Self-monitoring and reporting system refers to the requirement that polluting and emitting enterprises should install automatic monitoring equipment and its supporting facilities in accordance with the requirements of laws and regulations, and that if the automatic monitoring system has been inspected by the administrative entities and can operate normally, its data should be used as evidence for the administrative entities to issue emission licenses, conduct environmental statistics, on-site environmental law enforcement and other law enforcement actions, and should be made public in accordance with the regulations. Conversely, if the counterparts do not install automatic monitoring equipment or submit monitoring reports in accordance with the requirements, it is presumed that

---

[81] See Article 36, *Law of The People's Republic of China on Administrative Penalty*.

[82] See Liu Yi: *Why is environmental law enforcement so difficult? People's Daily*, January 13, 2005.

[83] Zong Jianshu: *How to keep the bottom line of environmental safety? China Environment News*, February 2, 2012 (3rd edition).

there is an illegal act of pollutant emission or carbon emission exceeding the standard. Consequently, they should undertake adverse legal consequences, such as administrative penalties. At present, a more mature technical condition and systematic foundation have been established in China for the establishment of a self-monitoring and reporting system for key polluting enterprises. In the field of environmental monitoring, Ministry of Ecology and Environment promulgated in 2005 the *Measures for the Administration of Automatic Monitoring of Pollution Sources* which requires key polluting enterprises to install automatic monitoring instruments and sets a series of provisions for the construction, operation and maintenance of automatic monitoring systems. The Ministry of Ecology and Environment issued in 2013 the *Measures for the Self-Monitoring and Information Disclosure by the Enterprises subject to Intensive Monitoring and Control of the State (for Trial Implementation)* which specifies the content and scope of self-monitoring by the key monitoring enterprises, and makes clear requirements for the disclosure, supervision and inspection of their monitoring information. In the field of carbon trading management, the self-monitoring by emission control enterprises, the verification by third-party institutions and the review by administrative authorities have been solidified and become a formal MRV legal system. For example, this has been clearly stipulated in the *Decision on the Pilot Project of Carbon Emission Trading in Beijing under the Premise of Strict Control of Total Carbon Emissions*,[84] which actually requires emission control enterprises to entrust third-party verification agencies to monitor their carbon emissions, thus shifting part of the burden of proven administrative penalties for carbon trading (not exceeding the legal carbon emission quota) to the administrative counterpart and alleviating to a certain extent the difficulties in obtaining evidence. Based on the valuable experience accumulated in the current system provisions, when the future conditions are available, provisions should be unified through legislation in the field of low-carbon environmental law enforcement to set up counterpart self-monitoring and reporting system. The counterparts of key pollution monitoring enterprises and carbon emission control enterprises are required to install automatic monitoring equipment, report to the administrative entities and receive a review, which can effectively alleviate the difficulties in collecting evidence for low-carbon environmental enforcement in the design of the procedural system.

vi. The procedural system of prior enforcement. Generally speaking, environmental protection departments and climate change management departments have no administrative enforcement powers and can only apply to the courts for enforcement.[85] Although the *administrative review Law* and *Administrative Litigation Law* of the PRC provide in principle that appeals during reconsideration and litigation will not stop the enforcement of the original specific administrative act, the court has the

---

[84] See Article 3, *Decision on the Pilot Project of Carbon Emission Trading in Beijing under the Premise of Strict Control of Total Carbon Emissions*.

[85] Although the new *Environmental Protection Law* of 2014 gave the environmental protection department administrative compulsory measures for sealing up and detaining, environmental protection department has no right of administrative enforcement, and many enforcement decisions had to be applied to the court for compulsory execution.

power to rule on exceptions and stay of enforcement. According to the *Interpretation on Several Issues concerning the Application of the Administrative Litigation Law of the People's Republic of China* in 2000, Article 94 provides that if the administrative organ applies to the People's Court to enforce the specific administrative act being sued during the litigation process, the court shall not enforce it. Since the courts in administrative litigation practice usually give priority to the application of the refined provisions of judicial interpretation, the principle of complaint without stay of execution is practically impracticable in the field of administrative coercion. The interaction of these two procedures often allows the counterparty to take full advantage of the process and try to delay the implementation of low-carbon environmental enforcement decisions, which has led to repeated enforcement embarrassments in practice, such as the collection of emission fines over a period of 19 months,[86] or even a decade to shut down polluting enterprises.[87] During this period, the counterparty cannot be stopped exceeding the standard emission of pollutants and greenhouse gases as usual. As for the difficulty of enforcement, relative departments shall consider the introduction of a prior enforcement system for low-carbon environmental administrative enforcement decisions involving shutdowns and closures under litigation law. Article 94 of the *Interpretation on Several Issues concerning the Application of the Administrative Litigation Law of the People's Republic of China* in 2000 provides that the court has the right to pre-emptively enforce administrative enforcement decisions based on low-carbon public interest considerations. Currently, this system has been partially implemented by several courts such as courts in Xi'an and Nantong, China, where local courts enforce administrative penalties and administrative orders involving the suspension of production, business, closure, and cessation of discharge, etc., from environmental protection administrations and law enforcement agencies for serious and persistent pollution.[88]

3 Construction of Low-Carbon Administrative Procedures

Administrative procedure legislation is essential for constructing low-carbon administrative procedures. At present, conditions are becoming ripe for the formulation of a unified administrative procedure code at the national level. In the future formulation of the administrative procedure code, we should fully incorporate the low-carbon requirements, establish the basic principles of low-carbon for the convenience of the

---

[86] Zhao Nan, *The Sewage Discharge Case of Tuopai Agricultural Products Company: The Penalty Exceeds the Original Penalty by Several Time*, *China Environmental News*, March 27, 2012.

[87] Liang Siqi, *Why a polluting enterprise cannot be shut down in ten years? Shenyang Evening News*, November 4, 2006.

[88] See Chen Xiangdong and Gu Jianbing: *Prior Enforcement of Nantong on Five Kinds of Environmental Pollution Behaviors First*, Jiangsu Legal News, July 9, 2013; Ning Jun, *Xi'an Central Court issued ten measures to combat pollution and reduce haze with judicial protection, and pollution of the environment can be ruled by the court to stop production first*, *Huashang Daily*, December 11, 2013.

people, and stipulate the basic systems of low-carbon administrative procedures, so as to unify all kinds of single Administrative Litigation Laws.

3.1 Establishing Simplified and Low-Carbon Procedural Principles

The basic principle of Administrative Litigation Law is "the spiritual core that runs through the legal norms of administrative procedure, commands and dominates the legal norms of administrative procedure."[89] It plays an important guiding role for the value orientation and basic system construction of administrative procedure. In terms of the mainstream view of the current academic community, the basic principles of Administrative Litigation Law include the principle of procedural justice, the principle of administrative openness, and the principle of participation. Among them, the principle of justice and the principle of administrative openness are mainly aimed at guaranteeing the minimum legal rationality of administrative procedures, and the principle of participation aims at enhancing the democratic legitimacy of administrative procedures, thus they fail to reflect the low-carbon value orientation of administrative procedures. In this regard, the formulation of Administrative Litigation Law should also establish the basic low-carbon and simplified principles, requiring that the setting and operation of administrative procedures should be chosen in a way with low resource and energy consumption as far as possible, in order to meet the procedural demands of the low-carbon era.

3.2 Basic Systems of Low-Carbon Administrative Procedures

The basic systems of administrative procedures are the legal rules generally followed by all kinds of administrative procedures. Based on the consideration of low-carbon development and convenient for the people, the following systems should be stipulated as the basic systems of low-carbon administrative procedures.

(I) **Convenient Jurisdiction System**

Jurisdiction system should provide for the shortest possible traffic distance between administrative entities and administrative counterparts participating in the administrative procedures, so as to reduce the resource consumption and carbon emissions on the way. In jurisdiction, it should be clearly defined that the general administrative affairs be governed by the county and municipal administrative entities for the first time, the provincial administrative entities can only take over the complex affairs or affairs with significant social impact, affairs crossing the administrative

---

89 Hu Jianmiao and Zhang Jiansheng: *On the Legislation of Administrative Procedure and the Basic Principles of Administrative Procedural Law*, *Zhejiang Social Sciences*, Issue 6, 1997.

division or involving significant public interest, etc. In terms of territorial jurisdiction, the existing system of jurisdiction over the domicile of the counterpart and the place where the act occurred should be changed into flexible and proximate territorial jurisdiction allowing the counterpart not restricted by the jurisdictional area and choose the nearest convenient area for affairs on its will. In addition, the administrative entities should also actively use the transfer of jurisdiction, and take the initiative to transfer administrative affairs which have been accepted but without jurisdiction to the competent authorities for processing in order to reduce the carbon footprint caused by the jurisdictional inconveniences.

(II) **One-time Notification System**

At present, the one-time notification system is mainly applied in the field of administrative licensing, and has not yet become a statutory requirement in a wide range of fields such as administrative penalties, administrative payments and administrative disclosure. The legislation on administrative procedures should be expanded and stipulate that all procedures involving the rights and obligations of the counterpart should be notified at one time, which should be upgraded to a universal requirement for all administrative procedures to reduce the unnecessary costs and carbon emissions of the counterpart who repeatedly go back and forth to get information.

(III) **Joint Processing System**

The joint processing system is currently mainly applied in the field of administrative licensing, which is of course should be expanded. In the unified legislation of administrative procedure, joint processing should be promoted as a general working mode and be commonly applied in a wide range of administrative fields such as administrative charge, administrative registration and administrative investigation (inspection), etc. This should become a compulsory provision. This system on the one hand reduces the carbon footprint of the transportation of the counterpart to and from different departments, and on the other hand reduces the carbon footprint of the resources of the counterpart to different departments for repeated submission of materials and the exchange and transmission of materials between departments, thus greatly reducing the greenhouse gas emissions in the process of procedures.

(IV) **Prescription System**

The current various separate Administrative Litigation Laws have made many provisions about the prescription system, but it is not perfect enough, which leads to the delay of the procedure progress of administrative organs in practice. In this regard, in addition to clearly specifying the minimum statutory time limit of administrative procedures, administrative entities should also be further vigorously advocated to timely handle or complete the procedures ahead of time as soon as possible within the prescribed time limit if the conditions permit, shall not intentionally delay the procedures to the deadline, and stipulate the legal responsibility of the administrative entities to exceed the procedural time limit.

(V) Tacit Declaration Procedural System

The taciturnity of the administrative organ within the statutory period should be regarded as an expression of intention that has certain legal effect. Articles 101 and 102 of the *Administrative Procedure Code of Macao* provide for the system of tacit approval and tacit rejection respectively. Tacit approval means that within the period prescribed by law, the administrative organ is deemed to have granted permission or approval without granting permission or approval to the counterpart's application or request. Tacit rejection means that if the competent administrative organ does not make a decision on the counterpart's request within the statutory period, the counterpart's request is deemed to be rejected. The tacit declaration procedural system enables the counterpart to realize the rights and fulfill the obligations without entering into formal legal procedures but only by the unilateral legal acts of the administrative entities or the counterpart, thus reducing the carbon emission caused by unnecessary counterpart activities during the procedure.

(VI) Summary Procedural System

At present, the application of summary procedure is still limited to the field of administrative punishment. According to the requirements for low-carbon development, efficiency and convenience for people, it is required to, on the basis of maintaining procedural justice, expand the application scope of the summary procedures in all administration management domains, especially in the beneficial administrative domain. In this regard, the unified administrative procedure legislation can provide that all the cases with clear facts and minor legal disputes, in the premise of not violating the legal prohibitions, can be applied to the summary procedure without too much restriction.

(VII) Electronic Procedural System

The electronic administrative procedure is a technical means to promote procedural low-carbonization. It goes beyond the restrictions of materials, time and space, and can minimize the carbon footprint during the procedural process. For the time being, the legislation can encourage and advocate administrative entities to adopt electronic administrative procedures in administrative permits and approvals, administrative decision execution, administrative inspection, and administrative legislation. And for the administrative acts in the relevant single Administrative Litigation Law, the procedural requirement of issuing a written decision letter should be modified to accommodate the paperless feature of the electronic administrative procedure.

In addition to the above basic systems, the legislation can also provide for special administrative procedures in the field of environmental protection and other low-carbon administrative management. For example, in response to the current difficulties in obtaining evidence for environmental protection enforcement, the legislation on administrative procedures can adopt alternative provisions to authorize the relevant law enforcement agencies to take evidence by means of automatic testing.

For another example, the legislation may provide that the court may first enforce administrative penalties and administrative enforcement orders such as suspension of production, suspension of business, closure, and cessation of discharge related to serious and persistent polluting acts.

Chapter 5
Improving the Administrative Legislation for Low-Carbon Regulation

Legislation refers to the activities of state organs with legislative authority according to law to formulate, modify or abolish laws, regulations, rules and other codes of conduct in accordance with legal procedures. In building a low-carbon society, legislation is undoubtedly the primary link in regulating and guiding members of society to comply with low-carbon requirements. At present, China's legislation on low-carbon development includes laws, administrative regulations, local regulations, rules, etc. And even a large number of normative policy documents included are formulated by the administrative organs for the purpose of establishing behavioral norms, some of which are interpretations and refinements of laws, regulations and rules, while others are normative documents introduced in time when laws, regulations and rules have not yet been formulated. Together, they constitute the entire system of legal norms for low-carbon construction.

China has enacted over ten laws in the field of environmental protection, energy and resources, circular economy and cleaner production, including *Environmental Protection Law* (revised in 2014), the *Law of the PRC on the Prevention and Control of Atmospheric Pollution*, the *Law of the People's Republic of China on Environmental Impact Assessment*, the *Energy Conservation Law* (revised in 2007), the *Renewable Energy Law* (revised in 2009), the *Law of the People's Republic of China on the Prevention and Control of Environmental Pollution By Solid Waste*, and *Law of the People's Republic of China on Promoting the Development of a recycling Economy*, and the *Cleaner Production Promotion Law*, providing foundation for the low-carbon legal system.

Comparatively speaking, there are a large number of administrative regulations, rules and government normative documents related to low-carbon construction. At the central government level, the State Council and departments directly under the State Council have promulgated a large number of administrative regulations and departmental regulations including the *Regulation on Energy Conservation in Civil Buildings* (2008), the *Energy Conservation Regulation for State-funded Institutions* (2008), *Interim Measures for the Administration of Low-Carbon Product Certification* (2013), *Interim Measures for Promotion and Management of Energy-saving*

S. Fang and B. Tan, *On the Administrative Law of China in Addressing Climate Change*,
https://doi.org/10.1007/978-981-19-7705-3_5

and Low-carbon Technology (2014), and *Interim Measures for the Administration of Carbon Emission Permit Trading* (2015), and to address climate change, they introduced the *Interim Measures on the Administration of External Cooperation to Address Climate Change* (2010), the *Interim Measures for the Administration of Voluntary Greenhouse Gas Emission Reduction Transactions* (2012), and in the field of cleaner production, they introduced *Measures for the Administration of the Clean Development Mechanism Fund* (2010) and the *Measures for the Operation and Management of China Clean Development Mechanism Projects* (2011). According to statistics, there are more than 30 administrative regulations and more than 200 departmental regulations concerning energy alone.[1] At the local government level, all provinces have administrative legislation for energy conservation, cleaner production and other related areas. In the context of the "target responsibility system" for low-carbon development in China, local governments have formulated a large number of government regulations and normative documents to implement regulations in order to meet the binding targets for energy conservation and emission reduction. Search for keywords "low-carbon", "energy conservation and emission reduction" in the "law retrieval system" of Peking University Center for Legal Information (Beida Fabao), we can find that as of June 2015, there were 18 laws enacted by the National People's Congress and its standing committee on low-carbon issues; 50 administrative regulations enacted by the State Council; 370 departmental regulations; 23 local regulations; and 4,501 local government regulations and local government regulatory documents.[2] Thus, it is evident that administrative laws and regulations, as well as government regulatory documents, account for the vast majority of the low-carbon legislation. The main reason is that "low-carbon" is a new topic that has not been taken seriously by human beings until recently and need to be urgently addressed, and low-carbon legislation is still at the early stage even in the world, lacking mature experience and still to be explored in depth, with new problems and new situations springing up. This requires administrative legislation, a simpler and more flexible legislative approach, to respond and handle. Looking from the respective characteristics of law-making and administrative legislation, the law-making cycle is longer and the procedure is strict, and the matters requiring legislation usually have developed very mature, which makes law-making somewhat lagging and difficult to timely handle the low-carbon problem. In contrast, the administrative legislation is flexible and convenient, experimental and adaptable, which can play an active role in adjusting and exploring experience for the formulation of low-carbon related laws at this stage.

This type of legislation is called "low-carbon administrative legislation", which refers to the activities of specific administrative organs to enact administrative rules and regulations on energy conservation, environmental protection and other low-carbon construction within their legal authority. Low-carbon administrative legislation is an important means for the government to fulfill its new role in promoting the

[1] Chen Zhen, *Energy Legislation of China: Difficult to Come Out*, *Energy Review*, 2013, Issue 3.

[2] China law info Database: http://www.pkulaw.cn/cluster_call_form.aspx?menu_item=law&Db=chl, accessed on June 27, 2015.

construction of a low-carbon society and regulating energy conservation and emission reduction activities, also an important component of the overall low-carbon legislation. At present, China's administrative organs have made great achievements in low-carbon administrative legislation, filled many legislative gaps in the construction of a low-carbon society, explored and summarized some successful experiences, which promoted and guided the construction of a low-carbon society in China. However, there are still some problems, which include: There are legislative gaps in low-carbon consumption such as the lack for comprehensive regulations; the existing low-carbon administrative legislation has a large number of "soft law" norms, which fails to guarantee the actual implementation effect; there are repeated content or inconsistency between different low-carbon administrative legislation, resulting in the waste of legislative resources and frequent legislative conflicts. These are still worth studying and improving. The details are described as below.

1 Strengthening the Administrative Legislation for Low-Carbon Consumption[3]

The current legislation in the field of low-carbon construction in China is relatively lagging behind in low-carbon consumption, and even the administrative legislation, which is easier and more flexible to enact, is yet to be improved. In fact, as some scholars put it: "consumption is the core of the environmental crisis".[4] The UN *Agenda 21* for Sustainable Development states that "the major cause of the continued deterioration of the global environment is the unsustainable pattern of consumption and production". The sixth meeting of the Central Committee's Leading Group for Financial and Economic Affairs, chaired by President Xi Jinping on June 13, 2014, clarified the basic elements of China's energy consumption revolution, aiming to achieve low-carbon development through the regulation of the consumption.[5] However, at present, China's low-carbon consumption is still mainly driven by policy, without the adjustment and guidance of legal norms.[6] In order to better regulate and promote low-carbon consumption, administrative legislation should now be strengthened to regulate and adjust low-carbon consumption.

[3] Part content of this section has been published in *Journal of Hubei University of Police* (2013) Issue 11 and *Journal of Hubei Administration Institute* (2014) Issue 3, titled *On the Justification of Government Guiding Residents' Low-carbon Consumption* and *On the Application of Compulsory Administrative Actions to Low-carbon Consumption* respectively.

[4] [U.S.] Shridath Ramphal, *Our Country, The Planet*, translated by Xia Kunbao et al., China Environmental Science Press, 1993 version, p. 13.

[5] In addition, the *Program of Action for the Energy Development Strategy (2014-2020)* issued by the State Council in 2014 also proposes to promote the "energy consumption revolution" in China.

[6] See Yang Jiejun, *Low-carbon Oriented Legal Adjustment and Collaboration: Necessity-based Analysis and Review on Reality*, *Law Review*, 2014, Issue 2.

1.1 Meaning of Low-Carbon Consumption

Low-carbon consumption is a compound word of consumption and low-carbon. Generally speaking, consumption refers to "the act and process by which people satisfy their needs through the use and consumption of various labor products."[7] low-carbon means lower carbon emissions. Therefore, low-carbon consumption in a general sense means that consumers consume labor products in a way that minimizes the carbon emissions. The low-carbon consumption discussed in this chapter is only limited to living consumption, and does not include productive consumption, which means that individuals or organizations "choose the consumption method with the lowest carbon emissions within their affordability when purchasing, using and disposing goods to meet their reasonable consumption needs."[8]

Referring to different consumption groups, low-carbon consumption can be divided into public institution low-carbon consumption and individual low-carbon consumption (including individuals and various social organizations other than public institutions).[9] The two differ in terms of their resources consumed, the way they consume, and their consumption objects. Public institutions' low-carbon consumption is financed wholly or partially by financial fund, while individual low-carbon consumption is financed entirely by their own costs; public institutions' low-carbon consumption is limited to office supplies necessary for performing public functions, while individual low-carbon consumption can be all kinds of living and working supplies based on the richness of social life and individual preferences; all these determine that the governing of the two should be different.

Referring to the fields of consumption, low-carbon consumption can also be divided into low-carbon consumption for clothing (including official working clothes), food (including official reception), housing (including public buildings and office premises), travel (including official travel) and other official supplies or private living and working supplies.

1.2 Current Status and Problems of the Administrative Legislation for Low-Carbon Consumption

China now has not too many specific legislation on low-carbon consumption, but there are a series of regulations on low-carbon consumption in public institutions, like the *Energy Conservation Regulation for State-funded Institutions*, while few systematic legislation and regulation has been introduced for individual low-carbon

---

[7] Lin Baipeng, *Dictionary of Consumption Economy*, Economic Science Press, 1991, p. 1.

[8] Xu Wei, *Justification of Government Guiding Residents' Low-carbon Consumption*, *Journal of Hubei University of Police*, 2013, Issue 11.

[9] Public institutions here include state agencies, institutions and organizations that use all or part of financial funds. See Article 2 of the *Energy Conservation Regulation for State-funded Institutions*.

consumption.[10] Although without doubt, when considering about dealing with the close relationship between low-carbon consumption and energy conservation, reduction of greenhouse gas emissions and environmental protection, some fragmented provisions on individual low-carbon consumption could still be found in relevant laws and regulations. The following is a brief analysis of the current administrative regulations for low-carbon consumption by public institutions and by private individuals, respectively.

(I) **Standards for Low-carbon Consumption in Public Institutions**

i. **Status of administrative legislation for low-carbon consumption in public institutions**

As a whole, China has abundant administrative legislation regulating low-carbon consumption in public institutions, which mainly includes administrative regulations such as the *Energy Conservation Regulation for State-funded Institutions, the Regulations on Rigorous Enforcement of Economy and Anti-Waste for the Party and Government Organs* and *Regulation on the Administration of the Institutional Affairs of Government*, and *Regulation on the Implementation of the Government Procurement, Regulation on Energy Conservation for Civil Buildings*, and normative documents like *Blueprint of Conserving Energy in Public Institutions During the 12th Five-Year Plan Period, Guidance on Comprehensively Promote the Reform of Public Service Vehicles*, and *Reform Plan of Official Vehicle System for Central and State Organs*. Among them, the *Energy Conservation Regulation for State-funded Institutions* provide more comprehensive and systematic regulations on low-carbon consumption in public institutions, covering energy conservation planning, energy conservation management, energy conservation measures, supervision and guarantee, etc.; the *Regulations on Rigorous Enforcement of Economy and Anti-Waste for the Party and Government Organs* provides more specific regulations on low-carbon consumption in party and government organs, which are an important part of public institutions, covering fund management, domestic travel and temporary travel abroad on official business (overseas), official reception, official vehicles, meeting activities, office premises, resource conservation, publicity and education, supervision and inspection, and accountability, etc.; the *Regulation on the Administration of the Institutional Affairs of Government* provides special regulations on low-carbon consumption in people's governments at all levels and their departments, including fund management, assets management, service management and legal liability etc. The *Regulation on the Implementation of the Government Procurement* provides regulations on low-carbon procurement by public institutions, including the parties involved in government procurement, methods, procedures and contracts of government procurement, questions and complaints, supervision and inspection,

[10] Some scholars, on the basis of sorting out the structure of China's low-carbon legal system, point out that currently most of China's low-carbon legal norms are for production but rarely involve consumption, and there is almost no legislation that regulates consumption behaviors. See Yang Jiejun and Cheng Yuyan, *Research on the Structure and Improvement of China's Low-Carbon Legal System*, Jiangsu Social Sciences, 2014, Issue 2.

legal responsibilities, etc. *Regulation on Energy Conservation in Civil Buildings* provides regulations on energy conservation in office buildings of state organs, including energy conservation in new buildings, existing buildings, and in the operation of building energy systems, and legal liability. The *Blueprint of Conserving Energy in Public Institutions During the 12th Five-Year Plan Period* provides a general plan for energy conservation in public institutions nationwide, including the guiding ideology, principles and goals of energy conservation in public institutions in the 12th Five-Year Plan, key areas and projects for energy conservation in public institutions, and supporting measures[11]; the *Guidance on Comprehensively Promote the Reform of Public Service Vehicles* and *Reform Plan of Official Vehicle System for Central and State Organs* have made special provisions for the official vehicles of Party and government organs.

The brief overview shows that the provisions in existing administrative legislation on low-carbon consumption in public institutions mainly focus on basic requirements, objectives and ways to achieve them, assessment, supervision and inspection, and legal responsibilities.

(i) Basic requirements, objectives and ways to achieve low-carbon consumption in public institutions

According to Article 3 of the *Energy Conservation Regulation for State-funded Institutions*, the basic requirements for low-carbon consumption in public institutions are to "reduce energy consumption, reduce and stop energy waste, use energy efficiently and reasonably"[12] and to protect the environment. Meanwhile, Article 3 of the *Regulations on Rigorous Enforcement of Economy and Anti-Waste for the Party and Government Organs* also defines waste behaviors of Party and government organs, that is, "party and government organs and their staff conduct unnecessary official activities in violation of the regulations, or use the public funds, assets and resources beyond the stipulated scope, standards and more than the extent required by the performance of official duties, or use them improperly".[13] In terms of specific targets, the *Blueprint of Conserving Energy in Public Institutions During the 12th Five-Year Plan Period* proposes that the main goal of energy conservation in public institutions during the "12th Five-Year Plan" is "to reduce energy consumption by 15% per capita and 12% per unit of floor area in 2015 from the energy consumption in 2010. These are general provisions of administrative legislation for low-carbon consumption in public institutions.

As for the above basic requirements and the ways to achieve the goals, the *Energy Conservation Regulation for State-funded Institutions*, the *Regulation on the Administration of the Institutional Affairs of Government*, the *Regulations on Rigorous Enforcement of Economy and Anti-Waste for the Party and Government Organs*, and

[11] See *Blueprint of Conserving Energy in Public Institutions During the 12th Five-Year Plan Period*, *Ningbo Energy Saving*, 2012, Issue 4.

[12] See Article 3 of the *Energy Conservation Regulation for State-funded Institutions*.

[13] See Article 3 of the *Regulations on Rigorous Enforcement of Economy and Anti-Waste for the Party and Government Organs*.

the *Regulation on the Implementation of the Government Procurement* have made a series of specific and special provisions, which mainly deal with energy-saving planning, low-carbon procurement, and low-carbon utilization of public property.

In terms of energy conservation planning in public institutions, the *Blueprint of Conserving Energy in Public Institutions During the 12th Five-Year Plan Period* provides an overall plan for energy conservation in public institutions nationwide, while Chap. 2 of the *Energy Conservation Regulation for State-funded Institutions* provides for the rulemaking body, basic content and implementation plans of energy conservation planning, decomposition and implementation of energy conservation targets and indicators, and annual energy conservation targets, etc.

In terms of low-carbon procurement for public institutions, the relevant legislation provides for the objects, procurement methods, procurement order and procurement cycle of low-carbon procurement for public institutions. In terms of procurement objects, Article 18 of the *Energy Conservation Regulation for State-funded Institutions* stipulates that during the procurement, public institutions shall give priority to energy-saving products or equipment, products conducive to environmental and resource conservation, and economically applicable goods, and prohibit energy-using products or equipment whose elimination the state has explicitly ordered.[14] In terms of procurement methods, Article 10 of the *Regulation on the Implementation of the Government Procurement* stipulates that the state promotes the use of information networks for electronic government procurement activities; Article 12 of the *Regulations on Rigorous Enforcement of Economy and Anti-Waste for the Party and Government Organs* stipulates that party and government organs shall actively promote electronic government procurement. In terms of procurement order, Article 18 of the *Energy Conservation Regulation for State-funded Institutions* provides for the strict implementation of the "giving priority" to energy-saving and environmentally friendly products in the procurement as stipulated in Article 51 of the *Energy Conservation Law*, and sets forth the requirement of "mandatory procurement"; Article 43 of the *Regulations on Rigorous Enforcement of Economy and Anti-Waste for the Party and Government Organs* also emphasizes the strict implementation of the compulsory procurement and giving priority to energy-saving products. In terms of procurement cycle, Article 15 of the *Regulation on the Administration of the Institutional Affairs of Government* sets out the requirements for shortening the procurement cycle, improving procurement efficiency and reducing procurement costs.

With regard to the low-carbon use of public property by public institutions, the legislation mainly defines the public property and the manner of use. As for public property, public institutions are required to use energy-efficient products. For example, Article 19 of the *Regulation on Energy Conservation in Civil Buildings* stipulates that public institutions "shall install and use energy-efficient lighting and electrical control devices in public corridors and staircases of buildings"; the *Notice of the General Office of the State Council on the Control of Excessive Packaging of Goods* requires administrative organs at all levels to take the lead in consciously

[14] See Article 18 of the *Energy Conservation Regulation for State-funded Institutions*.

resisting excessive packaging of goods. Article 34 of the *Energy Conservation Regulation for State-funded Institutions* specifically stipulates that: "The official vehicles of public institutions shall be equipped in accordance with the standards, giving priority to vehicles with low energy consumption, less pollution and using clean energy, and the vehicle retirement system shall be strictly implemented." As for the use of public property, public institutions are required to adopt an energy-saving approach to the use of public property. For example, Article 3 of the *Energy Conservation Regulation for State-funded Institutions* requires public institutions to adopt technically feasible and economically reasonable measures for energy use management; Article 29 of the *Energy Conservation Regulation for State-funded Institutions* requires public institutions to reduce the standby energy consumption of air conditioners, computers, copying machines and other electric equipment and to turn off electric equipment in a timely manner[15]; Article 34 requires public institutions to use official vehicles in accordance with the prescribed purposes and to actively promote socialization of official vehicle services, encouraging staff to travel by public transportation and non-motorized transportation means[16]; Articles 25, 28 and 29 of the *Regulation on the Administration of the Institutional Affairs of Government* have strict provisions on the registration, standards and configuration of official vehicles, the standards of official receptions, the number, scale, duration and mode of meetings, etc.; Article 26 of the *Energy Conservation Regulation for State-funded Institutions* encourages public institutions to " adopt contract energy management and entrust energy-saving service institutions to carry out energy-saving diagnosis, design, financing, renovation and operation management",[17] and Articles 14–17 stipulate that public institutions should implement energy consumption measurement, statistics, quotas and expenditure standards and other energy-saving management systems. In addition, Article 18 of the *Regulation on the Administration of the Institutional Affairs of Government* specifically provides for requirement on the minimum service life of the assets, etc.

(ii) **Assessment, supervision and inspection of low-carbon consumption in public institutions**

In terms of assessment, supervision and inspection of low-carbon consumption in public institutions, the *Blueprint of Conserving Energy in Public Institutions During the 12th Five-Year Plan Period* calls for "the establishment of an energy conservation target responsibility system and the decomposition of energy conservation targets at each level for implementation, encompassing the completion of energy conservation targets as an important part of the evaluation of relevant units, according to which, rewards and punishments will be implemented". Article 6 of the *Energy Conservation Regulation for State-funded Institutions* clearly states that "the person in charge of a public institution shall be fully responsible for the energy conservation work of the institution. The public institutions shall implement the target responsibility system

[15] See Article 29 of the *Energy Conservation Regulation for State-funded Institutions*.

[16] See Article 34 of the *Energy Conservation Regulation for State-funded Institutions*.

[17] See Article 26 of the *Energy Conservation Regulation for State-funded Institutions*.

and evaluation system, with the completion of energy-saving targets being encompassed in the evaluation of the work of the person in charge of public institution." Article 35 stipulates the specific content of the supervision and inspection of energy conservation in public institutions, including the development and implementation of annual energy conservation targets and implementation plans, energy consumption measurement and monitoring; the implementation of energy consumption quotas; the establishment of energy conservation management rules and regulations; the setting of energy management positions and the implementation of the energy management post responsibility system, as well as energy audits and the use of official vehicles. Articles 49–56 of the *Regulations on Rigorous Enforcement of Economy and Anti-Waste for the Party and Government Organs* also provide for a more comprehensive supervision and inspection mechanism for Party and government organs to enforce economy and anti-waste, specifying the subjects, responsibilities, contents, methods and procedures of supervision and inspection.[18] The main systems include: first, include the enforcement of economy and anti-waste into the annual reports of party committees and governments at all levels; second, deliberate the enforcement of economy and anti-waste of leading cadres as an important part of the meeting of democratic life and leading cadres' reports on their work and their efforts to perform their duties honestly[19]; third, at least once a year, a special supervision and inspection will be organized on the enforcement of economy and anti-waste; fourth, discipline inspection and supervision organs should strengthen the supervision and inspection of the enforcement of economy and anti-waste, the central and provincial, autonomous regions and municipalities directly under the Central Party Committee inspection team should strengthen the inspection and supervision of the work of the leading team of the relevant Party organizations and their members[20]; fifth, Party and government organs should establish and improve the enforcement of economy and anti-waste information disclosure system; sixth, promote and support the supervision of people's congresses and their standing committees, deputies to the National People's Congress, the People's Political Consultative Conference on the Party and government organs of the enforcement of economy and anti-waste; seventh, strengthen the supervision role of media of all levels and types and the public on the waste behaviors of Party and government organs and their staff.

(iii) **Accountability for violation of low-carbon consumption rules of public institutions**

In terms of accountability for violations of low-carbon consumption rules of public institutions, Articles 37–42 of the *Energy Conservation Regulation for State-funded Institutions* clearly enumerate the various situations in which public institutions

[18] See Article 49 of the *Regulations on Rigorous Enforcement of Economy and Anti-Waste for the Party and Government Organs*.

[19] See Article 50 of the *Regulations on Rigorous Enforcement of Economy and Anti-Waste for the Party and Government Organs*.

[20] See Article 52 of the *Regulations on Rigorous Enforcement of Economy and Anti-Waste for the Party and Government Organs*.

violate energy conservation regulations. The Article 57, Article 59 and Article 60 of *Regulations on Rigorous Enforcement of Economy and Anti-Waste for the Party and Government Organs* also well establish the strict conservation and waste accountability system for Party and government organs, specifying the party discipline, political discipline responsibility for waste behaviors. In addition, the *Regulation on Energy Conservation for Civil Buildings* also made provisions for legal responsibility for state organ office buildings in violation of the provision of energy conservation in new buildings, existing buildings, and in the operation of building energy systems.

ii. **Inadequate legislation for low-carbon consumption in public institutions**

At present, China's administrative legislation has a systematic regulation of low-carbon consumption in public institutions, but there are still some deficiencies that need further improvement, mainly in the government's low-carbon procurement and information disclosure of low-carbon use of public goods.

(i) **Inadequate low-carbon procurement regulations for public institutions**

In terms of low-carbon procurement for public institutions, Article 3 of *Government Procurement Law* stipulates four principles of government procurement, namely openness and transparency, fair competition, impartiality and honesty and integrity. However, it does not clearly establish the principle of low-carbon procurement or green procurement,[21] and only briefly mentions that government procurement should help "protect the environment" in Article 9, while the rest of the text does not highlight the requirement of implementing low-carbon procurement, this is also the case in *Regulation on the Implementation of the Government Procurement*. This is clearly not enough to effectively tune the government's low-carbon procurement activities. In terms of consistency in legislation, this is clearly incongruous with the *Energy Conservation Law*, the *Cleaner Production Promotion Law*, as well as the *Energy Conservation Regulation for State-funded Institutions*, the *Regulation on the Administration of the Institutional Affairs of Government*, and *Regulations on Rigorous Enforcement of Economy and Anti-Waste for the Party and Government Organs* which focus on requiring the government to strengthen low-carbon procurement. Meanwhile, the *Government Procurement Law* and the *Regulation on the Implementation of the Government Procurement* do not stipulate the legal liability of public institutions for failing to comply with the requirements of low-carbon procurement,

[21] Government green procurement means the intentional procurement of products and services that are pollution-free and conducive to healthy and circular economic development by the government to promote the sustainable economic development. See Jiang Aihua, *International Comparison and Reference of Government Green Procurement System*, *Finance & Trade Economics*, 2007, Issue 4. low-carbon procurement principle and green procurement principle are expressed differently, but their basic connotation is the same, both referring to the procurement of environmental-friendly and energy-saving products.

thus making government procurement shall be conducive to "environment protection" only an advocating rather than a mandatory norm.[22] Clearly this is something that needs to be improved.

(ii) **Absence of comprehensive and unified regulations on the basic scope, types and standards of official consumption**

To restrain low-carbon consumption in public institutions, first, it is necessary to clarify the basic scope, types and standards of official consumption and make them rule of law to serve as guidelines for official consumption of public institutions and their staff; at the same time, it is also an important basis for implementing inspection, evaluation and accountability for related violations. In this regard, although there are some provisions in the existing *Energy Conservation Regulation for State-funded Institutions*, *Regulation on the Administration of the Institutional Affairs of Government*, and *Regulations on Rigorous Enforcement of Economy and Anti-Waste for the Party and Government Organs*, they are rather not systematic and comprehensive. In dealing with this, administration should introduce legislation to define the scope of official consumption in public institutions, compile a comprehensive list or list of official consumption items and standards by type and level, and make it public.

(iii) **Provisions for disclosure of information on official consumption in public institutions are not yet sufficient**

The current legislative provisions lack openness and transparency of information regarding official consumption in public institutions. For example, Article 8 of the *Energy Conservation Regulation for State-funded Institutions* stipulates that "the public has the right to supervise the waste of energy in public institutions," but Articles 13 and 15 only stipulate that public institutions shall report their annual energy conservation targets and implementation plans to the institutions managing institutional affairs at the same level for the record, and submit a report on energy consumption for the previous year by March 31 of each year, however, without requiring making public.[23] This makes it difficult to realize the public's right to know and to effectively monitor the waste of energy resources by public institutions. In addition, the regulations on disclosing "the three public consumptions" of public institutions are not explicitly stipulated. The central government has been fully disclosing its "three public consumptions" since 2011, three years after the introduction of the *Regulations on Disclosure of Government Information*, while local governments have done poorly.[24] Analyzing from the legislative perspective,

[22] See Ju Yuhong, *Discussion on Legal System of Government Green Procurement—From the Perspective of Green Economic Development*, *On Economic Problems*, 2010, Issue 7.

[23] For this purpose, the National Government Offices Administration of the State Council formulated the *Statistical System for Energy Resource Consumption in Public Institutions* in 2009.

[24] Some scholars summarized the main problems currently existing in the disclosure of the "three public consumptions" by the government in China as: sidelining of government decrees, and delay in disclosure; content being general and brief, and lack of explanations; statements being narrow and covering different institutions each time; concepts being ambiguous and boundaries being

in light of the scope of information disclosure stipulated in Articles 9 to 13 of the *Regulations on Disclosure of Government Information*, it is unclear whether the information on official consumption of public institutions is included in the government information that can be disclosed. From the practice that the central government has made public the "three public consumptions" expense, this kind of official consumption of public institutions does not fall under the list of state secrets, and should be classified as information to be disclosed by public institutions. Thus, the *Regulations on Disclosure of Government Information* and the *Energy Conservation Regulation for State-funded Institutions* need to be further revised and improved in disclosure of information on official consumption by public institutions.

(II) Standards for Individual Low-carbon Consumption

For individual low-carbon consumption, there are no special provisions, the relevant laws and regulations in this regard only have some non-systematic provisions.

i. Main contents

(i) **Provisions for general obligations**. Existing legislation stipulated a large number of general obligations for individual low-carbon consumption. For example, Article 5 of *Law of the PRC on the Prevention and Control of Atmospheric Pollution* states that "All unit and individual are obligated to protect the atmospheric environment." Article 6 of the *Environmental Protection Law* states more clearly that "Citizens shall enhance their awareness of environment protection, live a low-carbon and frugal lifestyle, and consciously fulfill their obligations for environment protection." Similar provisions can be found in Article 24 of the *Energy Conservation Law*, Article 9 of the *Law of the People's Republic of China on the Prevention and Control of Environmental Pollution By Solid Waste*, Article 10 of the *Law of the People's Republic of China on Promoting the Development of a Recycling Economy*, and Article 8 of the *Water Law of the PRC*.

(ii) **Non-systematic behavioral requirements**. For individual low-carbon consumption, there are currently a number of behavior advocates and prohibitions. In terms of behavior advocates, Article 26 of *Law of the People's Republic of China on Promoting the Development of a Recycling Economy* and Article 23 of *Cleaner Production Promotion Law* provide that "catering, entertainment, hotels and other service enterprises should adopt energy-saving, water-saving and other technologies and equipment conducive to environmental protection, reduce the use or not to use consumer goods that waste resources and pollute the environment"; Article 34 of the *Electricity Law of the PRC* stipulates that "power supply enterprises and users shall comply with the relevant state regulations and take effective measures to ensure safe use of electricity, electricity conservation and planned use of electricity." As for prohibitions, for example,

---

blurred; attitude being arrogant and response being less; and lack of review and verification. See Li Zhanle, *Current Situation, Problems and Countermeasures of the Chinese Government's Disclosure of "Three Public Consumptions"*, *Social Sciences in Yunnan*, 2012, Issue 2.

Article 28 of the *Energy Conservation Law* stipulates that no unit shall implement a lump-fee system for energy consumption; the *Notice of the General Office of the State Council on the Control of Excessive Packaging of Goods* stipulates that circulation enterprises shall not purchase or sell excessively packaged goods, etc.

(iii) **Regulatory approach**. Currently, individual low-carbon consumption is mainly stipulated in different laws, rules and regulations in form of administrative guidance, administrative incentives, administrative confirmation, administrative contracts, administrative collection, etc.

i) **Administrative guidance**. Administrative guidance is the most common administrative tool used for individual low-carbon consumption, mainly through publicity and education, provision of information, demonstration and guidance, and incentives to guide the counterparts to low-carbon consumption. For example, in the purchase of consumer goods, the government encourages the public to purchase and use energy-saving products and products that are conducive to environment and resource protection through demonstration and promotion of energy-saving products, energy-saving publicity and training, and information services.[25] Energy conservation is popularized during in the use of consumer products through education and demonstration.[26] In order to give full play to the role of administrative guidance, financial subsidies or tax incentives are also often introduced, i.e., the administrative objective of promoting low-carbon consumption is achieved by incentives. This can be seen from national general provisions on fiscal and taxation and price policies guiding energy users and individuals in energy conservation, such as Article 66 of the *Energy Conservation Law* and Article 46 of the *Law of the People's Republic of China on Promoting the Development of a recycling Economy*; it is also reflected in the special provisions for specific targets, such as the tax exemptions for vehicles and vessels with small displacement, new energy vehicles and vessels and public transport vehicles and vessels in the *Vehicle and Vessel Tax Law of the PRC*, and the policies to encourage and support solar energy utilization systems and renewable energy development and utilization under Articles 17 and 18 of the *Renewable Energy Law*, etc.

ii) **Administrative incentives**. The administrative incentives aim to fully mobilize the general public's enthusiasm for low-carbon consumption by recognizing the advanced and motivating less advanced. According to the relevant provisions, the awardees of administrative rewards include both units and individuals with significant achievements in energy conservation management,[27] and they also

---

[25] See Article 60 of the *Energy Conservation Law*, Article 16 of the *Cleaner Production Promotion Law*, and the *Notice of the General Office of the State Council on the Control of Excessive Packaging of Goods*.

[26] See Article 5 of the *Energy Conservation Regulation for State-funded Institutions* and Article 3 of the *Regulation on Energy Conservation in Civil Buildings*.

[27] See Article 10 of the *Regulation on Energy Conservation in Civil Buildings*.

include the offence-reporter of units and individuals found with serious waste of energy.[28]

iii) **Administrative confirmation**. In the regulation of low-carbon consumption, administrative confirmation mainly refers to making authoritative certification of energy-efficient products, the functions of which are: first, certified energy-efficient products can be included in the government's priority or mandatory procurement list; second, energy-efficient products can enjoy national preferential policies, thus improving product competitiveness. For example, the government has implemented energy efficiency labeling for household appliances,[29] energy-saving product certification, issuance of energy-saving product certificates and energy-saving labels for energy-saving products.[30] This plays a fundamental role in promoting low-carbon consumption.

iv) **Administrative contract**. Administrative contracts, with their advantages of equality, voluntariness and negotiability, are also widely used in regulation of low-carbon consumption. In terms of low-carbon consumption in public institutions, public institutions can sign contractual energy management agreements with energy-saving service providers to improve the efficiency of energy consumption in public institutions.[31] In terms of individual low-carbon consumption, the government has the authority to regulate both the implementation of contractual energy management agreements between individuals and energy-saving service providers,[32] as well as agreements with companies to save resources and reduce pollutant emissions.[33]

v) **Administrative collection**. Administrative collection includes both taxes and fees. For the promotion of low-carbon consumption, China has introduced fuel taxes for individuals, and the tiered electricity, water and gas tariffs implemented nationwide in the past two years have, to a certain extent, regulated low-carbon consumption by means of charging fees.[34]

In general, although some means and measures are used to regulate individual low-carbon consumption, they are still rather fragmented and unsystematic, making them less effective.

---

[28] See Article 67 of the *Energy Conservation Law*.

[29] See Article 18 of the *Energy Conservation Law*.

[30] See Article 3 of the *Management Measures for Energy-saving Product Certification of the People's Republic of China*.

[31] See Article 26 of the *Energy Conservation Regulation for State-funded Institutions*.

[32] See the *Opinions on Accelerating the Promotion of Energy Management Contract and Promoting the Development of the Energy Conservation Service Industry*.

[33] See Article 28 of the *Cleaner Production Promotion Law*.

[34] See the *Guiding Opinions on the Pilot Implementation of Tiered Pricing for Household Electricity*, *Notice on Issues Related to the Management of Urban Water Supply Prices*, and *Guiding Opinions on Establishing a Sound System for Tiered Pricing for Household Gas*.

ii. Problems existing in individual low-carbon consumption legislation

(i) There are misunderstandings about the consumption concept

According to the traditional consumption concept, "consumers have the freedom to consume passively and actively, i.e., consumers have the right to be free from interference and are entitled to consume autonomously and consciously."[35] Specifically, how individuals consume should be solved through their own ability and market, without government intervention, let alone coercion. Due to this perception, it is deemed that the government should only promote individual low-carbon consumption through publicity and education, etc. However, this perception is not always true considering that it ignores the externality and publicity of the high-carbon consumption of individuals in our time. That is, under urgent environmental and energy resource pressures, individual high-carbon consumption can have negative impacts on the climate environment, and its adverse consequences are borne by the public, even if individuals pay the corresponding price for high-carbon consumption, it cannot compensate for the adverse consequences of their consumption behavior on the climate environment. In this regard, the market means alone cannot fully solve the problem, it must be accompanied by necessary and effective administrative regulatory means. From the perspective of practical effect, the market regulation and limited role of education and guidance promoted by government alone have not been able to yield a rather satisfying outcome of regulating citizens' low-carbon consumption. To this end, it is necessary to clarify the misconception of absolute freedom in private consumption, to understand the impact of private consumption on the environment and energy resources from the perspectives of externality and publicity, to understand the necessity and legitimacy of asking individuals practice low-carbon consumption, and to break away from the concept of absolute freedom and arbitrariness in private consumption. In turn, through relevant legislation, we can vigorously promote the consumption revolution with a variety of effective measures and restrict all members of society to widely carry out low-carbon consumption.

(ii) Preference for soft regulation, lack of hard regulation

Based on the aforementioned consumption concept, it can be found that a large number of the requirements for individual low-carbon consumption in China's legislation are soft regulations like publicity and advocacy, model guidance, contractual agreements, and incentives, etc. Despite of a very small number of taxes and fees that are mandatory, we still lacks administrative penalties and administrative coercion to regulate individual low-carbon consumption. Meanwhile, the setting of obligation of low-carbon consumption of individuals are always disjointed with setting of legal consequences. Existing legislation often only provides for general, abstract obligations for individual low-carbon consumption (such as protecting the environment, saving energy, etc.), without specifying the corresponding legal consequences of violating the obligations, or providing for specific obligations, but without specific

[35] Zhang Xiaoyi, "*Freedom of Consumption" from the Perspective of Political Science: Also on the Implications of Freedom of Ecological Consumption*, *Ecological Economy*, 2012, Issue 4.

legal responsibilities as a guarantee of fulfillment. For example, Article 40 of the *Law of the People's Republic of China on the Prevention and Control of Environmental Pollution By Solid Waste* stipulates that urban residents have the obligation to place household garbage at designated locations, but does not specify the legal consequences of violating this obligation. "The logical structure of legal norms should be composed of two elements: the pattern of behavior and the legal consequences."[36] This disjointedness between the obligatory pattern of behavior and the legal consequences makes the low-carbon consumption obligation only advocacy rather than a mandatory obligation, and administrative penalties, administrative coercion and other forms of compulsory regulation cannot be fully utilized.

(iii) **Lack of systematic legislation**

As mentioned above, China has a number of special administrative legislation regulating low-carbon consumption in public institutions, mainly including the *Energy Conservation Regulation for State-funded Institutions*, the *Regulations on Rigorous Enforcement of Economy and Anti-Waste for the Party and Government Organs*, the *Regulation on the Administration of the Institutional Affairs of Government*, the *Regulation on the Implementation of the Government Procurement*, the *Regulation on Energy Conservation in Civil Buildings*, and other administrative regulations. However, in contrast, there is a serious lack of administrative legislation regulating individual low-carbon consumption in China, except for an administrative regulatory document *Manual on Promoting Energy Conservation and Emission Reduction* issued by the Ministry of Science and Technology in 2007, there are no regulations specifically for individual low-carbon consumption, and only some scattered provisions in the *Law of the PRC on the Prevention and Control of Atmospheric Pollution, Energy Conservation Law, Environmental Protection Law, Law of the People's Republic of China on the Prevention and Control of Environmental Pollution By Solid Waste, Law of the People's Republic of China on Promoting the Development of a Recycling Economy, Cleaner Production Promotion Law*, the *Water Law*, the *Electricity Law of the PRC*, and other laws and regulations, and they are only abstract and principled regulations, resulting in a "regulatory limbo" between public low-carbon consumption and individual low-carbon consumption. This lack of legislation directly, specifically and systematically regulating individual low-carbon consumption will lead to the following consequences: first, a deficit in institutional supply, making the legal basis seriously inadequate to effectively promote individual low-carbon consumption behaviors, and failing to attract the attention of the government and society; second, the government's authority, duties and responsibilities to regulate individual low-carbon consumption are unclear, and the rights, obligations and responsibilities of individual low-carbon consumption are unclear; third, the

[36] "Three elements theory" should be adopted in the study of the logical structure of legal norm: The legal facts + normative model words + legal effect. See Liuyang, *The new theory about the logical structure of legal norm, Law and Social Development*, 2007, Issue 1.

legal regulation of individual low-carbon consumption is fragmented and asystematic, without forming an organic whole, thus directly hindering the effectiveness of the regulation.

1.3 Necessity of Strengthening the Administrative Legislation for Low-Carbon Consumption

The aforementioned problems of low-carbon consumption legislation in China, such as the emphasis on low-carbon consumption in public institutions rather than individual low-carbon consumption, the absence of mandatory regulation, the fragmentation of regulation, and the inadequate supply of institutions, call for the improvement and refinement of existing legislation, especially the strengthening of administrative legislation on low-carbon consumption. The necessity lies in the following aspects:

(I) **Consumption Can Generate Huge Carbon Emissions, and Legal Constraints on Low-carbonization must be Enhanced**

Household consumption is an important source of carbon emissions, with statistics showing that more than 80% of energy use and carbon emissions in the United States come from residential consumption and the economic activities associated with it. In China, carbon emissions from household consumption accounted for 42.17–49.21% of total carbon emissions from 1992 to 2007.[37] Consumption has an important counteraction on production, in that consumption is the driving force of production, while the purpose of production lies in consumption, and consumption plays a guiding role in the adjustment and upgrading of production. Therefore, we should pay attention to both low-carbon production and low-carbon consumption. As stressed by General Secretary Xi Jinping, we should actively promote China's energy production and consumption revolution, that is, production and consumption are the wings of a bird, wheels of a car, that shall be maintained balanced. In the process of promoting low-carbon consumption, we need to strengthen legislation in consumption, especially in individual low-carbon consumption, the reason lies not only in the counteraction role of low-carbon consumption on low-carbon production, but also in the carbon emissions generated by low-carbon consumption, especially individual low-carbon consumption.

(II) **Individual Low-carbon Consumption as a Moral Obligation has Limitations and Needs to be Reinforced by Legal Obligations**

In terms of autonomy, individuals enjoy freedom in consumption, i.e., the right to choose to purchase, use and dispose of goods on their own, a principle embodied in the provisions of Article 9 of the *Law of the People's Republic of China on*

[37] See Wang Qinhua, Zhang Zhiqiang and Qu Jiansheng, *A Review of the Scientific Assessment and Research on Household Carbon Emission*, Advances in *Earth Science*, 2013, Issue 12.

Protection of Consumer Rights and Interests.[38] Therefore, even if individuals are required to practice low-carbon consumption, it can only be a moral obligation. According to the American scholar Fuller, this is a "morality of aspiration" rather than a "morality of duty"[39]. Influenced by this, countries often adopt soft administrative means such as administrative guidance, administrative incentives or economic leverage means such as certain taxes, fees and fiscal incentives to guide low-carbon consumption. However, we believe that advocating low-carbon consumption only as a private moral obligation plays a limited role. First, the externality of consumption[40] creates a natural tension between freedom of consumption and ecological protection, and there is a "consumption-ecology" paradox,[41] based on the premise that individual consumption is unlimited while the ecological capacity that people share is limited. Individuals must assume social responsibility in consumption with corresponding restrictions. Second, private carbon consumption has not only externality, but also publicity. Publicity means that even if an individual pays the corresponding consideration, he still cannot completely eliminate the damage caused to others by his own carbon consumption. Take gasoline consumption as an example, if a person drives a private car with excessive exhaust emissions to and from work every day, even if he pays a certain amount of tax for gasoline consumption, it still cannot compensate for the negative impact of excessive carbon emissions on the atmosphere because it is only an ex-post compensation mechanism, which is void in many cases, especially for others who have already breathed in the toxic and harmful exhaust emissions from the car. In other words, the publicity of private carbon consumption shows in the conflict between the individual's right to freedom of consumption and the legitimate rights and interests of others, such as the right to health, and therefore should be included in the sharp adjustment of the legislation, because "publicity is the fundamental nature of public administration, which determines the goals of the

---

[38] See Article 9 of the *Law of the People's Republic of China on Protection of Consumer Rights and Interests* specifies that "Consumers shall enjoy the right of free choice of commodities or services".

[39] "The morality of aspiration is the morality of the good life, of excellence, of the fullest realization of human powers", and "It takes the highest state that human beings can reach as the starting point", while "The morality of duty starts from the lowest point, and establishes the basic rules that make an ordered society possible or enable an ordered society to achieve its objectives". [U.S.] Lon Luvois Fuller, *The Morality of Law*, translated by Zheng Ge, The Commercial Press, 2005, pp. 7–8.

[40] Consumption externality refers to the situation that the consumption behavior of an individual or a family affects others or the society, but in the whole socio-economic system, that individual or family does not make or obtain any compensation accordingly. See Li Jianxin, *An Analysis of Consumption Externality*, *Consumer Economics*, 2001, Issue 5.

[41] The "consumption - ecology" paradox means: "Consumption is the basic way of survival and development of mankind. If it is not restricted by morality, the endless consumption driven by desire will inevitably lead to the emergence of materialism and the rise of consumerism, thus causing the loss of morality and the destruction of the ecological environment which, as the basic premise of human survival and development, needs to be protected, and this also requires prudent power of morality, otherwise, consumption will be hindered and people must endure poverty and sacrifice development. See Zeng Jianping and Huang Yisheng, *Ethical Implications of "Consumption-Ecology" Paradox*, *Academic Journal of Zhongzhou*, 2013, Issue 7.

government and the orientation of administrative action".[42] Finally, morality is only a kind of "soft constraint", relying on moral constraints such as conscience condemnation and public pressure alone is not enough to promote individual low-carbon consumption, and a large number of examples in practice have demonstrated this, such as in the elimination of public spending on food and drink, and the prohibition of water and electricity waste, in which the moral self-discipline alone has played a limited role. Therefore, it is necessary to regulate individual low-carbon consumption by the "hard constraint" of law.

1.4 Improvement of the Administrative Legislation for Low-Carbon Consumption

(I) **Improve the Legislation for Low-carbon Consumption in Public Institutions**

China's administrative legislation has constructed a relatively comprehensive regulatory system for low-carbon consumption in public institutions, but it still needs to be improved in the following aspects.

i. **Improve the provisions of low-carbon procurement in public institutions**

The types, procedures, and methods of procurement of goods by public institutions will affect the consumption of resources and energy as well as carbon emissions of public institutions. Therefore, the procurement behavior itself should be included in the legislation, and the process and results of procurement behavior should be required to achieve low-carbonization, i.e., short procurement cycle, low cost, and economical, energy-saving and electronic ways of procurement for public goods should be adopted. Therefore, it is necessary to amend and improve the *Government Procurement Law*: first, it should establish the principle of low-carbon procurement; second, it should establish an electronic public bidding priority system; third, it should clarify the obligations of mandatory low-carbon procurement and corresponding legal responsibilities; fourth, it should guarantee the right of public participation.

First of all, the *Government Procurement Law* shall assimilate the low-carbon procurement concepts in the *Energy Conservation Law*, the *Energy Conservation Regulation for State-funded Institutions*, the *Cleaner Production Promotion Law*, the *Regulation on the Administration of the Institutional Affairs of Government*, the *Regulations on Rigorous Enforcement of Economy and Anti-Waste for the Party and Government Organs*, and other laws and regulations, and establish the principles of low-carbon procurement by drawing on the common practices[43] of green procurement of governments around the world. The low-carbon procurement principle is

[42] Zhang Kangzhi, *On "Publicity" and Its Realization in Public Administration*, *Southeast Academic Research*, 2005, Issue 1.

[43] Like provisions for green purchase in chapter 23 in *Federal Acquisition Regulation* of the United States of America, in *The Government Green Procurement Guide* of EU, in *The Law of Encouraging*

that state organs, institutions and organizations at all levels should choose low-carbon procurement methods and purchase low-carbon public goods for administrative use, when using public funds to purchase goods or projects in the procurement process. The low-carbon public goods for administrative use here should include not only the low-carbon goods stipulated in the prevailing laws, such as energy-saving and environment-friendly raw materials, fuels, equipment and products, but also low-carbon projects, such as green buildings or structures. The principle of low-carbon procurement shall be followed all-aroundly, including procurement subjects, procurement methods, procurement procedures, and procurement targets. Specifically, first, in terms of procurement subjects, the principle of low-carbon procurement applies not only to state organs, institutions and organizations at all levels as stipulated in the *Government Procurement Law*, but also to other subjects providing public services, such as social organizations and individuals, who may also refer to the *Government Procurement Law*. Second, in terms of procurement methods, the government, rather than simply requiring giving priority to centralized public bidding during the procurement of public goods for administrative use, should give flexibility to procurement method that generates less carbon emission as the case may be. Third, in terms of procurement procedures, it is necessary to shorten the cycle and reduce the formalities of government procurement, and to reduce the excess carbon emissions caused by formalism by strengthening the post-facto information disclosure, justification and monitoring mechanisms. In other words, the design concept of procurement procedures should give priority to efficiency, and prefer post-facto supervision procedures to cumbersome procedures in the midst of the matter, because with a sound post-facto supervision system, the possibility of malpractices of the purchaser will be greatly reduced, while the cumbersome procedures and excessively long cycle will sacrifice the low-carbon and economical value of procedures. Fourth, in terms of procurement objects, the government procurement of public goods for administrative purposes should include not only goods, but also works, which to a certain extent can deter local governments from building luxury buildings and pavilions.

Second, we should gradually give priority to the electronic public bidding system. According to Article 10 of *Regulation on the Implementation of the Government Procurement*, and electronic government procurement requirements given in *Overall Plan for the Construction of National Government Sourcing Management Trade System* and *Regulations on Rigorous Enforcement of Economy and Anti-Waste for the Party and Government Organs*, the financial sectors need to accelerate the construction of unified management and trading platform for national electronic government procurement. The *Government Procurement Law* should not only adhere to the existing procurement method of giving priority to public bidding, but also promote the electronic government procurement method in a timely manner, and gradually

the Procurement of Environmentally Friendly Products of South Korea, and in *Green Procurement Law* of Japan. See Qinpeng, *Government Green Purchase: Logic Point, Microcosmic Effect and Legal System*, *Journal of Social Science*, 2007, Issue 7.

give priority to the electronic public bidding method in future government procurement. The *Government Procurement Law* should establish the priority rule of electronic open tendering through exclusionary legislation, i.e. clearly stipulating the scope where E-government procurement is not required, for example, the case where the time required for E-government procurement cannot meet the urgent procurement needs of the user, and the case where the cost for E-government procurement (including the economic, time, human and material costs) is higher than the cost for direct procurement by the user. Except for the exceptions clearly stipulated by the law, all other cases are within the scope of E-government procurement.

Third, the mandatory low-carbon procurement obligations and the corresponding legal responsibilities should be clearly defined. The *Government Procurement Law* should clearly stipulate the legal obligations and legal responsibilities of purchasers for compulsory procurement of low-carbon administrative public property, and change the current authorization norms to mandatory norms, i.e. purchasers will bear legal responsibilities if they fail to perform the mandatory obligations of procuring low-carbon administrative public property. Specifically, Article 71 of the *Government Procurement Law* should add two situations where purchasers or procurement agencies should be held liable for the violation of mandatory low-carbon procurement obligations: that is, the behavior of changing the procurement mode of electronic open tendering into other modes without authorization and the behavior of intentionally procuring goods or projects that do not meet low-carbon standards.

Finally, the participation right of the public should be guaranteed. First, the low-carbon procurement information disclosure system should be improved. Public institutions should disclose to the public the information about the procurement of administrative public property by purchasers, to protect the public's right to know. Specifically, the entities for information disclosure are mainly public institutions that procure administrative public property; the scope of the disclosure should include the procurement results of administrative public property by the public institutions, e.g. the eight pieces of procurement information specified in Article 8 of the *Administrative Measures for Government Procurement Information Announcements*, and the reasons for government procurement of administrative public property; purchasers should actively disclose the information about the procurement of administrative public property, and disclose the same to the public through government bulletins, government websites, press conferences, newspapers, radio, television or other methods that are easy for the public to know such information; citizens, legal persons, or other organizations may apply to purchasers for disclosure of the above-mentioned government procurement information according to law; and if any purchaser fails to perform the obligation to disclose government information according to law, the counterparts have the right to apply for administrative review or file an administrative lawsuit. Second, the low-carbon procurement reason explanation system should be improved. This mainly includes: (i) explaining the reasons why the public institution chooses the procurement mode, the reason why the purchaser procures the goods or projects, the reasons why the purchaser chooses the winning bidder, the reason why the government procurement price is higher than the market price, and so on. (ii) The reasons should be actively explained by the government in general, and sometimes may be explained according to application. (iii) The reasons should be explained to not only the third parties who have an interest in government procurement, but also the general public who have no interest in it. (iv) Public institutions should explain the reasons in a timely manner, and in principle should explain them in written form. Third, it is required to stipulate and protect the public's right to make suggestions, the right to make complaints and impeachment, and the right to file a public welfare lawsuit with respect to low-carbon government procurement. The public should have the right to make reasonable suggestions on government procurement, and have the right to provide reference information sources for government procurement of goods and projects. Public institutions should give appropriate rewards to the public who provide constructive suggestions. The public also has the right to make complaints and impeachment to relevant state agencies and to file public welfare lawsuits to the people's court in their own names or in the name of the public against misconduct or negligence during government procurement.

ii. **Improving regulations on public institutions' low-carbon use of public property**

The "public property" here refers to all goods and resources used by public institutions. With the development of economy, more and more types of goods are used by public institutions in China, which may cause various kinds of waste. This is against the low-carbon consumption obligations of public institutions. Therefore, it is also very necessary to incorporate public institutions' behavior of low-carbon use of "public property" into the scope of legislative adjustments. The *Regulations on Rigorous Enforcement of Economy and Anti-Waste for the Party and Government Organs*, *Energy Conservation Regulation for State-funded Institutions*, and *Regulation on the Administration of the Institutional Affairs of Government* have all contained some provisions on the use of public property by public institutions. The basic principle is "rigorous enforcement of economy and anti-waste", and the control standard is "not exceeding the legal total amount/quota". For example, Article 4 of the *Regulations on Rigorous Enforcement of Economy and Anti-Waste for the Party and Government Organs* proposes "total amount control", and Article 16 of the *Energy Conservation Regulation for State-funded Institutions* provides the "energy consumption quota" system for public institutions. In addition, a large number of regulations on energy conservation and anti-waste are provided in Article 47 of the *Energy Conservation Law*, Article 25 of the *Law of the People's Republic of China on Promoting the Development of a recycling Economy*, Article 29 of the *Energy Conservation Regulation for State-funded Institutions*, Articles 25, 28, and 29 of *Regulation on the Administration of the Institutional Affairs of Government*, *Regulations on Rigorous Enforcement of Economy and Anti-Waste for the Party and Government Organs* and the Eight-point Rules of CPC Central Committee. However, in terms of the use of public property, the specific standards for energy conservation or waste are not complete and clear, and it is required to improve the *Regulations on Rigorous Enforcement of Economy and Anti-Waste for the Party and Government Organs*, *Energy Conservation Regulation for State-funded Institutions*, *Regulation on the*

Administration of the Institutional Affairs of Government and other supporting regulations, and to prepare a list of standards and methods that can be used to quantify the low-carbon utilization of all kinds of public property. For example, the standards for construction and use of office buildings of public institutions at all levels, standards for official business vehicles and travels, standards for official clothing and reception, standards for use of water, electricity and other energies, and standards for procurement and consumption of office supplies. The establishment of these standards can also provide benchmarks for recognizing the "waste" specified in the Regulations on Rigorous Enforcement of Economy and Anti-Waste for the Party and Government Organs, and the "luxury goods", "super-standard services", "luxury office buildings" and other similar items with fuzzy concepts that are prohibited by Article 14 of the *Regulation on the Administration of the Institutional Affairs of Government*. It is required to ensure all these standards are complied with and implemented through the reward and punishment mechanism.

(II) **Strengthening Special Legislation on Individual Low-carbon Consumption**

As mentioned above, the administrative legislation for individual low-carbon consumption in China has many defects, such as misunderstanding of regulatory concepts, lack of regulatory law sources, vagueness of regulatory standards, formulation of soft regulations, lack of hard regulations, and fragmentation of regulating methods. Due to the lack of special legislation on individual low-carbon consumption in China, the State Council should formulate the *Regulations on the Promotion of Citizens' Low-Carbon Consumption* in a timely manner by making use of the advantages of the convenience and timeliness of administrative legislation and making reference to the requirements of the *Energy Conservation Regulation for State-funded Institutions, Regulations on Rigorous Enforcement of Economy and Anti-Waste for the Party and Government Organs* and other administrative regulations for public institutions, to integrate and centralize relevant provisions currently scattered in numerous laws and regulations, and to impose comprehensive and systematic regulations on rigorous enforcement of economy and anti-waste against individual consumption, or may have relevant ministries and commissions and local governments formulate regulations on the promotion of citizens' low-carbon consumption first, and then enact uniform administrative regulations when the time is ripe. The basic framework of this administrative legislation on low-carbon consumption should include legislative purposes, legislative principles, legislative adjustment objects, legislative adjustment matters, adjustment methods, etc.

i. **Legislative purposes**

Determining the purposes of the administrative legislation on low-carbon consumption is a prerequisite for giving play to the regulating and leading role of legislation. The purposes of the administrative legislation restricting individual low-carbon consumption should include the following aspects:

(i) **Ensuring survival and development consumption**. The survival and development consumption is the basic consumption necessary for citizens to maintain their daily life. This basic consumption can be determined as an average value in terms of energy resource consumption and carbon emission standards, i.e. the per capita annual energy consumption and carbon emission standards necessary for individuals to maintain their average living standards within the range of total amount control. It is the basic consumption necessary for citizens to maintain their daily life and must be guaranteed. Therefore, individual consumption within this standard should be considered low-carbon consumption. Of course, even if individual consumption falls within this standard, there is still potential for energy conservation and emission reduction, for example, trying to adopt a low-carbon lifestyle that is most energy-saving and most conducive to environmental protection as far as possible within the standard control scope. However, in this regard, legislation can only require adopting an advocacy approach rather than a mandatory approach. That is to say, the degree of legal intervention is limited, and administrative entities can only be required to guide citizens through administrative education, administrative guidance and other flexible methods, while citizens have only moral obligation or legal advocacy obligation,[44] rather than mandatory obligation. Let's take the tiered water and electricity prices as an example. Tier-1 price is relatively low because it is for the basic water and electricity consumption necessary for citizens to maintain their daily life, i.e. a kind of survival and development consumption of individuals or organizations.

(ii) **Restricting luxury consumption and prohibiting wasteful consumption**. Different from survival and development consumption, luxury consumption is a kind of consumption that is beyond the basic consumption standards and excessively pursues enjoyment, while wasteful consumption is a kind of consumption that unnecessarily squanders, wastes, or abandons energy resources. The administrative legislation restricting individual low-carbon consumption focuses on restricting luxury consumption and prohibiting wasteful consumption.

The survival and development consumption is limited to the per capita annual energy consumption and carbon emission standards necessary for individuals to maintain their average living standards. The individual consumption that exceeds the average annual per capita energy consumption will be considered as luxury consumption, which is mainly reflected in some indicators of high-carbon life, for example, the monthly consumption of water, electricity, gas and other energies exceeding the basic quotas (the amount allowed to be consumed in the basic prices in the tiered prices), and the private procurement of cars with bigger engines, high-grade housing and luxury goods with high carbon emissions (standards for these products and their catalog may be

[44] The advocacy obligation is only a principled guide. It reflects the value judgment of legislators, but does not necessarily affect the behavior of actors, or backed by the coercive force of state or legal consequences. See Yang Shibing, *On Advocacy Legal Norms*, *Qilu Journal*, 2011, Issue 5.

approved and published by the state, and these products should be marked by manufacturers or sellers). Because luxury consumption and wasteful consumption have exceeded the limits of basic consumption necessary to maintain daily life, and have caused excessive or unnecessary consumption of limited energy resources, they should be restricted or prohibited. This should be not only a moral obligation but also a mandatory legal obligation. Therefore, legislation should strengthen the corresponding regulations. In addition to educating and guiding consumers in a flexible way, legislation must also limit luxury consumption and wasteful consumption by making full use of the means of imposing taxes and fees for purchasing carbon emission rights, administrative enforcement, etc. For serious waste behaviors in consumption, such as large amounts of food waste, diners may even receive administrative penalties, e.g. warnings and fines.

(iii) **Building a social life model that regards energy conservation and environment protection as an honor, and fully implements low-carbon consumption**. China's energy consumption revolution aims to achieve low-carbon development through the regulation of consumption links. It is a giant project that reshapes social consumption life. It cannot be achieved only through moral requirements and advocacy guidelines, but also in the implementation of institutional arrangements in the way of rule of law. To this end, the *Regulations on the Promotion of Citizens' Low-Carbon Consumption* should be formulated to regulate the behaviors of all members of society. Through the design of the legal right-obligation relationship and the code of conduct in legal responsibilities, it will make the social life model of low-carbon consumption legally institutionalized, thus effectively promoting the low-carbon consumption action that regards energy conservation and environment protection as an honor in the whole society.

ii. **Legislative principles**

(i) **The principle of proceeding from China's reality**. This principle requires that the administrative legislation for individual low-carbon consumption must be based on China's current national conditions. This has the following meanings. First, it is required to fully understand the necessity and urgency of promoting low-carbon consumption as people's legal obligation in China. This includes both international and domestic factors. In terms of international factors, China is the world's largest developing country and the world's biggest source of carbon emissions, and also a party to both *United Nations Framework Convention on Climate Change* and *Kyoto Protocol*. Now, the first commitment period where China does not undertake the compulsory international carbon emission reduction obligation has passed, and *China-US Joint Statement on Climate Change* has set a schedule for China's carbon emission reduction. It is extremely urgent for China to perform its carbon emission reduction obligation. This is an international legal obligation acknowledged by China as a country to the international community, while its performance can only be completed by all Chinese citizens to perform their shares after this obligation is transformed through domestic laws and shared by all citizens. In terms of domestic factors, China has determined that its carbon dioxide emissions per unit of GDP will be reduced by 40% to 45% by 2020, from the level in 2005,[45] and the *Comprehensive Work Plan for Energy Conservation and Emission Reduction in the 12th Five-Year Plan Period* and other relevant policies have clearly stated the specific tasks and measures for energy conservation and emission reduction. To guarantee the realization of these goals, tasks and measures, relevant laws and regulations need to be formulated and implemented. Second, China is a developing country with a large population. It is required to balance the relationship between economic and social development and energy resource conservation and ecological environmental protection while strengthening legislation that restricts individual low-carbon consumption. This requires not only promoting economic development by stimulating consumption and stimulating domestic demand, but also restricting unreasonable consumption that wastes energy resources and increases the pressure on the ecological environment. Therefore, legislation should guide low-carbon production and promote economic development from the perspective of vigorously stimulating low-carbon consumption. At the same time, restricting people's low-carbon consumption can also restrict the behaviors of wasting energy resources and destroying the ecological environment. Third, legislation on individual low-carbon consumption must stipulate low-carbon consumption patterns that are in line with the actual conditions of China. First, legislation should vigorously promote and revive the excellent traditional virtues of Chinese people, such as diligence and thrift, and make full use of them to give full play to the guiding role of spiritual beliefs. Second, legislation should focus on the elimination of some bad habits that exist in Chinese people's consumption, e.g. consumption comparison and waste of resources for maintaining a good reputation. Third, on the principle of "energy resource conservation and ecological environment protection", legislation should properly consider the consumption conditions, consumption habits and consumption preferences of people in different regions and different classes, to form a rich and diverse low-carbon consumption pattern. Fourth, the regulations on low-carbon consumption of Chinese citizens specified by legislation should be gradually improved. To a large extent, low-carbon consumption is a major change in people's lifestyle and habits. Since people are still unable to fully adapt to low-carbon consumption currently, legislation should not be separated from reality or make "one-size-fits-all" regulations, instead, it is a classified and gradually strengthened process.

(ii) **The principle of differentiation**. Low-carbon consumption involves different domains and entities, and the objectives and methods of regulation should be diversified, so the principle of differentiation should be implemented. China's

[45] See Li Shaohui, *Small-scale Thermal Plants with a Total of 60.06 Million Kilowatts Shut Down Nationwide*, *China Reform Daily*, January 7, 2010.

Program of Action for the Energy Development Strategy has clearly pointed out the "principle of differentiation", emphasizing the necessity of distinguishing the energy consumption characteristics of different regions and industries. Article 16 of *Energy Conservation Regulation for State-funded Institutions* also provides different energy consumption quotas and different expenditure standards for public institutions in different industries and different systems. Anthony, a British scholar, pointed out that "Environmental protection needs to be specific, because the cost of loss caused by pollution varies significantly in different regions and even in different areas of the same region. The reason is that regions differ from each other in the pollutant absorbing capacity of waters and air, ideal environmental quality and number of pollution sources."[46] The principle of differentiation applies not only to the management of energy conservation and emission reduction in public institutions, but should likewise be applied to the area of individual low-carbon consumption. The principle of differentiation means that the legislation should provide different low-carbon consumption standards and apply different regulation methods for different regions and entities. For example, different low-carbon regulation standards should be adopted for direct and indirect energy consumption and for the consumption in different regions with different development levels and conditions. Advocacy, incentive and other flexible regulation methods should be applied to promote the low-carbonization of survival and development consumption, while compulsory, punitive and other rigid regulation methods should be adopted to restrict or prohibit luxury and wasteful consumption. For different types of individual consumption, such as clothing, food, housing and transportation, different low-carbon requirements should be specified.

(iii) **Cooperative governance principle**. Promoting low-carbon consumption in the whole society is a systemic project that requires actions led by the government and participated by all citizens. It needs the state and society to cooperate with each other for public-private cooperative governance. Cooperative governance, also known as cooperative regulation or cooperative administration, is a supplement to and replacement of the traditional command and control regulation of the government.[47] The theory of cooperative governance changes the government-centered management style[48] and proposes a collaborative, cooperative, and complementary co-governance model that mobilizes social forces to positively interact with the government. For the regulation of low-carbon consumption in the whole society, legislation should construct a cooperative governance model; clearly specify the functions and responsibilities of

[46] [U.K.] Anthony I. Ogus, *Regulation: Legal Form and Economic Theory*, translated by Luo Meiying, China Renmin University Press, 2008 version, p. 170.

[47] Gao Qinwei, *Private Entity and Food Safety Standard Establishment—Based on the Legal Principles of Cooperative Regulation*, *Peking University Law Journal*, 2012, Issue 4.

[48] See Zhang Kangzhi, *On Participatory Governance, Social Autonomy and Cooperative Governance*, *Administrative Tribune*, 2008, Issue 6.

governments at all levels and relevant functional departments; state the collaborative functions of social organizations to bring into play the regulatory role of all social forces, including enterprises, institutions, consumer associations, industry organizations, rural and community grass-roots organizations, stores and restaurants; and specify the extensive participation of the public, and implement the regulation methods that work together with legal norms by applying social norms, such as conventions of citizens, rural rules and regulations, and industry regulations and charters of organizations.

iii. **Scope of matters for legislative adjustment**

The *Regulations on the Promotion of Citizens' Low-Carbon Consumption* should adjust the low-carbon consumption behaviors of private entities. The private entities here refer to citizens and organizations other than public institutions. Their low-carbon consumption behaviors, according to the classification of the *Manual on Promoting Energy Conservation and Emission Reduction* issued by the Ministry of Science and Technology of the People's Republic of China in 2007, can include behaviors associated with clothing, food, housing, transportation, and other daily commodities. The low-carbon consumption legislation for these five domains should put forward the most basic low-carbon requirements. For example, it should guide people to buy less unnecessary clothes, buy clothes made of low-carbon materials, and wash clothes in energy-saving methods in terms of clothing; require people not to waste food and implement the "empty plate" campaign in terms of food; require people to carry out low-carbon decoration in terms of housing; encourage people to buy small-displacement vehicles or new energy vehicles, and try to choose low-carbon travel modes by taking public transportation or non-motor vehicles in terms of transportation; and require people to reasonably and economically use water, electricity, gas, fuel oil, coal or other articles for daily use in terms of daily commodities.

iv. **Main regulatory methods for individual low-carbon consumption**

The regulatory methods that should be adopted for individual low-carbon consumption can be divided into three categories: flexible methods, such as administrative guidance and administrative award; rigid methods, such as administrative collection and administrative enforcement; and legal liability, such as administrative penalties.

(i) Flexible methods, such as administrative guidance, administrative award, and administrative contract, are mainly used to encourage citizens to actively implement low-carbon consumption through publicity, education, demonstration, guidance, benefit incentive, negotiation and collaboration, suitable for groups of survival and development consumption.
(ii) Rigid methods, such as tax collection and administrative enforcement, are mainly used to force citizens to implement low-carbon consumption to some extent by imposing property obligations and behavioral obligations on them, suitable for groups of luxury and wasteful consumption. The administrative collection against low-carbon consumption includes collecting fees and

collecting taxes. The state can levy the carbon tax or carbon fee on objects whose carbon emissions exceed the quotas. This has been implemented in foreign countries. For example, some EU member states, such as Finland, Sweden, Denmark, and the United Kingdom, have already levied taxes of carbon tax nature on the consumption of fossil fuels according to carbon emissions. Japan requires people to buy carbon emission rights before purchasing motor vehicles.[49] Relevant legislations are also available in China, such as the *Law of the PRC on the Prevention and Control of Atmospheric Pollution*, *Regulation on the Administration of Collection and Use of Pollutant Discharge Fees*, and *Measures for the Administration of the Charging Rates for Pollutant Discharge Fees*. These laws and regulations have provided the charging systems for the emission of atmospheric pollutants. Accordingly, the *Regulations on the Promotion of Citizens' Low-Carbon Consumption* should specify that a certain amount of carbon tax or carbon fee should be levied on individual carbon emissions exceeding the quotas. For some luxury consumer goods with high carbon emissions, in addition to their normal prices, a certain amount of carbon emission fees (i.e. purchasing the carbon emissions rights) can be levied in the sales process, or the carbon tax can be directly levied. For the energy supply that can be directly controlled by the public power of the government, such as tap water, electricity and gas supplies, if a citizen's consumption exceeds the unallowable limits, but he/she still refuses to make corrections after being warned, the government may strictly limit his/her consumption of water, electricity and gas within a certain period of time, i.e. taking the compulsory measures of supplying water, electricity and gas only necessary for maintaining his/her basic life within limited periods. For vehicles with excessive carbon emissions, forced scrapping may be implemented.

(iii) Administrative penalties and other forms of legal responsibility are mainly applied to behaviors that damage the ecological environment or cause serious waste in individual consumption. For example, for the behaviors of driving vehicles with excessive carbon emissions, or seriously wasting food, legislation should stipulate that administrative penalties may be taken, such as warning, recording illegal acts in carbon footprint files and disclosing to the public, and fining a certain amount. With regard to the implementation of administrative penalties, citizens are encouraged to report relevant clues, and then law enforcement agencies are responsible for the implementation. The implementation of minor penalties, such as warnings, recording illegal acts in carbon footprint files and disclosing to the public, can be authorized to some social organizations, e.g. neighborhood committees, village committees, hotels, and restaurants.

---

[49] See Xie Deliang, *Japanese People Must Buy Carbon Emissions Rights Before Buying Vehicles*, *Green Living*, 2013, Issue 9.

2 Resources for the Effective Implementation of Low-Carbon "Soft Law" Should Be Fully Allocated in the Law Formulation[50]

2.1 Application of Soft Law in the Construction of a Low-Carbon Society

Soft law is an emerging topic in jurisprudence research in recent years and a new kind of legal institutional supply in legislative practice. Professor Luo Haocai has pointed out that soft law "refers to those legal norms that may not have a complete effect structure and do not need to rely on the state to guarantee their implementation, but can produce social effectiveness."[51] Hard law has the advantages of stipulating clear rights, obligations and responsibilities, and effective implementation guaranteed by the coercive force of the state, and its important role in the mandatory promotion of a low-carbon society is self-evident. However, China currently has limited hard law in this area, while the development and application of soft law are very commonly seen in various low-carbon construction areas such as consumption reduction and emission reduction, circular economy, and low-carbon certification. In recent years, a large number of laws, rules, regulations and normative documents have been issued with names indicating soft law methods and names such as "promotion", "generalization" and "incentives" in the central and local governments to promote the construction of a low-carbon society. The laws introduced include the *Law of the People's Republic of China on Promoting the Development of a recycling Economy* and the *Cleaner Production Promotion Law*. In accordance with the *Law of the People's Republic of China on Promoting the Development of a recycling Economy* and *Cleaner Production Promotion Law*, almost all provinces and municipalities in China have formulated the corresponding local *Regulations* and *Implementation Measures*. For example, the *Regulations on the Promotion of low-carbon Economy in Anhui Province*, the *Regulations on the Promotion of Circular Economy in Shanxi Province*, the *Regulations on the Promotion of Cleaner Production in Yunnan Province*, the *Regulations on the Promotion of Cleaner Production in Tianjin*, the *Regulations on the Promotion of Cleaner Production in Shandong Province*, and the *Implementation Measures on the Promotion of Cleaner Production in Nanjing*, etc. The *Interim Measures for the Administration of Voluntary Greenhouse Gas Emission Reduction Transactions*, the *Interim Measures for the Management of Energy Conservation and low-carbon Technology Promotion*, and the *Interim Measures for Public Participation in Environmental Impact Assessment* formulated by the relevant departments of the State Council, as well as the *Measures for Energy Conservation Incentives in Shandong Province*, the *Trial Measures for*

[50] Part of this section has been published in *Studies in Law and Business*, 2013 (3), under the title of *On the Resource Guarantee for the Implementation of "Soft Law" in Public Law*.

[51] See Luo Haocai and Song Gongde: *Taking Soft Law Seriously—The General Theory of Public Soft Law and Its Practice in China*, *China Legal Science*, 2006 (2).

Energy Conservation Incentives in Guangdong Province, and the *Interim Measures for Energy Conservation and Emission Reduction Incentives in Beijing*, formulated by some local governments, are all soft law in nature. Administrative legislation accounts for a significant portion of these soft laws. The current situation shows that soft law is a widely used legislation to regulate the promotion of low-carbon development, and is gaining momentum. This is mainly because that, at this stage of low-carbon society construction, limited by the existing social conditions and people's awareness, the national low-carbon regulations should not be fully constrained by rigid coercive means, but should be gradually promoted by flexible methods such as advocacy, guidance and encouragement. In general, China and the world at large are still in the initial stage of building a low-carbon society, and the level of awareness and recognition of low-carbon economy and low-carbon life among members of the general society is generally not high. A 2012 statistical analysis of a sample of 3,489 found that the average percentage of those willing to accept low-carbon living and take action on climate change was less than 33%[52]; a survey conducted by the American Broadcasting Corporation on the general public's views on policy of increasing taxes on electricity and gasoline to reduce energy consumption also found that their support rates were only 20% and 32%, respectively.[53] Under such circumstances, if a hard law is enacted directly, there may be great social resistance and social conflicts. As Giddens has repeatedly reiterated, "fear is not necessarily the best motivator to get people to respond to climate change."[54] In this regard, lessons can be learned from Australia whose carbon tax legislation has been enacted and then repealed. After the Australian government announced its carbon tax proposal in May 2011, polls showed that more than 60% of the population opposed the carbon tax, with a support rate of only 30%.[55] In the face of low public support rating, the Australian government's decision to impose a carbon tax sparked a strong social backlash, with more than 5,000 trucks from across the country entering the capital Canberra in batches, honking their horns to oppose the carbon tax, and asking for re-election.[56] Facing huge social controversy, the Australian Senate finally passed a series of bills to repeal the carbon tax in July 2014.[57] In contrast to hard law, soft law favors guidance rather than coercion. For low-carbon construction, the progress could only be made gradually and it will be accepted by society gradually, it is now necessary to induce and motivate members of society through the enactment of soft laws.

---

[52] See Xie Hongzuo and Chen Tao: *Analysis on Factors Influencing Public Willingness to Act on Climate Change in China*, *China Soft Science*, 2012 (3).

[53] See Chang Genying et al.: *Public Perceptions of Global Warming and Support for Climate Policy in the United States*, *Advances in Climate Change Research*, 2012 (4).

[54] [UK] Anthony Giddens: *The Politics of Climate Change*, Translated by Cao Rongxiang, Social Sciences Academic Press, 2009, p. 160.

[55] Anonymous: *Why Australia's Carbon Tax Became a Target*, *International Financial News*, May 5, 2011 (Fourth Edition).

[56] See Li Jingwei: *Australian Trucks Rally Against Carbon Tax*, *People's Daily*, August 23, 2011.

[57] Anonymous: *Australia Repeals Carbon Tax Amidst Controversy*, Xinhuanet: http://news.xinhuanet.com/energy/2014-07/21/c_1111712703.htm, accessed January 3, 2015.

As a legislative phenomenon, soft law has been widely used in many areas of low-carbon society construction. However, the proliferation of such soft laws does not mean that they have been effectively implemented. Their implementation effectiveness after their enactment cannot be evaluated yet, and they have not received attention. This suggests that we should pay attention to the conditions to guarantee the effective implementation of soft law when a large number of soft laws are formulated, and there are obviously some areas that need to be studied and improved in this regard in the relevant administrative legislation.

2.2 *Proposal of Ensuring the Effective Implementation of Soft Law*

Soft laws enacted by the state have many similarities with hard laws: they are both enacted by the legislature in accordance with legal procedures, they both embody the will of the state, they both are norms of behavior for members of society, and both require universal compliance. In this sense, it can be said that "soft law is also law". However, there are also differences: soft law is flexible in terms of norms and requirements and is implemented without the use of state coercive power, and its formulation and implementation have more room for democratic consultation.[58] The most significant difference is whether their implementation relies on the coercive power of the state. The implementation of hard law relies on the coercive power of the state, while the implementation of soft law relies mainly on the self-restraint of members of society and the "non-coercive" enforcement of law enforcement agencies. However, how can members of society develop self-discipline in complying with soft law? How can the "non-coercive" enforcement by law enforcement agencies be guaranteed to be effective? In other words, how to ensure the effective implementation of soft law without relying on the coercive power of the state to form a unique law enforcement mechanism? This involves the resources on which the implementation of soft law depends. In a country's rule of law governance, the implementation of law usually requires two kinds of support resources, namely, oppressive resources and guiding resources. Oppressive resources are external violent powers, including systematic coercive and disciplinary regulations, law enforcement forces such as police, and judicial institutions such as courts and prisons. The guiding resources are the ideal goal, value pursuit, morality and ethics, public order and good customs, benefit distribution, human-based management and other inherent inspirational power contained in the law. Enforcement of hard law can use both types of resources, with oppressive resources serving as a bottom-line guarantee to compel members of society to comply with the law's provisions. Soft law, on the other hand, can only be implemented by fully mobilizing the guiding resources to win hearts of the members of the society. Guiding resources vary in sources and forms, and in general, they are

[58] See Luo Haocai and Song Gongde: *Taking Soft Law Seriously—The General Theory of Public Soft Law and Its Practice in China*, *China Legal Science*, 2006 (2).

the cohesion of society built by the state using various non-violent resources such as spiritual, material, and working methods. Guiding resources are inherent gravitation, which constitutes the fundamental basis for guaranteeing the implementation of the law. The implementation of the law based on guiding resources is the highest and optimal level of law implementation, because it is based on the harmonious implementation achieved by social members' active pursuit and positive response rather than against their will. By observing the content of the current low-carbon soft laws, we can see that the main guiding resources used are material benefits (including intellectual achievements and services, etc.) to guarantee implementation. Such low-carbon legislation rarely stipulates punitive legal liability (some punitive provisions are applicable to the government and not to the public) to guarantee implementation. The major method to guarantee its implementation is to reward those who achieve the legal target with certain material benefits or financial preferential policies, etc., in order to increase their motivation to comply with the law and enhance their incentive to take low-carbon actions. For example, the *Assessment Methods for Total Emission Reduction of Major Pollutants* developed by the Ministry of Ecology and Environment stipulates that "for the ones who deemed qualified in the assessment, the competent departments of environmental protection under the State Council, in conjunction with the development and reform departments and the financial departments shall give priority to increasing the financial support for pollution control and environmental protection capacity-building in the region."[59] The *Measures for Energy Conservation Incentives in Shandong Province* provides for an award of RMB 1 million for each unit and enterprise that makes outstanding contributions to energy conservation, an award of RMB 1 million for each major energy conservation achievement, and an award of RMB 50,000 for each excellent energy conservation achievement.[60] *Interim Measures for Energy Conservation and Emission Reduction Incentives in Beijing* and *Trial Measures for Energy Conservation Incentives in Guangdong Province* have similar provisions. The relevant departments of the State Council had promulgated the *Interim Measures for the Management of Energy Conservation and low-carbon Technology Promotion* aiming to accelerate the progress and popularization of energy-saving and low-carbon technologies, and guide energy-using units to actively adopt advanced and applicable new energy-saving and low-carbon technologies, new equipment and new processes, thereby promoting the economical use of energy resources, effectively alleviating the pressure on resources and the environment, and reducing carbon dioxide and other greenhouse gas emissions.[61] The Measures are mainly used as guiding resources for implementation through free technology promotion services, financial support and training, rather than relying on mandatory, punitive means. The *Measures for the Administration of the Paid Use of the China Clean Development Mechanism Fund* and *China's Special*

[59] Refer to Article 9 of the *Assessment Methods for Total Emission Reduction of Major Pollutants.*

[60] Refer to Article 14 of *The Measures for Energy Conservation Incentives in Shandong Province.*

[61] Refer to the *Interim Measures for the Management of Energy Conservation and low-carbon Technology Promotion* issued by the National Development and Reform Commission, *Renewable Resources and Circular Economy*, 2014 (2).

SciTech Campaign to Cope with Climate Change, on the other hand, mainly guide society to actively carry out low-carbon practices through the rational use of funds, increased investment in science and technology, greater financial support for scientific research and technology development on climate change, and strengthening the construction of science and technology infrastructure and condition platforms and other material resources.

However, it is not enough to merely rely on material benefit as guiding resources to guarantee implementation in the formulation of soft law. On the one hand, material benefit as guiding resources requires huge financial support, which is difficult to be continuously and universally used; on the other hand, the profit-oriented concept may develop in the society affecting by mere material benefit incentives. The practice of low-carbon activities is essentially a public good for the benefit of society, mankind and the future, which cannot be driven only by short-term material benefits for individuals. In addition to the necessary supply of material benefits, more diversified guiding resources need to be tapped to guarantee implementation.

2.3 Full Development of Guiding Resources

When formulating low-carbon soft laws, administrative legislation should pay due attention to the preparation of relevant guiding resources to guarantee the effective implementation of soft laws after their introduction; The guiding resources can be developed and applied from various aspects such as legislation content, legislation methods, government credibility, enforcement methods and law-abiding publicity.

(I) **The Use of Legislation Content as a Guiding Resource**

For soft law, good content is an important prerequisite for its effective implementation. If the formulation of soft law focuses on the textual presentation and institutional supply of guiding resources in the legislation, and comprehensively provides spiritual resources, material rights and interests resources and behavioral pattern resources, the citizens will consciously follow from their own interest and inner obedience, and thus providing strong guarantee to the smooth implementation of soft law.

i. From the perspective of spiritual resources, soft law should highlight the ideal goal, value orientation and moral ethics that members of the society pursue in common, and can meet the common interests of its members or can fairly deal with the interests among them, etc. It is the epitome of a society's core value system and the high cohesion of core values for members of society. The core values that carry the basic, stable, common ideal pursuit and value orientation of the social community are the common "spiritual home" of people. Some scholars have pointed out that core values, as the kernel of all values of social members, "will become the rules of behavior that social members follow and safeguard together, which will be internalized in the minds and hearts of social members, and then be well established as the value tradition and cultural spirit of social members, and carried forward from generation to generation."[62] It is not difficult to understand that in a country, the core values passed down will play a strong normative role for the members of the society, constitute the spiritual guiding force in the law, and help the law to be generally observed. The "leap forward to a new era of ecological civilization and building a beautiful China" proposed by General Secretary Xi Jinping recently[63] aims to guide the people of all ethnic groups to realize the common ideal of the Chinese dream of the great rejuvenation of the Chinese nation. The *Opinions of the CPC Central Committee and the State Council on Accelerating the Ecological Civilization Construction*, issued in April 2015, clearly put forward the idea of "making ecological civilization a mainstream social value", which has become the common vision of the whole Party and the whole nation, and constitutes the political ideology and moral ethics for building a low-carbon society and promoting low-carbon development. In modern China, facing the urgent situation of tightening constraints on energy conservation and emission reduction, serious environmental pollution, degradation of the ecosystem, and the increasingly prominent contradiction between development and population, resources and environment, it is in the long-term interests, fundamental interests and common interests of all people, to build a environment-friendly beautiful country featuring sustainable development for the benefit of future generations. In the process of formulating low-carbon soft law, the spiritual resource should be consciously used to win the hearts of the people, conform to the public opinion, and gather the people's strength, so that the low-carbon concept will take root among the members of the society and become a code of conduct that the members of the society will consciously abide by and spontaneously safeguard.

ii. From the perspective of material rights and interests resources, the content of soft law should meet the legitimate material rights and interests needs of the members of the society, in the position of working for the benefit of the people, and achieve a result with shared rights and interests. This requires adequate preparation of interest resources for the formulation of the soft laws, to fully coordinate the material interest resources so that they can be allocated fairly in the society, to benefit the people, and fulfill certain expectations on interests of the members of the society. In other words, respecting, safeguarding citizens' interests and reasonably inducing are an important condition for increasing citizens' identification with legal norms and inducing their compliance. A regression analysis of empirical data by some scholars suggested that the differentiation between citizens' environmental awareness and personal benefit realization is inversely correlated with the likelihood that awareness will translate into action. That is, the greater the differentiation between environmental awareness and benefit realization, the lower the likelihood of converting awareness into

[62] Liu Zheng and Liu Xingeng: *Exploring the Path of Realizing Socialist Core Values*, *Qiusuo*, 2011 (9).

[63] Zhou Shengxian: *Towards a New Era of Ecological Civilization—Learning from Comrade Xi Jinping's Important Discussion on the Construction of Ecological Civilization*, *Qiushi*, 2013 (17).

action.[64] This means that meeting the necessary personal interest needs can greatly increase the likelihood of translating people's low-carbon awareness to low-carbon behavior. Therefore, the formulation of low-carbon soft law should include sufficient resources for material rights and interests, including financial support, preferential policies, incentives, subsidies, etc., so as to encourage members of society to actively take low-carbon actions through benefiting the people.

iii. As for behavioral pattern resources, the behavioral norms set by soft law should fully consider and be as close as possible to the behavioral patterns already developed by members of society, such as the public order and customs shaped in economic activities, cultural and etiquette, social life interactions, etc.[65] These behavioral patterns are the rational paradigms that have been repeatedly proven to be effective and feasible by practice, which are highly replicable and transferable to the members of the society, and will be spontaneously accepted and carried forward by the members of the community, and are highly acceptable to the members of the community. According to the British philosopher Burke, tradition is "the crystallization of human wisdom" and "the foundation of social order". In this context, what Burke calls "tradition" includes at least the long-established public order and customs in social life.[66] The long-established public order and customs in a particular country, a particular nation or a particular social community are themselves highly recognized and accepted by the members as actual rules, which play an important normative support role in the "social effectiveness" of soft law, or the "factual binding force" of soft law. Soft law stipulating rules that are consistent with the daily patterns of behavior and public order and morals of members of a given community will provide resources guarantee to achieve widespread social compliance. This reminds us that the setting of low-carbon behavior patterns in soft law should give consideration to the convenience and easiness to implement in life. If the behavior patterns set by legislation completely conflict with people's long-established behavioral habits, which makes it extremely inconvenient and troublesome for the public to implement, they will hinder the effective implementation of the legislation. For example, the behavior pattern should be set in accordance with people's good customs of frugality. If the behavior pattern set by the legislation makes people pay too high a cost and brings a heavy burden, members of the society will not actively comply with it. The Ministry of Science and Technology of the PRC has

[64] See Liu Xiaozhong: *Household Appliance Replacement Decision and Empirical Research under Energy-saving Subsidy Policy in China*, pp. 39–40 of Master's Thesis of Southwest Jiaotong University, 2014.

[65] It is important to clarify that the public order and customs referred to here only refer to social norms without physical coercive power, excluding those customary laws that are enforced by clan power and religious power to ensure the implementation. Because the latter already has the "hard law" characteristic.

[66] See [UK] Burke: *Reflections on the Revolution in France*, Translated by He Zhaowu, Xu Zhenzhou and Peng Gang, The Commercial Press, 2010, p. 10.

prepared the *Manual on Promoting Energy Conservation and Emission Reduction* to help citizens use low-carbon air conditioners, and recommend that: in summer, "appropriately adjusting the air conditioner temperature without prejudice to the comfort helps us contribute to energy saving and emission reduction", "If the set-temperature of each air conditioner is increased by 1°C from 26°C recommended by the state, 22kWh electricity use and 21 kg CO_2 emission will be reduced per year.[67] That is to say, a behavior pattern that does not seriously affect the daily lives of citizens and is in line with frugal customs is very easy to be accepted and followed by the general public. This behavior pattern setting should be widely used in the development of low-carbon soft law.

(II) The Use of Legislation Approach as a Guiding Resource

The legislation approach also plays a pivotal role in the implementation of soft law. The scientificity of the methodology directly determines the quality of the soft law legislation, which further influences whether it will be generally observed. Therefore, to ensure the smooth implementation of soft law, the scientific legislative method is also a guiding resource that cannot be ignored. Specifically, soft law legislation in low-carbon area should include at least two aspects:

First, the appropriateness and timing shall be assessed before proposing the subject matters for regulation. In terms of the characteristics and functions of soft law, soft law norms that require compliance by members of society generally stipulate advocated, optional, exchangeable and negotiable rights and obligations, so soft laws are only suitable for such matters as the granting of rights and interests, consultation and cooperation, and behavior guidance of members of society.

Second, the formulation of soft law should pay attention to openness and consultation. In order to promote compliance with soft law by advocacy rather than coercion, it is necessary to understand the true will of the members of the society, so that they can be reasonably expressed in the soft law norms. Then, the process of soft law making should be fully open, with room for consultation. An open legislative process that allows for extensive and deep public participation can provide a platform for all parties to express their interests. This is conducive to drawing on a variety of views, understanding of different interests, thus achieving full explanation and persuasion; legislation content, achieved by full consultation and with consensus, helps coordination of contradictions and balance among different interests, thus wining extensive understanding, recognition and support from members of society. A high degree of democracy in the formulation of soft law ensures a foundation of wide public opinion, which ultimately creates favorable conditions for the effective implementation of soft law. In the construction of a low-carbon society, the social acceptance of energy conservation and emission reduction is still generally not high, the multiple interests of different social subjects are intertwined and overcomplicated, and there are inevitable differences and contradictions between private interests and public interests, and between different private interests in propositions on the content of

---

[67] Wang Xiexin: *A Brief Discussion on Low-carbon Construction and Use of Computer Classrooms in Primary Schools, China Information Technology Education*, 2010 (10).

legislation. Therefore, the formulation of low-carbon soft laws should emphasize more on openness and democracy, so that different interest subjects can engage in rational negotiation and debate on an equal basis in the legislative process, the government should properly balance the interests of all parties through sufficient explanation of reasons and publicity and persuasion, and actively develop the low-carbon awareness of participants, so as to provide a broad public opinion foundation and social support for the implementation of soft laws. The UK's low-carbon legislation has successfully applied this legislation approach with good results. During the proposal stage of the UK *Climate Change Act*,[68] the Department for Environment, Food and Rural Affairs (DEFRA) convened a "Citizens' Summit" for public consultation in the hope of reaching an understanding and consensus on low-carbon living through deliberation. Delegations of citizens from different regions of the UK have participated in this series of events. Before the deliberation, only nearly half of the participants think that "all of us" are responsible for tackling climate change. After full participation, communication and consultation, the participants holding the view rose to 83% at the end of the legislative deliberation[69]; the percentage of participants who agreed that "immediate action is necessary" increased from 65% at the beginning to 82% at the end; and the percentage of participants who said "I am well informed about climate change" more than doubled. This shows that the democratic process of legislation is conducive to better understanding and reaching maximum consensus, which will effectively support the effective implementation of the law and universal compliance.

(III) **The Use of Government Credibility as a Guiding Resource**

Effective implementation of soft law enacted by administrative legislation requires maximum guidance for active collaboration and cooperation of citizens. The involvement of the public depends on the degree of trust members of society have in government. Then, government credibility can be used as an important guiding resource.

Trust is "one of the most important comprehensive powers in society".[70] In economics, trust is the core of social capital,[71] and in jurisprudence, the principle of good faith is considered to be the king provision of law. Trust, as the essence of human social communication and rules of social life, demonstrates the law of social operation that the higher the degree of trust between members of society, the higher the level of harmony and cooperation will be. For the government and the members of the society, the credibility of the government can determine the degree of embracing and cooperation of the members of the society to its actions, which is a very important external condition for the general compliance of soft law. In exploring the value of

---

[68] The main contents of the *Climate Change Act* are to set goals and guidelines for the UK to build a low-carbon society, most of which are soft law norms.

[69] See [UK] Anthony Giddens: *The Politics of Climate Change*, Translated by Cao Rongxiang, Social Sciences Academic Press, 2009, pp. 118–119.

[70] G. Simmel, The Philosophy of Money, London: Routledge, 1978, pp. 178–179.

[71] See Zhang Weiying: *Information, Trust and Law*, Joint Publishing, 2006, p. 3.

administrative procedures, an American administrative law scholar has noted that "if there is a widespread feeling that an organ of government is making decisions arbitrarily or unfairly, that feeling can undermine public trust in that department and the voluntariness of compliance with its administrative decisions."[72] The sharp decline in government credibility due to integrity issues will reduce the compliance of the society with soft law. Soft law might be neither observed nor enforced. Therefore, enhancing the government's credibility is an important way to guarantee the implementation of soft laws. In terms of the formulation and implementation of low-carbon soft laws, the government should enhance its credibility in the following ways: First, various incentives for energy conservation and emission reduction stipulated in soft laws must be trustworthy, that is, they should be stable and sustainable to ensure that members of society trust and expect them. Second, the government should keep its word and must fully guarantee the various rights and interests of members of society and timely reward the ones contributing to energy conservation and emission reduction as stipulated in the soft law. Third, the government shall apply the soft law provisions equally and fairly to all the members of the society and shall not treat them in a biased or unfair manner. Fourth, the government should strictly restrain its own behavior according to the law, take the lead in energy conservation and emission reduction, and make a demonstration for the society in order to win the trust and support of the members of the society, so as to guide the whole society to comply with the provisions of the low-carbon soft law.

(IV) **The Use of Innovated Enforcement Methods as a Guiding Resource**

As a legal norm, soft law is "soft" but also needs to be enforced. However, it is significantly different from hard law enforcement: it obtains the consent and obedience of the parties without the application of coercive force, which requires appropriate enforcement methods different from hard law enforcement featuring command and obeying, enforcing and being enforced, punishing and being punished; more diverse ways need to be innovated to lead the public's willingness to accept, therefore, innovative enforcement methods are also an important resource to ensure the implementation of soft law. In this regard, *Administrative Coercion Law of the People's Republic of China* provides for an exemplary flexible approach to enforcement. The *Administrative Coercion Law of the People's Republic of China* is a hard law in nature, and all kinds of indirect coercive measures, direct coercive measures, and administrative coercive enforcement means provided for are the application of the state coercive power. However, flexible methods of enforcement are also provided for in the *Administrative Coercion Law of the People's Republic of China*. Taking

[72] Ernest Gellhorn Ronald M. Levin, Administrative Law And Process in A Nutshell, West Publishing CO. 1990, p.6.

"reminder to perform"[73] and "enforcement agreement"[74] as an example, the former is to inform and urge the parties without imposing coercive force, while the latter is agreed upon by the administrative compulsory organ and the parties involved through negotiation, with the purpose of allowing the parties to perform their obligations without imposing coercive force. Both are innovated enforcement methods of administrative coercion, and both are designed to achieve enforcement of the law in a manner that the public will readily accept. This humanized method of law enforcement that mobilizes the public to comply and accept should be fully applied to soft law enforcement.

Following the above-mentioned path, the innovative low-carbon soft law enforcement shall at least meet the following three requirements: First, the law enforcement should be based on equal interaction. That is, law enforcement officers shall fully communicate with the parties based on equality; on the one hand, respecting the human dignity of the parties, equality and personality is the ultimate way showing mutual care between people, and it's easy to eliminate the gap and sense of resistance and enhance the sense of closeness between parties through humanized soft law enforcement; on the other hand, it is conducive to achieving full explanation and persuasion, and also helps listening to and adopting the reasonable opinions of the parties, so that the parties are willing to comply. Second, the law enforcement approach shall encourage more collaboration and less command. On the one hand, the command-based enforcement in soft law will only produce legal effects when it is obeyed by the parties. If the person does not comply, the enforcement method is invalid. Therefore, command need to be minimized in soft law enforcement. On the other hand, soft law enforcement should resort more to negotiation, contract, and agreement to gain the parties' acceptance of the enforcement. In the low-carbon area, the National Development and Reform Commission of China announced the *Medium and Long-term Special Plan for Energy Conservation*, which clearly proposes "to promote new mechanisms for energy conservation based on market mechanisms, including voluntary energy conservation agreements", and has formulated the national standard for energy conservation agreements named *General Technical Rules for Voluntary Agreement of Energy Conservation* (GB/T 26,757–2011). This practice of using administrative contracts to implement the low-carbon obligations of the parties is a collaborative enforcement method for administrative agencies, and can be widely used in soft law enforcement. Third, law enforcement methods should be flexible and diverse. Soft law is generally not strictly binding, so there is a certain degree of freedom and flexibility in the way of enforcement. Law enforcement

[73] Reminder to perform "means that the administrative organ initiates the enforcement procedure and sends a notice to the administrative counterpart who has failed to perform the obligation according to the administrative decision, urging the administrative counterpart to perform the obligation within a certain period of time and giving a warning about the consequences of failure to perform the obligation". See Yuan Shuhong, Editor-in-Chief: *Tutorial on Administrative Coercion Law*, China Legal Publishing House, 2011, p. 104.

[74] An enforcement agreement is a way for the administrative enforcement authority to negotiate an agreement with the parties under certain conditions and for the parties themselves to perform their obligations as agreed.

agencies should create diverse ways of enforcement, apply them flexibly according to the person and the situation, avoid "one size fits all", and achieve the basic goal of substantive justice. For example, they could put themselves in the parties' positions and, where possible, provide them a variety of choices; when one solution will cause loss to the parties, other compensatory methods can be adopted in parallel to compensate for certain benefits, etc.

(V) The Use of Law-abiding Publicity and Education as a Guiding Resource

The effective implementation of soft law is closely related to the law-abiding awareness and self-discipline level of members of society. Soft law relies on conscious compliance by members of society, which puts forward higher requirements for them. Accordingly, the government should strengthen law-abiding publicity and education for its members of society, which naturally constitutes a guiding resource for the implementation of soft law. The *Decision of the CPC Central Committee on Several Major Issues on Comprehensive Promotion of Rule of Law* stipulates: "to promote the whole society to establish awareness of the rule of law. We should insist on popularization of law and law compliance as a long-term groundwork of the rule of law, in-depth publicity and education on the rule of law, guide the whole population to consciously abide by the law, resort to the law when encountering problems, and solve problems by the law." Law-abiding publicity and education can help citizens enhance faith in the law and develop the habit of acting in accordance with the law, which plays a fundamental role in guiding the soft law to be observed. Most of the soft laws currently enacted in China in the field of low-carbon development are timely regulations introduced in the short term to address climate change, but the corresponding law-abiding publicity and education are not yet sufficient. To this end, the effective implementation of soft law also requires extensive publicity and education on the rule of law in low-carbon construction throughout society. This must be done earnestly: first, use various forms to let members of the general public know that: low-carbon requirements put forward by the low-carbon soft law concern the common, fundamental and long-term interests of all, and it is urgent for the whole society to actively practice energy saving and emission reduction. For example, through warning propaganda, citizens can be shown and warned of the serious consequences of climate change and be made aware of the necessity of energy conservation and emission reduction; through experiential education, people can experience the risk of energy shortage and environmental degradation in an immersive manner to enhance their awareness of the urgency of energy conservation and emission reduction and their willingness to act; through exemplary guidance, exemplary figures and deeds that comply with low-carbon legislation and make outstanding contributions to energy conservation and emission reduction and ecological civilization construction can be promoted and commended, in this way, to guide the actions of the general public. Second, since soft laws are generally not enforced by the state, their effective implementation requires a higher law-abiding awareness and self-discipline level among members of society, and there is a strong positive correlation between the two. Therefore, when a certain low-carbon soft law is formulated, the awareness of law-abiding and self-discipline of the members applicable to its implementation should be fully measured. Only when the law-abiding awareness and self-discipline level of most members match the provisions regulated by the soft law, can the low-carbon legislation be smoothly implemented. Third, the administrative agencies should publicize need-to-know legal knowledge to the general public so that they understand that legal norms, be it in the form of hard or soft law, they are the embodiment of the will of the people and the code of conduct introduced by the state that should be observed. Compliance with the law should become the basic quality and minimum moral ethics of citizens in modern society, and everyone should "take pride in obeying the law and be ashamed of breaking the law", instead of passively complying with it because it is forced by the state or for fear of punishment.

In short, in the field of low-carbon construction, in order to be widely observed by members of the society, the soft law must embody common concern and interest of members of the society, with approach compatible with their law-abiding consciousness; this requires the full exploration and use of various guiding resources for soft law implementation at the time of law formulation.

3 The Model of Joint Legislation Should Be Fully Utilized for the Administrative Legislation in Low-Carbon Field

3.1 Basic Mode of Administrative Legislation in China

"Legislative mode refers to the customary approach to the creation of law by the legislative subject, and the principled standards followed in legislative activities throughout the legislative process by reference to previous practices."[75] It is generally divided into separate formulation mode and joint formulation mode according to the administrative legislative subject and operation mode. The separate formulation mode is an approach for an administrative legislature to formulate administrative regulations, departmental rules and local rules independently on matters within its scope of authority; the joint formulation mode refers to the joint legislation of more than two administrative legislatures on matters within the scope of authority of those administrative legislatures. According to the provisions of Article 81[76] of the *Legislation Law of the PRC*, the current joint administrative legislation in China only refers to the legislative activities in which relevant departments of the State Council jointly formulate regulations for matters within the scope of authority of those departments of the State Council.

[75] Wang Chunye: *Research on Regional Administrative Legislative Mode-In the Context of Regional Economic Integration*, Law Press China, 2009, p. 3.

[76] See Article 81 of the *Legislation Law of the People's Republic of China*.

In the administrative legislation in low-carbon field, both modes have been applied, but the separate formulation mode is generally applied. The joint legislation is relatively rare and is limited to central department regulations rather than local government regulations.[77] By examining the current situation that regulations are generally formulated separately by the central department and the local government in low-carbon field, some problems can be found.

(I) **Substantial Duplication of Content of Legislation**

The duplication exists in central department regulations (including normative documents at the corresponding level) and can be more reflected in local government regulations. For example, the *Detailed Rules for the Implementation of Energy Conservation Law in Railway Industry* issued by the former Ministry of Railways and the *Detailed Rules for the Implementation of Energy Conservation Law in Transport Industry* issued by the Ministry of Transport have a large proportion of same or similar expressions of in the contents. The determination standards for key energy consumption units are exactly the same, and they are defined as "energy consumption units with a total annual energy consumption of more than 5,000 tons of standard coal", failing to reflect the different pertinence for different industries. For example, the *Guiding Opinions on Further Strengthening Energy Conservation and Emission Reduction of Small and Medium Enterprises* issued by the Ministry of Industry and Information Technology and the *Notice on Energy Conservation and Emission Reduction of Small and Medium Enterprises* issued earlier by the National Development and Reform Commission have a large proportion of duplication in the contents, such as fully understanding the importance and urgency of energy conservation and emission reduction of small and medium enterprises, guiding ideology and work objectives, promoting the development of service industry and technology-based small and medium enterprises, optimizing industrial structures and improving energy conservation and emission reduction service systems, and exploring centralized pollution control modes, etc., the former is a rephrasing of the latter's relevant requirements from a micro perspective.

During the regulation constitution of local government, mutual replication is more common. For example, since the State promulgated the *Cleaner Production Promotion Law* and the State Council enacted the *Energy Conservation Regulation for State-funded Institutions*, almost all local governments have formulated "Implementation Opinions," "Implementation Rules" and Energy Conservation Regulations for State-funded Institutions for their provinces and cities, but the basic frameworks, contents and even texts are basically the same, many of which are duplicated from the superior laws or similar regulations of sister provinces and cities. The substantial duplication of legislative content is clearly a significant waste of legislative costs and fails to meet the low-carbon requirements.

---

[77] For example, the *Interim Measures for the Management of Low-carbon Product Certification*, the *Measures for the Management of China Clean Development Mechanism Fund* and *Measures for the Operation and Management of China Clean Development Mechanism Projects* in the field of clean production are all administrative legislative documents jointly formulated by departments.

(II) **Conflicting and Inconsistent Legislative Content**

The separate formulation mode means regulations are formulated by a department or local government. Administrative and legislative organs tend to consider from their own perspectives or interests, without considering the connection between the regulations and other relevant legislation at the same level. Some scholars have analyzed and pointed out that, in the field of coal legislation governed by the *Law of the PRC on the Coal Industry*, the main purport of administrative legislation such as the *Measures for the Administration of Coal Production License*, the *Regulations on Coal Mine Safety Supervision* and the *Special Provisions on Preventing Coal Mine Production Accidents* is safe coal production, coal management and operation, protection and supervision and management of mining area,[78] without involving the sustainable development, green and low-carbon development of coal resource, which is inconsistent with the legislative purport of other resource fields. Inconsistency of standards and contents occurs in the administrative legislation of local government on the same matter of the same level. For example, Tianjin and Beijing, both belonging to the Bohai Economic Zone, have inconsistent provisions on geothermal resources as a new energy in their respective government regulations. Article 2 of *Regulations on Tianjin Geothermal Resources Management* stipulates that geothermal resources "refer to the thermal energy that can be economically and reasonably developed in rocks and fluids buried in the crust below the ground of the city, including five types: Steam type, hot water type, geopressured type, dry-hot rock type and magmatic rock type." Among which, the hot-water geothermal resource refers to underground hot water with a flow temperature of more than 40 °C (including 40 °C). "However, Article 2 of *Beijing Geothermal Resources Management Method* stipulates that geothermal resources "refers to the thermal energy stored in rocks and fluids below the ground, including five types: Hot water type, steam type, geopressured type, magmatic rock type and dry-hot rock type." Where, the hot water geothermal resource refers to bedrock water with humidity above 25 °C (including 25 °C) and hot springs exposed naturally." The two standards could be said to be different. The inconsistent standards for hot water geothermal resource in two closely adjacent cities with the same natural conditions such as geography and climate will directly lead to conflict of interests: For example, for hot water geothermal resource under the border areas of the two cities, or hot water geothermal resource flowing between the two cities, the amount and intensity of exploitation will be different because of different standards, and the city with higher resource developing standards will suffer from the loss of interests in the utilization of natural resources. At the same time, such different standards will lead to unequal treatment for geothermal development enterprises in both cities.

The above problems are related to the contradiction between the comprehensiveness, openness, synchronicity of low-carbon requirements and the relative simple and closed mode of separate formulation in administrative legislation. The overall goal of low-carbon construction is to reduce carbon dioxide emissions in the atmosphere. As a natural ecosystem, the atmosphere is objectively not controlled by industry and

[78] See Yang Jiejun: *Problems and Bottlenecks in Contemporary China's Energy Legislation and the Countermeasures*, *Nanjing Journal of Social Sciences*, 2013 (12).

region. The global and systematic activities to control the atmosphere and reduce carbon dioxide emissions should be carried out synchronously by various industries and regions. In the relevant legislation, the boundaries between different administrative departments or administrative regions have to be eliminated. At the same time, the low-carbon construction involves a wide range of complex issues, covering almost all aspects of social life, and they are closely interrelated. Different administrative legislative subjects have different jurisdictions due to the division of regional management and specialization, forming a pattern of separation in legislation, which is not completely adapted to the systematicness and relevance of low-carbon social construction matters. If separate legislation is applied in low-carbon matters, there will be a large number of repeated, similar or even mutually duplicated principle clauses and basic frameworks, resulting in conflicting and inconsistent provisions on specific issues.

Based on the objective comprehensiveness and openness of low-carbon requirements, it is necessary for relevant administrative legislation to explore the model of broadening and widely applying legislative subjects to strengthen joint legislation to solve such above problems.

3.2 *Necessity of Joint Administrative Legislation in Low-Carbon Field*

The joint administrative legislation in low-carbon field refers to the administrative legislative mode of joint legislation and application of administrative legislation subjects with corresponding legislative authority in case of low-carbon matters involving commonality or cross-sector and cross-region. In the central government, the joint formulation of regulations by more than two departments is in accordance with the *Legislation Law of the PRC* and has a large number of legislative practices. It has not changed the existing administrative legislative authority in China. At present, it is necessary to explore how to apply it more widely and effectively in low-carbon field. At the local level, there is no legal basis for the joint formulation of cross-regional regulations by two or more governments with the regulation constitution right at the same level. However, there are a large number of theoretical studies[79] on

[79] Relevant monographs and papers include: Wang Chunye: *Research on Regional Administrative Legislative Mode-In the Context of Regional Economic Integration*, Law Press China, 2009; Ye Bifeng: *Legal Governance of Regional Economic Integration*, *Social Sciences in China*, 2012 (8); Chen Shuquan and Wu Jing: *Research on Cross-regional Administrative Legislative Mode in the Context of Regional Economic Integration*, *Journal of Ocean University of China (Social Sciences)*, 2011 (1); Rao Changlin and Chang Jian: *Collaboration of Regional Administrative Legislation in China: Real Problems and Institutional Improvement*, *Administrative Law Review*, 2009 (3); Wang Chunye: *On the Integration of Administrative Legislation and Route Selection in the Economic Region*, *Journal of South-Central University for Nationalities (Humanities and Social Science)*, 2009 (6); Wang Xuan: *Research on Regional Administrative Legislation*, CUPL Doctoral Dissertation in 2010, etc.

regional legal cooperation and some relevant legislative pilot explorations.[80] The new joint administrative legislative mode needs to be applied particularly in low-carbon field.

Strengthening joint legislation between departments facilitates the integration of low-carbon regulatory matters of the same purpose and similar content to make overall provisions for a jointly formulated regulation, which maximally save the overall legislative cost of developing same or similar regulations by departments. During the organization and implementation of the same regulation, departments need to make detailed and professional arrangements for the issuance of documents related to the work content of the departments, and omit the common and general contents such as the legislative purpose and principles that must be expressed in the format of inherent legislative text when formulating the regulation, thus reducing a large number of repeated provisions. At the same time, through full communication and interaction among all relevant departments, the joint legislation can greatly reduce the conflict or inconsistency and incoordination that occur during the regulation constitution by taking into account industrial characteristics, integrating professional knowledge and coordinating the interests of all parties, which not only optimize the legislative content, but also avoid the contradictions or loopholes arising from the implementation in the future.

It is needless to say that it is as necessary to strengthen the joint legislation between relevant local governments to greatly save the overall legislative cost and avoid the conflict of legislative contents as it is to make joint legislation between departments. However, its significance is more than that, because it is also particularly conducive to the extensive cooperation between administrative regions in the prevention and control of air pollution flowing in different regions. Several local governments in adjacent administrative regions, or several local governments that have reached a common goal of regional integration construction, will have more governance advantages by

[80] For example, in order to share administrative legislative resources, reduce administrative legislative costs and improve administrative legislative quality in Northeast China, Heilongjiang, Liaoning and Jilin signed China's first regional framework agreement on administrative legislative collaboration in 2006, the *Framework Agreement on Legislative Collaboration in Northeast China*, which adopts three main approaches: close collaboration, semi-close collaboration and decentralized collaboration. For the difficulties, hot topics and key legislative projects of government concern and public interest, a close collaboration mode is adopted, with the three provinces establishing a joint working group; for common legislative projects, a semi-close collaboration mode is adopted, with one province taking the lead in organizing the drafting and the other two provinces cooperating; for other projects of the consensus of the three provinces, each province shall legislate independently according to the actual situation of the province and the conditions are ripe for urgent formulation, with the legislative results shared among the three provinces. Over the past few years, focusing on promoting the revitalization of Northeast China, 22 legislative projects have been facilitated in scientific and technological progress, equipment manufacturing industry and non-public economic development, and the protection of migrant workers' rights and interests, breaking the regional blockade, maintaining market unity, promoting resource optimization, and accelerating regional coordinated and sustainable development. For example, Jiangsu Province, Zhejiang Province and Shanghai signed the *Minutes of the Seminar on Legal Collaboration between Jiangsu, Zhejiang and Shanghai* in 2007, which clearly defined the guideline of coordinating the common development of regional economy and society through joint legislation.

jointly making regulations and applying them jointly on relevant low-carbon regulatory matters than separate administrative legislation in these administrative regions. For example, it's impossible to bar the atmospheric resources within one specific area because of their mobility, while the place where air pollution occurs and the place where the damage lies are often not in the same administrative region, as is the case with many water resources. This urgently requires cooperative governance among the relevant administrative regions. In terms of low-carbon regulatory matters, on the one hand, standards and actions shall be unified; on the other hand, we should complement each other's advantages and balance interests. If each administrative region makes its own administrative regulations limited to its own region, the lack of communication and cooperation between each other will inevitably lead to various conflicts, which is not conducive to the comprehensive implementation of low-carbon construction. The comprehensiveness and synchronicity of low-carbon construction call for cooperation and co-governance between regions. Recently, the "Beijing-Tianjin-Hebei" environmental protection plan and the water pollution control of Taihu River Basin in the Yangtze River Delta Economic Zone issued by the state reflect such requirement. This also presents the necessity and feasibility of joint administrative legislation among local governments, and of the formulation of government regulations that can be uniformly and fairly implemented in the relevant regions.

3.3 Basic Thoughts on Improving Joint Administrative Legislation

Joint administrative legislation in low-carbon field encompasses both central and local levels.

(I) Joint Administrative Legislation at the Central Level

At the central level, China has the legal basis and practice for departments to jointly formulate regulations, but they are not widely used. In the field of low-carbon administrative legislation, in addition to submitting to the State Council for the formulation of administrative regulations, more joint formulation of administrative regulations between departments should be carried out in the future, so as to minimize the duplication and similar provisions made by a single department, due to the comprehensiveness of low-carbon matters, involving various fields, common and related issues, and high frequency of interactions between departments.

Article 81[81] of *Legislation Law of the PRC* is the legal basis for the central departments to jointly formulate regulations. According to the article, With regard to a matter that falls within the limits of power of two or more departments under

[81] Article 81 of the *Legislation Law of the PRC* stipulates: "With regard to a matter that falls within the limits of power of two or more departments under the State Council, the State Council shall be requested to formulate administrative regulations or the departments concerned under the State Council shall jointly formulate rules.".

the State Council, the State Council shall be requested to formulate administrative regulations or the departments concerned under the State Council shall jointly formulate rules. Administrative regulations are higher-ranking legal norms, and for comprehensive matters the legislative process is relatively longer. There are two standards for proposing to formulate administrative regulations: one is the cross-authority standard, that is, legislative matters involving the scope of authority of two or more departments, and therefore comprehensive; the second is the standard of mature conditions, which is derived from Article 8 of the *Regulations on Procedures for the Formulation of Rules*.[82] In a sense, the latter is more important. Then, it also establishes the applicable standards for the formulation of joint regulations by departments, i.e. cross-authority standard and contingency standard. The former is for legislative matters within the limits of power of two or more departments, and the latter is the adjustment and regulation of administrative rules in order to respond to new issues and situations in a timely manner when the conditions for the formulation of administrative regulations are immature. Accordingly, all regulations of legislative matters that meet the above two standards should be jointly formulated by the relevant departments. In which cross-authority standard should be strictly controlled. It not only refers to the legislative matters directly belong to the scope of cross-authority management between different departments, but also could be applied to the situation that the consequences of a department's decision on the matter may affect the normal exercise of another department's authority, or the decision on the matter will dovetail with the exercise of another department's authority.

Given that the joint administrative legislative mode involves joint legislation of more than two administrative organs, it is necessary to establish a long-term cooperation mechanism of joint legislation between departments in order to ensure quality. Such cooperation mechanism requires, first of all, the establishment of a special departmental joint legislative coordinating body in the organizational system, which is composed of personnel sent by the legal institutions of each department. This may help to form a fixed cooperation platform, the government needs to institutionalize and stabilize it, instead of applying the current working method of temporarily assigning personnel from relevant departments to participate because of a joint legislative task. Departmental joint legislative coordinating body should regularly convene plenary sessions on joint legislative work, inform the legislative planning and plans of different departments, especially projects requiring joint legislation, fully exchange legislative experience, study relevant legislative issues, establish joint legislative tasks, etc. In matters involving specific joint legislation, special working meetings of representatives of relevant departments should be held as required to carry out specific joint legislative work. In addition, it is necessary to establish mechanisms for sharing legislative information resources between departments, consultation mechanisms, advisory mechanisms, etc.

---

[82] Article 8 of *Regulations on Procedures for the Formulation of Rules* stipulates: "If some issues involve the scopes of power of at least two departments under the State Council and there is an immature condition for formulating the administrative regulations, the rules concerned shall be formulated jointly by the related departments under the State Council.".

(II) Joint Administrative Legislation at the Local Level

At the local level, the implementation of low-carbon joint administrative legislation is still a work worth exploring, as China's laws have not yet made clear provisions for such joint low-carbon administrative legislation at the local level. However, in view of the comprehensiveness of the low-carbon matters, which are often beyond the jurisdiction of a certain administrative region, it is necessary for local governments to strengthen cooperation and achieve comprehensive and effective regulation of low-carbon matters through the mode of joint administrative legislation in low-carbon regions.

i. **The legitimacy basis for cross-regional joint administrative legislation of low-carbon field between local governments**. The cross-regional joint legislation of local governments has to break the existing regional division of administrative legislation, which is different from the traditional administrative legislative mode of local governments formulating regulations separately, but it has a legal basis in terms of legal principle and legislative authority.

   In terms of legislative authority, local governments that carry out joint administrative legislation have the power to formulate regulations independently, which is explicitly granted by the Constitution, the *Organic Law* and the *Legislation Law* of the PRC. They carry out joint administrative legislation without institutional changes in legislative subjects, legislative authority, and legislative matters, but only with certain changes in the ways of application of legislative authority, i.e., the joint exercise of their respective legislative authority. At the same time, such change in the application of legislative authority is also a real demand, and such demand is supported by relevant laws. For example, Article 15 of the revised *Environmental Protection Law of the PRC* stipulates that a inter-jurisdiction "joint prevention and control coordination mechanism"[83] for environmental pollution and ecological damage shall be established. Although it is not a clear provision of joint legislation between local governments, the inter-jurisdiction "joint prevention and control coordination mechanism" naturally suggests that inter-jurisdiction joint administrative legislation can be used to strengthen and implement "unified planning, standards, monitoring, and prevention and control measures".

ii. **The relevant conditions of joint administrative legislation in low-carbon field**. The joint administrative legislation between local governments requires certain conditions. From the perspective of practicality, operability and effectiveness, cross-regional joint administrative legislation in low-carbon field by local governments usually shows the following relevance: First, the relevant local governments have a connected jurisdiction over a certain region. This is most evident in areas such as water resources protection and air pollution

[83] Article 15 of the *Environmental Protection Law* stipulates: "The State establishes inter-jurisdiction joint prevention and control coordination mechanism environmental for pollution and ecological damage to implement unified planning, standards, monitoring, and prevention and control measures.".

control. In terms of natural properties, water resources are fluid and often cross different administrative regions, so in terms of their governance and protection, the places where water resources flow through have jurisdiction, which forms the common jurisdiction of the relevant local governments in the region. For example, Taihu Lake flows through Jiangsu, Zhejiang and Shanghai, the three governments share the responsibility for the supervision of the waters of Taihu Lake flowing through their jurisdictions. Therefore, Jiangsu Province has specially issued the *Regulations on Prevention and Control of Water Pollution in Taihu Lake in Jiangsu Province*, Zhejiang Province has issued the system of supervision and protection of waters in Taihu Lake in the *Regulations on Prevention and Control of Water Pollution in Zhejiang Province*, but Shanghai has not issued special regulations. In this regard, the three governments can fully utilize the form of joint formulation of local government regulations to jointly govern and give full play to the synergy in governance. Second, the relevant local governments have close interests in a matter. For example, the existing economic zones in China such as Yangtze River Delta Economic Zone, Pan-Pearl River Delta Economic Zone, Bohai Economic Zone show the trend of integrated economic development with reasonable industrial layout, effective utilization of energy resources, and coordination of ecological and environmental protection in various places within the economic zones, thus forming common interest relationships. In this regard, separate legislation in the places can easily bring about inconsistency or "fragmentation" of provisions, which may harm the integrated development. This needs to be properly handled through the mode of joint legislation. Thirdly, the relevant local governments are geographically close to each other. This refers to the fact that the local governments in different administrative divisions are geographically close to each other and can also actively carry out joint administrative legislation on related matters based on common environmental governance, energy resource protection and effective utilization, as well as management and law enforcement cooperation needs.

Local governments with the above-mentioned circumstances are in a position to actively and extensively carry out joint low-carbon administrative legislation among them. Other local governments without such conditions can carry out separate administrative legislation according to local actual conditions and characteristics, and follow the path of low-carbon development consistent with local characteristics.

iii. **Ranking and form of joint low-carbon administrative legislation**. According to the existing practice of regional legal cooperation, the current regional administrative legislation is mainly limited to the provincial government level, and the form of cooperation adopted is to jointly formulate administrative agreements rather than formal administrative regulations through Joint meetings, which can be further promoted and developed. For municipal-level local governments with rules formulation right, joint administrative legislation should also be actively carried out on matters such as coordinated protection of cross-regional waters and coordinated governance of cross-regional air pollution in the construction of low-carbon society, based on common interests and shared responsibilities. In terms of legislative form, the current form of administrative agreements between local governments through joint meetings can be considered as a preliminary exploration of low-carbon joint administrative legislation. Administrative agreements between local governments are not yet standard administrative legislation, with weak legal effects, binding only the subject of the agreements-the administrative organs in the region, and not directly defining the rights and obligations of the counterpart.[84] In addition, administrative agreements are mostly principled provisions, failing to achieve the adjustment effect that legal norms have in terms of standardization and applicability of specific matters. Therefore, it is necessary to gradually develop the administrative agreements between local governments into the form of joint regulation, to form a legal norm with stronger stability, normativity, enforcement and coercion power.

iv. **Procedures of Joint Administrative Legislation in Low-carbon Fields**. Cross-regional low-carbon joint administrative legislation can rely on the mature regular meeting mechanism or joint meeting system of relevant local government executive heads to exchange, discuss ideas and finally reach an agreement on low-carbon matters that need to be solved by joint legislation. The joint administrative legislation among local governments basically follows the current administrative regulation formulation procedure, but some additional jointly-formulated procedures are required:

At the legislative planning stage, when the local governments formulate legislative plans, it is necessary to identify projects belonging to regional joint legislation and to reach a consensus on such projects through the joint meeting system of local governments to form a joint legislative task.

At the legislative drafting stage, it is necessary to negotiate to determine a local government to take the lead in legislative drafting work, or each local government to undertake the task of legislative drafting separately, and then finally organize meetings to revise and improve it in a centralized manner. A special team can also be established by local governments to carry out legislative drafting work.

At the review stage, the legal institutions of each local government shall firstly review or audit and make amendments to the draft legislation, then exchange and inform each other of the review or audit results, and form a legislation draft of administrative regulation for review on the basis of consensus.

Finally, at the consideration and adoption stage, the jointly-formulated local government regulations shall be adopted by each local government in accordance with their legislative authority to establish the legal status and effectiveness of the regulations, and then submitted to the joint meeting of local governments to reach a unanimous resolution and signed jointly, so that they are applicable to the regions under the jurisdiction of each local government. After the adoption of the regulations jointly formulated by local governments, the regulations also need to be filed. According to Article 98 (iv) of the *Legislation Law of the PRC*, in

[84] See Ye Bifeng, Editor-in-Chief: *Administrative Agreements-Research on Cooperation Mechanism between Regional Governments*, Law Press China, 2010, p. 198.

addition to being filed by the State Council, local government regulations shall also be submitted to the corresponding Standing Committee of the People's Congress at the same level for filing.

v. **Effectiveness Level of Joint Administrative Legislation in Low-carbon Fields**. The effectiveness of regulations formulated jointly by local governments is superior to those formulated separately by local governments, with reference to the definition of the effectiveness of the departmental regulations jointly formulated by the departments of the State Council in the *Legislation Law of the PRC*. This determines that, in the event of a conflict of contents between the regulations formulated separately and regulations formulated jointly by local governments, the regulations formulated jointly shall be used as the benchmark for modification, or only the regulations formulated jointly shall be applied. However, regulations jointly formulated by local governments have inferior legal force than local regulations in the region.

Chapter 6
Improving the Administrative Licensing for Low-Carbon Regulation

1 Role of Administrative Licensing in the Construction of a Low-Carbon Society

1.1 Special Functions of Administrative Licensing in Implementing Low-Carbon Regulation

The construction of a low-carbon society is related to the sustainable economic and social development of China, and is inseparable from the well-being of Chinese people. Every social entity has the responsibility to actively participate in the construction of a low-carbon society. The government should give full play to its overall planning, leading and regulating roles. As an important administrative regulatory method, administrative licensing has unique advantages and functions in controlling carbon emissions and promoting green development. Administrative licensing has the feedforward control function of screening and admittance and the concurrent dynamic adjustment function, that is to say, it can not only support the promotion of energy conservation & emission reduction activities by licensing, but also prohibit the behaviors of energy resource waste and high carbon emissions by not licensing. It is an important means for the government to make full use of low-carbon regulation. The unique functions and advantages of administrative licensing in the construction of a low-carbon society are reflected in the following aspects.

(I) **Screening and Filtering Functions**

According to Article 2 of the *Law of the PRC on Administrative Permission*, the term "administrative licensing" as mentioned in the present Law refers to the acts that the administration permits, upon examination according to law, the administrative counterparts to engage in special activities according to their applications. Therefore, administrative licensing is essentially a matter of market access, and its functions are to screen different market entities and to filter unqualified market entities through examination according to law. In the context of building a low-carbon society, the

S. Fang and B. Tan, *On the Administrative Law of China in Addressing Climate Change*,
https://doi.org/10.1007/978-981-19-7705-3_6

primary role administrative licensing plays is to exclude market entities that will carry out non-low-carbon behaviors in the access process to achieve the "interception" effect.

According to Article 19 of the *Law of the People's Republic of China on Promoting the Development of a recycling Economy*, if a market entity that will engage in the design of process, equipment, products and packages does not meet the requirements of reducing the consumption of resources and the generation of wastes or relevant national mandatory standards, it naturally can not be approved by competent national authorities to carry out market operation. In addition, Articles 22 and 23 of the *Law of the People's Republic of China on Promoting the Development of a recycling Economy* also reflect the screening and filtering functions of administrative licensing in the construction of a low-carbon society.

(II) **Dynamic Adjustment Function**

The major function of the administrative licensing is to exclude market entities that will carry out non-low-carbon behaviors in the access process, but this only means that market entities that have the conditions to carry out low-carbon behaviors are retained, and it is uncertain to some extent whether they will always engage in the production and operation activities according to the low-carbon requirements after obtaining the licenses. Thus, the administration is required to make dynamic adjustments to the administrative licenses that have been granted. Articles 10, 49, 61, 62, 64, 65, 66, 67 and 69 of the *Law of the PRC on Administrative Permission* reflect the dynamic adjustment function of administrative licensing in various forms, such as change, suspension or revocation of administrative licenses.

Specifically, for the construction of a low-carbon society, the dynamic adjustment function of administrative licensing works through: (i) change of administrative licenses. According to Article 49 of the *Law of the PRC on Administrative Permission*, the administration that makes the licensing decision shall not approve the application of a licensee for change of the administrative license against legal conditions or standards. For example, according to Article 10 of the *Environmental Protection Law of the People's Republic of China*, pollution prevention and control facilities in any construction project should be designed, constructed and put into use together with the main construction project, in order to control the pollution that may be generated in the construction project. Therefore, the pollution prevention and control facilities of an enterprise should match its production capacity and scale. If an enterprise expands its business scope and scale (subject to change of administrative license) for more profits, but it does not improve the capability of its pollution prevention and control facilities accordingly, the administration naturally can not make the decision to grant the change of license. During the process, the administration, by making the decision on whether to grant the change of administrative licenses, actually plays a role of dynamic adjustment of the administrative license, realizing the second "interception" of the market entities that may carry out non-low-carbon behaviors. (ii) Revocation or suspension of licenses. Revocation or suspension of licenses is a form of administrative penalties stipulated in the *Law of The People's Republic of China on Administrative Penalty*, and also a reflection of the function of dynamic adjustment of administrative licenses. For example, in order reduce and control pollution, Articles 51, 53 and 54 of the *Law of the People's Republic of China on Promoting the Development of a recycling Economy* provide for the revocation or suspension of licenses. By revoking or suspending the license, the administration can revoke or temporarily suspend the qualification of market entities that have carried out non-low-carbon behaviors, thus realizing the control of non-low-carbon behaviors.

1.2 Shortcomings of Existing Administrative Licensing in Low-Carbon Vision

Administrative licensing, as an important means for administrative entities to promote the construction of a low-carbon society, has unique functions and advantages that are difficult to be replaced by other administrative actions. Therefore, it is necessary to give full play to the role of administrative licensing in the construction of a low-carbon society. However, the existing legal system for administrative licensing in China still lacks the low-carbon vision, and its legislative purposes, basic principles, as well as the establishment and implementation of administrative licenses lack the guidance of low-carbon vision. Furthermore, in reality, too many administrative licenses are established and the administrative licensing procedures are repeated and complicated. This not only imposes many unnecessary burdens on the administrative counterparts, but also greatly deviates from the requirements of low-carbon administration and low-carbon society, and weakens the effectiveness of administrative licensing activities and their functions in guiding and regulating the administrative counterparts to engage in low-carbon behaviors.

In order to meet the requirements of the "low-carbon era" and to provide institutional norms for low-carbon licensing, the "low-carbon" vision must be incorporated in the legal system for administrative licensing and the "low-carbon administration" vision must be implemented in the perspectives of legislative purposes, basic principles and examination standards.[1] However, the current *Law of the PRC on Administrative Permission* does not embody the value of low-carbon administration: First, its legislative purposes do not contain the low-carbon value orientation. According to Article 1 of the *Law of the PRC on Administrative Permission*, one of its legislative purposes is to "safeguard public interests and social order," however, the Standing Committee of the National People's Congress has not exercised its interpretation right, and the State Council has not issued any implementation rules to explain what are "public interests" and "social order", and whether the public welfare promoting environmental protection and low-carbon development is included is unknown. The consequence of this is that a large number of administrative licenses that violate the principles and standards of low-carbon administration appear in practice. Second,

---

[1] Fang Shirong and Sun Caihua, *On the "Low-Carbon" Concept of Administrative Law*, *Truth Seeking*, 2010 (12).

the basic principles of the *Law of the PRC on Administrative Permission* lack the low-carbon vision. According to Articles 4, 5, 6 and 8 of the *Law of the PRC on Administrative Permission*, the administrative licensing system shall follow the principle of statutory licensing, the principle of publicity, fairness, and impartiality, the principle of facilitating convenience and high efficiency, and the principle of reliance interest protection. However, these traditional principles of administrative law can only facilitate administrative licensing activities to meet the minimum legal rationality, such as fairness and justice, but obviously cannot respond to the challenges of risk prevention in the context of global climate change, or meet the new functional requirements for the contemporary government to promote low-carbon economic development and low-carbon society construction. Third, the low-carbon standards are not included in the examination of legal conditions according to the *Law of the PRC on Administrative Permission*. Article 38 of the *Law of the PRC on Administrative Permission* provides in principle that the conditions for granting an administrative license are "the application complies with the legal conditions and standards". With respect to whether the "legal conditions" include environmental protection, energy conservation & emission reduction, pollution prevention, and promotion of ecological balance, the Standing Committee of the National People's Congress and the State Council have not made any legislative interpretation or formulated any implementation rules to clarify. As a result, a large number of applications that do not meet low-carbon standards are granted administrative licenses, and the advantages and functions of administrative licensing as a feedforward regulation approach are not effectively used in preventing environmental risks and promoting low-carbon development.

The problems mentioned above are also reflected in the practice of administrative licensing. It is reflected as follows.

First, from the perspective of the establishment of administrative licenses, some organs that have no right to establish administrative licenses establish administrative licenses in the form of departmental regulations and documents in violation of the *Law of the PRC on Administrative Permission* in order to pursue benefits of examination and approval,[2] resulting in excessive administrative licenses. On the one hand, the public administrative system that maintains the operation of administrative licensing is a large energy consumption and carbon emission system, and the illegal establishment of administrative licenses increases the waste of resources and carbon emissions in the operation and management of administrative entities. On the other hand, excessive administrative licenses impose unnecessary burdens on the administrative counterparts. To obtain administrative licenses, they must travel back and forth and submit application materials. This greatly increases the administrative licensing costs and environmental costs.

[2] Article 1 of the *Decision of the State Council on the Sixth Group of Administrative Examination and Approval Items to be Cancelled and Adjusted (GF No.52 [2012])* has put forward a specific requirement: "Administrative permits set in violation of the provisions of the Administrative Permission Law in the form of departmental regulations, documents, etc., shall be corrected within a time limit", and also "a dynamic clearing mechanism for approval projects shall be established".

Second, from the perspective of the implementation of administrative licensing, due to the vague definition of the connotation and scope of administrative license in the *Law of the PRC on Administrative Permission*, a large number of non-administrative license approvals appeared beyond the reach of *Law of the PRC on Administrative Permission*, which leads to things like repeated approvals, deliberate disassembling of approvals that violate the principles of legal proceedings, convenience and high efficiency. The current administrative licensing procedures are cumbersome, inefficient and time-consuming, thus greatly reducing the efficiency of administrative licensing and increasing the burden of administrative participants and the carbon emissions of administrative licensing procedures.

In addition, the low-carbon value orientation is still not highlighted in the administrative approval system reform in China currently. Facing the fact that excessive administrative approvals are set, and approval procedures are complicated and seriously overlapped in China, CPC Central Committee and local party committees and governments have always been emphasizing and promoting the administrative approval system reform. For this, both the Third and Fourth Plenary Sessions of the 18th CPC Central Committee have put forward clear requirements.[3] In recent years, in order to promote the administrative approval system reform, the State Council has successively canceled and adjusted a large number of administrative approval matters, and delegated some to lower levels.[4] However, in terms of the objectives of the administrative approval system reform that is promoted in an all-round way currently, they emphasize "stimulating market vitality",[5] "improving and strengthening macro-management, making the government management more scientific",[6] and "working for the convenience and benefits of the people",[7] but objectives of promoting "low-carbon administration" and "energy conservation & emission reduction" are rarely mentioned. However as early as 2010, the State Council clearly put forward in the *Notice on Making More Efforts to Ensure the Realization of the Target on Energy Conservation and Emission Reduction of the Eleventh Five-year Plan* that "Energy conservation & emission reduction indicators are legally binding indicators," and "Each region and department should highlight energy conservation & emission reduction in the work". In the process of promoting the construction of a

[3] For detailed information, please refer to Part 4 of the *Decision of the Central Committee of the Communist Party of China on Some Major Issues Concerning Comprehensively Deepening the Reform* and Part 3 of the *Decision of the CPC Central Committee on Some Major Issues Pertaining to Comprehensively Promoting the Rule of Law*.

[4] For detailed information, please refer to GF No.52 [2012], GF No.19 [2013], GF No.27 [2013], GF No.39 [2013], GF No.44 [2013], GF No.5 [2014], GF No.27 [2014], GF No.50 [2014], GF No.6 [2015], GF No.11 [2015], GF No.27 [2015], GF No.29 [2012] and other documents.

[5] Li Keqiang: The teleconference address on streamlining administration procedures, cutting red tape, *Streamline Administration, Delegate Power, Strengthen Regulation and Improve Service to Deepen Administrative Reform and Transform Government Functions*.

[6] *Notice of the General Office of the State Council on Dividing the Tasks for Implementation of the Plan for Institutional Reform and Functional Transformation of the State Council* (GBF No.22 [2013]).

[7] *Notice on Issuing the Key Points of Deepening the Reform of the Administrative Examination and Approval System in 2014* (WZB No.32 [2014]).

low-carbon society, the government should first introduce the concept of low-carbon administration to guide the low-carbonization of its own administrative activities. For example, there is an urgent need of the introduction of the concept into the administrative activities like administrative approval system reform.

2 Construction of Low-Carbon Administrative Licensing System

Forming the idea of "low-carbon development" in administrative licensing system is of great significance for the government to implement low-carbon guidance and low-carbon regulation. In order to cope with the risk of energy depletion and the environmental risk of global climate change and to reflect the concept of low-carbon administrative licensing, administrative licensing proceedings should embody the low-carbon development value in the contents and results. This is mainly reflected in three aspects. First, the administrative licensing setting should be low-carbonized, that is, to cancel administrative licenses that fail to conform to the *Law of the PRC on Administrative Permission*, fail to adapt to the economic and social development and fail to meet the requirement of low-carbon society construction in strict accordance with the principle of legal licensing, the principle of rationality and the principle of low-carbon administration. Second, the administrative licensing procedure should be low-carbonized, that is, to realize low-carbonization in examination procedures, examination time limits and examination methods according to the requirements for construction of low-carbon procedures. Third, the administrative licensing implementation should be low-carbonized, that is, to actively encourage the applications of administrative licenses that can promote the development of low-carbon economy and low-carbon society, and open up a quick-examination channel for these applications.

2.1 Low-Carbonization of Administrative Licensing Setting

(I) Administrative Licensing Needs to Be Low-carbonized

The administrative power consists of the following five elements: the elements of source, subject, operation, counterpart and the material support.[8] And the exercise of the administrative licensing in a specific domain needs to be guaranteed by the above five elements, which will generate a large number of administrative costs and energy consumption. The costs and consumption are reflected in the following aspects: First, the *Law of the PRC on Administrative Permission* has clearly defined the legal

---

[8] Fang Shirong, Qi Jiangang: *Research on the Power Constraint Mechanism and Its Legalization*, Chinese Financial and Economic Press, 2001:16.

norms that can set administrative licenses,[9] but in reality, except for administrative legislation, other normative government documents (minutes of meetings, policy documents and even speeches, comments and directions of leaders) may become the basis for the setting of administrative licenses. The huge number of normative documents, from its planning, drafting to writing, consume lots of resources and energy. Second, an administrative subject itself is a huge energy-consuming and carbon-emitting entity. In order to guarantee the exercise of the administrative licensing, it needs to set up a corresponding organizational structure and be staffed with a certain number of civil servants. Excessive administrative entities may only increase the consumption of resources and energy. Third, the implementation of administrative licensing procedures (methods, steps, sequences and time limits) requires material supports, and the lengthy and unnecessary procedural arrangements will increase the resource and energy consumption of the participants (administrative entities and administrative counterparts). This deviates from the purpose of low-carbon society construction. Fourth, in order to guarantee the effective exercise of the administrative licensing authority, administrative entities need to consume certain public expenses on equipment and property. This also belong to the consumption of resources and energy.

Therefore, in order to reflect the low-carbon value in administrative licensing, it is required to reasonably institute administrative licenses in strict accordance with laws, and not to institute licenses for the matters that can be effectively regulated by the market mechanism, that can be managed by industry organizations based on self-discipline, and that can be resolved by the administration through post-supervision, to minimize administrative licensing. At the same time, a large number of existing non-administrative license approvals and administrative licenses instituted beyond the authority need to be canceled comprehensively and extensively, to control carbon emissions from the source and achieve low-carbon self-control.

(II) **Low-carbonization of Administrative Licensing Setting**

According to the above theory, administrative licensing is a resource and energy consuming administrative activity, and the resource and energy consumption in the administrative licensing process needs to be controlled in the low-carbon administration and low-carbon society. Low-carbonization of administrative licensing setting is the first step to achieve this goal. It mainly includes the following aspects: (i) Canceling unnecessary administrative licenses. In accordance with the guidelines of the Third Plenary Sessions of the 18th CPC Central Committee, unnecessary administrative licenses should be canceled on a large scale. In general, for the matters that can be effectively regulated by the market mechanism, that can be managed by industry organizations based on self-discipline, and that can be resolved by the administration through post-supervision, licenses should not be instituted and those

[9] The *Law of the PRC on Administrative Permission* limits the legal basis for setting administrative license to laws, administrative regulations, local regulations and regulations of the people's governments of provinces, autonomous regions and municipalities, as detailed in Articles 14 and 15 of the Law.

that have been instituted should be canceled in a timely manner. (ii) Merging and standardizing necessary administrative licenses. Administrative licenses that need to be retained should be merged according to the principle of simplification provided that they can be merged in order to avoid too many and excessive licenses. In addition, administrative licenses should be comprehensively standardized to guarantee the normal proceeding of their institution.

2.2 *Low-Carbonization of Administrative Licensing Procedure*

The elements of administrative procedures practically refer to the step, time limit, method and sequence of the exercise of administrative power,[10] i.e. it is stipulated that administrative power needs to be exercised in a certain manner and within a certain time limit. The administrative licensing procedure itself is a huge energy-consuming process, and its start-up and operation require a certain amount of material resources as the guarantee. Procedures are clarified by the rules and can be improved through the designing of specific rules.[11] Therefore, in order to realize the low-carbonization of administrative licensing procedure, low-carbonization should be one of the measurement criteria for the legitimacy of administrative licensing procedures, and simpler and more economical administrative licensing rules should be designed. For administrative licensing matters that really need to be retained, administrative licensing procedures should be streamlined to improve licensing efficiency and reduce resource and energy consumption under the premise of ensuring procedural justice.

(I) **Low-carbonization of Administrative Licensing Examination Process**

The low-carbonization of administrative licensing examination process mainly includes two aspects:

i. **The low-carbonization of examination of general administrative licensing procedures**. For general administrative licensing procedures, on the one hand, formality procedures should be deleted to the maximum extent, and on the other hand, some steps with strong relevance or high repeatability should be merged according to the characteristics and functions of the licensing procedures. The deletion of non-essential red tape in the licensing process can not only effectively benefit the work of enterprises and the public, but also reduce the consumption of resources and energy. This requirement is reflected in handling "them jointly or in a concentrated way" stipulated in Article 26 of the *Law of the PRC on*

[10] Jiang Mingan: *Administrative Law and Administrative Litigation Law*, Peking University Press and Higher Education Press, 2002: 260.

[11] See Ji Weidong: *The significance of Legal Procedures-Another Thought on the Law Construction in China*, *Social Sciences in China*, 1993(1).

Administrative Permission.[12] In addition, innovative measures are taken in the administrative approval system reform in some regions of China, for example, the "certificate and business license joint handling mechanism" implemented in Wenzhou and the "parallel examination and approval system" implemented in Shanghai for construction projects.[13] For the approval process involving multiple government departments or units, the joint approval or regular countersignature system can be actively implemented,[14] while for approval steps with strong relevance, the method of one-time document receipt, combined examination and one-time conclusion should be adopted to save administrative licensing management costs and reduce unnecessary energy consumption.

ii. **Establishing summary administrative licensing procedures**. By reference to the summary procedure for administrative penalty, it is feasible to consider establishing a summary procedure for *Law of the PRC on Administrative Permission*, to shorten the administrative licensing process and reduce the consumption of energy resources. The *Law of the PRC on Administrative Permission* does not contain the term "summary procedure" in its text, but actually, it has recognized the applicability of summary procedure, as provided in Article 34. According to the content, what is stipulated in that article is exactly the summary procedure for administrative licensing. The scope of application of the summary procedure for administrative licensing should be further expanded and clarified. The administration could consider to clearly list the administrative licensing matters applicable to summary procedure in the the *Law of the PRC on Administrative Permission*, and the specific steps and time limits of the summary procedure need to be clearly stipulated. In practice, administrative licensing authorities in some regions of China have begun to apply the summary procedure for specific administrative licensing matters. For example, in June 2014, Zhejiang Provincial Bureau of Quality and Technical Supervision approved the pilot on-spot issuance of some provincial production licenses for industrial products in Shaoxing, Zhejiang. For the 14 products of 9 categories listed, the summary procedure of "license issuance before verification" is adopted, that is, after an enterprise has made commitments against the license obtaining conditions and product quality requirements, the license-issuing authority issues the administrative license on the spot without carrying out the on-site inspection in advance, and then the Bureau of Quality and Technical Supervision conducts on-site inspections and sample tests against that enterprise. This greatly simplifies the licensing process while ensuring the quality and safety of industrial products.[15] Considering there are a wide variety of administrative licensing matters with different

[12] See Article 26 of the *Law of the PRC on Administrative Permission*.

[13] For detailed information, please refer to WZB No.32 [2014] and HFB No. 46 [2010].

[14] Fang Shirong: *Legal Issues of the Reform of the Administrative Examination and Approval System in China, Chinese Cadres Tribune*, 2002 (3).

[15] Summary procedures for industrial approval license for pilot projects in Zhejiang, website of General Administration of Quality Supervision, Inspection and Quarantine: http://www.aqsiq.gov.cn/zjxw/dfzjxw/dfftpxw/201406/t20140606_414610.htm, accessed on June 23, 2015.

characteristics in China, and licensing procedures are not unified, it is impractical to establish a detailed summary procedure for administrative licensing that is in line with the characteristics of each administrative licensing matter. Therefore, it is suggested that the *Law of the PRC on Administrative Permission* should first stipulate in principle that summary procedures should be applied to administrative licensing matters that meet specific conditions, Clearly list the administrative licensing matters and conditions applicable to the summary procedure, and make general provisions for the steps, time limits and methods of the summary procedure.[16] The norm basis should be set first, and the summary procedure for specific licensing matters should be further specified, but it should meet the general standard for the application of the summary procedure in the *Law of the PRC on Administrative Permission*.

(II) Low-carbonization of Administrative Licensing Time Limit

The time limit of the administrative procedure is not only related to the administrative management cost, but also has a significant impact on the interests of administrative counterparts. Therefore, in order to minimize the procedural costs of the administrative entities and the administrative counterparts, and ensure that the administrative licensing process conforms to the low-carbon value, the administration needs to set a timely, rapid and efficient licensing time limit with strict legal liability.

i. **Minimizing the time limit of each procedure as much as possible during the implementation of administrative licensing**. Articles 32 and 42 of the *Law of the PRC on Administrative Permission* clearly stipulate the legal time limit for application and examination of administrative licenses,[17] but in practice, the time limit requirements for a large number of administrative licenses are not followed, and it is common to break the time limits, as is presented in the provisions of Article 14 of the *Regulations of Shanghai Municipality on Registration of Real Estate*, which was formally implemented on July 1, 2009.[18] In the provision, once the real estate registration agency believes it needs to check the real estate on the spot, the real estate registration time limit may exceed twenty days without an upper limit. This obviously exceeds the 20-day examination period stipulated in Article 42 of the *Law of the PRC on Administrative Permission*, and brings about the increase of costs of both administrative entities and counterparts, including the consumption of resources and energy.
ii. **Clarifying the legal liability for violating the provisions on time limits**. The *Law of the PRC on Administrative Permission* clearly stipulates the time limit of each link in the administrative licensing process, however, they are null and void because there is no supporting provision on the legal liability for violating these time limits. Therefore, the legal liability system for licensing time limit shall

---

[16] Zhang Shufang: *On Administrative Summary Procedure*, *Journal of East China University of Political Science and Law*, 2010 (2).

[17] See Articles 32 and 42 of the *Law of the PRC on Administrative Permission*.

[18] See Article 14 of *Regulations of Shanghai Municipality on Registration of Real Estate*.

be clearly defined, stipulating that if the administrative licensing matter is not timely handled within the legal time limit, the administrative licensing authority should undertake the compensation liability, and relevant responsible personnel and staff should be investigated for their legal liability.

(III) Low-carbonization of Administrative Licensing Methods

In addition to the low-carbonization of administrative license setting, procedures and time limit, the construction of a low-carbon society can also be promoted through the low-carbonization and greening of the operating methods of administrative licensing, the which could focus on the implementation of E-government.

We are now living in an information society, and the administration should carry out administrative activities with the methods that can adapt to the society. The traditional methods of administrative licensing are not in line with the concept of low-carbon society because they cause serious waste of paper resources and occupation of physical spaces.[19] Through the implementation of E-government, the administrative license applicants and implementation authorities can complete the license application, examination and handling processes in data messages through computers, communication networks, and other modern information technologies. This is simple and easy to do and reduces unnecessary consumption of energy resources. The hot topic "Sealing makes leg broken"[20] on the Internet some time ago exactly reflects the disadvantages of traditional administrative licensing methods. This kind of continuous rush for a simple signature and seal not only consumes a large amount of human, material and financial resources of the applicant, but also generates a large amount of carbon emissions and energy consumption. This obviously contradicts the value and requirements of "low-carbon administration".

In fact, the *Law of the PRC on Administrative Permission* has already put forward advocacy norms for "E-government", e.g. the provisions in Articles 29 and 33. In order to promote E-government, the administrative licensing implementation authorities need to promote concept of administrative efficiency in the long run, devote greater effort in the construction of E-government infrastructure and investment, to realize the construction of standardized and intensive E-government administrative procedures and improve their utilization efficiency.

---

[19] Xie Jing: *Service Applicant Promotion of Electronization of Patent Application-the interpretation of Provisions on electronic patent applications, China IP News*, September 3, 2010.

[20] *"Sealing makes leg broken" Calls for Simple Approval Rights*, Xinhua Net: http://news.sina.com.cn/o/2012-06-08/093924558380.shtml, accessed on June 23, 2015; *How Many Odd Certificates Are Left for People to Run off Their Feet After Streamline Administration*, Xinhua Net: http://news.xinhuanet.com/local/2015-05/18/c_127811314.htm, accessed on June 23, 2015.

2.3 Low-Carbonization of Administrative Licensing Implementation

The functions of administrative licensing in the construction of a low-carbon society can be realized not only through the institution and procedures of administrative licensing, but also the implementation of administrative licensing.[21] Compared with the low-carbonization of administrative licensing setting and procedures, the low-carbonization of administrative licensing implementation emphasizes that administrative entities, as the power-execution entities,[22] regulate and restrict the behaviors of counterparts by "examining whether the applicant has the qualification and condition for the exercise of rights" according to the low-carbon standards, that is, the prior examination of the administrative licensing implementation authorities becomes a precondition for the administrative counterparts to enter the industries that are related to environmental public welfare or engage in the activities with specific restrictions that affect environmental interests. The implementation of administrative licensing is more likely to bring into play the unique advantages and functions of administrative licensing as a feedforward method in dealing with climate change risks.

The low-carbonization of administrative licensing implementation mainly includes the following two aspects:

(I) **Clearly Setting "Environmental Protection" as One of the Criteria for Administrative Licensing Examination, and Emphasize the Low-carbon Value in the Administrative Licensing Examination**

Currently, the low-carbon value is not involved in the legislative purposes, basic principles and examination standards of the *Law of the PRC on Administrative Permission*. The principle of legitimacy and principle of rationality of the traditional administrative law, as the minimum legal rationality, can not adapt to the severe situation of climate change and the new functional requirements for government risk prevention any more. Therefore, the standard and connotation of administrative licensing examination should change with the development of the economy and society. The content of the "environmental protection" standards for administrative licensing examination can be instituted based on the definition of ecological benefits given by the World Business Council for Sustainable Development (WBCSD), which should mainly include seven aspects: "reducing the material consumption of products and services, reducing the energy consumption of products and services, reducing the emission of toxic substances, increasing the recycle and reuse of materials, trying to use renewable energy, increasing the durability of products, and enhancing the service intensity of products".[23]

---

[21] See Bai Guixiu: *Research on Environmental Administrative Licensing System*, Intellectual Property Publishing House, 2012, 1.

[22] Fang Shirong, Sun Caihua: *On the Government Function and Administrative Acts of Promoting the Construction of Low-Carbon Society*, *Law Science*, 2011 (6).

[23] See Liu Fudong, Zhu Xuezhong: *Research on the Patent System Based on Low- Carbon Development Orientation*, *China Soft Science Magazine*, 2011 (7).

(II) Setting Up a Green Quick-examination Channel for Administrative License Applications That Meet the "Environmental Protection" Standards

On the premise of implementing strict and scientific examination according to law, the quick-examination channel aims to shorten the license examination period, merge and simplify examination steps, save the procedural costs for the counterparts, quickly promote the construction of low-carbon environmental protection projects and the application of low-carbon green technologies and products, and advocate and encourage low-carbon production and low-carbon consumption throughout the society. Take the green patent quick-examination mechanism as an example. Green patents have unique advantages and functions in stimulating the innovation of low-carbon technologies, preventing the excessive consumption of natural resources, and promoting the transfer and popularization of low-carbon technologies. However, since the *Patent Law of the People's Republic of China* does not grant green patent licensing any privilege currently, the patent examination period can be as long as 36–48 months in practice. This greatly undermines the enthusiasm of individuals and units for the innovation of low-carbon technologies and weakens the effect of low-carbon technologies in promoting energy conservation and emission reduction. Therefore, in order to give full play to the key role of green patents in coping with climate change, it is necessary to learn from foreign experience to set up a quick-examination channel for green patents in the *Patent Law of the People's Republic of China* to improve the examination efficiency. The green patent quick-examination procedure should mainly include three links: First, when applying for a patent, the applicant should submit an authentication report issued by a third-party authentication institution to certify that patent conforms to the green quick-examination standard. The third-party authentication institution should be an expert group entrusted by China National Intellectual Property Administration, an environmental protection department, or a non-governmental organization with authentication qualifications. Second, the first examination and substantive examination shall be combined. Once the green technology has passed the preliminary examination, the China National Intellectual Property Administration will initiate the substantive examination of the patent ex officio without the need for the applicant to put forward an application for substantive examination. Thirdly, after the substantive examination, if it is determined that a patent right can be granted, the decision shall be made with the least delay possible. At the same time, other citizens or legal person shall be given the right of objection. For patent applications that have passed the green patent quick-examination channel, other citizens or legal person may file an objection to the Patent Re-examination Board if they believe that the approved patent will lead to significant harm to the environment, but the objection shall not suspend the patent rights already approved. If the opposition is sustained, the Patent Re-examination Board may declare the patent invalid. On the basis of clarifying the steps of quick-examination, it is required to shorten the time limit of each examination link in the patent examination practice in China, so as to shorten the examination period of green patents, promote the rapid and wide implementation of green patent technologies, and maximize the benefits of environmental protection.

3 Green Patent Licensing System in Low-Carbon Construction

3.1 Traditional Environmental Administrative Licensing and Green Patent Licensing

In order to implement the *Law of the PRC on Administrative Permission* implemented since July 1, 2004, the former Ministry of Ecology and Environment of the PRC issued HF [2004] No. 119 *Announcement on the Issuance of Administrative License Items to Be Retained* on August 27, 2004, which clearly lists 31 administrative licenses to be implemented by the competent administrative departments of environmental protection. Among them, there are 18 administrative licenses instituted by environmental protection laws, e.g. *Environmental Protection Law of the People's Republic of China* and *Law of the People's Republic of China on Prevention and Control of Water Pollution*, 6 administrative licenses instituted by administrative laws and regulations on environmental protection, e.g. *Regulation on the Supervision and Management of Civil Nuclear Safety Equipment* and the *Regulations on the Nuclear Materials Control of the PRC*, and 7 administrative licenses instituted by the normative documents of the State Council for environmental protection (e.g. *Decision of the State Council on Establishing Administrative Licenses for the Administrative Examination and Approval Items Really Necessary to Be Retained*) needed to be retained and meeting the provisions of the *Law of the PRC on Administrative Permission*. According to the *Announcement*, on the one hand, the existing laws and regulations concerning the institution and implementation of administrative licenses for environmental protection are relatively scattered, with different effects, and lack unified and complete environmental administrative licensing procedures. On the other hand, the traditional environmental administrative licenses instituted by environmental protection laws and administrative regulations in China are mostly the approval of specific industrial activities involving national security and public safety, or market access qualification approval, and are mostly the administrative licenses at the application examination stage. There is a lack of widely applicable environmental administrative licenses that actively stimulate units or individuals to engage in environmental protection activities and the administrative licenses for supervision and management stages.

In contrast, the green patent system implemented by the patent administration department under the State Council, through which patent rights are granted to low-carbon environmental protection technologies, plays an increasingly prominent role in stimulating the innovation of environmental protection technologies and energy conservation and emission reduction. Although the green patent license is not an environmental administrative license implemented by the environmental protection administration department in the traditional sense, it plays an irreplaceable positive role in preventing and controlling pollution, and promoting energy conservation & emission reduction and environmental protection. First, unlike the negative pollution prevention and control method, i.e. the environmental protection administration department examines applicants' qualifications to engage in specific industries or activities, the green patent administrative license gives patentees exclusive rights to their inventions and innovations, thus actively stimulating units and individuals to engage in the innovation of environmental protection technologies and and truly reflecting the dominant position of units and individuals in building a low-carbon society. Second, the green patent license is an administrative license of process sense. It includes not only administrative licenses at the application examination stage in the traditional sense, but also administrative licenses at the patent application stage, such as the compulsory license for patent implementation and the license for patent promotion and use. The green patent license system gives full play to the supervision and management of licensees and the protection of environmental public welfare, so as to maximize the benefits of environmental protection.

3.2 Active Role of the Green Patent System in Addressing Climate Change

The legal system affects the environment by regulating and guiding the ways of production and people's daily life. The green patent system is a typical example for this. The system plays an active role in coping with climate change, which is mainly reflected in the following three functions: low-carbon technology innovation and incentive function, replacement function, and technology transfer and promotion function.

(I) **Low-carbon Technology Innovation and Incentive Function**

The application and development of environmental protection technologies are considered a fundamental means to effectively address the challenges of global climate change. On the one hand, technology innovation can improve the resource utilization rate and decrease the dependence of development on traditional fossil energy. Especially, low-carbon technologies, such as wind energy, solar photovoltaic, clean carbon energy and bioenergy conversion, have facilitated the development of alternative energy products and services and their efficient transportation and utilization, thus greatly reducing the negative impact of human activities on the climatic environment. But on the other hand, technology, as a "double-edged sword", also has negative impacts on the ecological environment while improving human's ability to understand and transform nature. For example, traditional high-energy-consumption technologies pursue high yields. This cuts the relevance among technological production, consumption and natural ecological balance, and eventually results in the deterioration of the ecological environment. Therefore, it is necessary to re-examine the functions and goals of technologies. The development and application of technologies must be an act of kindness. When applying and promoting technological achievements, we should maximize their potential to promote harmony between human beings and nature within the bearing capacity of the climatic environment.

The generation and development of the patent system are inextricably linked with the development of technology. First, the patent system originates from the development of technology. Since technology research and development require a large amount of time and funds and face high risks, a powerful intellectual property protection system will serve as a driving force and cornerstone for technology innovation and development. Second, with the development of technology, the number of the objects protected by the patent system are expanding accordingly. Third, the patent system unifies internal and external technology innovation incentives. On the one hand, the patent system creates scarcity on purpose through legal compulsion,[24] i.e. it allows the patentees to control product prices by giving them exclusive rights, thus inherently stimulating innovation, research and development of technologies with high-cost and high-risk. On the other hand, the patent system grants the technology innovators patent right to prevent their patent achievements from being "hitchhiked" by others at a very low cost, thus preventing technology imitation and plagiarism, and providing external guarantee for technology innovation incentives.

The green patent system introduces "green", "low-carbon", "environmental protection" and other relevant elements to the current patent system, which links the patent system and low-carbon development, and regulates non-ecological technology innovation and "hitchhiking" behaviors, thus stimulating the innovation and investment in green technologies and low-carbon technologies.

(II) **Replacement Function**

The green patent system itself cannot directly reduce human dependence on natural resources, but the objects protected by it can reduce human dependence on natural resources and the negative impact on the climatic environment. The patent system encourages the production of ecological technology products with low dependence on natural resources and high dependence on knowledge and technology, thus promoting the transformation of economic development from resource based "resource economy" to knowledge and human resource based "knowledge economy". On the one hand, in the development of "knowledge economy", intellectual property rights constitute the core.[25] That is to say, the more new knowledge, technologies and more intellectual property rights you own, the more advantages you will have in economic competition. On the other hand, the property rights system can be used to protect and encourage knowledge and technology innovation. Intangible intellectual achievements can be transformed into transferable and identifiable "property."[26]

---

[24] See Michael A. Heller, *The Tragedy of the Anticommunist: Property in the Transition from Marx to Markets*, 111Harv. L. Rev, 1997.

[25] Liu Jianwen: *Knowledge Economy and Legal Transformation*, Law Press·China, 2001, 187.

[26] Chen Wenxuan: *Boundary of Patent Rights-Semantic Interpretation of claims and Policy Adjustment of the Scope of Protection,* Intellectual Property Publishing House, 2014.

By guaranteeing the holders' rights to possess, use, benefit from and dispose of such "intangible property", the intellectual property law system enables the creation, application and protection of knowledge and technology. Therefore, in the context of the growing resource depletion and environmental crisis, it is necessary to develop knowledge economy to replace resource economy. The intellectual property system, especially the patent system, can be used as the cornerstone of the existence and development of the knowledge economy, and knowledge and technology innovation can be relied on to replace or reduce the consumption of natural resources, thus achieving the goal of low-carbon development.

(III) The Function of Facilitating Low-carbon Technology Transfer and Promotion

The modern intellectual property system has two legislative purposes. The first purpose is to protect private rights. Intellectual property rights are the rights enjoyed by civil subjects to their intellectual achievements recognized by the private law, and intellectual properties as non-material objects of intellectual property rights are respected and protected by national laws.[27] The second purpose is to balance interests. The protection of intellectual property rights is limited. The intellectual property law system, through the appropriate intervention and application limitation of national public rights on intellectual property rights, ensures that the public can obtain general knowledge and information and realizes the balance of interests between subjects of rights and obligations and between individuals and society. Therefore, China also needs to clarify that intellectual property legislation has a public purpose.[28] In addition to establishing the goal of balancing private interests and public interests in legislative purposes, the intellectual property law system should also impose restrictions on the application of intellectual property rights in terms of scope. With respect to the patent system, the balance of interests is reflected in the restrictions of the patent system itself, such as the disclosure of patent information, compulsory license, promotion and use, and facilitating the transfer, promotion and diffusion of low-carbon technologies. Hence, the functions of the green patent system in facilitating the transfer and promotion of low-carbon technologies are mainly realized in the following three ways.

First, the specifications and application documents of green patents are the detailed descriptions of inventions, and their disclosure makes information and new technologies widely disseminated, and indicates the ways for third parties to find the patentees, thus reducing the transaction costs of patent transfer.

Second, the risk of patented low-carbon technology transfer is smaller, and the *Patent Law of the People's Republic of China* has stipulated clear provisions on their transfer, which makes it easy for the parties to draw up contracts for technology transfer. Compared with low-carbon technology without patent protection, technology transferees prefer to choose technologies protected by green patents.

---

[27] See Wu Handong: *The Multi-Attribute and Research paradigm of Intellectual Property Rights*, *Social Sciences in China*, 2011(5).

[28] As stipulated in Article 1 of the *Patent Law of the People's Republic of China*.

Finally, the green patent system grants patentees monopoly rights for a period of time, but it also increases the costs of acquiring patented technologies and developing new technologies. While in view of public welfare, low-carbon technologies should be used in the practices of statutory compulsory licensing and promotion under specific circumstances, as the implementation of low-carbon technologies is conducive to the protection of the environmental rights of the whole society. In this way, low-carbon technology achievements can be applied for a wider range.

3.3 Construction of Green Patent System

According to the *Law of the PRC on Administrative Permission*, the administrative licensing procedure mainly includes the application, examination and supervision of administrative licenses, while the patent law system established by the *Patent Law of the People's Republic of China* includes three links: patent application, examination and utilization. Hence, the construction of green patent system should mainly include three aspects: first, the greening of the patent application system, second, the greening of the patent examination system, and third, the greening of the patent utilization system.

(I) Greening of the Patent Application System

The greening of the patent application mainly includes the greening of patent application resources and event sources and the greening of application methods.

First, according to the principle of environmental protection and prevention, in order to avoid or reduce environmental risks and to prevent pollution from the source, a green patent application resource and event source information disclosure mechanism should be established to ensure the technologies to be granted patent rights are environmentally friendly. In addition to the disclosure of the patent application specifications and claims as required by the *Patent Law of the People's Republic of China*, the green patent application should also disclose the environmental impact assessment submitted and the sources of genetic resources used in the patent. Among them, the disclosure of the environmental impact assessment mainly includes the disclosure of resources and event sources, such as raw materials used in the green patent applied, production and manufacturing processes, valid terms and subsequent treatment methods. In addition, the disclosure of the sources of genetic resources of the patent application should be clearly stipulated, as genetic resources[29] not only maintain the reproduction, variation and evolution of species and ecosystem, but also have the functions of eliminating pollutants and protecting ecological environment. In order to protect genetic resources and prevent them from being illegally acquired

---

[29] See Article 26 of the *Implementing Regulations of the Patent Law of the People's Republic of China*.

or used by others, it is necessary to disclose genetic resources at the patent application stage to guarantee the exclusive patent right of the applicant to use the genetic resources.

Second, low-carbon administration requires administrative entities not only to play a leading role in promoting the construction of a low-carbon society and but also to ensure low-carbonization in their own administrative activities. Therefore, the greening of the patent application system also includes the low-carbonization of the patent application activities. Article 6 of the *Administrative Measures for the Priority Examination of Invention Patent Applications* issued by China National Intellectual Property Administration in 2012 clearly stipulates that invention patent applications that may be subject to priority examination shall be those applied electronically. However, except for those subject to priority examination, in China, a large number of invention patent applications are still in written form. Article 10 of the *Patent Law of the People's Republic of China* stipulates that where the right to apply for a patent or a patent right is assigned, the parties concerned shall conclude a written contract. Article 30 also stipulates that any applicant who claims the right of priority shall make a written declaration. Article 2 of the *Implementing Regulations of the Patent Law of the People's Republic of China* stipulates that the procedures stipulated in *the Patent Law of the People's Republic of China* and the *Implementing Regulations of the Patent Law of the People's Republic of China* shall be handled in writing or in other forms stipulated by the patent administration department under the State Council. Therefore, at present, the patent application and examination in China are still approved in written form, and with the rapid growth of the number of patent applications, it can be expected that a large number of paper resources will be wasted and a lot of physical space will be occupied.[30] In order to realize the low-carbonization of patent administration activities, it is necessary to amend the *Patent Law of the People's Republic of China* to clarify that the patent application and examination shall be made mainly in electronic form, and if necessary, in written form.

(II) Greening of the Patent Examination System

The greening of the patent examination system forms the basis for the construction of the green patent system and is also a precondition for the implementation of green patents. The greening of the patent examination system includes the greening of the patent examination standards, the greening of the green patent examination procedures and the greening of the patent examination forms.

i. Greening of the patent examination standards

According to the *Patent Law of the People's Republic of China*, the legislative purposes and basic principles in Chap. 1 "General Provisions", and Chap. 2 "Requirements for Grant of Patent Right" have no clear provision on the low-carbon development goals of the patent law system. Besides, in the technologies or methods for which no patent right shall be granted in Article 25 of the *Patent Law of the People's*

[30] Xie Jing: *Service Applicant Promotion of Electronization of Patent Application-the interpretation of Provisions on electronic patent applications*, *China IP News*, September 3, 2010.

Republic of China, the inventions that pollute the environment or seriously waste energy or resources are not included.[31] Although the newly revised *Guidelines for Patent Examination* in 2014 expanded the interpretation of "utility" in Article 22 Requirements for Grant of Patent Right of the *Patent Law of the People's Republic of China*, and then further interpreted "positive effect" as "positive and beneficial effect on economy, technology and society", it is still unclear whether the "positive effect" in the *Guidelines for Patent Examination* includes the significant contribution of the patent application to the construction of a low-carbon society and environmental protection. In addition, on the premise that the *Patent Law of the People's Republic of China*, the *Implementing Regulations of the Patent Law of the People's Republic of China* and the *Guidelines for Patent Examination* have not explicitly listed "environmental protection" as a legal criterion for patent examination, the traditional standard of "novelty", "inventiveness" and "practicability" are still used in patent examination. While "Environmental friendliness" is a criterion that will be used by the patent administration when examining the patent but enjoying free verdictive right in a large scope. Thus, in practice, some non-ecological or even anti-ecological technical inventions have been granted patent rights.

The standard for patent examination are not static, and its connotation should evolve in line with economic and social development. With the enormous consumption of natural resources, the growing environmental crisis, public awareness of environmental protection is also on the rise. Article 27 of the TRIPS Agreement signed by member states in 1994 specifies that member states may not grant patents for inventions "where the prevention of commercial exploitation of such inventions in their territories is necessary to preserve public order or morals, including to protect the life or health of human beings, animals or plants, or to avoid serious damage to the environment". Therefore, in order to respond to the requirements of low-carbon economy and social development, to meet the principles of "prevention", "prudence" and "safety" of environmental protection, and to curb technologies or methods that pollute the environment at the source, the "environmental protection" criterion may be added to Article 22 Requirements for Grant of Patent Right of the *Patent Law of the People's Republic of China*. Or "environmental protection" could be clearly stipulated as the basic connotation and requirement of "practicability" in the *Guidelines for Patent Examination*, and the examination of the possible impact of the applied patent on the environment must be conducted in the examination of "practicability". Or "no patent for inventions that severely pollute the environment or waste energy and resources shall be granted" may be clearly stipulated in Article 25 of the *Patent Law of the People's Republic of China*.

In addition to separately establishing the general clauses such as the environmental protection objectives of the patent legal system, the "environmental protection" standard of patent examination or excluding the technologies and methods that violate the basic principles of environmental protection in the legislative purpose and basic principles in Chap. 1 "General Provisions" and Article 22 " Requirements for Grant

[31] Zhu Xuezhong: *On Low-Carbon Development and Improvement of Patent Law in China, Intellectual Property*, 2011 (6).

of Patent Right" or Article 25 "No Patent Shall be Granted" of *the Patent Law of the People's Republic of China,* a further definition of the specific content of the "environmental protection" standard and the basic requirements for environmental protection examination is needed:

Firstly, the specific connotation of the "environmental protection" standard for patent examination shall be defined. In this regard, China can draw on the definition of ecological benefit by the World Business Council for Sustainable Development (WBSCD) and clarify in the *Guidelines for Patent Examination* the "environmental protection" requirements in the patent examination, taking into account the actual situation of China's economic and social development and environmental protection.

Secondly, the requirements of green patent system on the applicant shall be clearly stipulated in the *Implementing Regulations of the Patent Law of the People's Republic of China.* Firstly, the patent applicant is required to list the environmental impact evaluation of the invention in the patent specification which can be made by a legally qualified environmental impact evaluation institution. The environmental impact evaluation must include the descriptions of the raw materials used in the patent, the manufacturing process, the service life and the follow-up treatment methods. Secondly, other citizens or legal person shall be clearly given supervision power. Once a citizen or legal person finds that the environmental impact evaluation of the invention patent with a patent power is false, and sufficient evidence is available to prove that the implementation of the patent will lead to significant harm to the environment, he or she may apply to the Patent Re-examination Board to declare the patent invalid. Where the environmental impact evaluation has been found to be false and the approved patent has a negative impact on the environment, the Patent Re-examination Board may declare the patent invalid. Thirdly, "environmental protection" shall be included in the patent examination standard. According to the patent specification, technology or method can be independently patented if it contributes more to environmental improvement and green and low-carbon development than previous inventions.

ii. **Greening of green patent examination procedures**
(i) **Green patent quick-examination mechanism**
i) **Legal system of patent examination procedures in China**

The essence of the elements of administrative procedures refers to the manner, step, time limit and sequence of the exercise of administrative power, i.e. it is stipulated that administrative power needs to be completed in a certain manner and within a certain time limit. The greening of the patent examination procedures refers to the development of quick-examination channel for green patent applications under the premise of strict and scientific examination in accordance with the law, so as to minimize the green patent examination time limit, combine and simplify the examination steps, and ensure a more rapid examination of low-carbon and environmental protection patents. There are practical reasons for building a green patent quick-examination mechanism in China: on the one hand, the green patent technology is rapidly updated and their research and development may cost applicants a lot of time and money while facing high-risk failures. Thus, in order to encourage the innovation of green technology and enable it to play a key role in response to climate change, a rapid examination channel is needed to improve the efficiency of the examination and the current serious climate change situation. On the other hand, according to the patent examination time limit stipulated in the *Patent Law of the People's Republic of China*, green patent is not granted preferential rights. According to Article 34 of the *Patent Law of the People's Republic of China*, the publication time limit after preliminary examination by the patent administration department under the State Council is 18 months, and Article 35 stipulates that within three years from the date of application for an invention patent, the patent administrative department under the State Council may conduct a substantive examination at the request of the applicant or on its own initiative. In practice, the current time limit of the invention patent examination is generally 36–48 months. Even though the time for granting a patent can be shortened to 12 months by putting forward an early publication statement and simultaneously an early examination at the substantive examination stage in accordance with Article 34 "early publication of the application" of the *Patent Law of the People's Republic of China*, and having it approved, very few patents have been approved by early examination because the current scope of approval is extremely limited.

ii) **The practice of green patent rapid examination system at home and abroad**

At present, various incentives have been adopted in different countries to stimulate green technology innovation, among which the accelerated examination mechanism of green patent has become the core of the reform of the patent administrative examination system in various countries. On May 12, 2009, UKIPO announced that from that day, applicants can apply for accelerated examination of green patent technology in response to climate change. Green patent applications that are approved will be examined in a "green channel", with the inspection and examination being carried out in a single process and the substantive examination initiated by the Intellectual Property Office ex officio, taking only 9 months from the date of putting forward the patent application to obtaining the patent right.[32] In response to the severe climate change situation, the Korean Intellectual Property Office has also established an ultra-rapid examination mode for green patent applications, for which three requirements must be met: Firstly, the subject of rapid examination of green patent must be the type of technology specified in the Eight Acts established by the Korean government to address environmental issues; secondly, a special panel of technical experts appointed by the Korean Intellectual Property Office will conduct a technical evaluation of the patent and produce an prior technical report to determine whether the patent is eligible for the ultra-rapid examination mode; thirdly, applicants need to apply online for ultra-rapid examination of green patents via the internet to save paper and implement patent licensing low-carbonization. In general, the examination

[32] He Juan: *From Green Technology to Green Patents-Whether a special patent system is needed for climate change*, Intellectual Property, 2010 (1).

time limit in Korea is 17 months, but it can be shortened to 1 month if the patent is under the ultra-rapid patent examination mode.[33]

Although there is no "green channel" for rapid examination of green patent in the *Patent Law of the People's Republic of China*, local and national patent administrative departments have issued normative documents and departmental regulations related to the accelerated examination of green patent. In order to be in line with the proposals of the *Decision of the People's Government of Sichuan Province on Strengthening the Work of Energy Conservation* and *Comprehensive Working Schemes on Energy Conservation and Emission Reduction of the People's Government of Sichuan Province*, Sichuan Intellectual Property Service Promotion Center established a rapid channel for energy conservation and emission reduction patent applications at the Chengdu Agency of China National Intellectual Property Administration in 2007, specifying that five types of technologies can be applied to the accelerated patent application process. However, this rapid channel does not specify the specific procedures for the rapid application and examination of energy conservation and emission reduction patents.[34] On June 19, 2012, China National Intellectual Property Administration issued the *Administrative Measures for the Priority Examination of Invention Patent Applications* (hereinafter referred to the *Measures*), in which Article 4 clearly lists four types of invention patent applications that can be given priority examination.[35] Among them, the first and second types of invention patents given priority examination are directly related to energy conservation and environmental protection technologies. However, the *Measures* are still insufficient: on the one hand, from the perspective of the objects that can apply priority examination, the *Measures* do not make out a green technology classification table, and the classification of green invention patent applications that given priority examination is not clear and targeted, thus leading to an unclear scope of green patent applications that can be applied for priority examination procedures; on the other hand, from the perspective of priority examination procedures, Article 7 of the *Measures* stipulates that a prior examination procedure shall be added to the intellectual property offices of provinces, autonomous regions and municipalities before the priority examination of the four types of patent applications which is contrary to the original intention of the green patent rapid examination mechanism to minimize the examination steps and shorten the examination time limit, thus greatly reducing the implementation effect of priority examination.

---

[33] See the website of China National Intellectual Property Administration: *The UK plans to accelerate the approval procedures of patent applications for green environmental protection technology*, http://www.sipo.gov.cn/wqyz/gwdt/201110/t20111027_626642.html, accessed on June 7, 2015.

[34] The website of China National Intellectual Property Administration: *Sichuan Intellectual Property Office Has Established a Green Channel for the Application of Energy Conservation and Emission Reduction Patents*, http://www.sipo.gov.cn/dtxx/gn/2007/200804/t20080401_359832.html, accessed on June 9, 2015.

[35] See Article 4 of the *Administrative Measures for the Priority Examination of Invention Patent Applications*.

iii) Construction of green patent quick-examination system in China

Although there are differences in the green patent examination procedures established by various countries, a consensus has been reached on the development of a "green channel" for green patent rapid examination. Although Article 16 of the *Law of the PRC on Administrative Permission* empowers local rules and regulations to make specific provisions for the implementation of administrative licensing within the scope of the administrative licensing matters set by the upper-level legislation, in order to maintain the unification of the legal system and practice of patent examination, it is recommended that the *Patent Law of the PRC* should clearly stipulate the quick-examination mechanism to green patent applications, and that the *Implementing Regulations of the Patent Law of the People's Republic of China* and *Guidelines for Patent Examination* should specify the objects to which quick-examination applies and the specific procedures.

Firstly, the objects to which green patent quick-examination applies shall be stipulated. In 2010, WIPO issued the Green Inventory of International Patent Classification (IPC Green Inventory), in which green technologies are presented according to a hierarchy structure, comprising seven main subjects: alternative energy production, transportation, energy conservation, waste management, agriculture and forestry, administration and management or design. A number of technical sub-categories have been established under these seven subjects. China National Intellectual Property Administration can draw on the green technology classification methods issued by WIPO and Patent Offices in other countries, and refine them in conjunction with the low-carbon and environmental-friendly technologies listed in *Administrative Measures for the Priority Examination of Invention Patent Applications*. Therefore, a green technology classification system table that is in line with the reality of patent applications in China will be made to provide clear guidance to applicants and clear examination guidance to examiners.

Secondly, the green patent quick-examination procedures shall be stipulated. The operational elements of administrative procedures mainly include the method, step, sequence and time limit of the exercise of administrative power. Therefore, the green patent quick-examination procedures shall mainly specify the method, time limit, specific step and sequence.

First, the green patent examination procedures shall be disclosed. The basic feature of the construction of the patent system lies in the use of disclosure to curb monopolies, where the disclosure is comprehensive and clear.[36] The disclosure of green patent information includes not only the disclosure of general patent application documents such as claims and specifications of the applicant at the patent application stage, but also the disclosure of information on the implementation status of the patent examination procedures. As some scholar has pointed out in China, although the *Administrative Measures for the Priority Examination of Invention Patent Applications* have been issued by China National Intellectual Property Administration in

[36] Liu Chuntian: *Intellectual Property Law*, Peking University Press and Higher Education Press, 2010: 162.

2012, other citizens or legal persons can not find any written materials or data information on the status of implementation of the priority examination procedures for patent applications by all means.[37] This, to some extent, also increases the cost of promoting green patent and public's duty of care to avoid infringement.

Second, the time limit for green patent examination shall be shortened. Although the examination time limit for green patent varies among countries, all the countries have reduced and consolidated the examination steps based on the general procedures for patent examination and significantly reduce the examination time limit. Thus, in order to ensure a more rapid grant of green invention patents, China should try to shorten the examination time limit of invention patents by taking into account the specific situation of patent examination in China.

Third, the step and sequence of green patent examination shall be simplified: First, when applying for a patent, the applicant should submit an authentication report issued by a third-party authentication institution to certify that patent conforms to the green quick-examination standard. The third-party authentication institution should be an expert group entrusted by China National Intellectual Property Administration, an environmental protection department, or a non-governmental organization with authentication qualifications. Second, the first examination and substantive examination shall be combined. Once the green technology has passed the preliminary examination, the China National Intellectual Property Administration will initiate the substantive examination of the patent ex officio without the need for the applicant to put forward an application for substantive examination. Thirdly, after the substantive examination, if it is determined that a patent right can be granted, the decision shall be made with the least delay possible. At the same time, other citizens or legal person shall be given the right of objection. For patent applications that have passed the green patent quick-examination channel, other citizens or legal person may file an objection to the Patent Re-examination Board if they believe that the approved patent will lead to significant harm to the environment, but the objection shall not suspend the patent rights already approved. If the opposition is sustained, the Patent Re-examination Board may declare the patent invalid.

(III) **Greening of Patent Application System**

The application and protection of patents is the foothold of the patent system. The *Outline of the National Intellectual Property Strategy* issued by the State Council in 2008 clearly states that the government should "guide and support market entities in creating and applying intellectual property rights", "promote the transformation of various innovations and inventions", make the "effective application" of intellectual property rights the basic policy of the national intellectual property strategy and "encourage the transformation and application of intellectual property rights" as one of the important strategic measures to implement the national intellectual property strategy. In this way, the value of green patent can only be realized through

[37] Li Weiwei: *Evaluation and Improvement of the Implementation of the Rapid Examination System for Green Patent Applications*, *Journal of Huazhong University of Science and Technology*, 2014 (3).

the implementation and application of the patent. Based on the *Patent Law of the People's Republic of China*, the legal system of patent application mainly includes three aspects: protection of patent rights, compulsory licensing for patent implementation and promotion and application of patents. Based on the public welfare nature of green patent technology itself and the benefit balancing function of the patent system, the purpose of greening in the application stage of green patent is to limit patent rights and promote the wide implementation of green patent technology, so as to maximize the benefits of environmental protection. The greening of the application of green patent mainly includes three aspects: compulsory licensing for green patents, promotion and application of patent, and greening treatment after patent infringement.

i. **Compulsory licensing for green patent**

The fundamental purpose of the establishment of a patent compulsory licensing system is to prevent the abuse of the patent right enjoyed by the patentee by limiting their rights. And the green patent compulsory licensing indeed refers to the effective and wide implementation and use of green patent technology that is explicitly listed in the classification system in advance, based on limiting patent abuse and promoting the public interests.

(i) **The legitimacy for compulsory licensing for green patent**

First, from the perspective of the legislative purpose and goal of the patent legal system,[38] the patent system is not purely a technical rule or a tool to stimulate innovation and economic development, but a unity of purposefulness and instrumentality. It is the balancing function of the patent right that constitutes the legitimacy of the patent system: on the one hand, the patent system, as a fundamental legal institution of civil law, aims to compulsorily guarantee the exclusive monopoly right of the patentee to the invention patent by law to obtain benefits for a certain time limit; on the other hand, there are limitations to patent right, where the State achieves a balance between individual interests and the public interests by limiting the private nature of patent right through public rights. The "Compulsory License for Exploitation of Patent" provided for in this chapter of the *Patent Law of the People's Republic of China*, that is, the restriction of patent right, reflects the value of balancing the interests of the patent system.

Next, the patent right itself has a monopolistic property. On the one hand, some patentees fail to effectively use their patent rights after obtaining a green patent

[38] The legislative purpose of patent legal system reflects the balance between the protection of patent right and the preservation of public interests. For instance, Article 7 of the TRIPS Agreement defines the objective as "contributing to technological innovation as well as technology transfer and communication", "to the mutual benefit of creators and users of technological knowledge and to the development of social and economic welfare as well as the balance of rights and obligations." Article 1 of the *Patent Law of the People's Republic of China* has stipulated the objective as "protecting the legal rights of Patentee, encouraging innovation and creation, promoting the application of invention and creation, improving the innovation ability, promoting scientific and technological progress as well as economic and social development.".

licensing, and no other entity is able to use this scarce resource given the protection of patent right, leaving the low-carbon technologies unused and resulting in causing waste; on the other hand, overly aggressive patent protection leads to patent manipulation as well as preventing potential competitors from entering the market, resulting in increased costs for subsequent inventions. As a result, to break patent monopolies and reduce the costs of technological innovation, patent compulsory licensing is required to limit patent rights.

Finally, the low-carbon technologies protected by green patents are of public interest, as the wide application of low-carbon technologies will effectively address the serious situation of climate change, promote energy conservation and emission reduction, and safeguard human environmental right. When environmental right, a fundamental human right, is in conflict with patent right, patent rights should give way to fundamental human right. Consequently, the existence of environmental rights is, to some extent, a limitation on patent rights. A compulsory licensing system for green patent is required based on safeguarding human environmental rights and achieving environmental justice.

(ii) **Construction of a compulsory licensing system for green patent in China**

Currently, the laws, regulations and rules relating to the compulsory licensing system of patent implementation in China mainly include the *Patent Law of the People's Republic of China*, the *Implementing Regulations of the Patent Law of the People's Republic of China* and *Measures for the Compulsory Licensing for Patent Implementation* published by China National Intellectual Property Administration in 2012. Although all three legal documents specify the legal situation for compulsory licensing for patent, that is, compulsory licensing for patent abuse, compulsory licensing for public interest and compulsory licensing for dependent patent, none of them explicitly includes green patent that promotes environmental protection and low-carbon development in their contents. Furthermore, in current practice, compulsory licensing has not yet been fully implemented in other areas, except for pharmaceutical patent for specific diseases, which have been implemented in some countries. In China, no application for compulsory licensing has yet been made by any institution or individual.

The construction of a compulsory licensing system for green patent mainly includes the clarification of the scope and procedures of green patent compulsory licensing. Both *Implementing Regulations of the Patent Law of the People's Republic of China* and *Measures for the Compulsory Licensing for Patent Implementation* have clearly stipulated the procedures for compulsory licensing of patent implementation. At present, green patents that promote environmental protection and low-carbon development should be included in the scope of compulsory licensing in the *Patent Law of the People's Republic of China*, *Implementing Regulations of the Patent Law of the People's Republic of China* or *Measures for the Compulsory Licensing for Patent Implementation*. Articles 48, 49, 50 and 51 of the *Patent Law of the People's Republic of China* provide for four types of compulsory licensing for patent implementation respectively: compulsory licensing for patent abuse, compulsory licensing for public interest, compulsory licensing for pharmaceutical products of public health, and compulsory licensing for dependent patents. As Article 50 of the *Patent Law of the People's Republic of China* has specified that the object of compulsory license for patent implementation is "medicine", it is therefore suggested that green patents be included in the compulsory licensing for patent abuse, compulsory licensing for public interest and compulsory licensing for dependent patent.

i) **Compulsory licensing for patent abuse**

According to Article 48 of the *Patent Law of the People's Republic of China*, there are two main legal situations of compulsory licensing for patent abuse.[39] Additional regulations should be added to provide that when a major environmental treatment project is involved and the patentee abuses the green patent or fails to effectively apply the patent within a legally reasonable time limit, the patent administrative department under the State Council shall grant the applicant institution or individual who is qualified to implement a compulsory licensing for green patent.

ii) **Compulsory licensing for public interest**

Article 49 of the *Patent Law of the People's Republic of China* has specified the circumstances in which compulsory license for patent exploitation can be granted. It is recommended that the "state of emergency", "extraordinary case" and "public interest" be clearly explained in the *Rules for Implementation of the Patent Law of the People's Republic of China* or *Measures for the Compulsory Licensing for Patent Implementation,* and that a situation in which a major environmental pollution accident may endanger the life and health of the public be included in the "state of emergency" or "extraordinary case" for compulsory licensing. The "public interest" should be subdivided into the basic interests of citizens, such as the survival environment, and the circumstances in which compulsory licensing are exploited in the public interest shall be clearly listed, such as the case with significance of saving energy and reducing carbon emissions.

iii) **Compulsory licensing for dependent patent**

In addition to Article 51 of the *Patent Law of the People's Republic of China*, which provides for the granting of a compulsory licensing for the exploitation of the preceding invention or new model, in order to achieve innovation and progress in green patents, the legislation may be extended on the basis of the existing regulations: when a later patented invention is more significant than the preceding patented invention in improving the environment, promoting low-carbon and enhancing scientific and technological progress; and when the later granted patent right is dependent on the former patent right for its exploitation, a compulsory licensing to exploited the former invention may be granted by the patent administrative department under the State Council upon application by the latter patentee."

In addition, a clear regulation should be made that if it is not clear whether a green patent belongs to the legal compulsory licensing situation as specified in the *Patent*

[39] See Article 48 of the *Patent Law of the People's Republic of China.*

Law of the People's Republic of China, the patent administration department of the State Council, that is, the compulsory licensing authority for patent implementation, shall make the judgment.

ii. **Promotion and application of green patent**

In order to achieve a balance between the interests of the individual and the public interest as well as to limit the private attribute of the patent right, Article 14 of the *Patent Law of the People's Republic of China* explicitly takes the promotion and use of patents as the basic way of patent application. As opposed to compulsory licensing, for the applicable circumstances, the ones of the promotion and application of patent are limited to safeguarding and promoting "*national interests or public interests*"; for the manner of implementation, the promotion of patent is implemented by the people's government at or above the provincial level ex officio, rather than on the basis of an application by an institution or individual[40]; for the object of patent exploitation, the object of patent promotion is limited to invention patents of state-owned enterprises and institutions. Although the promotion and application of patent enjoys unique advantages in stimulating technological innovation, industrializing patent achievements and maximizing social benefits, Article 14 of the *Patent Law of the People's Republic of China* only specifies the applicable circumstances, implementation methods and applicable objects for the promotion of use, without specifying its detailed application circumstances and operation procedures in the *Implementing Regulations of the Patent Law of the People's Republic of China* revised subsequently, making the patent promotion and application system a "*beautiful vase*".

The promotion and application of green patents will effectively break the technical monopoly held by the patentee, and maximize the positive impact of green technology innovation in the climate change context in terms of energy conservation and emission reduction, pollution prevention and control, and promotion of ecological balance, so as to achieve a balance between patent rights and environmental rights. Therefore, it is of practical significance to construct a promotion and application system for green patent in *Implementing Regulations of the Patent Law of the People's Republic of China*. The construction of a promotion and application system for green patent mainly includes two aspects: firstly, to clarify the scope of patent promotion by defining "national interest" and "public interest", and secondly, to refine the rights of intervention and boundaries of the relevant departments of the State Council and the people's governments above the provincial level in the promotion and application of patents, so as to make the promotion and application system for patent practicable. In the specific definition of "national interest" and "public interest" in the *Implementing Regulations of the Patent Law of the People's Republic of China*, and in defining which invention patents are those of great significance to the national interests or public interests, we can draw on Article 8 "Principles" of the TRIPS Agreement to define public interests as those relating to public health and nutrition and of vital importance to the promotion of social, economic and technological development. In addition, further refinement and listing should be made to

[40] See Li Yuxiang: *Research on Patent Promotion and Application, Intellectual Property*, 2011 (4).

include green patents that are conducive to pollution prevention and control, energy conservation and emission reduction, and environmental improvement in the "invention patents of great significance to national interests or public interests". In addition, on the premise that the *Patent Law of the People's Republic of China* grants the relevant departments of the State Council and the people's governments at or above the provincial level the right to initiate the promotion of patents and the State Council the final say on the promotion and application of patents, the *Implementing Regulations of the Patent Law of the People's Republic of China* need to further restrict the requirements for the intervention of the government public power. Reference can be made to Article 31 of the TRIPS Agreement, which stipulates that the application by the government or a third party approved by the government of a patent that is not authorized by the patentee is limited to "cases of national emergency or other extreme emergency or for public, non-commercial purposes". On the one hand, it prevents the government from excessively interfering with private rights through patent promotion, and on the other hand, it further clarifies the circumstances under which patent promotion is applicable, making the patent promotion system more practicable.

iii. **Greening treatment of patent infringement**

Based on the *Patent Law of the People's Republic of China*, patent application includes not only the legal application of patent rights, such as the use and disposal of patent application by the patentee within the scope of legal authority, the compulsory licensing exploited by the patent administrative department under the State Council, and the promotion and application of the patent approved by the State Council, but also the illegal application without patentee's permission. Thus, the greening of patent application also includes the greening of the relief system for patent infringement, which mainly includes the greening treatment of infringing tools, the greening treatment of infringing products and careful use of the replacement of calling off an infringement with punitive compensation.

(i) **Greening treatment of patent infringing tools**

At present, both the *Patent Law of the People's Republic of China* and the *Implementing Regulations of the Patent Law of the People's Republic of China* do not stipulate the disposal methods of infringing tools used by patent infringers, but in accordance with Article 134 of *General Principles of the Civil Law of the PRC*, the People's Courts may seize property and illegal gains from illegal activities when hearing civil cases; Article 48 of the *Copyright Law of the People's Republic of China* also stipulates the disposal methods of illegal tools in copyright infringement cases; Article 60 of the *Trademark Law of the People's Republic of China* stipulates that if the industrial and commercial administrative department determines that an infringement is established, then it shall order the confiscation and destruction of the tools used in the manufacture of infringing goods and the falsification of the registered trademarks. Thus, the disposal method of patent infringing tools determined by China's law is "confiscation and destruction". However, considering low-carbon, environmental protection and public interest, patent infringement tools cannot simply be "destroyed". A more resource-conservation and low-carbon method should be adopted for the disposal of patent infringing tools. Reference could be made to Article 46 of the TRIPS Agreement, which stipulates that judicial authority has the right to dispose of materials and tools used in the production of infringing goods "except commercial channel in a method that reduces the risk of further infringement without compensation". While the *Patent Law of the People's Republic of China* and the *Implementing Regulations of the Patent Law of the People's Republic of China* stipulate the treatment of patent infringing tools as "disposed except commercial channel", which has a broader connotation and is more flexible and more suitable for environmental interpretation and low-carbonization.

(ii) **Greening treatment of patent infringing products**

Although the *Patent Law of the People's Republic of China* and the *Implementing Regulations of the Patent Law of the People's Republic of China* do not stipulate the specific treatment methods of patent infringing goods, in accordance with Article 134, Paragraph 3 of the *General Principles of the Civil Law of the PRC*, the People's Court may "seize property and illegal gains from illegal activities". Article 48 of the *Copyright Law of the People's Republic of China* stipulates that for copyright infringement that harms the public interests, the copyright administrative department shall "confiscate the illegal gains and confiscate and destroy the infringing copies". Article 60 of the *Trademark Law of the People's Republic of China* stipulates that if the industrial and commercial administrative department determines that an infringement is established, it shall order the confiscation and destruction of the tools used in the manufacture of infringing goods and the falsification of registered trademarks. Therefore, the disposal method of patent infringing products determined by China's law is "confiscation and destruction". However, a disposal method system is not established, i.e. in which cases the infringing goods should be confiscated and in which cases they should be directly destroyed. Nor does it stipulates how to further dispose of the infringing goods after confiscation, and lacks consideration of the impact of disposal of infringing goods on the environmental public interest.

Although the Patent Law of the People's Republic of China and the Implementing Regulations of the Patent Law of the People's Republic of China do not involve the disposal of patent infringing goods, Article 27, Paragraph 3 of the *Regulation of the People's Republic of China on the Customs Protection of Intellectual Property Rights* systematically stipulates the green disposal methods after the customs confiscates the infringing goods.[41] In addition to the specific method of "disposal except commercial channel" or "destruction" of infringing goods, Article 46 of the TRIPS Agreement also stipulates that the disposal of infringing goods "shall take into account the necessary balance between the severity of the infringement and the remedy decided, as well as the interests of third parties". Thus, in terms of the disposal of intellectual property infringing goods, both the *Regulation of the People's Republic of China*

[41] See Article 27 Paragraph 3 of the *Regulation of the People's Republic of China on the Customs Protection of Intellectual Property Rights*.

on the Customs Protection of Intellectual Property Rights and the TRIPS Agreement have taken into account the balance between the protection of the interests of intellectual property owners and resources effective utilization.

With reference to *Regulation of the People's Republic of China on the Customs Protection of Intellectual Property Rights* and the provisions of the TRIPS Agreement as well as the existing legal system for the disposal of infringing goods in China, the greening of the disposal of patent infringing goods in China should mainly include two aspects: first, the disposal methods and the specific application situation of infringing goods confiscated and directly destroyed, and the specific disposal method after confiscation shall be stipulated in the *Patent Law of the People's Republic of China* and the *Rules for Implementation of the Patent Law of the People's Republic of China*; second, the principle of balance of interests in the disposal of patent infringing goods shall be established, i.e. considering the interests of third parties and social public interests on the basis of protecting the dominant position and rights of the patentee. It means that infringing goods must not be simply destroyed, but should be used to our best advantage, thus to achieve resources conservation and low-carbon development.

(iii) **Greening treatment of patent infringement**

Article 134 of the *General Principles of the Civil Law of the PRC* sets out "call off an infringement" as one of the ways in which an infringer can assume civil liability, and Article 60 and 66 of the *Patent Law of the People's Republic of China* clearly stipulate that the disposal method of patent infringement is "call off an infringement". No matter as a bearing method of substantive civil legal responsibility or temporary restraining order, "call off an infringement" aims to remedy the legitimate rights and interests of the right holder. But for patent infringement, especially green patent infringement, it should not simply be prohibited. If the infringement is deliberately called off, it may lead to major damage to public interests, such as serious damage to environmental interests. Therefore, "call of an infringement" shall be carefully applied for the disposal of patent infringement. Punitive damages shall be applied instead for relief if the public interests obviously exceed private interest of the patentee.

Public interest considerations should be taken into account when dealing with violations of the law, as reflected in the *Law of the PRC on Administrative Permission* and the *Administrative Litigation Law*, such as paragraphs 2 and 3 of Article 69 of the *Law of the PRC on Administrative Permission* and Article 74 of the new *Administrative Litigation Law of the PRC*, which both contain detailed provisions. Thus, the illegal administrative acts shall not be "revoked" when the public interests are obviously more important than private interests or the administrative order. Greening treatment of patent infringement means that the remedy methods for patent infringement shall not be limited to simply "calling of an infringement", fully balancing the private interests and public interests. When calling off an infringement will lead to significant damage to the public interests and environmental protection, it should be used carefully and punitive damages should be implemented to make up the loss of the patentee.

Chapter 7
Administrative Guidance for Innovative Low-Carbon Regulation

1 Practical Difficulties in Administrative Guidance for Promoting Energy Conservation & Emission Reduction Among Citizens

1.1 Role of an Individual Citizen in Energy Conservation and Emission Reduction

In-depth implementation of the energy conservation and emission reduction campaign is not only an important part of the strategic deployment of "promoting low-carbon and circular development" and "forming an environmental-governance system involving the government, enterprises and the general public"[1] proposed in China's 13th Five-Year Plan, but also a powerful measure to realize the "green development" and "comprehensive conservation and efficient use of resources"[2] of the Fifth plenary session of 18th CPC Central Committee. The actions of the state in promoting the development of a low-carbon society are mainly presented in two ways: on the one hand, for all kinds of enterprise legal persons and other organizations, the state has formulated and implemented a series of compulsory behavioral rules to regulate their production and organizational activities by creating specific models of rights and obligations, adjusting the relationship of low-carbon social development and achieving the goal of energy conservation and emission reduction; on the other hand, for the general citizens, the state has mainly guided them to low-carbon consumption and set up the concept of low-carbon life through non-compulsory means such as encouragement and advocacy. It should be said that every

[1] The Fifth Plenary Session of the 18th Central Committee of the Communist Party of China passed the *Recommendations of the Central Committee of the Communist Party of China (CPC) for the 13th Five-Year Plan for Economic and Social Development of the People's Republic of China.*

[2] *Communiqué of the Fifth Plenary Session of the 18th CPC Central Committee*, http://www.news.xinhuanet.com/fortune/2015-10/29/c_1116983078.htm, December 4th, 2015.

S. Fang and B. Tan, *On the Administrative Law of China in Addressing Climate Change*,
https://doi.org/10.1007/978-981-19-7705-3_7

citizen has an "obligation not to harm others" when emitting greenhouse gases and an "ethical and moral responsibility"[3] to actively practice low-carbon consumption for the society as a whole and for future generations.[4] However, considering the limited legal intervention in citizens' lives and the actual needs of China's rapid economic and social development, it is not appropriate to incorporate all the behaviors of citizens in the development of a low-carbon society into the compulsory legal regulation, in contrast, it is more necessary and feasible for the state to guide citizens to live a low-carbon life through "administrative guidance" and other "flexible" behavioral approaches. Meanwhile, the "Jevons Paradox" in energy economics shows that without lifestyle changes, increased energy efficiency may lead to higher energy consumption. It tells us that we cannot rely too much on technological innovation to reduce energy consumption.[5] Analyzing the trend of carbon emission in China from 2001 to 2009, we can find that the total amount of carbon emission has increased sharply since 2001, while the emission intensity has been decreasing, from 3.2 tons of CO_2 emission per tone of standard coal in 2001 to 2.2 tons of CO_2 emission per tone of standard coal in 2009. We can see that China's energy utilization is being optimized, but total carbon emissions are rising.[6] This bears out the "Jevons Paradox". This shows that how to properly resolve the conflict between "increasing consumption spending" and "energy conservation and emission reduction" can not only rely on the technological innovation of enterprises, but also the change of citizens' lifestyle and social behavior. In the absence of rigid institutional conditions for regulating carbon emissions for citizens, such as administrative permits, administrative penalties and administrative coercion, the overcoming of the "Jevons paradox" relies heavily on the role of administrative guidance.

1.2 Shortcomings of Administrative Guidance in Effectiveness

Administrative guidance refers to the administrative organ, within its authority or jurisdiction, using guidance, advice, suggestion and other "flexible" way to achieve certain administrative purposes.[7] In order to implement the *Notice of the State Council on Issuing the Energy Conservation and Emission Reduction Plan during the "Twelfth Five-Year Plan" Period*, which proposes "to carry out an in-depth national

[3] [US] Donald A. Brown: *Ethical Obligations of Individuals to Reduce Greenhouse Gas Emissions*, translated by Shi Jun and Dong Jingqi, *Yuejiang Academic Journal*, Vol. 5, 2012.

[4] [US] Donald A. Brown: *Ethical Obligations of Individuals to Reduce Greenhouse Gas Emissions*, translated by Shi Jun and Dong Jingqi, *Yuejiang Academic Journal*, Vol. 5, 2012.

[5] Lazarus A. *To cool a sweltering earth: Does Energy Efficiency Improvement Offset the Climate Impacts of Lifestyle? Energy Policy*, 2010, (38).

[6] See Zhao Dingtao, Guo Tao, and Fan Jin: *Determination and Evolution of Embedded Carbon Footprint of Chinese Urban Residents*, *Systems Engineering*, Vol. 5, 2012.

[7] See Yang Haikun and Huang Xuexian: *A Comparative Study of Administrative Guidance*, *China Legal Science*, Vol. 3, 1999.

campaign for energy conservation and emission reduction", the State Council in September 2013 formulated the *Air Pollution Prevention and Control Action Plan*, which clearly proposes "to actively carry out various forms of publicity and education to popularize the scientific knowledge of air pollution prevention and control"; The Ministry of Environmental Protection issued the *Breathe Together & Work Together—Citizen Code of Conduct* on August 13, 2014, advocating citizens to adhere to low-carbon travel, green consumption and develop power saving habits; The Ministry of Environmental Protection has set the theme of Environment Day 2015 as "Practice Green Living" to propagandize the message of "practicing green living" through the intense publicity on Environment Day, so that the majority of citizens' awareness of green lifestyle can be consciously transformed into practical action. Local governments and relevant departments also actively use administrative guidance as a "flexible" way to promote the concept of low-carbon life for citizens, such as in May 2014, the Luqiao Traffic Police Brigade in Taizhou City, Zhejiang Province, carried out "low-carbon icon" and "civilized driving icon" selection event in the district to minimize private car travel and advocate low-carbon travel. In June 2014, Wuzhou City, Guangxi Power Supply Bureau distributed energy-saving publicity materials, issuing energy-saving lamps and explaining electricity saving to guide citizens to save electricity and use electricity scientifically, advocating the concept of energy-saving and emission-reduction. A series of administrative guidelines adopted by various administrative organs and departments from the central to the local level to achieve the goal of energy saving and emission reduction have been effective in promoting a low-carbon lifestyle, however, the problem is, the majority of citizens know what "low-carbon" is and how to live a low-carbon life, but it is difficult to internalize their knowledge of low-carbon life and put them into practices.

In general, citizens' intrinsic motivation to practice low-carbon consumption, energy conservation and emission reduction is still insufficient, and the effectiveness of the government in building a low-carbon society through administrative guidance is greatly reduced. For example, according to the survey data of the statistics of residents of low-carbon lifestyle consumption launched by Zhejiang Huzhou Consumer Protection Commission in 2010, on the use of disposable plastic bags, 15.47% of people use every time, 43.27% of people will use most of the time, while people refusing to use only accounts for 21.53%.[8] Another example, according to the results of a survey on low-carbon awareness conducted by scholars in Tianjin in 2012, 8% of the respondents were familiar with the meaning and content of low-carbon consumption, 83% said they had heard of low-carbon consumption, and only 9% had never heard of low-carbon consumption, which means that 91% of the respondents know about and are aware of low-carbon consumption to some extent. However, only 31% of the surveyed citizens said they often concerned about low-carbon consumption, environmental protection and energy saving, and only 28% practice low-carbon

[8] See Huzhou Consumer Protection Commission survey report on low-carbon lifestyle consumption, China Consumers Association website: http://www.cca.org.cn/jmxf/detail/24082.html, visited on December 4, 2015.

consumption motivated by individual consciousness.[9] Although the factors affecting citizens' low-carbon consumption, energy conservation and emission reduction are very complex, in terms of the characteristics and functions of administrative guidance, there is still a need for further exploration and innovation on how to strengthen the implementation effectiveness of this "flexible" administrative regulation and explore the resources to guarantee its implementation.

2 Conversion of Administrative Guidance Concepts in Low-Carbon Era

2.1 Concepts of Existing Administrative Guidance

Traditionally, administrative guidance is defined as a non-coercive administrative action in the doctrine, which determines that administrative guidance cannot achieve the predetermined behavioral effect in time like administrative punishment and administrative coercion. Whether the administrative guidance will take effect depend on the degree of acceptance of the administrative guidance content by the administrative counterpart and on whether the counterpart can voluntarily follow the administrative guidance, and it does not authorize the administrative subject to promote the realization of the effect of administrative guidance through mandatory means. The non-compulsory nature of administrative guidance makes it hard to make great difference. And the specific content of the administrative guidance also focuses on the procedures, methods or means of administrative action, but seldom demanding effect of administrative guidance. Influenced by the traditional administrative guidance concepts, the current administrative guidance on citizens' energy conservation and emission reduction in China has the following two characteristics: on the one hand, it focuses heavily on the setting of the process of citizens' energy conservation and emission reduction guidance, but rarely mentions the expected effect to be achieved by the guidance. For example, the Section V of the *China's Policies and Actions for Addressing Climate Change (2012)*, "Participation of the Whole Society" provided detailed requirements on publicity, education and guidance to address climate change, but there is no provision for evaluating and summarizing the actual effect of these efforts on promoting energy conservation and emission reduction among citizens. On the other hand, there is a lack of provisions on the responsibility mechanism to urge the implementation of administrative guidance, that is, through the establishment of the corresponding assessment and disciplinary system to monitor and spur the administrative organs to make sure that administrative guidance takes effect. Relevant laws and policies in China like *Energy Conservation Law*, *Law of the People's Republic of China on Promoting the Development of a recycling Economy*,

[9] Huang Guozhu, Zhu Tan and Lu Diyin: *Survey Analysis of Urban Residents' low-carbon Awareness—Based on Data from 1894 Questionnaires in Tianjin*, *The World of Survey and Research*, Vol. 11, 2013.

and *Notice of the State Council on Making More Efforts to Ensure the Realization of the Target on Energy Conservation and Emission Reduction of the Eleventh Five-year Plan* generally require government departments at all levels to "carry out energy conservation publicity and education, popularize the scientific knowledge of energy conservation, enhance the awareness of energy conservation among all people", "encourage and guide citizens to use energy-saving, water-saving, material-saving and environmentally friendly products and recyclable products" and "advocate the concept of green consumption and moderate consumption", all of which are guidance applicable to administrative departments on how to implement the administrative guidance, without specifying the responsibility system for administrative guidance. From the above two aspects, we can see that the current administrative guidance on energy conservation and emission reduction in China still need to be improved in that it focus on the process rather than the actual effect.

2.2 Result-Oriented Should Be Highlighted in Administrative Guidance

Scientific researches show that the irreversibility of climate change will affect the ecosystems and socio-economic systems on which human beings depend, and consequences of which will lead to irreversible disasters. So, we must take proactive behavioral measures to reduce carbon emissions beforehand and prevent consequential harmful effect. At the same time, we shall correct the "invalid" administrative guidance concept, and pay more attention to the actual effect of administrative guidance. If the implementation of administrative guidance only focuses on the procedure and ignores the actual effect, it will lead to a huge waste of administrative costs, and strictly speaking, it is an kind of illegal administrative act. Because the counterparts of the administrative guidance of energy conservation and emission reduction are often not fixed ones, the guidance involves large number of people from all walks of life, and requires a large amount of human, material and financial resources. Therefore, administrative guidance to motivate citizens to save energy and reduce emissions must pursue for optimal results in terms of cost-benefit.

Theoretically, administrative guidance, as an administrative act, has the essential characteristics of administrative acts, i.e. through the adjustment of the counterparts' behavior to achieve the goal of specific administrative management. For a long time, administrative organs have, due to the non-compulsory nature of administrative guidance, always focused on the process of administrative guidance while ignoring to achieve specific administrative goals; it is obviously a cognitive misalignment. Therefore, the relation between the results and means of administrative guidance must be re-conceptualized. To fulfill the fundamental requirement of administrative actions to achieve the administrative objectives, a concept of result-oriented administrative guidance shall be set up: that is, the means and methods of guidance shall serve for rather than outshine the administrative purposes. Administrative guidance should be results-oriented, proposing targeted, innovative methods, and focus on achieving the social benefits of obtaining a positive response from those being guided. To this end, internally, the administration should require the administrative guidance subject to establish a target responsibility system, and through performance assessment, accountability and other mechanisms to enhance the effective implementation of the guidance with motivation and responsibility; externally, develop a variety of targeted, diversified guidance methods to induce the entire population to practice energy saving and emission reduction.

3 Strengthening the Pertinence of Administrative Guidance

3.1 Crux Analysis of Existing Administrative Guidance

Currently, administrative guidance in China is not closely related to the needs of the daily life of its citizens. Administrative guidance fails to give adequate and targeted guidance about the long-time wrong attitude of the public about environmental protection as shown by their thoughts and life norms. Hence, pro-environmental publicity of the administrative authorities fails to strike a responsive chord with many citizens.[10] Effects of administrative guidance are not quite satisfactory. Currently, there are several obstacles that exist in the ideas and life norms of individuals to prevent them from taking initiative to embrace energy conservation and low-carbon lifestyles. Administrative authorities must provide highlighted guidance to tackle the obstacles.

(I) **The Idea of Ignoring Future Impacts of Climate Change**

It has become an indisputable fact in science that the crisis of climate change is urgent. In the recent ten years, many authoritative scholars (including many Nobel Laureates) have warned as if by prior agreement that mankind may only have the time of one or two generations to take effective actions to avoid this global ecological disaster.[11] According to the prediction of Intergovernmental Panel on Climate Change (IPCC), global warming caused by consumption of fossil fuels may accelerate and sea level will rise 0.2–0.6 m by the year 2100. This means the environment in which one-tenth of the world's population live will be seriously threatened at that time.[12] However, citizens are not mindful of possible danger in times of peace so they, as individuals, are unable to rationally realize seriousness of the climate crisis due to limits of

[10] Wang Jianmin & Wang Junhao, *Factors Affecting Public's Low-carbon Consumption Mode and Government's Management and Control Policy, Management World*, 2011 (4).

[11] See [Australian] David Shearman & Joseph Wayne Smith, *The Climate Change and the Failure of Democracy* (Wu Xishen and Li Nan, Trans.), Social Sciences Academic Press, 2009, p.7.

[12] IPCC, *Climate Change 2007: Forth Assessment Report*, at http://www.ipcc.ch/.

perspective, thoughts and information.[13] Some researchers found that physiologically the nature of human beings determines that it is very hard for them to think with a long-time perspective and generally they only habitually make judgements for immediate gains and losses.[14] In addition, different from the specific and realistic risks in such areas as nuclear, finance and terrorism, ecological risks are mainly predicted through scientific models and imagined experiments. The thoughts are "counterfactual".[15] The risks cannot be directly encountered in daily life and hence cannot bring a real sense of crisis. It is hard for the general public to take the risks seriously. Many people think that the coming day of these potential public risks to the lives of them as individuals is far distant. The risks are problems for the future generations to consider. Therefore, they ignore the risks that may be caused by further climate change.

(II) The Inactive Attitude That "An Individual Is Too Weak to Achieve Anything"

One the one hand, the low-carbon concept for protecting the environment will be most effectively implemented due to cumulative effect of the acts of individuals. On the other hand, triviality of an individual's acts themselves brings about the inactive public attitude. A nation-wide survey in the UK conducted by a scholar in 2008 showed that although many people were concerned about global climate change, many of them believed that "humans are not having that much impact."[16] A similar survey conducted by Chinese scholars also showed that nearly two thirds of the respondents thought that "this task that benefits all mankind is too arduous and small actions cannot contribute a lot to it" and "a person's power cannot bring much change".[17] It can be found that many people have not fully and positively recognized the impacts of the pro-environmental actions that they may take as individuals. In addition, the publicity nature of the pressure brought by climate change in contrast with individuality of citizens as individuals creates a big room for citizens to evade their responsibilities and therefore makes the citizens lack the confidence in and the driving force for taking low-carbon actions. From the perspective of administration management, the formation of the above situation is greatly due to the citizens' information deficit for low-carbon actions. They cannot fully get such relevant information as the potential of their energy efficient actions and the contributions made by such actions, for example, the utility of the energy efficient and emission reduction actions taken by them in daily life and what collective effect can be achieved by

---

[13] For example, an individual's limits of perspective, nonprofessional thinking and lack of information.

[14] Some researchers found that they usually do not look beyond two generations after them. See E.O. Wilson, *The Future of Life*, London: Little Brown, 2002.

[15] [UK] Anthony Giddens, *The Consequences of Modernity* (Tian He, Trans.), Yilin Press, 2011, p. 116.

[16] Ipsos-MORI, public attitudes to climate change 2008. Retrieved November 18th, 2012 from http://www.ipsos-mori.com/Search.aspx?usterms=public%20attitudes%20to%20climate%20change.

[17] Wang Jianmin&Wang Junhao, *Factors Affecting Public' s Low-carbon Consumption Mode and Government's Management and Control Policy*. *Management World*, 2011 (4).

concerted actions of all citizens. Therefore, they develop an idea that the influence of an individual's actions is trivial. At the same time, when facing the energy conservation and emission reduction tasks announced by administrative authorities, citizens will unconsciously compare the tasks with the low-carbon actions taken by them in daily life. This will further consolidate the huge gap between an individual power and the public target.

(III) The Psychology of "Hitchhiking" and "Conformity"

"Hitchhiking" refers to the behavior of some citizens where they do not act actively while expect to benefit from the actions of others. "Conformity" refers to the act of people that sit on the fence, do not act actively but align their acts with others to fit in with the group. People with these two mindsets influence each other causing a "prisoner's dilemma" where no one takes the lead to take low-carbon actions, that is, "I do not take low-carbon actions but expect others to take" and "I won't take low-carbon actions until others have". Climate change is a public problem and also an external problem. This is an important reason for developing the psychology of "hitchhiking". Responding to change of the climate is viewed as responding to the change of "public goods".[18] No matter you act or do not act, environmental bonus brought by energy conservation and pro-environmental actions is shared by the entire society and is not exclusively owed. This makes some citizens to form the mindset that if they do not act actively, they can also benefit from the actions of others. Someone ever vividly drew an analogy: "if money is raised to repair the road of a village and you do not contribute, the consequence may be that you are prevented from using the road; however if money is raised to improve air quality of the village and you do not contribute, no one can restrain you from breathing in improved air of the village."[19] In addition, the psychology of "hitchhiking" is related to a lack of public spirit and selfish attitude on social responsibility because "the single raindrop never feels responsible for the flood". The reason for "conformity" is that the public goods attribute of dealing with climate change will make the actions of individuals or some people benefit all, at the same time, the person that conserves energy and reduces emissions needs to pay certain costs. Considering the unfair consequence that one may "suffer losses" because other people may "hitchhike", a person that may potentially take action to conserve energy and reduce emissions eventually decides to not to do anything until most people do. What's more, although many people have a correct understanding, they are limited by the overall pressure in the group and do not want to become isolated individuals due to being different. Many people also do not have the courage to follow their own hearts to do the right thing and therefore have to choose to align their behaviors with those of most people around them.

---

[18] Wang Jun, *Literature Review of Climate Change Economics. World Economy*, 2008 (8).

[19] Mao Cui& Mao Chunchu, *An Ultimate Query on Energy Conservation, China South Grid*, December 27, 2010.

(IV) The Liberal Consumption View

Individuals' carbon emissions primarily come from daily consumption, and currently most citizens hold a concept of liberal consumption, which is shown by the personal liberty in desire-based consumption[20] and by the personal liberty in money saving consumption. Desire-based consumption refers to consuming far more material or spiritual products than what is basically needed in life for enjoyment of material things and spiritual stimulation. The products are usually high-carbon products that waste resources and are extravagant. They think it is purely their personal freedom to choose how they spend as long as they have the ability to consume the products and are willing to bear the corresponding costs. They will not consider the excessive depletion of resources and energy and carbon emissions caused by the consumption, since they are not mandatorily pressed to do so. With regard to money saving consumption, the factor that the consumer considers is to save money on expenses. Of course, the intention aligns with energy conservation and emission reduction in some cases. For example, using a bicycle means spending less than a motor vehicle and emits less carbon dioxide. However, such a consumption does not completely align with energy conservation and emission reduction in many cases. For example, traditional household appliances are cheaper than new energy efficient household appliances that support environmental protection. The former may end up saving more money but are not good as the latter for energy conservation and emission reduction. Consumers have the right to buy the former to save money but this is not good for energy conservation and environmental protection of the entire society. Therefore, people upholding this concept of consumption shows they fail to actively get involved in the drive to achieve energy conservation and emission reduction. In addition, consumers with the mindset of saving money in consumption also shows they fail to fully realize the long-term economic benefits brought by low-carbon and energy efficient consumption and also shows their "loss aversion" tendency. "Loss aversion" refers to the tendency of people to prefer small imminent losses or gains than greater gains or losses in the future.[21] They abandon long-term benefits brought by low-carbon consumption because money can be saved in present consumption.

In general, the aforesaid concepts of liberal consumption are related to traditional awareness of rights with individual freedom as the center. People think they pay bills of the things they buy for themselves and this has nothing to do with the interest of others and this is an area subject to absolute autonomy.

[20] Liu Fushen & Guo Lingling, *Costs of Existentialism Under the Rule of Consumerism Hegemony, Humanist Magazine*, 2005 (4).

[21] See John Broome, *Discounting the Future, Philosophy & Public Affairs*, 1994, Vol. 23, pp. 128–156.

3.2 *Strengthening the Pertinence of Administrative Guidance*

The government must give targeted administrative guidance to promote the people to change the aforesaid norms and ideas.

(I) **Strengthening Efforts to Warn People of and Admonish People for Negative Consequences of Climate Change**

With regard to the citizens' ignorance of the risks of climate change and their wrong idea that they should not be mindful of future danger in times of peace, administrative authorities should pay attention to warning them of the serious consequences reasonably brought by their ignorance—to be ruthlessly punished by laws of nature and responsibilities to be imposed by stricter laws in the future. Administrative authorities should comprehensively use direct ways to guide the people to directly and intuitively realize the dangerous consequences of climate change and the urgency to prevent it from happening.

(II) **Actively Using Information Tools to Direct Individuals to Correctly Realize Their Potential for Taking Low-carbon Actions and Their Contributions to Driving Low-carbon Development**

It is believed in environmental psychology that " Pro-environmental behavior will become a more attractive alternative when positive consequences are attached to it."[22] With regard to the idea that an individual's power is not worth mentioning, when administrative guidance is given, information concerning individuals' contribution to energy conservation and emission reduction should be fully conveyed to convince them of the significance of their individual low-carbon actions so as to increase their confidence level, interest and motivation. For example, fully displaying the enormous impact brought by concerted efforts of all citizens and providing feedbacks about individuals' contributions to energy conservation and emission reduction to stimulate their enthusiasm for competition.

(III) **Taking Great Pains to Direct Consumers to Change Liberal Consumption That is not Low-carbon**

For desire-based consumption, targeted administrative guidance must be given to restrain it because the needs it satisfies are "false needs" beyond basic needs of life.[23] The resources exhausted and the large amount of carbon dioxide emitted into the atmosphere for satisfying such needs should have been completely avoided. Different

---

[22] Wokje Abrahamse, Linda Steg, Charles Vlek, Talib Rothengatter, *A Review of Intervention Studies Aimed at Household Energy Conservation*, *Journal of Environmental Psychology*, 2005, Vol. 25, p. 278.

[23] [US] Herbert Marcuse, *One-Dimensional Man* (Zhang Feng & Lv Shiping, Trans.), Chongqing Publishing House, 1988, p. 6.

from desire-based consumption, money saving consumption is an interest-balancing choice made by profit-driven citizens. Based on this, the highlight of administrative guidance is to help citizens to correctly view the relationship between money-saving and low-carbon development and tell them the money saved at the moment is less than the long-term economic benefits brought by low-carbon consumption. For the "loss aversion" tendency, administrative guidance should provide appropriate inducement (for example, reducing taxes levied on buying energy efficient ad pro-environmental products and providing preferential price) or lead them to choose a way of consumption that saves money and can also reduce the level of carbon emissions.

(IV) Creating a Social Environment Where Hitchhiking Is Prevented and How to Act Actively Should Be Modeled for People That Tend to "Conform to Others"

With regard to the mindsets of "hitchhiking" and "conformity", the highlight is to reduce the chance for "hitchhiking". Through administrative guidance, administrative authorities can establish low-carbon social organizations that are of proper size and have clear boundaries to restrain "hitchhiking" phenomenon. Low-carbon social organizations are like numerous cells of the society. They can turn energy conservation and emission reduction, an abstract social responsibility, into a specific responsibility of the cells, because it is more convenient to allocate responsibilities clearly and equitably among organizations of certain size and convenient for them to mutually supervise each other and reduce "hitchhiking". The two mindsets of "hitchhiking" and "conformity" are closely related, so solving the problem of "hitchhiking" can also help some people that conform to break free of the worry of having "hitchhikers" to some extent. At the same time, administrative guidance can also use typical exemplification to actively direct people that "conform" to act. The basic characteristic of people with "conformity" mindset is that they may sit on the fence but they are willing to follow others to act. The typical exemplification of energy conservation and emission reduction as provided by administrative guidance just provides positive examples and targets for these people to imitate and hence impels them to initiatively follow the examples to change their behaviors to low-carbon lifestyles. The UK Department for Environment, Food and Rural Affairs (DEFRA) pointed out after a "Defra Survey of Public Attitudes and Behaviors Toward the Environment" that: for people that are more dependent on behaviors becoming the norm before they will act (14% of the respondents who said "I do a couple of things to help the environment. I'd really like to do more, well as long as I saw others were."), exemplification should be provided to guide them.[24]

[24] See Department for Environment, Food and Rural Affairs, *A Framework for Pro-Environmental Behaviors*, London: HMSO, 2008.

4 Path of Innovative Administrative Guidance

If administrations want to duly promote citizens to adopt low-carbon behaviors, the ways of providing administrative guidance should be innovated. Currently, administrative authorities mainly provide inducement[25] to persuade people to adopt low-carbon behaviors but this method has some limitations. A lot money needs to be spent to make inducement play its due role so it is hard to widely use inducement in the long run. Therefore, administrative guidance should be provided in various innovated ways instead of one.

4.1 Use Warnings to Provide Guidance

Giving warnings to provide administrative guidance is to warn people of and admonish people for the serious consequences of climate change to promote them to realize the urgency and necessity to reduce emission and improve energy efficacy. Warnings are mainly used to deal with people's ignorance of the risks of climate change. The types of warnings include:

(I) **Use Examples to Warn People of Possible Dangers**

Generally, it is rare for the general public to directly see climate change crisis in their daily life, so particular events need to be used to warn people of the danger. It is pointed in media psychology that "when abstract risks from climate change that are of statistical significance are linked with specific hot issues and a clear-cut way of response, they can help the public very vividly feel the pressing danger."[26] Relevant authorities in China have begun to use this kind of guidance in practice. For example, they have organized to broadcast such programs as *Global Warming—The Prophecy is Coming True*, and Facing Up With *Global Warming.*[27] These programs have played a certain role in warning and educating the public. However, for the examples used, improvement is still needed in terms of content and communication. As far as content is concerned, it's not enough to only show dangerous consequences that may occur in relevantly distant future such as sea-level rise and distinction of species. The emphasis should be put on national conditions of China. The major examples chosen should be

[25] For example, encouragement and rewards and other inducement measures are used for such low-carbon behaviors of citizens as saving energy, saving water, green consumption and planting trees in related laws such as Articles 8 to 9 of the *Law of the PRC on the Prevention and Control of Atmospheric Pollution*, Article 67 of the *Energy Conservation Law* and Article 48 of the *Law of the People's Republic of China on Promoting the Development of a recycling Economy*, Article 6 and Article 16 of the *Cleaner Production Promotion Law of the PRC* and Article 12 of the *Forestry Law of the PRC*.

[26] See [UK] Atony Giddens, *The Politics of Climate Change* (Cao Rongxiang, Trans.), Social Sciences Academic Press, 2009, p. 127.

[27] Video retrieved September 27th, 2013 from: http://www.video.sina.com.cn/v/b/2406971-1258065320.html; http://www.tv.cntv.cn/video/C39278/3237626666194fb68838eae06f74aaec.

regions and things that show people's lives have been seriously affected by drought, smog, pollution and things like those, as they can be better understood by Chinese citizens. "Compared with unfamiliar risks and unobvious risks, familiar risks and obvious risks are thought to occur more easily and can get more attention."[28]

(II) **Use Direct Experiences to Warn People**

People usually tend to believe what they personally experience. According to the law of cognition, when an individual uses his/her own experience as the base to perceive risks, negative feelings related to the experience will "rapidly, accurately and rationally" drive the individual to be aware of the risks.[29] Studies about consumption psychology also found that in consumption, "how low-carbon awareness is developed affects the gap between awareness and behavior. When low-carbon awareness is developed through personal experience and practice, the awareness can be used to better predict low-carbon consumption mode. Otherwise, when the awareness is mainly developed through hollow preaching in books, the predictive power of the awareness is much lower."[30] This is enlightening for giving administrative guidance: that is, organizing citizens to take part in activities to bring immersive experience to them and make them develop a sense of crisis about climate change and make them to adopt low-carbon behaviors. For example, establishing low-carbon education bases to simulate such dangerous scenarios of climate change as inundated sea banks, drought, cyclone, and flood where people can visit and experience; setting aside a "day for experiencing depletion of energy resources" when the use of water, power and gas is stopped to make the people feel the crisis of clime change.

(III) **Warn People of Legal Responsibilities to Be Borne**

Imposing legal responsibilities is also an important way of regulating individuals in the society. With the problem of climate change becoming more and more serious, the ethical obligation of conserving energy and reducing emission will hence become a mandatory legal obligation. Where necessary, China will adopt such "hard regulations" as imposition, punishment and enforcement. *The Vehicle and Vessel Tax Law of the PRC*, which was revised in 2011 and first stipulated that progressive tax rate shall apply to vehicles and vessels tax based on displacement, and the *Regulations Banning Smoking in Public Places* and other regulations that have been successively enacted by various local authorities are to some extent caused by increasingly serious resource and environmental crisis. Legal regulations may impose mandatory obligations on citizens and reduce and impair their vested rights and interests. This can better prompt people to actively adopt low-carbon behaviors. Therefore, vivid cases

---

[28] [US] Cass R. Sunstein, *Risk and Reason* (Shi Shuai, Trans.), China University of Political Science and Law Press, 2005, pp. 41–43.

[29] See Paul Slovic, Melissa L. Finucane, Ellen Peters & Donald Macgregor, *Risk As Analysis and Risk As Feelings: Some Thoughts About Affect, Reason, Risk and Rationality*, *Risk Analysis*, 2004, Vol. 24, pp. 311–322.

[30] Wang Jianmin& Wang Junhao, *Factors affecting public' s low-carbon consumption mode and government's management and control policy*. *Management World*, 2011 (4).

in administrative guidance can be used to warn people of legal responsibilities so as to guide citizens to spontaneously take actions to conserve energy and reduce emissions.

4.2 Use Restraints to Provide Guidance

Using restraints to provide guidance means using certain restraint means to prevent, alleviate and restrain high-carbon consumption behaviors. This mainly applies to hedonistic high-carbon consumption. While encouraging consumption and stimulating domestics demand, China needs to consider energy conservation and emission reduction more. Administrative guidance should be provided to direct the society to restrain high-carbon consumption. The following restraints could be made:

(I) **Restraint Based on Reputation Mechanism**

Reputation is an important social asset of a person. Due to certain consideration of reputation, people will restrain their behavior to play a guiding role. Therefore, administrative guidance can put reputation pressure on citizens that have high-carbon consumption behaviors through reputation mechanisms and hence displays a restraining role. First, standards of average personal carbon emission for daily or monthly activities of citizens should be estimated and announced (which standards may vary for people across different regions) to advocate citizens of strictly following low-carbon standards in their daily consumption. Second, citizens should be regularly informed of data of carbon emissions generated through their daily behaviors such as clothes, food, accommodation, and travel[31] and they should be told how they should do to meet the standards. Third, individuals that have high-carbon consumption behaviors should be warned of their reputation, for example, using carbon label on invoice, tax invoice and package to remind citizens of high-carbon consumption. Last, publicly disclosing carbon emission information of concerned people to put reputation pressure on their serious high-carbon consumption behaviors to use public opinions to restrain high-carbon consumption. For example, for manufacturers that waste energy and resources to produce consumer products with needlessly excessive packaging and individuals that unreasonably use excessive amount of water, power, and gas in unit time, management departments should publish their names within a certain scope to warn them of reputation risk.

---

[31] The *Manual on Promoting Energy Conservation and Emission Reduction* prepared by the Ministry of Science and Technology of the PRC is a good example. It conducted publicity about the effects of saving energy from six aspects of life, that is, clothes, food, accommodation, travel and use. It tells people if one avoids buying a piece of unnecessary clothing, 2.5 kg standard coal can be saved and emission of carbon dioxide can be reduced by 6.4 kg; if one reduces food waste by 0.5 kg (take rice as an example), 0.18 kg standard coal can be saved and correspondingly emission of carbon dioxide can be reduced by 0.47 kg. Retrieved October 20th, 2013 from the website of the Ministry of Science and Technology at http://www.most.gov.cn/ztzl/jqjnjp/qmjnjpsc/qmjnjpsc-ml.htm, visited on October 20th, 2013.

(II) **Restraint Based on Payment Mechanism**

Government's price restraint policy also plays an important role in guiding consumption behavior. As early as 2003, German began to implement a container-deposit scheme for metal pop cans, disposable drink bottles and other contains whose recycle rates are low. When buying all mineral water, beer and soda water that are packaged in plastic bottles and pop cans, consumers need to pay a corresponding deposit (a deposit of €0.25 for volumes of less than 1.5 L).[32] The deposit can be refunded when empty bottles and cans are returned. In China, the General Office of the State Council of the People's Republic of China issued a *Notice about Limiting Production, Sales and Use of Plastic Shopping Bags*, requiring "all retail places for any commodity such as supermarkets, shopping malls and trade markets should charge a fee for plastic shopping bags and are forbidden to provide plastic shopping bags for free." All these measures can guide consumption behaviors of the society, that is, effectively restrain use by "charging".

Guidance provided by restraining is different from guidance provided by warning: the former highlights on warning and admonishing citizens to make citizens subjectively restrain consumption and the latter highlights on objectively restraining citizens' consumption directly. With regard to the different functions of the two types of guidance, they can be used flexibly in practice.

4.3 Use Organizations to Provide Administrative Guidance

Using organizations to provide guidance means organizing the society to widely establish low-carbon organizations of certain size (for example, low-carbon communities, low-carbon companies, low-carbon organs, low-carbon school campuses, low-carbon car buff associations and associations of low-carbon volunteers) where low-carbon responsibilities can be allocated to the low-carbon organizations and each member in the organizations can be urged to conserve energy and reduce emission. This can effectively discourage hitchhiking mindset and remove the worry of some people that conform to behaviors of others that they might be hitchhiked. From the perspective of working highlights, organizational functions of administrative guidance include the following: first, administrative authorities should guide and support various types of low-carbon organizations; second, administrative authorities should guide low-carbon organizations to prepare village rules, civilian regulations and code of self-discipline for energy conservation and emission reduction; third, administrative authorities should guide citizens to do various types of activities targeted at energy conservation and emission reduction. For example, government authorities or third parties entrusted by government authorities can advocate low-carbon

[32] Author unknown, *How rubbish is sorted in foreign countries. Kaifeng Daily*, July 9, 2010.

knowledge to low-carbon organizations, demonstrate methods of energy conservation and emission reduction, and provide services for energy conservation and emission reduction. We can take low-carbon community as an example to explore how to use organizations to provide administrative guidance.

"Low-carbon community refers to an area where there is a leading microclimate and a recyclable and sustainable energy structure. It can be understood as extension of the concept of (constructing) specific aspects of urban spatial structure of a low-carbon city."[33] Compared with other social organizations, low-carbon communities have their own unique advantages. First, communities are the smallest unit and cells of a city, it is easier and flexible for them to promote low-carbon technologies, policies and lifestyles. Second, it is easier to make democratic decisions about energy conservation and emission reduction for a community-based mode of operation. Therefore, the decisions are more proper and acceptable and can be really supported and implemented by the public. Thirdly, localized actions make it easier for individual public to participate in community energy conservation and carbon reduction. They also make it convenient for members of the communities to share experience, communicate with each other and exchange information and also to integrate energy conservation and emission reduction into their daily life. Last, the efforts to conserve energy and reduce emission is progressively made from a bottom to top way, which helps to form grid governance and scale effects for energy conservation and emission reduction. China has made arrangement through its *Work Plan for Greenhouse Gas Emission Control during the 12th Five-Year Plan*. According to actual conditions of various places, efforts have been made to set up many ecological low-carbon communities in the places, for example, Beijing Fengtai District Changxindian Low-Carbon Ecological Community, Shanghai Chongming Dongtan Ecological Community and Guangzhou Asian Games City. With regard to the problem of how to help to build low-carbon community, the solution of organizational guidance is promising. Lucie and Bradley, environmental scholars from the UK put forth a theoretical framework for building low-carbon communities in the paper *Building Capacity for Low-carbon Communities*. They thought that encouraging communities and their members to take responsibilities for their carbon footprint involves four capacity dimensions: first, cultural capacity, that is, "legitimacy of sustainability objectives in light of the history and values of a community"; second, organizational capacity, that is, "values of the organizations active within a community and resulting support available for community action"; third, infrastructural capacity, that is, "provision of facilities for sustainable living by government, business and community groups; Fourth, personal capacity, that is, "members' resources for community sustainability (e.g. understanding, skills, values, enthusiasm of individuals)".[34] Administrative guidance is very appropriate for developing such capacities. Organizational guidance should be devoted to strengthening the four capacities of low-carbon communities: (i) depend on sub-district offices and residents committees to actively build pilot low-carbon

[33] Ma Yuting, *Low-carbon Communities in Foreign Countries*, *Economy*, 2010 (11).

[34] Lucie Middlemiss, Bradley D. Parrish, *Building Capacity for Low-Carbon Communities: The Role of Grassroots Initiatives*, *Energy Policy*, vol. 38, 2010, pp. 7559–7566.

communities and guide and help communities to prepare conventions on the habit of self-discipline for energy conservation and emission reduction to strengthen "organizational capacity" of low-carbon communities. (ii) help communities with publicity and education, guide communities to collectively prepare plans for energy conservation and emission reduction through democratic consultations, set up platforms for communities to exchange and share information to increase the influence of low-carbon communities to strengthen "cultural capacity" of low-carbon communities. (iii) provide energy conservation and emission reduction guidance to communities, assist communities training their members about low-carbon living skills, and reward leading members of communities to strengthen "personal capacity" of low-carbon communities. (iv) With regard to community building, provide suggestions about planning such things as low-carbon transportation, saving energy, and carbon sink management, provide technical support for retrofitting existing buildings for energy conservation and energy recycling, and earmark money in fiscal budget to provide material guarantee to strengthen "infrastructure capacity" of low-carbon communities.

4.4 Use Effect Feedback to Provide Guidance

Using effect feedback to provide guidance refers to using effects brought by energy conservation and emission reduction measures to direct citizens to inspire and motivate them about low-carbon behaviors. This method is appropriate for directing people to change the negative attitude that "an individual's power is too weak" for building a low-carbon society. When feedback about effects brought by energy conservation and emission reduction behaviors is used to provide guidance, emphasis should be put on the following feedback:

(I) **Feedback About the Effects Brought by Collective Energy Conservation and Emission Reduction Behaviors**

Failure to understand the collective effects brought by concerted actions is one of the reasons why some people negatively think that "an individual's power is too weak". Therefore, administrative guidance should provide feedback to the society about the collective effects brought by individual's energy conservation and emission reduction efforts. In fact, "reducing carbon dioxide emission is a process where the people have the power of changing the future."[35] For example, statistics show the Chinese households would save more than 70,000 million kwh electricity a year if they generally used energy efficient lights; the Chinese households would save more than 40,000 million kwh electricity a year if more than one hundred million refrigerators in their homes were all replaced by energy efficient refrigerators. The

[35] Remarks by Achim Steiner, Executive Director of the United Nations Environment Programme. Chen Yuanyuan, *What we do and say today will influence the future—record ten moments of people taking part in environment protection in 2009. China Environment News*, December 30, 2009.

total electricity saved by the aforesaid two actions would be equal to the electricity generated by more than one hydroelectric power plant at the Three Gorges Dam in a year.[36]

(II) Feedback About the Effects Brought By An Individual's Energy Conservation and Emission Reduction Behaviors

Individuals have an information deficit about the effects accumulatively brought by their daily energy conservation and emission reduction behaviors. This is another reason causing them to have the wrong idea that "an individual's power is too weak". This also calls for timely feedback provided by administrative guidance. Government authorities can use data models about the effects brought by individuals' energy conservation and emission reduction behaviors to provide predictive responses, that is, inform the citizens of the energy conservation and emission reduction effects brought by their relevant low-carbon behaviors through a simulation calculation performed of the data. Take the *Manual on Promoting Energy Conservation and Emission Reduction* issued by the Ministry of Science and Technology of the PRC as an example, based on scientific assessments, it predicted the potential of citizens to conserve energy and reduce emission in their daily activities associated with clothes, food, accommodation, travel and use. In addition, low-carbon organizations can be used to set up schemes for tracking and feeding back some carbon footprint of their individual members. Organizations can regularly feedback to their departments about the accumulative effects achieved by the water, electricity, fuel and gas saved by the departments as shown by average energy conservation and emission reduction rates of the organizations.

(III) Provide Feedback About Comparative Results of Energy Conservation and Emission Reduction Behaviors

A foreign team studying environmental psychology did an experiment comparing the consequences brought by pro-environmental behaviors. The participants were divided into several groups based on their neighbors and friends. In a two-year period, some groups were regularly provided feedback about their own pro-environmental information and also shared pro-environmental information of others. Results of the experiment showed that the groups that received comparative results respectively used 16.9%, 7.6% and 6.7% less gas, electricity and water than the groups that did not received comparative results and waste disposed by the former was 32.1% less than that disposed by the latter.[37] The study showed that providing feedback about comparative results helps to motivate people to adopt pro-environmental behaviors. In this example, people were guided to adopt pro-environmental behaviors through providing them with feedback about comparative results of pro-environmental behaviors.

---

[36] Zou Wenbin, *Great potential of households to conserve energy and reduce emissions. Modern Guangxi*, 2008 (7).

[37] See Staats, H., Harland, P., & Wilke, H. A. M. *Effecting Durable Change: A Team Approach to Improve Environmental Behavior in the Household, Environment and Behavior*, 2004, Vol. 36, pp. 341–367.

4.5 Use Exemplification to Provide Guidance

Using exemplification to provide guidance means using examples to guide the society to conserve energy and reduce emission. Specifically, the following can be exemplified:

(I) Exemplify Low-carbon Methods

The most direct and effective way of exemplification is to teach easy and economical pro-environmental methods to citizens and promote them to adopt the methods. Richard A. Winett and other scholars from the United States prepared a 20-min television program dramatizing conservation strategies. The program was regularly broadcasted to 150 households in 9 weeks. The result showed that these families accepted the strategies broadcasted in varying degrees and reduced the amount of electricity used by 9–20% on average.[38] As far as exemplifying methods are concerned, attention should be given to the following three aspects. First, highlight should be given to operability of the low-carbon methods exemplified. Existing media programs present more about the significance of low-carbon development and harms of climate change. They seldom specifically introduce specific energy conservation and emission reduction methods which are most needed by the citizens in their daily lives. Therefore, administrative guidance should pay attention to exemplifying operable pro-environmental methods through various ways. Second, the energy conservation and emission reduction methods to be introduced should be simple and cost effective. Conserving and reducing emission naturally needs money. If the cost is too high, people will be discouraged. Therefore, the methods to be provided through administrative guidance should be easy for the people and should be able to reduce their costs. Third, the methods to be used to conserve energy and reduce emission should be introduced through lively and vivid means. Currently, some exemplifying guidance is provided in a dull and boring way and is mostly provided through data and slogans rather than through ways that people love. It is hard to make the audience in the society interested.

(II) Exemplify Low-carbon Ethics

Exemplification of low-carbon ethics is to guide behaviors of the citizens through fostering low-carbon ethics and setting low-carbon examples. It specifically includes the following. First, making spontaneously conserving energy and reducing emission as a new ethical paradigm. Traditional ethics focuses on regulating social relationship between people, for example, helping others, cherishing one's job and being devoted to one's work, respecting the old and loving the young, and returning found money. Theses traditional requirements about what is ethical cannot completely meet the requirement of harmonious co-existence between nature and mankind. Therefore, people's behavior of conserving energy and reducing emission has the "ethical

[38] Winett, R. A., Leckliter, I. N., Chinn, D. E., & Stahl, B., *Reducing Energy Consumption: The Long-term Effects of a Single TV Program*, *Journal of Communication*, 1984, Vol. 34, pp. 37–51.

dimension"[39] of climate justice in the context of climate change. The *Implementation Outline of Civic Morality Construction* issued by the Central Committee of the Communist Party of China in 2001 has made "environmental protection" to be covered by social morality as what is required at the time. With regard to the social morality in the new era, we still need to enrich its content, integrate its system of code of behaviors, induce its values and its contributions to the good future of nature and mankind so as to form a low-carbon ethical system for people to conserve energy and resources, protect ecology of the nature, and shoulder social responsibilities. At the same time, efforts should be made to promote it in the whole society. Second, setting low-carbon examples in the society. Currently, there have been many exemplars that actively adopt low-carbon behaviors in real life,[40] but they are not praised as role models by the nation, which is not conducive to leading the majority of social members to carry out energy conservation and emission reduction. The role models selected are limited to people who are "Samaritans ", people who "boldly do what is righteous", people who are "honest and credible", people who are "devoted and willing to sacrifice", and people who show "filial piety".[41] The administration should widely publicize pro-environmental behaviors of low-carbon role models to promote the people in the society to learn from them.

[39] Chen Xilin, "*A Low-carbon Era" that has an Ethical Dimension, West China*, 2009 (6).

[40] Liu Chao & Ma Qian. *A Volunteer Has Practically Lived a Low-carbon Life for More Than Twenty Years*. China.com.cn. Retrieved November 12, 2013 from http://www.news.china.com.cn/live/2012-11/11/content_17096346.htm.

[41] *Implementation Method of Selecting and Praising the Fourth National Ethical Models*. Publicity Department of the CPC Central Committee. Retrieved November 12, 2013 from http://www.wenming.cn/ddmf_296/jj_ddmf/201304/t20130413_1172823.shtmlf.

Chapter 8
Application and Development of Administrative Penalties in Low-Carbon Field

Administrative regulation used by government to promote the construction of a low-carbon society manly works through two mechanisms: first, a cooperation and voluntariness based mechanism that is represented by administrative guidance and administrative contract; second, a unilateral mandatory mechanism that is represented by administrative penalty and administrative enforcement. In the unilateral mandatory mechanism, administrative penalty plays an important and indispensable role. It is widely used in administrative law enforcement. In the following sections, the issue of how to effectively use administrative penalty in the construction of a low-carbon society and how to improve its use will be further explored.

1 Application of Administrative Penalties in Energy Conservation and Emission Reduction

1.1 Legal Provisions of Current Administrative Penalties

In order to promote the construction of a low-carbon society, China has prepared a series of laws and regulations about resources, energy and environmental protection, etc. Currently, except the general provisions concerning administrative penalties as contained in the *Law of the People's Republic of China on Administrative Penalty*, legal provisions directly related to administrative penalties for regulating low-carbon development are mainly distributed in legislation in two aspects, that is, legislation about energy and resource conservation and pollution control legislation.

(I) **Administrative Penalties Contained in Legislation About Energy and Resource Conservation**

(i) **Energy Conservation Law**. *Energy Conservation Law* that was adopted in 1997 and revised in 2007 involves many administrative penalties, including

S. Fang and B. Tan, *On the Administrative Law of China in Addressing Climate Change*,
https://doi.org/10.1007/978-981-19-7705-3_8

warning, fine, cancellation of business license, and ordering for suspension of production or business.[1]

(ii) **Law on Renewable Energy**. Fine, as an administrative penalty, is mainly stipulated in Article 29 of the chapter concerning "Legal Liability" of the *Renewable Energy Law of the PRC* promulgated in 2005.

(iii) **Law on Promoting the Development of A Recycling Economy**. Corresponding administrative penalties for various types of behaviors that are against the obligation of resource and energy reducing, recycling and reusing are stipulated in the legal liability section of the *Law of the PRC on Promoting the Development of a recycling Economy* that was promulgated in 2008. The main administrative penalties include fine, confiscation of illegal proceeds, cancellation of business license.[2]

(iv) **Law on the Coal Industry, Electricity and Water**. The "legal liability" sections of the *Law of the PRC on the Coal Industry, Electricity Law* and *Water Law* of the PRC all involve penalties related to energy and energy conservation. The main penalties include fine, confiscation of illegal proceeds, ordering to suspend production and business.[3]

(II) Administrative Penalties in Pollution Control Legislation

Low-carbon administrative penalties in pollution prevention and control legislation covers a wide range of areas, including the following provisions closely related to climate change:

(i) **Environmental protection law**. Illegal acts concerning environmental pollution are more severely punished in the *Environmental Protection Law* that is most recently revised in 2014.[4] First, where an illegal behavior continues, the behavior can be fined consecutively on a daily basis.[5] Second, where a major illegal behavior should occur, an order for suspension of business or closure may be given.[6] Third, where a major illegal act should occur but the act does not constitute a crime, the act can be punished according to relevant laws and regulations and the concerned people may also be detained by public security authority.

(ii) **Cleaner production promotion law**. The *Cleaner Production Promotion Law* that was adopted in 2002 and revised in 2012 mainly stipulated the administrative penalty of fines.[7]

---

[1] See Articles 68 to 80 of *Energy Conservation Law*.

[2] See Articles 51, 52, 53, 54 and 56 of the *Law of the PRC on Promoting the Development of a recycling Economy*.

[3] See Article 59 of *Law of the PRC on the Coal Industry*, Article 62 of *Electricity Law of the PRC* and Articles 68 and 71 of *Water Law of the PRC*.

[4] See Article 59 of *Environmental Protection Law*.

[5] See Article 60 of *Environmental Protection Law*.

[6] See Article 63 of *Environmental Protection Law*.

[7] See Articles 39 and 41 of the *Cleaner Production Promotion Law*.

(iii) **Water law and water pollution prevention and control law**. *Water Law of the PRC* and *Law of the People's Republic of China on Prevention and Control of Water Pollution* stipulate such administrative penalties as fine, order for demolition, restoration to original state, order for correction about illegal discharge of pollutants into relevant waters.[8]

(iv) **Law on the prevention and control of air pollution**. *The Law of the PRC on the Prevention and Control of Atmospheric Pollution* is a basic law regulating air pollution. The law stipulates many forms of penalties such as fine, canceling qualification certificate, order for stopping illegal acts, controlling or eliminating air pollution within a specified period of time, confiscating and destroying illegal equipment, mandatory demolition, canceling production and import quota.[9]

As far as existing stipulations of laws are concerned, currently there has been basically an administrative penalty system about low-carbon regulation. The system is characterized by a great variety of penalties and by many ways of using the penalties. However, when existing administrative penalties are inspected, it can be found that they still have some shortcomings and they cannot fully meet the need for low-carbon regulation.

1.2 Analysis on Main Shortcomings of Administrative Penalties

Current administrative penalties in the field of energy conservation and emission reduction mainly have the following shortcomings:

(I) **Lacking Administrative Penalties for Individual Citizens**

Currently, administrative penalties mainly apply to legal persons and organizations and obviously lack punishments for individual citizens. For example, totally twenty-two articles in the chapter "Legal Liability" of the *Law of the People's Republic of China on Prevention and Control of Water Pollution* stipulated administrative penalties. However, most of the penalties are targeted at organizations and units. Only the second paragraph of Article 81 involves penalties for individual citizens.[10]

[8] See Articles 67 and 73 of *The Law of the People's Republic of China on Prevention and Control of Water Pollution.*

[9] See Articles 45 to 51 of *The Law of the People's Republic of China on Prevention and Control of Water Pollution.*

[10] Article 81 of the *Law of the People's Republic of China on Prevention and Control of Water Pollution* stipulates that "If an individual swims, fishes or conduct any other activities that may cause pollution to the water body of drinking waters within the same, the competent environmental protection department of the local people's government at or above the county level shall order him/her to cease and desist from the violation and may impose on him/her a fine of not more than 500 yuan.".

Among the relevant laws and regulations about energy conservation and emission reduction, most of them almost stipulate no administrative penalty for illegal acts of individual citizens. Although some of the legal provisions involve obligations of individual citizens for low-carbon development and environmental protection, the provisions are mostly limited to abstract obligations and obligations that citizens are advocated to shoulder. No corresponding penalties and legal liability are provided as a guarantee. For example, Article 6 of the *Environmental Protection Law* and Article 9 of the *Energy Conservation Law*. Aside from these two articles, there are no specific provisions of penalties to hold citizens liable when they do not perform their statutory obligations.

Without doubt, it is the obligation and duty of every citizen to actively get involved in building a low-carbon society and conserve energy and reduce emission according to laws. In fact, among total social consumption of resources and energy, a great proportion is consumed by citizens. As far as emission of greenhouse gas and pollutants are concerned, citizens almost emit equal amount of greenhouse gases and pollutants as corporate bodies and other organizations do. For example, in terms of energy and resource consumption, panel data of total energy consumption of the urban residents of China increased from 231 million tons standard coal in 1999 to 565 million tons standard coal in 2004 (1 ton standard coal is almost equivalent to 1.9 tons of carbon dioxide), increasing from 19 to 31% as a percentage to overall social primary energy consumption.[11] According to pollutant emission data as shown in *2013 Communique on Environment of China*, residential chemical oxygen demand emission reached 8.899 million tons, amounting to 37.8% of total chemical oxygen demand emission of China and was over twice as much as industrial chemical oxygen demand emission. Residential ammonia-nitrogen discharge reached 1.414 million tons, amounting to 57.4% of total residential ammonia-nitrogen discharge of China and more than 470% of industrial ammonia-nitrogen discharge (Table 1).[12] It can be found that it is far from enough for existing administrative penalties to only target at low-carbon behaviors of body corporates and other organizations. In order to effectively respond to climate change and construct a low-carbon society, behaviors of individual citizens need to be similarly controlled.

Currently, China is still exploring on how to build a low-carbon society. Based on acceptability of citizens and the consideration that new things gradually develop in an orderly way, present low-carbon behaviors of citizens are mainly regulated through inducements such as administrative awards. It is undeniably easier to use inducements to direct citizens to adopt low-carbon behaviors. Theoretically, however, the role played by inducements tends to weaken with time passing by. US scholars Dwyer and others randomly selected 220 volunteers that often used automobile in Washington. They divided the volunteers into two groups, an experimental group and a control group, to conduct an experiment about reducing mileage for energy

---

[11] Wang Yan & Shi Minjun, *Total energy consumption of Chinese urban households, Resource Science*, 2009 (12).

[12] *2013 Communique on Environment of China*. Ministry of Ecology and Environment of the PRC. Retrieved January 19th, 2015 from http://jcs.mep.gov.cn/hjzl/zkgb/2013zkgb/.

Table 1 Main pollutants in effluent water discharged in China 2013

COD (0000 omitted, unit: ton)					Ammonia-nitrogen (0000 omitted, unit: ton)				
Total amount	Industrial source	Residential source	Agricultural source	From collective treatment sites	Total amount discharged	Industrial source	Residential source	Agricultural source	From collective treatment sites
2352.7	319.5	889.8	1125.7	17.7	245.7	24.6	141.4	77.9	1.8

conservation. The experiment lasted four weeks. Participants that reduced the number of miles they drove their automobiles by more than 5% every week would be rewarded $ 9 to $ 12 according to the percentage reduction in miles. At the end of the fourth week, the champion with the most mileage reduction will receive a reward of $41. The results showed that under given conditions, experimental participants reduced their miles driven by 11% in the four weeks on average while the miles driven by control participants increased by 21% on average. However, the achievement made by the experimental group disappeared in the following 28 days of follow-up observation with cancellation of the monetary reward. Some scholars conducted economic analysis of the material reward for the power conservation behaviors and found that "marginal returns brought by the rewards diminished over time".[13] This is not only true in environmental protection, a similar situation also occurred in traffic management in China. On July 5th, 2013, Taizhou Public Security Bureau took a humanistic law enforcement measure to "friendly remind" the people who breached parking restrictions for the first time of their wrong behaviors instead of issuing them a parking ticket. This was in fact a way to guide concerned people not to breach parking restrictions by offering the inducement of exempting them of parking tickets. The humanistic measure worked effectively and reduced the number of breaches of parking restrictions. However, nothing lasts forever. According to statistics of traffic management authorities, totally 11,697 breaches occurred three weeks after the month when the measure was taken while 10,686 breaches occurred in June, the month before the measure was taken. This means the inducement of "exemption of ticket for the first breach" worked in a short period of time but contrarily increased the number of breaches by 10% in a long run. At last, it had to be cancelled.[14] A psychological explanation to the above-mentioned phenomena is that rewards cannot internalize such duties as energy conservation and environmental protection into a strong attitude.[15] In view of this, in addition to administrative incentives such as soft guidance, administrative penalties are still needed as rigid restraint and a guarantee to effectively force citizens to perform pro-environmental and low-carbon obligations.

(II) **Lacking Consideration of Climate Change Risk Prevention**

Ecological risks from climate change such as energy crisis and environmental pollution are uncertain. Long-term effects of some impacts are still unknown. They are, to some extent, beyond our understanding and cannot be explain by science at the moment, showing four aspects of uncertainty. First, degree of impact. Specific harms of climate change and environmental pollution can only be eventually revealed after a long period of time or after the harms are actually felt. They are not obviously shown in real life. Second, probability of occurrence, that is, science and technologies can

[13] Lou McClelland, Stuart W. Cook. *Energy Conservation Effects of Continuous in-home Feedback in all-electric Homes*. *Journal of Environmental Systems*, vol. 9, 1979, pp. 169–173.

[14] Wang Weijian (2013, August 6). *Why Taizhou Stopped Flexible Law Enforcement*. *People's Daily*.

[15] [US] Michael Leippe & Philip Zimbardo (2007). *The psychology of attitude change and social influence*. Deng Yu, (Xiao Li & Tang Xiaoyan, et. al.,Trans.) (pp. 47–53). Posts and Telecommunications Press.

not accurately predict how much impact can climate change brought on environment. Third, complex cause-and-effect relationship, that is, cause-and-effect relationship between eventual consequences and acts of a single organization or an individual, one of the factors causing the consequences, cannot be proved through sufficient evidence, for example, it is hard to prove the cause-and-effect relationship between the heavy snowfall in South China in 2008, an extreme climate event, and high-carbon emission acts of some organizations or individuals. Currently, it is only possible to infer the correlation between the two theoretically by science and technology. At the same time, some harmful effects of ecological risks are irreversible, that is, as long as the harmful effects work in reality, it is neither possible to restore the reality to its original state nor find replacement. This brings new requirements for administrative penalties when they are used for low-carbon regulation. Traditional concepts about administrative penalties should be abandoned, for example, use of administrative penalties should only be limited to the aftermath of harmful consequences and there should be a direct cause-and-effect relationship between illegal acts and harmful consequences. The emphasis should be placed on preventing harmful consequences from occurring. The major thing to consider is to prevent risks.

Ecological risks are uncertain and the harmful consequences brought by the risks are irreversible, so the government should actively act and take necessary actions to prevent possible major ecological harms, that is, lacking scientific certainty should not be used as a reason for refusing to take or delaying taking effective regulatory measures to prevent ecological risks. The urgent need to prevent ecological risks bring a new task to government regulation. With regard to administrative penalty, a basic tool used for government regulation, more consideration should be given to risk prevention. The main things concerned in administrative penalties that are intended to prevent risks are different from those concerned in administrative penalties that are intended to punish harmful consequences caused. The latter, which is based on certainty, require that there must be facts of harmful consequences and conclusive evidence proving cause-and-effect relationship between illegal acts and harmful consequences. The former is based on uncertainty and are used to address unknown risks. The features of the former include: first, what is considered for imposing administrative penalties is not occurrence of harmful consequences but occurrence of illegal acts; second, what is considered for imposing administrative penalties is not confined to direct cause-and-effect relationship between illegal acts and harmful consequences but highlights on risk of the illegal acts with harmful consequences or on the multiple cause-single effect relationship between acts and consequences; third, the basic aim of administrative penalties is to avoid occurrence of harmful consequences or reduce degree of the harmful consequences. This will provide law enforcement authorities with great discretion. When preliminarily finding that an illegal act may cause harmful consequences or even bring more serious problems, law enforcement authorities may intervene ahead of time and use a proper kind of punishment to intervene in time. In the practice of environmental protection law enforcement, this model of preventive administrative punishment has been explored. An unidentified strong odor was noticed in Dakengkou Village, Wushi Town, Qujiang District, Shaoguan in May, 2011. The villagers all said the strong odor came from

Sheng Zhao Mining Co., Ltd. near the primary school. The strong odor had made many people have adversely effects of coughing and headache. The Environmental Protection Bureau investigated into the issue on the site on May 27th. It ordered the company to first stop production and be monitored 24 h a day. The company was not allowed to begin production before it was proved not to be source of the strong odor.[16] The case showed the characteristics of preventive penalty to some extent. The environmental protection bureau takes "the company was not ruled out to be source of the strong odor" as the factual basis, which was obviously just a result of preliminary investigation; at the same time, currently, there have no codes and regulations promulgated about monitoring odious materials. The environmental protection bureau judged that the company released the odious gas based on the people's sense of smell. However, in order to prevent the great risk that may occur at any time and endangered lives and health of the villagers and students of the primary school (once a disastrous accident had occurred, the harms and consequences would be irreparable), the environmental protection bureau first imposed the penalty of ordering the company to stop production in case of absence of conclusive evident and direct and clear cause-and-effect relationship (the highlight was put on an obvious possibility or non-exclusion). The emphasis was obviously placed on preventiveness rather than exemplariness of the penalty. This is a new idea about penalty. It is applied to the field of low-carbon development and environmental protection. Based on the principle that administrative penalty should be regulated by law, more consideration of preventing risks should be given to administrative penalties so as to effectively respond to ecological risks in a low-carbon era.

(III) **Lack Legal Liability for Restoring Ecology**

"The twenty-first century should be a century for environmental restoration and regeneration."[17] Ecological restoration is an important requirement in sustainable development. Carbon dioxide emission or environmental pollution events may lead to serious adverse changes in the physical, chemical or biological functions of the ecological environment itself. Artificial measures must be taken to address such adverse changes that are against the law of nature.[18] However, from the above reflective thinking about the administrative penalties for low-carbon and environmental protection, it can be found that a concept of administrative order penalty is still adhered to when administrative penalties are inflicted. In this practice, punishment to be inflicted on the person that breaches laws is partially emphasized and ecological restoration of natural environment, climate and resources is neglected. From the perspective of legislation, except few provisions of few laws such as *Law*

[16] Anonymous Author, *Many Companies are Stopped or Have Their Business Suspended Due to "Producing Stranger Smells" in Shaoguan.* China News Service Guangdong. Retrieved January 25, 2015 from http://www.gd.chinanews.com/2011/2011-06-02/2/116618.shtml.

[17] Wang Canfa (2002), *Environmental Legislation of A New Type is Needed in An Era of Environmental Restoration and Regeneration. Journal of Zhengzhou University*, (2).

[18] Zhu Xiao (2007). *Reflections on Legal Embarrassment of the Administrative Fine Imposed in the Songhua River Water Pollution Incident —From the Perspective of An Accountability System for Compensating Ecological Damage, Legal Science*, (3).

of the People's Republic of China on Prevention and Control of Water Pollution involve such administrative penalties requiring restoration such as making correction within a specified period of time and eliminating pollution,[19] other legislation in the sector of low-carbon and environmental protection only generally inflicts such preventive and punitive administrative penalties as fine, order for suspension of production or business, cancellation of license and even administrative detention illegal counterparts that damage the environment or have high-carbon emissions. These traditional administrative punishment measures are deterrent and preventive methods dealing with the present and future, and there is no direct remedy for the atmospheric resources that have been polluted and damaged in the past. The newly revised *Environmental Protection Law* in 2014 has greatly strengthened the administrative punishment for environmental violations, but there is still no administrative punishment for restorative responsibility.

Since the polluter does not bear the responsibility of treatment and repair in administrative punishment, the costs of fines or suspension of production, or even closure are often only a small part of the ecological environment loss caused by it. The biggest problem with these traditional ways of punishment is that the environmental pollution and damage can not be effectively controlled. Take the "Water Pollution Incident in the Songhua River" that caused a sensation through out China in 2006 as an example. On November 13th, 2005, an explosion suddenly took place at a nitrobenzene rectifying tower in a phenol and phthalic anhydride plant of Sinopec Jilin Oil Products Company. In this explosion, about 100 tons of benzene substances (benzene, nitrobenzene, etc.) flowed into the Songhua River, which not only seriously polluted the water quality but also badly influenced the lives of the people in the region along the river. Some polluted water flew into Amur River in Russia, causing a diplomatic dispute.[20] Among the administrative penalties applicable to the case, the maximum fine would not exceed one million Chinese yuan according to the *Rules for Implementation of Law of the People's Republic of China on Prevention and Control of Water Pollution*. The Ministry of Ecology and Environment of the People's Republic of China also made a decision on administrative punishment according to the highest standard of 1 million yuan. However, a fine of one million yuan was a drop in the bucket compared to the money needed to repair the damage. The government more than 10 billion yuan to treat the pollution in the Songhua River. Only in the year 2011 up to 800 million yuan was spent.[21] The money was actually paid by all tax payers. It was obviously extremely unfair. Of course, Sinopec Jilin Oil Products Company might not be the only company that caused the pollution of the Songhua River. However, compared with the 10 billion yuan needed for the cleanup

---

[19] See articles 76 and 80 of *Law of the People's Republic of China on Prevention and Control of Water Pollution*.

[20] Anonymous Author. *The Songhua River Suffered a Major Water Pollution Incident*. Xinhua Net. Retrieved January 20th, 2015 from http://www.xinhuanet.com/society/zt051124/.

[21] Zhang Jian. *Ji'lin Province Will Invest 11 Billion Yuan in Preventing and Treating Pollution in the Songhua River*. Xinhua Net. Retrieved January 20th, 2015 from http://news.xinhuanet.com/fortune/2012-05/10/c_111925645.htm.

and restoration, the one million yuan fine paid by the company was only a very small portion.

In view of the difficulties faced by the current traditional punishment methods (especially fines), many scholars raise a countermeasure of using continuous fines calculated on a daily basis, which was adopted in the *Environmental Protection Law* revised in 2014. This continuous punishment on a daily basis is to prevent and deal with illegal acts by increasing the illegal cost of enterprises. However, continuous fines calculated on a daily basis is only a kind of fine, which has limited regulatory effect on the behavior of illegal subjects. Fixing damage to ecological environment needs relevant remedial actions and a large number of human and material resources. Accumulative penalty cannot replace treatment and work to directly restore ecological environment. Therefore, administrative penalty requiring restoration of ecological environment should be introduced to make polluters to shoulder the liability of treating pollution in ecological environment and making compensation so as to achieve dual effects of deterring illegal acts and fixing damaged ecological environment.

The above deficiencies of administrative punishment in the field of low-carbon environmental protection largely stem from the lack of adaptation to the changes of low-carbon requirements and clear focus in the purpose of administrative punishment in this field. The purpose does not adapt to the change to low-carbon requirement and also does not point to an emphatic direction. Rudolf Von Jhering, the founder of sociological jurisprudence, has long pointed out that purpose is a core concept of legal philosophy and also the creator of the entire law.[22] Therefore, the prerequisite of overcoming the defects of existing administrative penalties is to determine exactly the purpose of inflicting administrative penalties in low-carbon development and environmental protection. As a general rule, when setting liability of administrative counterparts for low-carbon development and environmental protection, the following logic should be followed. Firstly legal provisions should be prepared for a preventive purpose to warn administrative counterparts of not breaching legal regulations concerning energy conservation and emission reduction and to protect the ecological environment in the macroscopic points of view; secondly, if an administrative counterpart violates law, administrative organs should immediately stop the violation, reducing the damage caused to ecological environment as much as possible; if the act of an administrative counterpart has caused serious impacts on ecological environment, the administrative penalty should require the person to restore ecological environment; Thirdly, if the purpose of restoring ecological environment cannot be fulfilled, administrative penalty should be inflicted in a way to achieve the purpose of getting compensation for ecological environment. Based on such a logic, the purposes of administrative penalties in low-carbon development and environmental protection should include preventive purpose, inhibitory purpose, compensatory purpose and restorative purpose.

---

[22] Rudolf von Jhering, *Law As a Means to an End*, Isacc Husik (Translator), Gaunt Inc., 1998, Author's Preface, pp. II V, IV II.

(i) **Preventive purpose**

Law can prevent possible illegal acts because of its unique internal structure and operating principle. With regard to internal structure of law, it is an organic system consisting of legal concepts, legal principles and legal rules. The role of legal rules is to regulate acts of social entities through specifically stipulating their rights and obligations and corresponding legal consequences.[23] Regardless of their type, the purpose of legal rules is to guide people to do determined acts. When choosing to do a certain act, people are able to predict what legal consequence their act may cause, that is, protection or sanction, so people can choose the behaviors that are protected by law according to prediction of the consequences brought by the acts.

When administrative penalties for low-carbon development and environmental protection are concerned, they, of course, have the general attribute of legal rules. They can direct the behaviors of social entities through clearly stipulated legal provisions, behavior patterns and legal consequences so as to fulfill the purpose of preventing illegal behaviors. The preventive role of administrative penalties for low-carbon development and environmental protection works in the following three ways: (i) General prevention before implementation of administrative penalties. This preventive role works for all entities in the society. In modern society, due to the two functions of law, that is, regulation and protection, all entities in the society should know the contents of law (especially, behavioral patterns and legal consequences stipulated therein). Social entities can reasonably arrange their behaviors to avoid illegal behaviors through understanding such information like the subject, conditions and forms of administrative penalties. (ii) Prevention of specific offenders. Once the behavior of a social entity does not conform to the behavioral pattern stipulated by administrative penalty, administrative organs will choose an appropriate way to punish the behavior. The entity of the behavior will bear certain or some specific adverse consequences, for example, when an administrative counterpart violates the law to discharge pollutants beyond statutory limits, administrative organs may choose a reasonable penalty from the many types of penalties such as warning, fine, order for suspension of production and business, cancellation of license or permission, and detention. The adverse consequence that the violator of law must bear now exist as the cost of the violation of the social order and the interests of the third party. Bearing adverse consequences by law breakers can effectively remind them of avoiding the adverse consequences, which can help to prevent their future violation of law to some extent. (iii) Prevention of illegal behaviors of other social entities during and after infliction of administration penalties. Although administrative penalties can generally prevent people from illegal behaviors before they are implemented, this does not mean every social entity will follow the guidance of law to reasonably arrange their behaviors. In fact, when choosing behavioral patterns, many social entities tend to

[23] In Jurisprudence, legal rules are generally divided into obligatory rules, authoritative rules and compound rules from the perspective of nature of legal rules; and divided into regulatory rules and rules of criteria from the perspective of the way of their existence; and into regulative rules and constitutive rules from the perspective of function. Jurisprudence Editorial Group (2010). *Jurisprudence* (pp. 38–41). People's Education press& Higher Education Press.

be more affected by legal evaluation of behavior patterns of other social entities, in addition to the influence of behavior habits, value pursuit and other factors. Through implementation of administrative penalties, the status of punished ones can be intuitively felt and known by other social entities. Implementation of administrative penalties is good for widely preventing illegal behaviors of other social entities.

From the perspective of promoting the construction of a low-carbon society, the overall prevention before the implementation of administrative punishment is the most valuable way. Among the three ways how administrative penalties work, the preventive role played by administrative penalties of the type specified in the above (ii) and (iii) need the precondition of existence of an "illegal behavior". Illegal behavior means harm to environment and resources. Even if measures are taken to control or eliminate the harm, social costs have been caused. Therefore, consideration should be given to introduce administrative penalties that are able to intervene before ecological risks occur.

(ii) **Inhibitory purpose**

Inhibitory purpose of administrative penalties is mainly shown by existing administrative penalties. All administrative penalties inflicted by administrative organs are for the purpose of preventing illegal behaviors from harming the environment. Using preventing harmful behaviors as the purpose of inflicting administrative penalties can, to some extent, prevent companies, organizations and individuals from having polluting behaviors through huge fines and liability for severe consequences. This plays an important role for energy conservation and emission reduction. Therefore, currently the principal purpose of administrative penalties is still to prevent illegal behaviors, but this purpose cannot be fully fulfilled due to the following factors: first, some types of administrative penalty do not play an inhibitory rule; second, there are limited types of administrative penalties that have an inhibitory role.

(iii) **Restorative purpose**

Administrative penalties in low-carbon environmental protection should have a restorative purpose because ecology and environment are special. Ecological and environmental elements are essential and rare for mankind. This requires that quality of the ecology and environment that is damaged by illegal acts of administrative counterparts be restored to the greatest extent. Restoring quality of the ecology and environment means making damaged ecology resume or almost resume to a state before the damage occurs so as to maintain its normal ecological and environmental functions. However, the types of penalties in the current legislation such as warning, fine, order for suspension of production and business, temporary seizure or cancellation of business license and detention cannot meet such a requirement. Therefore, there should be administrative penalties that require such legal liability that help to restore ecology.

(iv) **Compensatory purpose**

Similar to restorative purpose of administrative penalties for low-carbon environmental protection, compensatory purpose focuses on quality of ecology and environment damaged by administrative counterparts. However, these two purposes are fulfilled in different ways. Restorative purpose emphasizes damaged ecology and environment themselves more and requires measures that can directly help to restore ecology and environment be taken. Compensatory purpose is more about indirect restoration of damaged ecology and environment and there are procedures of conversion involved. When being found, illegal acts have practically jeopardized ecological environment. At the moment, adopting administrative penalties that has a preventive purpose is unable to reverse the damage that has been caused. However, administrative penalties that have a compensatory purpose can overcome the deficiency and provide homogeneous compensation for harm that has been caused. This kind of administrative penalties that has a compensatory purpose impose huge liability on illegal actors for the consequence they caused. Once their illegal behaviors cause serious harm to the environment, they shall not only be liable for their jeopardizing behaviors themselves but also for making homogeneous compensation for the harm caused by their behaviors.

Compared with the purposes and requirements of administrative penalties for low-carbon environmental protection, existing Chinese administrative penalties are limited in terms of purpose. This is mainly reflected by their emphasis on inhibitory purpose and the lack of attention to preventive, restorative and compensatory purposes. This unreasonable situation is in urgent need of change.

2 Developing Administrative Penalty Systems for Ecological Protection

2.1 Establishing Penalty Principles for Preventing and Remedying Damages

(I) Legislative Significance of the Principle of Preventing and Remedying Damages

Administrative penalties are typical adverse administrative actions, whose implementation will inevitably result in deprivation of rights or interests of specific administrative counterparts, so a series of basic principles must be strictly followed. Currently, the basic principles of administrative penalties established by *Law of the People's Republic of China on Administrative Penalty* and other relevant laws and regulations about administrative penalties include the principle that administrative penalty should be regulated by law, the principle of fairness and openness, the principle of combining punishment with education, the principle of no-double punishment for one wrongdoing, and the principle of protecting lawful rights and interests of concerned party.[24] These principles are established based on the following two purposes: first, restrain illegal misuse of punitive right, secure administrative punishments are fair and appropriate, and guarantee legitimate rights and interests of concerned parties are not jeopardized; second, prevent lawbreakers from relapsing into past illegal behavior through disciplinary and education, and warn people to follow the legal order maintained by administrative penalties. Of course, these traditional principles for administrative penalties are correct and no problem has occurred when they are used for administrative penalties in the past. However, obviously there are limitations if there are only these two basic purposes for establishing and implementing administrative penalties for energy conservation and emission reduction in ecological environmental protection. This would mean preventing infringement caused by illegal behaviors and remedial measures for the infringement are taken lightly. However, such prevention and remedy are an important concept and a purpose that need to be highlighted in administrative penalties in the field of protecting ecological environment, that is, using administrative punishment to effectively prevent the risk of infringement or further infringement, and to take remedial and restorative measures for infringement caused. Therefore, a new principle of "preventing and remedying damages" should be established in this field to make up for the deficiency in the traditional basic principles and to guide the improvement of the types and application methods of administrative penalties.

The principle of preventing and remedying damages involves two things, that is, preventing impairment from occurring and taking remedial measures for impairment. From the perspective of preventing impairment, illegal acts that waste energy and resources and have high emissions of carbon dioxide will cause harmful consequences of environment degradation and ecological damage whose effects are long term and hard to be reversed. Even if fix is made to some extent whose costs are extremely high. Therefore, preventive role of administrative penalties must be highlighted so as to avoid occurrence of impairment as much as possible or reduce impairment to its lowest level. From the perspective of taking remedial measures for impairment, the ultimate purpose of punishing illegal behaviors destroying ecological environment is to ensure a good ecological environment. The purpose can be reliably fulfilled through fixing damage to ecological environment caused by illegal

[24] Scholars also summarize the principles of administrative penalties differently. For example, Professor Jiang Ming'an summarizes the principles of administrative penalties as the principle that administrative penalty should be regulated by law, the principle of parity and openness, the principle of combining punishment with education, the principle of guaranteeing rights of administrative counterparts, the principle of separating functions, and the principle of no-double punishment for one wrongdoing. Professor Yang Jiejun summarizes the principles of administrative penalties: the principle of fully respecting human rights, the principle of justice, the principle that administrative penalty should be regulated by law, the principle of no-double punishment for one wrongdoing, the principle of proportional punishment, the principle of individualized punishment, the principle of offenders are the same with the punished, the principle of combining punishment with education, and the principle of separating adjudicative right of punishment from enforcement right of punishment. See Jiang Ming'an (Ed.) (2005). *Administrative Law and Administrative Litigation Law* (pp. 312–314). Peking University Press& Higher Education Press; Yang Jiejun (1995). *Order·Power and Legal Control—a Study on Administrative Penalty Law* (pp. 203–219). Sichuan University Press.

behaviors because this makes administrative penalties to not just focus on punishment but to directly implement remedies or promote illegal actors to actively take remedial measures through punishment. This isn't what can be achieved through traditional penalties such as warning, fine, confiscation, cancellation of license, and suspension of production or business because warning and fine cannot fix impairment that has been caused. Such penalties as cancellation of license and suspension of production or business, however, just prevent law breakers from further impairment and are also unable to fix impairment that has been caused. Therefore, the function of fixing repaired ecological environment must be enhanced and ways of administrative penalties should be improved. At the same time, damaging ecological environment is a serious thing. Damaged environment needs a long time to recover and it is hard and costly to restore ecological environment. Therefore, administrative penalties shouldn't just require that lawbreakers shoulder such obligations as reputational damage (for example, warning), deprivation of property (for example, confiscation of property and fine), limiting behaviors (for example, cancellation of license and suspension of production or business) and no recidivism, the penalties should also require they must shoulder the obligation of restoration and taking remedial measures for impairment.

(II) Legislative Requirement of the Principle of Preventing and Remedying Damages

Principles of administrative penalties are like threads that run through legal relations in administrative penalties. They reflect the purpose and value of administrative penalties and are the basis for existence of specific rules of administrative penalties. Principles of administrative penalties are abstract and are reflected through specific provisions of administrative penalty laws. The concept of prevention and remedy is not fully reflected by existing administrative laws and regulations which also lack provisions about prevention and remedy. Therefore, the principle of preventing and remedying damages must be added for administrative penalties for low-carbon development and corresponding legal provisions must also be added to ensure the spirit of this principle run through the penalties imposed for low-carbon development.

First, the scope of application of fines should be expanded to ensure remedies for impaired ecological environment. The fine-related provisions of existing *Law of the People's Republic of China on Administrative Penalty* and relevant low-carbon laws and regulations require that illegal actors shall pay a certain amount of money to the country. The sum is limited to cover loss caused by their illegal behaviors and not such costs of manpower and materials to be paid for making up for the loss. For traditional illegal behaviors, such provisions about fine can meet the need of resuming social management order; however, for illegal behaviors against low-carbon development, the scope covered by such fine is obviously too narrow and is hard to meet the need for money to be used to resume natural ecological system. Therefore, according to the principle of of preventing and remedying damages, it is suggested that the scope of application of the fines stipulated in low-carbon laws and regulations for environmental pollution and wasting resources and energy should be expanded to cover cleanup, fixation, compensation and restoration, and incidental expenses. Administrative organs can choose coverage of fines according to severity of the illegal behaviors of illegal counterparts. For example, Article 59 of *Environmental Protection Law* reflects the concept of remedy to some extent, but the provision should be made more specific. Therefore, content about compensation and restoration should be added to the provision, that is, a paragraph that goes[25] "This fine refers to a punitive fine for compensation and restoration." should be added after the second paragraph.[26] At the same time, the concept of a punitive fine for compensation and restoration should be defined in the Supplementary Provisions of the law.

Second, new types of administrative penalties should be added to reflect compensatory purpose of administrative penalties. Because it is costly to fix the ecological environment and also takes a long time, it is suggested that such types of administrative penalties as order for participating in replacement programs and order for participating in ecological compensation programs should be added and definitions of these types of penalties should be added in supplementary provisions of corresponding laws. This is mainly targeted at illegal behaviors that seriously pollute the environment and it is difficult to achieve rectification or it is too costly to make rectification but remedial measures can be taken through eco-compensation programs. Such illegal behaviors can be punished through such types of administrative penalties as ordering counterparts of such behaviors to take part in replacement programs or eco-compensation programs. For example, adding "and order them to adopt replacement programs" to Article 83 of *Law of the PRC on Energy Conservation*[27] and also adding the definition of replacement programs in the Supplementary Provision of the law.

Third, there should be more ways of implementation to reflect restorative purpose of administrative penalties. When impaired by illegal activities, ecological environment should be maximally restored because it is rare and vital for mankind. This is how traditional administrative penalties are different from those in a low-carbon era. Therefore, the scope of "agency performance" can be expanded to allow performance by a third-party substitute or allow eco-restoration through "carbon neutrality" to fix polluted eco-environment maximally. For example, the following sentence can be added to Article 76 of *Law of the People's Republic of China on Prevention and Control of Water Pollution*: "if size of the fine is too big for a business, homogeneous compensation may be made for the pollution through 'carbon neutrality'."[28]

---

[25] Article 59 of *Environmental Protection Law* stipulates: "The above-mentioned fines shall be implemented in accordance with laws/regulations and take into considerations of operating cost of pollution control facilities, direct loss of violation activities and revenues of such violations".

[26] Zhang Jigang (2014). *Improving Ways of Shouldering Criminal Liability for Public Environmental Hazard Crimes. Journal of Liuzhou Normal College*, (6).

[27] Article 83 of *Law of the PRC on Energy Conservation* stipulates that "Where a key energy-using unit, without justifiable reasons, refuses to comply with the requirement for rectification, as provided for in Article 54 of this law, or fails to fulfill the requirement after rectification, it shall be fined not less than 100,000 yuan but not more than 300,000 yuan by the department in charge in energy conservation".

[28] Article 76 of *Law of the People's Republic of China on Prevention and Control of Water Pollution* stipulates that " Where a unit commits one of the following acts, the competent environmental

Last, there should be provisions about preventive administrative penalties targeted at individual illegal acts of citizens. Although existing provisions about administrative penalties are also targeted at illegal administrative counterparts, preventive purpose of penalties is not reflected by corresponding provisions about penalties. It is hard to effectively prevent the future illegal acts of the counterpart. This is especially true for the chapters about liability in low-carbon laws and regulations. Possible ecological risks of illegal behaviors of administrative counterparts are not considered. Therefore, preventive provisions about penalties for illegal behaviors of individual citizens can be added in laws and regulations about energy and resource conservation and pollution prevention and control. The following provisions can be added: if citizens should seriously waste resources and energy, fail to discard wastes and household garbage according to regulations, and engage in "alienated consumption of energy and resources such as too much excessive consumption and luxurious consumption, administrative organs should disclose their violation in the places where they work and live and in public places. If their acts of should cause bad influence and greatly influence others and the society, administrative organs should record their acts in their personal credit record. Where they should cause serious consequences and refuse to correct, administrative organs should, in addition to fines, adopt mandatory measures to demand them to regularly and quantitatively take part in environment treatment efforts under the supervision of competent environment authority." Adding the above provisions can effectively prevent individual citizens from having illegal behaviors against low-carbon development and effectively warn and educate social public so as to form a good atmosphere where energy and resources are conserved and ecological environment is protected.

2.2 *Strengthening Administrative Penalties Against Law-Breaking Citizens*

Chinese citizens consume a great portion of China's energy and resources and emit a great portion of China's pollutants and green gases, so administrative penalties targeted at illegal behaviors of citizens must be added to and strengthened by existing low-carbon laws and regulations.

Currently, administrative penalties should at least cover the following categories of behaviors of individual citizens: (i) seriously waste energy and resources. In Germany, citizens are not allowed to waste food. If they are found to waste food, any person has the right to report them, and they will be fined according to regulations. It was reported that some Chinese tourists wasted food in Germany and were

protection department of the local people's government at or above the county level shall order it to cease and desist from the violation and to take control measures within a time limit to eliminate the pollution, and shall impose on it a fine. If the unit fails to take the said measures on the expiration of the time limit, the said department may designate another unit capable of putting such pollution under control to do the job instead, and the expenses entailed shall be borne by the violator".

fined DM40 to DM50.[29] (ii) fail to discard wastes and household garbage according to regulations and affect recycling of wastes, for example, do not classify wastes according to regulations and discard them at will. Currently many countries have promulgated laws about reasonable disposal of household wastes, for example, if a citizen violates Wastes Disposal Law and litter in Japan, he/she will be detained by the police and fined 30,000–50,000 Japanese yen.[30] (iii) consumptive behaviors that seriously affect environmental protection, for example, smoking in public places, and driving motor vehicles with excessive emissions.

With respect of penalty types and specific punitive measures to be selected, reputational penalty and behavioral penalty can be mainly used with combination of appropriate property penalty.

(i) **Reputational penalties**

Reputational penalty refers to sending warnings to lawbreakers or disclosing their violations by administrative organs so as to warn them of or admonish them for their behaviors through effects on their reputation, honor and credit. For individuals, reputation is an important social asset. Illegal behaviors can be punished and restrained through reputational pressure on lawbreakers. Currently, reputational penalties are mainly warnings or admonishments given by administrative organs to administrative counterparts that have breached their low-carbon and pro-environmental obligations. However, due to enforcement mechanism, the influence of such penalties is limited because they are only known by administrative organs and administrative counterparts themselves. Information about administrative counterparts' illegal acts are not widely made known to the public. Therefore, it is hard for administrative counterparts to take the penalties seriously so effects of the penalties are very limited. Reputational penalties are even marginalized and become dispensable. Therefore, reputational loss of administrative counterparts brought by reputational penalties should be increased so that administrative counterparts are forced to correct their illegal acts due to greater mental pressure and reputational loss. Specifically, this can be done through the following means: (i) disclose violations. Citizens breaking their low-carbon and pro-environmental obligations should be warned, admonished, persuaded and educated, and information of their violations should also be published within a certain scope to bring mental pressure to them. For example, administrative organs can publish names of the citizens that often litter and waste energy and resources through website and newspaper to publish information of their violations in the places where they work. In addition, administration organs suggest that the organizations they work should take actions about them. (ii) record information of violations in personal credit history. The reason why the effects of reputational penalties were not obvious was mainly that no actual loss and deterrence were brought to violators. Therefore, credit rating system can be additional used as an appropriate

[29] Anonymous Author (2013, January 29), *There Are Ways to Contain Food Waste, South Korea Promotes the Use of Smaller Bowls. Guangzhou Daily*.

[30] Hai Zhou (2013, March 19). *How do Foreign Countries Sort and Recycle Household Garbage?, Shenzhen Special Zone Daily*.

means to improve deterrence of reputational penalties and really realize the dual role of punishment and education.[31] For example, low-carbon and pro-environmental activity can be a factor that affects personal credit score. When citizens receive such reputational penalties as warning and admonishment due to illegal behaviors against low-carbon and pro-environmental practice, the penalties should be recorded in their credit history. When the bad records reach a certain number, credit reporting agencies can reduce their personal credit ratings and share the information with other administrative management authorities, which directly affects such personal activities of them as seeking jobs, promotions and obtaining credit loans.

(ii) **Behavioral penalties**

Traditional behavioral penalties in administrative penalties mainly refer to ability penalties, that is, depriving certain behavioral capacities or qualifications of administrative counterparts, for example, order for suspension of production or business and temporary withholding or canceling of license or permits. Behavioral penalties that apply to environmental violations of citizens should be behavioral penalties in a broader sense, that is, penalties are completed by ordering citizens to actively adopt certain pro-environmental actions and they combine education with punishment. Some scholars found through researches that how citizens develop their pro-environmental awareness significantly affects their actual behaviors. When developed from practical experience, such an awareness can obviously play a greater role in encouraging them to adopt pro-environmental behaviors. If developed through hollow preaching, such an awareness obviously plays a weaker role in encouraging them to adopt pro-environmental behaviors.[32] The purpose of behavioral penalties is to gradually make citizens develop a low-carbon awareness and habit through actual involvement in pro-environmental actions so as to imperceptibly restrain environment violations and improve energy efficiency. Many behavioral penalties have emerged in enforcing administrative penalties for environmental violations in recent years. For example, citizens in Guangdong Nanzha Community had long had the habit of dumping and littering rubbish at random. The government spent more than five million yuan a year on cleaning but the effect was not ideal at all. Then the community introduced a new punitive measure—"those who randomly litter rubbish will be punished by cleaning the community for one hour". After implementation of the measure, sanitation conditions of the place were obviously improved.[33] A similar case also occurred in enforcing administrative law about urban environment in Shenzhen. A citizen was fined 50 yuan for randomly litter rubbish. At last he was permitted to clean three streets because he was in a difficult financial situation.[34]

---

[31] See Liao Dan (2013), *Research on Administrative Penalties for Environment Violations*, Master dissertation of Chongqing University.

[32] Wang Jianmin& Wang Junhao (2011), *Factors Affecting Public' s Low-carbon Consumption Mode and Government's Management and Control Policy*, *Management World*, (4).

[33] Lei Yuanquan (2013, May 24). *Humen Nanzha Community Adopts a New Measure for Managing Environmental Sanitation*, *Dongguan Times*.

[34] Xiao Shitan (2003, May 31). *"Behavioral penalties" Can be Used to Stop Spitting*, *Jiangnan Times*.

People who illegally put up small ads in some cities, which is an urban phenomenon that is hard to cure as "psoriasis", are ordered to clean a certain area as a punishment. The effect is good.[35] The experience for these effective practices should be summarized in time and be fixed and institutionalized through legislation to form a new type of penalty so as to better regulate citizen's environmental behaviors and urge them to adopt low-carbon pro-environmental lifestyles.

2.3 Introducing Precautionary Administrative Penalties to Prevent Ecological Risks

Due to uncertainty of ecological risks and irreversibility of their consequences, the environment precautionary principle should be introduced in addition to the principle that administrative penalty should be regulated by law. The environment precautionary principle comes from *International Environmental Law* and gradually extends its use to various types of administration regulation. The environment precautionary principle was created based on looking back at traditional environmental policy of "pollution first, treatment afterwards" and is intended to avoid possible future harm to the environment through comprehensive preventive measures. The principle is clearly stipulated in many international conventions and bilateral and multilateral treaties. The *World Conservation Strategy* of 1980,where a package of preventive environmental policies are proposed, states "these policies require that actions be taken before the environment is damaged"; Nairobi Declaration adopted by the United Nations in 1982 states that "Prevention of damage to the environment is preferable to the burdensome and extensive repair of damage already done." The principle is also much talked about in international law documents such as *the United Nations Convention on the Law of the Sea* and *the World Charter for Nature*. In the field of climate change, the principle is also introduced into *the United Nations Framework Convention on Climate Change*.[36] Although the principle is stipulated in various types of international conventions, there is still no consensus about its specific regulatory connotations. Different types of international conventions and legal documents in different applicable fields of the principle are also different about how strict the principle should be used. According to degree of strictness of using the principle, the principle can be theoretically divided into two types: the weak precautionary principle and the strong precautionary principle. The weak precautionary principle states that absence of conclusive evidence about a risk or sufficient technical certainty should not bar the taking of precautionary measures in the face of a possible harm.[37] As typically summarized by the *1998 Wingspread Declaration* proposed by environmentalists, the strong precautionary principle states: "When an activity raises threats

---

[35] Li Mu (2012). *On the Offset of Administrative Counterpart's Obligations*, *Law Review*, (5).

[36] See Sub-Article 3 of Article 3 of the *United Nations Framework Convention on Climate Change*.

[37] Peng Feng (2012). *Re-examination of the "Precautionary" Principle in Environmental Law*. *Journal of Beijing Institute of Technology (Social Sciences Edition)*, (2).

of harm to human health or the environment, precautionary measures should be taken even if some cause-and-effect relationships are not fully established scientifically. In this context the proponent of an activity, rather than the public, should bear the burden of proof."[38]

However, either the strong precautionary principle or the weak precautionary principle has deficiencies. Both of them need to be looked back and improved. A common fatal problem with them is their incoherent logic, which may paralyze relevant actions. This is mainly reflected in the following aspects. First, if, as required by the strong precautionary principle, a risk maker must shoulder the responsibility of proving that their activities are absolutely harmless. This may make the activities in some fields paralyzed. Second, measures taken to prevent a risk almost always go with substitute risks in any case. Strict use of the strong precautionary principle may result in excessive regulation and causes "what one gets on the roundabouts, he loses on the swings". For example, the United States forbade the use of DDT (a pesticide) to prevent it from destroying the food chain of carnivorous birds in the 1960s, but killing pests by DDT is one of the most effective ways of preventing and controlling malaria. Another typical disproof lies in the field of drug administration. If the government took stringent preventive measures about production of new drugs, this would also deprive people of the hope of being cured of ineradicable diseases and gain health (and even life) through new drugs. In these scenarios, strict use of the strong precautionary principle undoubtedly brings more risks. This is not what was original intended for implementing the precautionary principle. The cautious attitude of "Better safe than sorry" leads to an undesirable situation as described by the proverb "He who hesitates is lost".

Due to deficiency of it as far as its use is concerned, the precautionary principle can be used for administrative penalties about environmental violations from the following aspects. (i) In terms of preventive strength, currently the weak precautionary principle should be used. Although China having made world-renowned achievements in its economic development since its reform and opening-up, China is still the largest developing country in the world. China still has the "primary task" of improving people's standard of living and strengthen its comprehensive national power. Its only way of fundamentally solving the issue of green gases emission and environmental protection is through development. Therefore, when imposing administrative penalties, it is necessary to balance the relationship between preventing ecological risks and economic development. It is not right to bluntly use the strong precautionary principle, which may stifle vitality of social and economic development. (ii) In terms of application and behavior pattern, use of the precautionary principle should be further limited based on the weak precautionary principle. The precautionary principle does not apply to all administrative penalties for environmental violations. It only applies to serious ecological risks that cannot be dealt with in advance by the principle that administrative penalty should be regulated by law. When the principle is practically used, theories about specific potential damage

[38] Carolyn Raffensperger and Peter L. deFurr, *Implementing The Precautionary Principle: Rigorous Science and Solid Ethics, Human & Ecological Risk Assessment*, 933, 934, 1999.

offenses in criminal law can be referred to. As far as administrative penalties for pro-environmental violations is concerned, use of the principle should only be confined to behaviors that bring obvious and immediate risks to the ecological environment and health of the residents, for example, the act of burning straw, which should be monitored and receive administrative penalty to prevent smog. With regard to the requirements of preventing risks, currently common requirements include, among others, using the best feasible technologies, the best environmental practice, considering cost effectiveness, social economic benefits, and looking for substitutive methods.[39] Administrative counterparts that fail to meet such minimum preventive requirements can be judged as having "specific" potential ecological damage. Therefore, administrative penalties can be imposed on them based on the principal of precautionary principle. Preventive administrative penalties cannot be randomly given to people whose behaviors are deemed as having abstract potential damage. (iii) In terms of burden of proof, based on the "privilege against self-incrimination" and the consideration of avoiding putting too heavy burden of proof on counterparts in public law, the burden of proof is still on administrative organs. However, the uncertainty characteristic of ecological risks should also be considered to appropriately lower the standard that requires administrative organs to prove wrongdoings through investigation. Take the aforesaid Shaoshan strong odor case as an example, although temporarily the environmental protection bureau couldn't conclusively determine that the strong odor came from Shengzhao Mining Co, Ltd., it was urgent to eliminate the potential harm to the health of the surrounding residents and to the surrounding environment. Therefore, the environmental protection bureau could use identification of the residents and their adverse symptoms as a sufficient condition for it to investigate and gather evidence. In fact, there had been a similar case involving administrative penalties for environmental violations in 1992 where Xiamen Environmental Protection Bureau adopted a similar practice. It neither had scientific monitoring data nor a national or local standard about atmospheric environment quality, so it requested the Ministry of Ecology and Environment about whether administrative penalties should be imposed on Lota Group for its emission of waste gases according to strong reactions of surrounding residents. The Ministry of Ecology and Environment replied that "(you) can refer to the methods used by foreign countries to identify and determine the odious pollutants according to the people's sense of smell and sensory judgment."[40] This was, in fact, a decrease of the criteria of the investigation for inflicting administrative penalties in case of uncertain risks and technical difficulties. (iv) In terms of punitive measures, the main penalties to be used should be behavioral penalties such as order for suspension of production and business because of the following two reasons. First, precautionary prevention is to prevent harmful consequences from occurring in advance, so the penalties must be able to stop corresponding behaviors. Second, it

---

[39] Peng Feng (2012), *Re-examination of the "Precautionary" Principle in Environmental Law*, *Journal of Beijing Institute of Technology (Social Sciences Edition)*, (2).

[40] The Supreme People's Court (1993), The case where Lota Group was inflicted administrative penalties by Xiamen Environmental Protection Bureau for emitting most odious gases. In *Volume one of the anthology of adjudicated cases in China 1993*, People's Court Publishing House.

is hard to concretely determine in advance severity of potential damage and probability of its occurrence so other penalties such as fines give the administrative organs too much discretion but a lack of basis for imposing the penalties.

Currently, reference can be made to some administrative penalties of China where the precautionary concept has been introduced. For example, Article 91 of the *Road Traffic Safety Law* 2014 stipulates that "Whoever drives a motor vehicle after drinking alcohol shall be temporarily withheld of his/her motor vehicle driving license for six months and be concurrently imposed upon a fine of not less than 1000 yuan but not more than 2000. Whoever drives a motor vehicle after drinking alcohol again after being punished for such act shall be detained for not more than ten days and be concurrently imposed a fine of not less than 1000 yuan but not more than 2000 yuan, and be revoked of his/her motor vehicle driving license." In the stipulation, drunken driving has not actually caused a traffic accident, but the driver still receives administrative penalties for which the purpose of the legislator is to prevent safety risk brought by drunken driving. Likewise, it is stipulated in the first paragraph of Article 25 of the *Law on Prevention and Control of Environmental Pollution by Solid Waste* that imported solid wastes shall be managed through catalogs of classified solid wastes. Imported solid wastes shall be managed based on their categories according to *Directory of National Hazardous Wastes, Prohibited Catalogue on Import of Solid Waste, Restricted Category on Import of Solid Waste that Can be Reused as Raw Material* and *Automated Registration Category on Import of Solid Waste that Can be Reused as Raw Materia.* Penalties are stipulated in Article 43 of the *Administrative Measures for the Import of Solid Wastes.*[41] It can be found through analysis that precautionary purposes are contained in these categories and directories. Article 8 of the *Administrative Measures for the Import of Solid Wastes* is intended to forbid importing polluting wastes for which currently no standard has been prepared so as to prevent uncertain potential hazards to the environment. The 84th category of solid wastes as specified in *the Prohibited Catalogue on Import of Solid Waste* is "other unlisted solid wastes", which means all solid wastes which cannot be proved to be harmless to health and the environment through existing inspection and test technologies are forbidden to be imported and those who do not follow this catalogue will be given administrative penalties. In addition, Article 2 of the *Directory of National Hazardous Wastes* clearly stipulates that such dangerous wastes as corrosive, toxic and inflammable wastes are included in the directory but it also stipulates in the last paragraph of the article that dangerous wastes that "have possible hazard characteristics, are likely to cause adverse effect on the ecological environment or personal health" are not excluded. This no doubt shows a management mechanism for preventing potential pollution. Through the above legislation, we can get valuable institutional experience for improving precautionary measures to be used in administrative regulation of environmental violations. The experience can be assimilated when future administrative penalty system is improved and developed.

[41] Refer to Article 43 of the *Administrative Measures for the Import of Solid Wastes.*

2.4 *Establishing Administrative Penalties for Ecological Restoration*

"Protective function of law is realized through two means: first, punishing illegal and criminal acts, and second, recovering infringed rights and obtaining redress for the infringement."[42] Administrative penalties for ecological restoration need to be established due to the ecological restoration requirement of current environmental governance and the shortcomings of traditional administrative penalties. It is also required in the *Resolution of the Central Committee of the Communist Party of China on Major Issues Concerning the Enhancement of All-round Law-based Governance* approved at The fourth Plenary Session of the 18th Communist Party of China Central Committee that "laws and regulations improving among other things, ecological compensation and prevention of pollution of soil, water, atmosphere, and protection of the oceanic ecological environment should be improved". In fact, the concept of "restorative justice"[43] in criminal law can provide us with a helpful reference. The concept of " restorative justice" in criminal law is designed to redress the condition that traditional criminal punishment puts undue emphasis on getting offenders punished and maintaining order and neglects restoration of legal interests infringed by criminal acts. Instead of derogating the interests of criminals and punishing them, it focuses on repairing damage caused to crime victims, hence re-balance the social interests harmed by criminal acts. Restorative justice practice has also emerged in China in recent years, for example, the case prosecuted in Chongqing in 2006 where Qiu Tianshi and Zhou Xinlong were not punished by imprisonment but by planting trees, which caused heated discussion. Such scholars as Professor Ma Kechang and Professor He Jiahong thought that provisions of laws were not rigidly followed, and on the contrary, the concept of restorative justice was flexibly used in the case. The sentence not only involved a punishment of the offenders but also involved protection of rights and interests of the victim, which better realized the purpose of criminal justice of protecting legal interests.[44] The *Law of the People's Republic of China on Administrative Penalty* has dual legislative purposes of "safeguarding the public interest and social order". However, traditional administrative penalties are in the scope of penalties against violations of the order, which can maintain social order very well but cannot fully safeguard the public interest. Both administrative penalty law and criminal law are public laws in nature and are inflicted by the state. They are of similar purpose and mechanism. Therefore, there is no harm to refer to the concept of restorative justice to realize the purpose of administrative penalties of maintaining order and also restore damaged legal interests by introducing the method of restorative justice.

---

[42] Sun Guohua.,& Zhu Jingwen, *Jurisprudence,3rd ed,* China Renmin University Press, 2010, p. 51.

[43] Zehr, H. B., Toews. *Critical Issues in Restorative Justice.* New York Criminal Justice Press and UK Willian Publishing, 2004, pp. 161–161.

[44] Hao Shaohong, *Legal Analysis of Two Typical "Restorative Justice" Cases*, Master's degree thesis of Lanzhou University, 2011.

Administrative penalties that impose the legal liability for restoration theoretically originated from the legal responsibility for the restoration of the status quo ante in civil law. However, they are fundamentally different from the civil liability of restoration to status quo ante in terms of their objectives and specific composition. The liability to restore status quo ante is a tort liability and is "intended to restore a right holder to the status quo ante".[45] It is a remedy pattern that is mainly realized through restoration of ownership rights to property and reparation. In general, the holder of the liability is the infringer of a right. The legal liability for ecological restoration imposed by administrative penalties, however, is a complicated liability system and has connotations different from those of the civil liability of restoration to status quo ante. First, the legal liability for ecological restoration requested by an administrative penalty is not directed at replacing or filling in any particular environmental object, but at the restoration of the functions of any particular ecosystem services.[46] This is because ecological objects such as the natural environment and climatic resources constitute a functional system. Once ecological objects are damaged, the damage cannot be corrected by simply restoring any particular point of damage or replacing the same with objects of the same kind. They need to be redressed from a holistic approach. For example, water and soil loss and carbon sequestration loss caused by the illegal cutting of a great number of forest trees by a company cannot be simply redressed by supplementary planting of trees. On the contrary, many remedial measures (for example, enclosing the hillsides to facilitate afforestation, protecting the secondary forest, artificial afforestation, constructing a network of shelterbelts) need to be taken to resume the functions of the damaged ecosystem from the perspective of the ecological status of the entire forest. With regard to this, although "compensate by planting trees"[47] is stipulated under the *Forest Law of the People's Republic of China* (hereinafter "*Forest Law*") as an administrative penalty, this is not enough to truly repair the ecosystem functions and services of a forest by simply restoration to the status quo ante. Second, the legal liability for ecological restoration requested by an administrative penalty is not only directed at recovery of ecosystem functions and services but is also directed at compensating surrounding people affected by environmental damage. It is known to all that environmental damage has broad and far-reaching negative impacts on the life and survival of surrounding people. With regard to this, aside from enforcing civil liability for infringement of environmental laws and regulations against a particular defendant, the defendant also needs to assume administrative

[45] Wang Feng, *On Restoration as a Civil Remedy*, *Wuhan University journal: Philosophy and Social Sciences Edition*, no.4, 2012.

[46] "Ecosystem services" means all resources needed by human beings for survival and development eventually come from nature's ecological system. Nature's ecological system not only directly provides us with various raw materials or products (for example, food, water, oxygen, wood, and fiber) for our survival, but also has such functions as regulating climate, purifying air, conserve water resources, conserving water and soil, breaking wind and fixing sand, alleviating natural disasters, and protecting biodiversity, which hence provides a good ecological environment for human to survive and develop. All ecosystem products and services that contribute to the survival of huma beings and improvement of their quality of life are collectively called ecosystem services.

[47] See Article 39 of the *Forest Law of the People's Republic of China*.

liability to pay compensation to a non-specified or potential group of victims. Third, the legal liability for ecological restoration requested by an administrative penalty is incidental. When it is pursued by an administrative body against a violator, it is pursued in conjunction with other traditional administrative penalties. For example, a company discharges industrial wastewater into a lake. The administrative agency tasked with environmental protection will impose a penalty for restoration on it such as ordering it to clean the water pollution and purify the water body and will also concurrently impose other traditional administrative penalties on it according to law such as fining it, ordering it to stop production or business operation or close down. The main reason is traditional administrative penalties such as property-based penalties and behavioral sanctions are in the scope of penalties against violations of the order. In these penalties, the legal interest infringed by a violator is the order of environmental administration. While in a penalty requesting for restoration, the legal interest infringed by a violator is the integrity of the ecosystem. Based on the difference of the legal interest infringed, the two categories of administrative penalties should be assessed concurrently and are not mutually replaceable.

Globally, restorative legal liability have been available in the legislation of many countries with a developed level of nomocracy, which sets up a good example for us to establish relevant administrative liability to be imposed. For example, there is a chapter in the *Environment Act 1995* of the UK which provides for the liability of companies to remediate contaminated land and abandoned mines and the liability of them to restore contaminated land and abandoned mines to their original state. Germany specially launched a *Mine Restoration Act* to require that developers should restore and regenerate damaged lands and natural landscapes. There are also many detailed provisions about environmental restoration and regeneration in the United States such as *Resource Conservation and Recovery Act*, *Surface Mining Control and Reclamation Act*, and *Comprehensive Environmental Response, Compensation, and Liability Act*.[48] The legal liability for ecological restoration requested by an administrative penalty in China can be assumed by taking actions or by paying reparation:

(i) Administrative penalty of taking actions for restoration

For violations related to low-carbon emission and environmental protection, administrative penalties of restoration should first require that the violator independently take remediation actions for restoration, that is, administrative penalties requiring taking actions for restoration are in the scope of behavioral sanctions in a broader sense. Administrative penalties requiring taking actions for restoration take on many forms and have an open system architecture. In consideration of the current status of administrative enforcement of law related to low-carbon emission and environmental protection in China, emphasis should be put on the use of two types of penalties: i) performance by a third party on behalf of the violator, which mainly applies to the

[48] See Wang Canfa, *New Environmental Legislation is Needed in Times of Environmental Restoration and Regeneration, Journal of Zhengzhou University: Philosophy and Social Sciences Ed*, no.2, 2002.

sector of pollution treatment, that is, requiring the violator to entrust a third-party treatment servicer appointed by the government to be administratively responsible for carrying out the restorative actions required by the penalty. During the entire process, the violator should correspondingly cooperate with the treatment work done by the actual servicer. Due to comparatively limited professional capacity, time, and energy, the violator is usually unwilling or unable to independently perform the obligation of ecological restoration imposed by administrative penalties. Therefore, it is required that the mechanism for entrusting performance by a third party can promote the violator to timely and effectively perform the obligation imposed by the penalties. At present, a series of mechanisms related thereto have been practiced in China. For example, a mechanism for outsourcing pollution treatment has been enforced among the organizations and units in the Wujin District of Changzhou since 2005.[49] Now hundreds of organizations and units have begun to implement the mechanism. The mechanism of outsourcing pollution treatment to a third party requires that polluters must sign a contract about outsourcing their pollution treatment work with organizations and units that are qualified for doing pollution treatment work. The environmental protection organ is responsible for assessing and determining the amount of pollution discharged by the polluters, setting reasonable standards for amounts of emissions allowed, determining the amounts of fees to be paid to the outsourced vendors, and, during the entire process, supervising payments of pollution treatment fees from the polluters to the outsourced vendors that have signed a contract with the polluters. Pollution treatment outsourcing not only makes pollution supervision and administration easier but also reduces the efforts needed for pollution supervision and administration. In January 2015, the General Office of the State Council issued the *Opinions on Advocating the Treatment of Environmental Pollution by Third Parties* to further confirmed the practice of outsourcing pollution treatment to third parties. ii) Carbon neutrality. At present, the concept of carbon neutrality is thought to be the best way to solve the problem of carbon dioxide emissions. At this stage, violators that exceed GHG emissions standards to discharge greenhouse gases can choose to use carbon naturalization programs such as planting trees, carbon capture and storage, and purchasing carbon emission quota to achieve the purpose of restorative penalties. During the process that carbon neutrality programs are used to carry out restorative actions required by penalties, administrative entities first need to use the MRV mechanism to detect the amount of GHG excessively emitted by the violator and demand the counterpart to offset the carbon emissions excessively discharged. Then the administrative entities supervise and recheck the offsetting data through a certain verification system.

(ii) **Administrative penalty of compensatory restoration**

When the concerned party is incapable of taking action for restoration, the administrative penalty of compensatory restoration can be used. An administrative penalty

[49] Zhu Demi, *Taking Water Pollution Prevention and Control of Taihu Basin as an Example to Illustrate formation of the cooperative relationship between Local Government and Organizations and Units*, *Journal of Shanghai Administration Institute*, no.1, 2010.

of compensatory restoration means imposing a fine on the violator to cover the ecological damage caused thereby. In a traditional civil liability system for environmental infringement, only particular interested parties that sustain economic or health loss due to environmental pollution can obtain reparation for damages in environmental infringement. With regard to loss or degradation of the functions of ecosystem services due to environmental pollution and high carbon emissions of a violator, non-specific counterparts that are indirectly harmed thereby cannot get compensated for their loss. For example, after the occurrence of the above-mentioned Water Pollution Incident in the Songhua River, Wang Jin, Gan Peizhong, and other environmental scholars initiated a civil public interest lawsuit against Sinopec Group, requesting the court to sentence Sinopec Group to indemnify 10 billion Chinese yuan to set up a fund for treating the pollution of the Songhua River basin and restore the ecological balance of the Songhua River basin. However, the court rejected the case.[50] With regard to ecological loss that still can be redeemed through monetary compensation, the loss should be further redeemed through a penalty of compensatory restoration because "it is better late than never" for mending. Generally speaking, fines imposed for compensatory restoration include the following: In general, the fines to be imposed due to imposition of the penalty of compensatory restoration should include the following: i) A clearing fine. This is imposed to remove pollutants and greenhouse gas emissions, and eliminate the harm caused by illegal acts to the ecological environment or prevent the harm from expansion. Due to characteristics of ecological damage, reversing harmful consequences of the damage must be done by professional law enforcement authorities. In most cases, the violator does not have the ability and energy to reverse the same, and the resulting administrative cost needs to be included in administrative penalties. In this regard, there have been rules concerning collecting clearing costs in the judicial practice of foreign countries.[51] ii) A fine for repair work. Removal of pollution only temporarily prevents harm from escalation and achieving the purpose of restoration relies on further work to be done for ecological repair. This involves a reparation fine. The fine is inevitably for further treating and taking further remedial actions for polluted or damaged ecological environment, making it able to regain its functions before the pollution, and ensuring that the polluted environment regains life and restores vitality and can be reused by human beings.[52] Specifically, the repair work involves bio-remediation, phytoremediation, physical remediation, chemical remediation, ecological remediation, and carbon neutrality. iii) A fine for reparation and settlement. The fine is collected for paying reparations to non-specific victims who cannot obtain reasonable reparations through an environmental infringement lawsuit. The main factors used to calculate

[50] See Liu Xiaoxing, *Amendments to PRC's Civil Procedure Law Open a Door to Public Interest Environmental Litigation, China Environment News*, Nov. 6, 2012.

[51] See Zhu Xiao, *Reflective Thoughts on Legal Embarrassment of the Administrative Penalty Inflicted for Water Pollution Incident in the Songhua River—from the Perspective of Ecological Damage Compensation Liability System, Legal Science*, no. 3, 2007.

[52] See Zhou Qixing, et.al., *Ecological Restoration*, China Environmental Science Press, 2006: 3–8.

the amount of such a fine mainly include the number of people surrounding environmental pollution, and direct or potential loss of property and health, etc. iv) An incidental fine. This is a fine imposed on the violator of the law and mainly refers to the costs of administrative organs that are caused when they perform such activities as assessment and monitoring during the process of law enforcement. Enforcement of the restorative penalty is a very professional activity. Such activities as assessing polluting behaviors, detecting harm caused by pollution need considerable administrative costs, which should not be paid by the government by using the money of the taxpayers, and should be included in administrative penalties and be paid by the violator themselves. Finally, a fine fund management system should be established for the penalty of compensatory restoration so that fines can be collected and managed uniformly, and fines are guaranteed to be used for repairing the ecological environment.

In addition, when it is, in fact, hard to reverse the damage caused by illegal acts to the ecological environment or the cost of reversing the damage is too expensive, a restorative penalty on the violator can be realized through alternative projects. In this regard, the Supplemental Environmental Projects created by the Environmental Protection Agency can provide us with a useful reference. Supplemental environmental projects are environmentally beneficial projects included as part of a settlement for administrative penalties. Violators can voluntarily agree to undertake such projects related to their violations in place of part of the penalty that they are required to pay for the violations. They do this in exchange for a lighter punishment by the environmental protection agency, excluding the measures that the violator must take in order to comply with the law. In this sense, supplemental environmental projects and replacement administrative punishments are different but they achieve the same result, that is, both of them do not directly correct and resume legal environmental obligations of the violator, but replace obligations of the violator through other projects.[53] According to the EPA's practice of its projects, such alternative restorative penalty can at least use the following types of projects: (i) Public health. Public health projects mainly provide health checkups and medical services to residents that may or have been affected by environmental violations, to reduce the harm caused by the violations. (ii) Environmental compliance promotion. These are projects requiring a violator to provide training or technical support to other members of the regulated community when pollutants discharged through illegal acts are hard to be thoroughly cleaned and it is hard to resume the original services and functions of the ecosystem. The violator should use technical devices of pollution control that go beyond applicable statutory environmental requirements to better prevent and reduce the emissions of contaminants in future production and operation, and thereby offsetting the environmental consequences caused by the violations. (iii) On a site with geographic proximity but different from the site where the violations occurred. These are projects used to replace the performance of restoration obligations by resuming or repairing the ecosystems of a site with geographic proximity that may have been

[53] See Zhang Jianyu, Yan Houfu, Qin Hu, *Selected US Environment Law Enforcement Cases*, China Environmental Science Press, 2013: 54–60.

adversely affected by the violations. For example, the violator pays to repair a piece of wetland, or establish or invest in a protected area for endangered animals. (iv) Environmental funding. These are projects where the violator provides donations and support to fund other projects that are conducive to low-carbon emission and environmental protection, for example, sponsoring environmental organizations for social welfare, funding low-carbon environmental research of universities or research institutions.

2.5 *Adding Administrative Penalties for Ecological Compensation*

Taking actions to make homogeneous compensation for the damage and negative effects caused shows the profound meaning of compensatory purpose. After an administrative counterpart breached the law of energy conservation and curbing carbon dioxide emissions, this can remind him/her that he/she not only needs to stop the infringement, be subject to a fine, and also to make homogeneous compensation for the damage caused. In the field of energy conservation and emission reduction, such homogeneous compensation requires long-time input of money and labor, which increases the cost of the administrative counterpart and hence plays a deterrence role to some extent. In this field, the compensatory purpose of administrative penalties can be realized through behavioral sanctions. Only through certain acts can compensation be made to the environment. As a behavior sanction, ordering an administrative counterpart to take remedial measures is an important way to realize such a purpose. For a violator that violates the law that promotes energy conservation and curbs carbon dioxide emissions, the administrative organ can order the violator to take compensatory measures for ecological environment damage. Ecological compensation projects can be used to fulfill such a purpose.

(I) **Purpose of Ecological Compensation Projects**

Currently, there is no uniform definition of ecological compensation. Although scholars have different definitions, through comprehensive analysis, it is concluded that ecological compensation is a means to encourage people to maintain and conserve the ecological system through economic incentives. With such a means, problems affecting ecological benefits can be externally solved to some extent. At the same time, fair development of the society can be kept and hence the goal of maintaining good ecological development can be fulfilled.

(II) **Application of Ecological Compensation Projects**

To realize the compensatory purpose of administrative penalties, an ecological compensation mechanism can be tentatively incorporated in the administrative penalties imposed on violators of the law. From the perspective of the compensatory purpose, it is not enough to only inflict property-based penalties on organizations or units that are held responsible for environmental pollution. Although the money collected through such means as confiscation and fines can be indirectly used to make up for and repair ecological environment damage, the long term experience shows us little effect has been achieved through such a practice. The infringers can tentatively be converted to participants of compensatory projects, that is to say, letting the organizations and units that have violated the law that promotes energy conservation and curbs carbon dioxide emission participate in eco-compensation projects. For example, companies and units that have seriously damaged the ecological system should actively participate in such projects as protecting natural shelter forests, restoring farmland to forest, and projects of constructing other key ecological public welfare forests. The eco-compensation mechanism shouldn't be limited to forests only, and it should also cover ecological protection of grassland, wetland, nature conservation zones, ocean, and agriculture, etc. Administrative organs can decide on what ecosystem in which organizations and units should get involved in different regions based on characteristics of their trade, the location of business and production activities, and the nature of their operational activities. An ecological compensation mechanism managed by a special management agency should be established. The establishment of the mechanism should be targeted at the characteristics of forests and be based on such well-established disciplines as sociology, economics, and ecology. The mechanism can be based on regional divisions to prevent people in a region to shift responsibility to others or pass on the cost of treating the environment to others. The mechanism can alleviate the degradation of the ecological environment, reduce cross-region conflicts of various departments, and avoid unreasonable use of ecological resources due to administrative division of regions.[54] These measures are important protection for a good forest eco-compensation mechanism.

[54] Li Wenhua, Li Fen, *Current Research on Forest Ecological Compensation and Outlook*, *Journal of Natural Resource*, Sep., 2006.

Chapter 9
Application and Development of Administrative Enforcement in Low-Carbon Field

Administrative enforcement is a traditional administrative act that is widely used in many types of administration fields. It indispensably plays an effective regulatory role in the government's efforts to build a low-carbon society and restrain the whole society to improve energy conservation and reduce carbon dioxide emission. Since promoting energy conservation and curbing carbon dioxide emission is a new administrative work that has just appeared recently, it is not well-supported by some provisions of existing legislation about administrative enforcement. Therefore, research, improvement and innovation are needed in this regard.

1 Function of Administrative Enforcement in the Field of Energy Conservation and Emission Reduction

Administrative enforcement in *Administrative Coercion Law of the People's Republic of China* includes administrative enforcement measures and implementation of administrative enforcement. Administrative enforcement has the following functions in the field of energy conservation and emission reduction based on analysis of the principle of administrative enforcement.

First, preventive function. In the field of energy conservation and emission reduction, the preventive function of administrative enforcement is mainly reflected by administrative enforcement measures. According to the *Administrative Coercion Law of the People's Republic of China*, administrative enforcement measures are mainly intended to "prevent the destruction of evidence" and "avoid damage", etc., all having an eye to "prevention". In the field of energy conservation and emission reduction, such a preventive function can prevent wasting of energy, exceeding-standard high-carbon emissions, hazardous consequences or danger, and destruction of evidence by lawbreakers in the process of being investigated.

S. Fang and B. Tan, *On the Administrative Law of China in Addressing Climate Change*,
https://doi.org/10.1007/978-981-19-7705-3_9

Second, blocking function. In the field of energy conservation and emission reduction, the function of administrative enforcement of blocking illegal acts or harmful consequences is also achieved by administrative enforcement measures. Administrative enforcement measures can effectively "stop illegal acts" and "prevent escalation of danger". In the field of energy conservation and emission reduction, their blocking function is reflected by timely stopping various acts of wasting energy and high carbon emission, and preventing harmful consequences from continuing or escalating.

Third, restorative function. In the field of energy conservation and emission reduction, the restorative function of administrative enforcement is mainly realized through implementation of administrative enforcement. Various types of waste of energy resources and high-carbon emissions essentially harm the legal interest of ecological balance and energy conservation. Since ecological resources are not just a type of "property", ecological benefits driving from them belong to the whole society and even the ecological circle of the nature outside of the human world.[1] Therefore, in the field of energy conservation and emission reduction, the entities that cause energy and resource waste and high carbon emission usually need to perform certain restorative duties to try to repair damaged environment and ecological function. In fact, some laws of China have stipulated legal restoration responsibilities in ecosphere, for example, Article 60 and Article 61 of the *Environmental Protection Law*. As one of the branch laws that are most closely related to ecological and environmental protection, administrative law also needs certain means to restore infringed and damaged environment, resources and ecological balance. As far as administrative enforcement is concerned, such a requirement can be met by two administrative enforcement methods under *Administrative Coercion Law of the People's Republic of China*, that is "removal of obstructions or restitution" and "agency performance". The two means apply to regulating energy and resource waste and high-carbon emissions. It is self-evident that "removal of obstructions or restitution", a means of implementing administrative enforcement, has a clear restoration intention, while "agency performance" as a means of regulation is also clearly based on the *Administrative Coercion Law of the People's Republic of China*. Therefore, administrative organs should emphasize the restorative role of administrative enforcement in the field of energy conservation and emission reduction. They should make reasonable arrangements according to different fields, proceedings and features of the issues of energy conservation and emission reduction to make "removal of obstructions or restitution" and "agency performance" be more pertinent and operable.

[1] See Article 50 of the *Administrative Coercion Law of the People's Republic of China*.

2 Application of Current Administrative Enforcement

According to provisions of the *Administrative Coercion Law of the People's Republic of China*,[2] there are many types of administrative enforcement measures and ways of administrative enforcement implementation. As far as the field of energy conservation and emission reduction is concerned, administrative enforcement measures and administrative enforcement implementation are mainly applied as follows:

2.1 Application of Administrative Enforcement Measures

(I) **Closing Down and Detainment**

Closing down and detainment are a measure taken by state administrative organs to verify, seal or seize relevant facilities and equipment of companies and public institutions that cause or may cause pollution. The purpose is to make the act of discharging pollutants terminate due to lack of necessary material conditions and energy conservation and emission reduction can be successfully realized. Such a mandatory administrative measure is mostly stipulated in environment related laws of China such as the *Environmental Protection Law*, *A Law of the PRC on the Prevention and Control of Atmospheric Pollution*.[3]

Generally speaking, Closing down and detainment are targeted at relevant facilities and equipment that are discharging pollutants, and not at other facilities and equipment. The procedure for closing down and detainment generally involves making such a decision and delivering the decision in writing. The procedure can be done very easily. Since closing down and detainment are targeted at facilities and equipment that are discharging pollutants, which will make the work of discharging pollutants stop due to lack of basic equipment. Therefore, once the measure is implemented, the effect is very obvious.

(II) **Freezing Deposits and Remittances**

Freezing deposits or remittances is a typical administrative enforcement measure clearly stipulated under the *Administrative Coercion Law of the People's Republic of China*. The role of the measure is to control circulation of the money in the bank accounts of an administrative counterpart. It generally applies to the situation where the concerned party may illegally transfer or conceal property, for example, the situations stipulated under Article 38 of the *Law of the People's Republic of China on the Administration of Tax Collection*.[4] As a type of administrative enforcement measure, freezing deposits or remittances is also used in the field of environmental

[2] See Articles 9 and 12 of *Administrative Coercion Law of the People's Republic of China*.

[3] See Article 25 of *Environmental Protection Law of the People's Republic of China*.

[4] See Article 38 of *the Law of the People's Republic of China on the Administration of Tax Collection*.

protection in China to some extent. According to Article 79 of the *Energy Conservation Law* of China, if a construction entity violates construction energy conservation standards, the construction administrative department shall inflict on it an administrative penalty of paying a fine. If the construction entity can pay the fine but refuses to pay it, the construction administrative department may take such an administrative enforcement measure of freezing the assets with the cooperation of banks and other financial institutions to ensure the fine can be collected through administrative enforcement by money transfer.

(III) Mandatorily Stop the Supply of Electricity, Water and Gas and Other Energy

Although mandatorily stopping the supply of electricity, water and gas and other energy is not a measure that is clearly stipulated in the *Administrative Enforcement Law* of China, it has been used in practice. It is even clearly stipulated in some local regulations and mostly in regulatory documents of local governments. For example, Article 51 of the *Regulations of Zhejiang Province on Prevention and Control of Water Pollution*. It is also clearly stipulated in the *Plan for Energy Conservation and Emission Reduction Work of the Organs Directly Subordinated to the Municipal People's Government* issued by Ezhou City, Hubei Province that organs directly subordinated to the municipal people's government that fail to fulfill energy conservation and emission reduction targets will be subject to power rationing. In order to effectively control companies' work for conserving energy and reducing emissions and meet the target of energy conservation and emission reduction, many local governments take the mandatory measure of stopping energy supply against highly polluting and energy-intensive industries such as power rationing. For companies and units that waste energy and pollute the environment, such measures as power rationing "pull the plug" on the actions, directly limit energy supply from the source. Such measures are preventive actions taken by administrative organs to exercise their power, and are forced to be accepted by the concerned party. Therefore, these measures are intrinsically a type of administrative enforcement measures. As things stand, the measures such as electricity rationing taken by various localities are marked by the following features. First, having an obvious intention of having the mission accomplished. When the deadline for meeting the target of energy conservation and emission reduction is approaching, electricity rationing, in general, is widely implemented in various localities, with an obvious intention of making organized efforts to concentrate on meeting the target quickly. Second, expanding the application of power rationing. In order to meet the target of energy conservation and emission reduction, some local governments expand the application scope of electricity rationing in practice and even ration the supply of power that are used by residents for their everyday life. With regard to these two prominent problems, the state corrected inappropriate use of such measures as power rationing. For example, the General

Office of the State Council issued an *Urgent Notice of Ensuring Residential Power Use and Normal Power Supply and Demand* in 2010.[5]

2.2 *Application of Administrative Enforcement Implementation*

(I) **Enforcement Penalty**

Enforcement penalties are widely applicable in the practice of administrating energy conservation and emission reduction practices in China. When an administrative counterpart fails to duly pay relevant taxes, fees or fines determined by an administrative organ in connection with energy conservation and emission, a fine or overdue fine is imposed on a daily basis to promote the counterpart to perform the obligation in time. According to Article 59 of the *Environmental Protection Law* of China, where an enterprise or public institution is fined due to illegal discharge of pollutants, and refuses to pay the fine without a proper reason, the administrative organ may impose impose continuous fines calculated on a daily basis according to the original amount of the fine. The purpose of the said "impose continuous fines calculated on a daily basis" is to promote the concerned party to pay the original fine without delay, so the fine is an enforcement penalty in nature. The characteristics of enforcement penalties are mainly reflected in two aspects: enforceability and property obligations. On the one hand, an enforcement penalty is based on the fact that the concerned party is obligated to pay taxes and fines. When the party fails to duly pay the taxes and fines, the administrative organ can use enforcement penalties to urge the obligated entity to duly perform the obligation. On the other hand, the application of enforcement penalties is limited to additional imposition of fines and overdue fines, both of which are execution penalties that are imposed as a property obligation in nature.

(II) **Agency Performance**

Agency performance is a means of administrative enforcement implementation that is widely used in the field of energy conservation and emission reduction in China.[6] Different from enforcement penalty that is directed at property obligations, agency performance is directed at behavioral obligations, that is, obligations of take certain

[5] Recently, in few places, the reasonable need of power supply by companies for their normal production and by residents for their normal life is restricted, and thermal units are prevented from generating power. This is against the original intention of saving energy and reducing emissions, and is also not helpful for the efforts to push energy conservation and emission reduction to continuously go on in a deeper way. Vital interests of the people are also jeopardized seriously and safe operation of the power grid is endangered. This is a mistake and must be correctly immediately. Power supply of key users should be immediately resumed such as power supply for people's daily life. In order to effectively maintain the normal power generation and supply, it is not allowed to illegally interfere in a power grid's dispatching and power generation.

[6] See Article 25 of the *Regulations of Hubei Province for Environmental Protection*.

actions. If, in the field of energy conservation and emission reduction, the concerned party has the obligation of taking measures to stop energy waste and high-carbon emission, the obligation of dealing with resulting harmful consequences, or the obligation of removing obstructions and reinstitution, but obligated entity does not perform such behavioral obligations. In this case, the owed actions will be done by others instead and the expense shall be borne by the obliged entity. The obligated entity must also be responsible for legal consequences of such substitute performance. In general, the prerequisite for a agency performance is that the act can be performed by someone else at all. If performance of the act is irreplaceable or the act can only be carried out by the obligated party himself, there is no agency performance. In the case of agency performance, the act can be carried out by a third party other than the obligated entity or by the ordering administrative organ.

2.3 *Administrative Enforcement in Special Legislation for Energy Conservation and Emission Reduction*

The above-mentioned types of administrative enforcement are general types of administrative enforcement stipulated in the *Administrative Enforcement Law*. Aside from such types of enforcement, there are also some other types of administrative enforcement measures or administrative enforcement implementation that are stipulated in many special legislation in the field of energy conservation and emission reduction but not listed in the *Administrative Coercion Law of the People's Republic of China*.

(I) **Mandatory Dismantling and Scrapping**

Mandatory dismantling is a mandatory measure taken by an administrative organ to legally dismantle the facilities and equipment that prevent energy conservation and emission reduction, and to make them stop operation. Mandatory dismantling is specially stipulated in the *Law of the People's Republic of China on Prevention and Control of Water Pollution* to prevent and control water pollution.[7] Mandatory dismantling is somewhat similar to agency performance in their mechanisms of action. Both deal with obligations that should have been fulfilled by a violator but are done by other entities on behalf of the violator. Mandatory scrapping is a mandatory measure taken by an administrative organ to destroy the product that has reached its end of life and, if used continuously, will seriously endanger the environment or increase energy consumption. For example, in order to promote energy conservation and emission in the transportation industry, systematic provisions about mandatory scrapping of motor vehicles are stipulated in the *Standard for Compulsory Scrapping*

[7] See Article 75 of the *Law of the People's Republic of China on Prevention and Control of Water Pollution*.

of Motor Vehicles. The characteristic of mandatory dismantling and mandatory scrapping lies in physically removing energy intensive carriers that are highly polluting and hence fundamentally terminating the pollution due to elimination of the carrier.

(II) Mandatory Disclosure of Environmental Information of Companies

According to Article 2 of the *Measures for the Publicity of Environmental Information* of China, there are two types of environmental information: environment information of the government and environmental information of companies. As a means of administrative regulation, only environmental information of companies can be disclosed. As far as disclosure mechanism of environmental information of companies is concerned, there are two mechanisms for disclosure, that is, autonomous disclosure and mandatory disclosure. Autonomous disclosure refers to autonomous and willing disclosure by a company of its environmental information to the outside based on considerations of corporate social responsibility, social ethics and its own interest and development. In the modern society, the importance of corporate environmental information is self-evident. Whether there is disclosure of corporate environmental information to the outside and to what extent corporate environmental information is disclosed affect the building of ecological environment. The effects of mechanism of autonomous disclosing of corporate environmental information is mainly dependent on subjective value judgement of the company itself, which is impossible to fundamentally guarantee stable ongoing operation of the mechanism. Therefore, mandatory disclosure of corporate environmental information is needed.

The prerequisite for mandatory disclosure of corporate environmental information is that a company has a corresponding obligation of disclosing its environmental information. The legal status of a company as the main body disclosing corporate environmental information has been confirmed by some laws and regulations of China. For example, Article 55 and Article 62 of the *Environmental Protection Law* of China, and Article 20 of the *Measures for the Publicity of Environmental Information*. What is stipulated in Article 9 of the *Measures for the Publicity of Environmental Information by Enterprises and Public Institutions* is also similar to what is stipulated in Article 55 of the *Environmental Protection Law*.[8] Therefore, companies have a legal obligation of disclosing their environmental information. When such an obligation is not performed, the mechanism for mandatorily disclosure of the same becomes necessary. The competent environmental administrative organ can require a company to disclose its environmental information by ordering it to disclose its environmental information directly, disclosing environmental information of the company on behalf of it, or imposing administrative penalties on the company for non-disclosure of the same. These are all important measures that can be used by a competent administrative organ to implement mandatory disclosure of environmental information, which provide a certain guarantee for the mechanism of mandatory disclosure of corporate environmental information and also help to make the mechanism exercise a mandatory role.

---

[8] See Article 9 of the *Measures for the Publicity of Environmental Information by Enterprises and Public Institutions*.

(III) **Publicize Facts of a Violation**

Trust shows "the overall strength of an enterprise within the society".[9] In economics, reputation is the core of social capital.[10] At present when competition is especially intense in the economic field, credit is one of the most important and core capitals of a business. With development of the times, the importance of credit will become more and more prominent. For a company, good credit is, no doubt, a "pass". Lack of credit may cause performance loss and even bankruptcy. As an indirect way of administrative enforcement, the reason why the publication of illegal facts can play an important role is rooted in the capital attribute of "credit" under the condition of market economy. As a scholar pointed out, "publicizing facts of a violation can be said to be an indirect mandatory means to ensure the fulfillment of administrative obligations. It forces a violator to perform its obligations by using pressure caused by social accusations."[11]

In order to promote energy conservation and emission reduction, the local governments in some places of China have used such indirect administrative enforcement of publicizing facts of a violation. A batch of polluting companies in Nanjing were closed in 2011, and the names of the first batch of 173 companies that needed rectification were publicized in local mainstream media. The publication of the facts of a violation made the batch of companies suffer from huge social pressure. They abandoned the inactive attitude mostly adopted in the past and turned to cooperate with the environmental protection agencies to make rectifications.[12] The important reason they changed attitude might intrinsically be they feared the government might inflict further punishments. However, it was also an unneglectable factor that this could prevented the harm that exposure might cause to their credit and hence their operational profits. However, such a case also indirectly showed that publishing facts of a violation, as a means of indirect administrative enforcement, is not often used by relevant authorities. Otherwise, there wouldn't be the phenomenon that there were a batch of companies discharging pollutants. Publishing facts of a violation, as a new means of implementing administrative enforcement that can effectively regulate energy conservation and emission reduction, should be more widely used. With regard to this, a scholar pointed out "currently in a time of social transformation with a more pressing ecological and environmental crisis, the effective mechanism of publishing a name list of companies that need to make rectification for polluting should be fully used for the work of energy conservation and emission reduction."[13]

Due to the aforesaid special roles, publishing facts of a violation, as a means of implementing administrative enforcement, has been clearly stipulated in the newly

[9] G. Simmel, The Philosophy of Money, London: Routledge, 1978, pp. 178–179.

[10] See Zhang Weiying, *Information, Trust and Law* (Sanlian Book Store, 2006), 3.

[11] Zhang Zhiyuan, *Publishing of Facts of a Violation as a Means of Implementing Administrative Enforcement*, *The Jurist*, no. 1 (2012).

[12] See Song Jinping et al., *The Environmental Protection Storm of Closing 75 Polluting Companies in Nanjing Showed the Power of Publication*, *Xinhua Daily*, July 8th, 2011.

[13] Zhang Zhiyuan, *Publication of Facts of a Violation as a Means of Implementing Administrative Enforcement*, *The Jurist*, no. 1 (2012).

revised *Environmental Protection Law*.[14] Compared with the original law, this should be an innovation made in the new *Environmental Protection Law*. This helps to provide publishing facts of a violation, as a means of enforcement, an important role played in energy conservation and emission reduction.

2.4 Shortcomings of Current Administrative Enforcement

Administrative enforcement is an important means of regulation to promote energy conservation and emission reduction. However, from the current administrative enforcement provisions in the field of energy conservation and emission reduction, there are still some deficiencies. This is mainly reflected in the following aspects:

(I) **Subjects to Which Administrative Enforcement Applies are Restricted to a Narrow Scope**

Energy conservation and emission reduction is a common obligation of all members of the society that not only include various types of organizations such as state organs, companies and public institutions, but also include a great number of individual citizens. All these are subjects that are regulated by low-carbon emission related laws. According to regulations of administrative enforcement in the field of energy conservation and emission reduction, the regulation of administrative enforcement applies mainly to companies and public institutions and is barely targeted at individual citizens. Scope of the type of subjects regulated by administrative enforcement is narrow, resulting in the acts of individual citizens that cause energy waste and high-carbon emissions are not constrained. However, the reality is that with continuous social and economic development, consumption ability and demand of citizens rapidly improve. They contribute more and more significantly to energy consumption and carbon emission. At the same time, due to the great number of individual citizens and some unreadable and wrong habits traditionally developed in consumption, the total usage of energy and carbon emission are huge, inevitably causing excessive depletion of energy resource and affect the ability of ecological environment to support people. Therefore, strong regulation is needed, and it is not right for administrative enforcement, an important means of regulation, to be targeted at companies and public institutions only, but not individual citizens.

(II) **Lack Variety of Exiting Types of Administrative Enforcement**

Although currently there are many types of administrative enforcement in the field of energy conservation and emission reduction, there are still not enough statutory types of administrative enforcement measures and administrative enforcement implementation. They can neither fully cover the various issues in the field of energy conservation and emission reduction, nor widely cover the various procedures in regulating energy conservation and emission reduction, which causes regulation gaps.

[14] See Article 54 of the *Environmental Protection Law*.

When establishing the types of administrative enforcement, as an important means of promoting energy conservation and emission reduction, efforts should be made to cover important nodes in the field and the types of administrative enforcement should have pertinence to common and important issues, and should be practically effective. Therefore, it is not right to be confined to existing types of administrative enforcement. There should be more diversified innovative administrative enforcement measures and means of administrative enforcement implementation. There should be at least three categories of basic factors that cause energy waste and high carbon emissions, that is, factors related to the subjects, factors related to materials and behavioral factors. The subjects are the actors that cause waste of energy resources and high-carbon emissions. There are two types of subjects, that is, organizational entities such as companies and public institutions and individual citizens. Material factors are various types of material resources used and consumed by the subjects that waste energy resources and discharge carbon dioxide, as waste of energy and high-carbon emissions come from consumption of material resources. Behavioral factors refer to the types of behaviors and behavior patterns of the subjects causing carbon emissions that are adopted in the process of transferring and using materials. In order to control energy and resource waste and high-carbon emissions, there should be corresponding administrative enforcement measures and administrative enforcement implementation that are rightfully apply to the different factors. If it is not possible to choose appropriate administrative enforcement, regulatory gaps will occur due to lack of various or pertinent types and methods of administrative enforcement.

In terms of existing regulations of China on administrative enforcement, there are not sufficient types of appropriate administrative enforcement in the field of energy conservation and emission reduction. For example, administrative enforcement that has pertinence to factors of the subjects are rare. There is a lack of diversified types of administrative enforcement that are targeted at the factors of material and behavior. Therefore, if there are no correspondingly appropriate administrative enforcement measures and types of administrative enforcement implementation for the many types of subjects, fields, behaviors and a wide range of issues that are involved in energy conservation and emission reduction, energy and resource waste and high-carbon emissions cannot be effectively constrained.

(III) Occasional Occurrence of the Phenomenon That Administrative Enforcement Measures Are Illegally Established and Applied

In view of the severe environment and resource conditions of China, the government at various levels make meeting the target of energy conservation and emission reduction an important part of its performance assessment to intensify the efforts to promote energy conservation and emission reduction.[15] In the process of fulfilling

[15] It is clearly pointed out in the *12th Five-year Plan for Energy Conservation and Emission Reduction* issued by the State Council in 2012 that: the State Council will organize people to assess energy conservation and emission reduction objectives and responsibilities of a provincial people's government every year. Results of the assessment are important for comprehensive assessment of the team

the target, some administrative enforcement measures are illegally established and implemented in some places. For example, going beyond the legal right to randomly establish the administrative enforcement measure that supply of water, electricity, gas, and other energy to companies can be mandatorily stopped, or beaching Article 43 of the *Administrative Coercion Law of the People's Republic of China* to stop the supply of water, power, heat, and gas, etc. that are used in everyday life of residents to force an administrative counterpart to perform a relevant obligation.[16] The discretionary establishment or application of such administrative enforcement measures in various places are illegal. According to Article 9 and Article 10 of the *Administrative Coercion Law of the People's Republic of China*, even if it is necessary to make mandatory stoppage of supply of water, electricity, gas and other energy a statutory administrative enforcement measure, this can only be done through laws and administrative regulations.[17] Therefore, such provisions and practices reflected in some local regulations, regulations of local governments and regulatory documents of the government need to be reviewed and abolished.

3 Improvement of Administrative Enforcement in Low-Carbon Field

The aforesaid shortcomings of administrative enforcement will greatly affect the important role played by such means of administrative regulation in the field of energy conservation and emission reduction of China, and will also infringe upon legal interests of administrative counterparts. Therefore, improvement is needed.

3.1 Individual Citizens Should Be Included in the Scope of Administrative Enforcement

It has been established in some existing laws, regulations and policies of China that citizens are a type of important obligatory subjects in the field of energy conservation and emission reduction. This is also stipulated in the *Environmental Protection Law*

---

of leaders and the leading carders of the province, and will also be incorporated into performance management of the government. An accountability system is implemented.

[16] For example, in order to meet the target of "energy conservation and emission reduction", Zaoqiang County of Hebei Province began wide-scale power outages since October, 2010. There was only 4-h power supply to residents of the entire county in a day. There was no power supply in the remaining time of the day. See http://www.hcvw.cn/index.php?m=content&c=index&a=show&catid=116&id=15249, last site visit on October 6th, 2015. Xingye County, Guangxi Province also limited power supply to the residents in the same period in order to meet the target of energy conservation and emission reduction. See http://news.163.com/10/0921/21/6H4TDLNJ00014JB5.html, last site visit on October 6th, 2015.

[17] See Article 9 of the *Administrative Coercion Law of the People's Republic of China*.

and the newly revised *Law of the PRC on the Prevention and Control of Atmospheric Pollution*.[18] The "obligation of environmental protection" stipulated in these laws also naturally includes the obligation of energy conservation and emission reduction. In addition, it is clearly required under the *12th Five-year Plan for Energy Conservation and Emission Reduction* "deeply carry out the national action plan for energy saving and emission reduction". The status of citizens as the main body for the obligation of energy conservation and emission reduction is highlighted. The issue concerning obligations of citizens in building a low-carbon society has been noticed by administrative law scholars of China and they have made some pertinent suggestions.[19]

However, with regard to the measures of promoting citizens to fulfil the obligation of energy conservation and emission reduction, currently, the citizens are mainly urged to conserve energy and reduce emission through such "soft" measures as publicity and encouragement. This leads to a serious consequence, that is, the obligation of energy conservation and emission reduction that should have been performed by citizens are not effectively performed, causing the obligation of energy conservation and emission reduction to be only an advocated obligation. A big dissonance between such a situation and increasingly higher energy consumption and carbon emission is observed. In the modern society, citizens' demand and ability in consumption increase rapidly. They are contributing more and more to energy consumption and carbon emission. That is to say, it is not enough for the obligations of the citizens to conserve energy and reduce emissions to be advocated only. The obligations should be somewhat mandatory. For a citizen that fails to perform such an obligation, appropriate administrative enforcement should be used to make the citizen perform the obligation. As shown by administrative enforcement in the sector of energy conservation and emission reduction in China, application of administrative enforcement is mainly confined to companies and public institutions. It is rare for administrative enforcement to target at individual citizens. This makes it hard to strongly constrain energy-wasting energy and high carbon emission behaviors of the citizens.

In fact, it is ethically and legally justifiable to include citizens that fail to perform the obligation of energy conservation and emission reduction into the subjects of administrative enforcement. On the one hand, "when discharging greenhouse gases into the atmosphere, an individual is obligated to not to harm others. Each individual that is capable of reducing greenhouse gas emissions is ethically obligated to reduce greenhouse gas emissions and is also obligated to limit his greenhouse gas emissions to a fair share of safe global emissions."[20] That is to say, energy conservation and emission reduction is an ethical requirement of mankind, and reflects the subjectivity of people as human beings. It is also a code of conduct that must be followed and

---

[18] See Article 6 of the *Environmental Protection Law*.

[19] See Fang Shirong and Tan Binglin, *On Administrative Guidance for Promoting Low-Carbon Action of Citizens*, *Legal Science*, no. 2 (2014).

[20] Donald A. Brown, *Ethical obligations of individuals to reduce greenhouse gas emissions*, *Yuejiang Academic Journal*, trans. Shi Jun and Dong Jingqi, no. 5 (2012).

should not be rejected. It helps to meet such an ethical requirement to make the subjects of administrative enforcement include citizens that do not perform the obligation of energy conservation and emission reduction. Among the measures provided for in the administrative law that can ensure satisfaction of this ethical requirement, although administrative enforcement is a means that is not prioritized, it is indispensable(basic). Since, from a legal perspective, citizens' environmental protection obligations stipulated in such laws as the *Environmental Protection Law* and the *Law of the PRC on the Prevention and Control of Atmospheric Pollution* include the obligation of energy conservation and emission reduction, there should be corresponding legal responsibilities. According to such laws, however, there are still no clear legal responsibilities that correspond to the energy conservation and emission reduction obligation of a citizen. Therefore, it is legally justifiable to impose administrative enforcement on those who fail to perform the obligation of energy conservation and emission reduction.

3.2 *Types of Innovative Administrative Enforcement*

In order to give full play of its safeguarding role in energy conservation and emission reduction, administrative enforcement should cover all factors and procedures of energy conservation and emission reduction with nothing left uncovered. However, it can be found from the *Administrative Coercion Law of the People's Republic of China* that administrative enforcement measures and the means of administrative enforcement implementation cannot meet such a requirement. New statutory types of administrative enforcement need to be added based on the special requirements of energy conservation and emission reduction. This can be analyzed from two aspects of administrative enforcement stipulated in the legislation:

(I) **Establishing New Types of Administrative Enforcement Measures**

i. **Adding administrative enforcement measures targeted at factors of the subjects**

The subjects that produce waste of energy resources and high carbon emissions mainly include two types: organizational entities such as companies and public institutions and individual citizens. These two types of subjects are very different in terms of the organization and behavior patterns. They should be differentiated when establishing administrative enforcement measures for them.

For organizational entities that produce waste of energy resources and high carbon emissions, the corresponding organizational enforcement measures against them include cracking them down and suspending or limiting their qualification:

(i) **Cracking down.** For an organizational entity that produce waste of energy resources and high carbon emissions, the organizational entity should be cracked down through such means as banning it according to law, and destroying or closing it. In general, the administrative enforcement measure of cracking down an organizational entity applies to the situation where the entity itself is illegal. For example, administrative organs often cancel or destroy various types of small workshops and illegal dens that make counterfeits due to food safety. The organizational entities are physically eliminated as unlawful operators. In fact, such "illegal dens" and "illegal workshops" that concern food sanitation often that produce waste of energy resources and high carbon emissions. Aside from these, organizational entities that are unlawful but seriously waste energy resources and emit high levels of carbon dioxide widely exist. For example, small plants, workshops, and dens that illegally extract coal and other mineral resources, and illegally produce and process plastic bags. The most effective regulatory method for such illegal organizational entities that produce waste of energy resources and high carbon emissions is to physically eliminate them, so as to fundamentally eliminate the behaviors of seriously wasting energy resources and emitting high levels of carbon dioxide.

(ii) **Suspension or restriction of qualification.** The so-called suspension or restriction of qualification refers to temporarily suspending or restricting an organizational entity's qualification for doing certain activities by means of permits to prohibit or restrict it from doing activities that may cause waste of energy resources and high carbon emissions. For example, in order to promote energy conservation and emission reduction in the industrial sector, and accelerate the elimination of equipment with outdated production capacity and high energy-consumption, the Ministry of Industry and Information Technology of the People's Republic of China has successively announced several *Catalogue for Eliminating Outdated High Energy Consuming Electromechanical Equipment (Products)* since 2009. For the administrative organs regulating energy conservation and emission reduction, it is necessary for them to refer to the catalogues to adjust the qualifications and business scopes of the enterprises engaging in production and manufacture of electromechanical equipment (products), and restrict them from engaging activities that can cause waste of energy resources and high carbon emissions. In this regard, the State Council or the National People's Congress could compile and publish a list of behaviors of companies that produce waste of energy resources and high carbon emissions, and gradually suspend or restrict these behaviors through adjusting permits.

For individual citizens with behaviors that produce waste of energy resources and high carbon emissions, such behaviors of them can be regulated only through qualification permits.

ii. **Adding and improving administrative enforcement measures targeted at behavioral factors**

(i) **Mandatory security**

Different from function of the security system in civil law that is used to ensure fulfillment of debts, security (mandatory security) in administrative law is more of reflecting administration privileges and emphasizes the protection of public interests. As an important legal system, mandatory security is widely used in the administrative practice of China, for example, in the field of taxation administration.[21] In addition, mandatory security system is also stipulated in such laws and regulations of China as *Customs Law of the PRC* and the *Regulation of the People's Republic of China on the Customs Protection of Intellectual Property Rights.*

Security in civil law is different from that in administrative law in terms of scope of application, form, and implementation procedures. However, they hold the same kind of principle and purpose: that is, certain predetermined means (security in civil law and mandatory security in administrative law) are used to preventing possible risks in the future and better protect interests of the security setter. Currently, the violations in the field of energy conservation and emission reduction in China are mainly handled through passive ex post response. It is relatively rare to have active ex ante prevention in place. This is far from meeting the intrinsic requirement of the nature of environment and ecology. For environmental and ecological operation mechanism, once its elements are harmed or damaged, it is impossible or difficult to have them repaired. Therefore, as far as environmental and ecological maintenance mechanism is concerned, proactive ex ante prevention is always better than passive ex post response. In order to avoid possible waste of energy resources and high carbon emissions, administrative organs should "lay up for a rainy day" and take the initiative to prevent and control waste of energy resources and high carbon emissions through the ex-ante prevention mechanism of mandatory security. Considering the effectiveness of mandatory security, the subjects to which mandatory security applies should be mainly limited to companies. Specifically, the mandatory security in the management practice of energy conservation and emission reduction can be handled with reference to the following ideas:

First, time of starting mandatory security. Security is a promise made by a guarantor about its succeeding behaviors. Security should be provided before commencement of succeeding behaviors. In the field of energy conservation and emission reduction, mandatory security is mainly a guarantee provided by a company to ensure that it will not waste energy resources and emit a high level of carbon dioxide. The start-up time can be considered in the process of applying for business license. In the process, operation of the company has not started yet, and no waste of energy resources and high carbon emissions are caused. Requiring it to provide mandatory security can restrain its subsequent operational activities. Moreover, putting the start-up time of the mandatory security in this link can felicitate the business, reduce the times for the company to go back and forth, and also correspondingly reduce work load of the administrative organ. All these are basic manifestations of low-carbonization.

Second, form of security. There are mainly five forms of security in civil law, that is, guarantee, mortgage, pledge, lien, and deposit. Compared with guarantee and mortgage, pledge, lien and deposit are created for the creditor over the guarantor's movable or immovable property, with more obvious intention of securing rights and

---

[21] See Article 38 of the *Law of the People's Republic of China on the Administration of Tax Collection.*

interests of the creditor and more restriction placed on the guarantor. Therefore, pledge, lien and deposit should be mainly considered for mandatory security in the field of energy conservation and emission reduction. This requires that companies should provide one of the three forms of security to the administrative organs in the process when they are trying to have their incorporation registered and approved. The security is provided to ensure that their subsequent production and operational activities will meet the requirements of energy conservation and emission reduction, and they will control the behaviors that produce energy resource wastes and high carbon emissions to reduce the negative impacts on ecological environment.

Third, supervision of security and responsibility. Mandatory security is a kind of supervision for a company. It reminds the company that its production and operation should meet the requirements of energy saving and emission reduction to reduce waste of energy resources and high carbon emissions. However, whether the company can follow the requirements to organize production and operational activities also depends on some other factors, such as market risks and awareness of corporate social responsibility. Therefore, the company needs to be supervised about its performance of its guaranteed obligations. If the company fails to perform the obligations as stipulated in the provisions of the security, the administrative organ can dispose the movable and immovable property of the company that are involved in the three forms of security, namely lien, pledge and deposit, as a means to regulate its breach of the guaranteed obligations.

(ii) **Traffic restrictions**

With intensifying traffic congestion and environmental pollution of cities, restrictions on the forms of transportation such as vehicles began to be widely used to as a compulsory measure. Beijing introduced odd–even license plate rules during the Olympic Games in 2008. That was the first time a big Chinese city issued tail number limits. After that, Tianjin, Shanghai, Nanchang, Guiyang, Shijiazhuang and other cities successively implemented driving restrictions. The measure was included as one of the ten measures introduced by the State Council for air pollution prevention and control in 2013.[22] It can be found from this that the restrictions on the driving of such means of transport as motor vehicles may increasingly become normal and extend to other places. The use of means of transport such as various types of motor vehicles and boats will cause enormous consumption of energy resources and high carbon emissions. Especially with gradual opening of low-altitude airspace of China in the future, there will be a large number of private aircraft, which will inevitably make energy-saving and emission reduction in the field of transportation a new focus of work.[23] In response to this new trend and new situation, the administrative organs have to make plans and arrangements.

---

[22] It is pointed out in the 9th measure of the ten measures that "heavy air pollution weather should be treated as emergency events of local governments that need urgent response. Local governments should take such measures as limiting production and emissions of heavy polluters and driving restrictions based on air quality."

[23] In 2010, the State Council and the Central Military Commission jointly printed and issued the *Opinions on Deepening the Reform of China's Low-altitude Airspace Management*. This drew the

Of course, there are still some legal disputes regarding restrictions on the traffic of various means of transport such as vehicles, boats, and private aircraft. In view of the fact that academically there are relatively more researches done on restrictions of the traffic of vehicles, restrictions on the traffic of vehicles are taken as an example to analyze the legal issues faced by various types of means of transportation. Some researchers show disapproval towards vehicle restriction. It is believed that restrictions on the traffic of vehicles are a restriction on property rights of citizens, basic rights of citizens, which are not legally justified.[24] Some scholars question the measure from the perspective of its implementation effect.[25] Some researchers agree on the good motivation of the measure, and deem that this measure needs to be further improved in the implementation process.[26]

The authors of this article believes that restrictions on the traffic of vehicles are justifiable to some extent: (i) the measure has been widely used in the administrative practice of China, and is supported by policy and law. The executive meeting of the State Council mentioned above has provided policy support for the measure. The measure was included in the air pollution prevention and control measures adopted at the meeting. *Law of the People's Republic of China on Road Traffic Safety* provides a corresponding legal basis for the measure.[27] It can be found that it is not right to think that the measure is totally not legal and justifiable. In addition, although the provision of the previous two drafts of the *Law of the PRC on the Prevention and Control of Atmospheric Pollution* that authorizes local governments to impose restrictions on

curtain on the work of China to fully develop its low altitude airspace resources and promote the development of navigation. In 2014, the State Council and the Air Traffic Control Commission of the Central Military Commission held a meeting on reforming national low altitude airspace management and decided to fully open the airspace below a true altitude of 1000 m in 2015 based on exiting pilot programs.

[24] Li Songfeng, *Analysis of Constitution Compliance of the Order of Restricting the Traffic of Motor Vehicles, Xiamen University Law Review 19*; Mo Jihong, *There Should be Public Interest Justified by the Restrictions on the Traffic of Motor Vehicles*, no. 5 (2008); Yang Shilin, *Restrictions of the Traffic of Motor Vehicles before and after the Olympic Games—Analysis of the Nature and Legitimacy of the Order of Restricting the Traffic of Motor Vehicles*, in *the Study of Chinese Constitutional Events (4)*, ed. Han Dayuan (Law Press, 2010), 228–230; *No Legalization for Beijing Restrictions on the Traffic of Motor Vehicles, Disputes about Reasonableness of the Restrictions are Worthy of Reflection, Legal Daily*, March 23, 2009; Zhong Jinjun, *The Disadvantages of Beijing's Restrictions on the Traffic of Motor Vehicles Continues Outweighs the Advantages, China Reform Daily*, March 31, 2009.

[25] Zhao Xiaoguang, Xu Zhencheng, Wang Xuan, and Wang Junneng, *Analysis of the Impacts of the Restrictions on the Traffic of Motor Vehicles on Ari Quality, Journal of Safety and Environment*, no. 4 (2010); Hu Jing, *Diagnostic Analysis of Causes Attributing to Guaranteed Atmospheric Environment in Beijing during the Olympic Games*, Environmental Science master's thesis, Beijing Industrial University, 2009; Li Anding, *Restrictions on Traffic of Motor Vehicles: Advisable but Should not be Enforced, The Economic Observer*, October 20th, 2008, 36.

[26] Ling Weici, *Legalization for Normalizing the Restrictions on the Traffic of Motor Vehicle from the Perspective of Administrative Law, Legal Science*, no. 2 (2015); Zhang Xiang, *Restrictions on the Traffic of Motor Vehicles, Restrictions on Property Rights and the Principle of Proportionality, Legal Science*, no. 2 (2015); Yao Hui, *Limitation on Ownership in the Odd–even License Plate Policy for Vehicles, The Jurist*, no. 5 (2008).

[27] See Article 39 of the *Law of the People's Republic of China on Road Traffic Safety*.

traffic of motor vehicles has been deleted in the newly revised version of the law, this does not mean that the law completely prohibits the practice of imposing restrictions on traffic of motor vehicles. Deletion of the provision of the law that authorizes local governments to impose restrictions on traffic of motor vehicles from the formal text of the law is not intended to completely prohibit imposing restrictions on the traffic of motor vehicle, but to prevent local governments from imposing restrictions on the traffic of motor vehicles arbitrarily and roughly. In fact, the law has left room for restricting the traffic of motor vehicles.[28] It is stipulated in the law to "take measures", but it does not clearly define the type or scope of the measures, so the measures are open-ended to some extent. The restriction of motor vehicles is obviously a measure that can be taken according to its nature. What's more, it helps for local governments to reach environmental quality standards within a time limit. (ii) Restricting the traffic of motor vehicles, as a mandatory administrative measure, has a legal basis. Motor vehicles of the citizens are not only a means of transportation, but also their lawful property. Lawful property rights are basic constitutional rights of citizens. Therefore, restricting the traffic of motor vehicles will restrict such basic rights of the citizens. This is a basic reason why many scholars have a negative attitude about restricting the traffic of motor vehicles. The analysis is not entirely unjustified. Does this mean that there is no legal basis for restricting the traffic of motor vehicles? The answer is no. In fact, restricting the traffic of motor vehicles has an adequate legal basis: first, the theory of rights in conflict. A citizen has many types of basic rights, which leads to conflicts between them. According to competing rights theory, when a person's two or more basic rights conflict, the rights that are more important in a hierarchy of value should be protected first. Putting restrictions on the traffic of motor vehicles is an effective measure to curb serious environmental pollution of a city. The measure involves two types of basic rights of a citizen, that is, property rights and the rights to life and health. On the one hand, the measure jeopardizes a citizen's property rights, basic rights of the citizen; on the other hand, it guarantees and promotes the citizen' rights to life and health. Compared with property rights, the rights to life and health are obviously more important and the protection of such rights should be prioritized. Second, the theory of social obligations of property rights. Citizens have lawful property rights to their motor vehicles. In general, public power of the state should not infringe or set obstacles to such rights. However, the lawful property rights of citizens are neither absolute, nor free from any restriction. As a type of right, property rights also contain corresponding social obligations. The theory of social obligations of property rights holds that: in order to maintain social justice, property rights should make self constraint; while advocating his freedom to property, an individual should also make his property contribute to realization of social welfare, that is, able to promote the realization of survival of all humanity with dignity.[29] Currently at a time when the situation of high energy resource consumption and high carbon emissions is becoming more severe, the restriction of motor vehicles

---

[28] See Article 14 of the *Law of the PRC on the Prevention and Control of Atmospheric Pollution*.

[29] See Zhang Xiang, *Restrictions on the Traffic of Motor Vehicles, Restrictions on Property Rights and the Principle of Proportionality*, *Legal Science*, no. 2 (2015).

essentially reflects the promotion and emphasis of the social obligation of energy conservation and emission reduction borne by citizens' property rights.

Similarly, restricting the traffic of other high-emission means of transportation that have high energy consumption levels is also done out of a similar reason. In short, restricting the traffic of the means of transport can be used as an administrative enforcement measure for conserving energy and reducing carbon emissions in the sector of transportation. Of course, practically there are some procedural and methodological shortcomings in the scheme of restricting the traffic of motor vehicles. Improvements are needed. In order to better guarantee the effects of restricting the traffic of various means of transportation, it is necessary to improve social acceptance of the restrictions by ensuring transparency of the process and participation of the citizens in the process.

iii. **Adding and improving administrative enforcement measures targeted at the factors of material**

(i) **Make the administrative enforce measure of limiting the supply and use of energy resources statutory**

According to the relevant provisions of China's *Administrative Enforcement Law*, the administrative enforcement measures that restrict the supply and use of energy resources such as electricity, gas, and water can only be established by laws and administrative regulations. Such measures cannot be established by local regulations, local government regulations and regulatory documents of governments. However, the reality is such administrative enforcement measures are often illegally established and applied in different localities. In order to avoid and control the occurrence of such illegal situations, the following two measures should be taken: firstly, such stipulations in some local regulations, local government regulations, and regulatory government documents should be reviewed and abolished, and such practices should be abolished; secondly, making the administrative enforcement measures that limit the supply and use of energy resources statutory.

There are two ways to make administrative enforcement measures that limit the supply and use of energy resources statutory. First, making limiting the supply and use of energy resources a part of the *Administrative Compulsion Law* of China. This can be realized by amending the *Administrative Compulsion Law*, that is, clearly making limiting the supply and use of energy resources an administrative enforcement measure that is in parallel with "closing downing premises, facilities or properties", "seizure of properties", "freezing deposits and remittances", etc. Second, correspondingly interpret "other administrative enforcement measures" in Article 9 of the *Administrative Compulsion Law, and* include limiting the supply and use of energy resources as an administrative enforcement measure. This can be done by promulgating detailed rules or methods concerning the implementation of the *Administrative Compulsion Law* by the State Council.

Due to the emergence of welfare administration, the production and life of various social subjects are greatly constrained by various resources provided by administrative organs. Since China adopted the policy of reform and opening up more than

30 years ago, there has been change to the distribution of social resources. However, the government is still the largest controller of social resources, such as coal, electricity, oil, gas, and water.[30] Although administrative enforcement can be used to restrict the supply and use of energy resources, it still needs to be used with caution. In view of the significant impact of restricting the supply and use of energy resources, there should be corresponding restrictions on the use of the measures. First, restrict the decision-making body of the measures. According to the *Administrative Coercion Law of the People's Republic of China*, the measures of "stopping the supply of water, power, and gas" stipulated in the *Regulations of Zhejiang Province on Prevention and Control of Water Pollution* are illegal, but it is desirable to limit the decision maker of such measures to "people's governments at or above the county level". The restriction can prevent the chaos caused by too many decision makers, and is also helpful to ensure that decisions about the supply and use of energy resources are cautiously and scientifically made. For cross regional administrative divisions decisions need to be made about restricting energy resource supply and use across, they should be reported to the common administrative organ at a higher level and the decisions should be made by the common administrative organ. Second, specify the prerequisite for making a decision to restrict the supply and use of energy resources. Once a decision of restricting the supply and use of energy resources is made, it will seriously influence the production and life of companies and public institutions. Therefore, it should be clearly made when such an administrative enforcement measure is used. In general, application of such a measure can only be considered when the concerned party has behaviors of serious wasting of energy resources and emitting high levels of carbon dioxide and such behaviors cannot be controlled through other measures. Third, optimize decision-making process. First, establishing hearing process. When making a decision to deny supply to a company, a hearing can be held to widely listen to opinions and suggestions of the person in charge of the company, employees of the company and other stakeholders. Second, explaining to companies why supply stoppage is ordered. Administrative organs must explain to a subject at which the supply stoppage is directed the legal basis and evidences of such stoppage.

(ii) **Add reasons that funds can be frozen**

Freezing funds (deposits and remittances) is an administrative enforcement measure stipulated in the *Administrative Coercion Law of the People's Republic of China*. Generally, the measure applies to situations where the concerned party has relevant property obligations but may illegally transfer or conceal property. The measure can be widely used for promoting energy conservation and emission reduction. This is because consumption of energy resources and carbon emissions themselves are material activities, which are highly dependent on various material resources. Acquisition

[30] It needs to be explained that in order to promote market reform, China has separately established several companies in the fields of coal, power, oil, gas, water and other resources to be responsible for the work of supplying and managing such resources. As is known to all, marketization of these companies is limited. To a large extent, they are still an extension of the government and have certain administrative functions.

and use of the material resources need to be supported by money. Energy resource consumption and carbon emissions are more notably influenced by funds in today's highly developed market economy, so the important role of freezing funds in the field of energy conservation and emission reduction should be fully displayed. However, the above-mentioned limitations on the scenarios where funds can be frozen actually hinder its due role in regulating energy conservation and emission reduction, which requires that the application of the administrative enforcement measure of freezing funds should be expanded. In addition to the original applicable circumstances, the money to be used by a concerned party to purchase outdated equipment that does not meet low-carbon environmental protection requirements should also be included in the freezing scope.

There is legal basis for including funds of a concerned party to be used to purchase outdated equipment in the scope of freezing. The said legal basis mainly refers to Article 46 of the *Environmental Protection Law* and *Law of the PRC on the Prevention and Control of Atmospheric Pollution.*[31] China's establishment of a system for eliminating processes, equipment and products that seriously pollute the environment helps it to promote its environmental protection work. The implementation of the system is mainly ensured via such measures as forced scrapping, dismantling, confiscation, and fines. However, these safeguarding measures are all ex-post remediation in nature, and cannot prevent the concerned party from purchasing, producing, selling and using these processes, equipment and products. The problem needs to be addressed at the source. Including the funds used by the concerned party to purchase outdated processes, equipment and products in the scope of freezing is a way to address the problem at the source. It can prevent the concerned party from purchasing, producing, selling, and using these processes, equipment and products that do not meet the requirements of environmental protection from perspective of the fundamental element of funds. This is very conducive to promoting energy saving and emission reduction of enterprises.

(iii) **Mandatory relocation**

A company is a huge material entity comprised of people, property, materials, and space. It is a very important source of energy resource consumption and high carbon emissions. The layout of industries in a certain period of time significantly influences energy resource consumption and high carbon emissions, so ongoing adjustment of the original layout of industries is needed to meet the requirements of energy conservation and emission reduction. To this end, a series of policies and measures concerning relocation of corporate polluters have been successively promulgated in different localities, such as the *Implementation Measures of Beijing Municipality to Push for the Relocation of Polluting Companies and Companies Creating a Public Disturbance and Accelerating the Adjustment of Industrial Structure*, and the *Notice on the Regulations of Relocating Polluting Enterprises (Projects) in Nanjing for Treatment*. Chongqing Municipal People's Government issued the *Opinions on Accelerating Implementation of the Work of Relocating Key Enterprises in the Main*

[31] See Article 46 of *the Environmental Protection Law*.

Urban Area that have Potential Environmental Pollution and Safety Hazards in 2004. The document provided more detailed regulations about the relocation of enterprises.

According to the policies and documents issued by local governments, the relocation of enterprises with high energy consumption and high emission pollution generally adopts a mode that is a combination of induced relocation and supervision. Government-induced relocation means the government encourages and induces the polluting companies to relocate with subsidies and preferential policies. Since it is not legal for an administrative organ to mandatorily demand a company that waits and sees or refuses to move to relocate, administrative organs can only strengthen supervision and urge them to relocate as early as possible. Many factors need to be considered by a company when it decides whether to relocate or not, for example, relationship between it and the government, operating cost, and market competition. As a for-profit organization, the fundamental factors considered are costs and benefits. Relocation generally means increase of production and transportation costs for a company, which is essentially against its nature of pursing profit. In case of government-induced relocation, only when subsidies provided by the government and preferences offered by policy of the government are theoretically greater than or equal to relocation cost of a company can the company has the willingness to relocate. But the problem is that the benefits provided by the government's financial and preferential policies are always limited, and the problem is made worser due to a huge number of heavy polluting and highly consuming companies. Therefore, government-induced relocation of polluting companies has limitations. Although it is infiltrated with the concepts of equality and consensus, it cannot fully guarantee eventual completion of relocation by the companies that should be relocated. However, energy conservation and emission reduction concern public interests and relocation success or failure of polluting companies directly affects realization of such public interest. Therefore, for the government, it must have the power to force polluting companies to relocate, that is, once inducement of the government fails, the ultimate choice will be forcing the companies to relocate.

(II) Adding and Improving the Means of Administrative Enforcement Implementation

i. Adding non-property enforcement penalty of the category of qualification restriction

There are mainly two forms of enforcement penalties in China: additional imposition of fines and late fines. Enforcement penalties are targeted at concerned parties who fail to perform their statutory obligations or determined by administrative decisions to have the obligations of making payments. Enforcement penalties can force the concerned parties to perform their obligations by imposing new obligations of making payments. Obviously, both imposed fines and late fees are enforcement of monetary penalties, but the problem is that with the development of society, the restraining effect of such type of enforcement penalties on some obligors is declining. On the one hand, with economic and social development, the influence of monetary wealth on some social subjects who get rich first has weakened to some extent. However, it is stipulated in the *Administrative Coercion Law of the People's Republic of China* that "the amounts of imposed fine or late fee shall not exceed the amount of the pecuniary payment obligation", which will inevitably affect the deterrent effect of the enforcement penalty itself. To this end, we should consider adding non-monetary qualification restriction enforcement penalties.

Eligibility restrictions are generally restrictions put on a certain eligibility (such as credit, consumption, employment, education, etc.) of obligors if they refuse to perform their legal obligations. As a new way of implementing administrative enforcement, eligibility restrictions frequently appear in China's legislation. For example, Article 39 of the *Regulations of Beijing Municipality for Recruitment of Soldiers*, and similar provisions in the *Regulations of Hubei Province for Recruitment of Soldiers*. For such eligibility restrictions, some scholars think they are an innovation for the way of administrative enforcement implementation, and also a new development of the theory of administrative enforcement.[32] In addition, extravagant spending of enforcees is specifically restricted in the *Certain Provisions of the Supreme People's Court on Restricting Extravagant Spending of Enforcees* promulgated in 2010. It can be found from the provisions that the restrictions on eligibility for extravagant consumption have essentially been a means of mandatory enforcement implementation, and a safeguarding measure to urge enforcees to perform their obligations in time.

Eligibility restriction is used as a new type of administrative enforcement implementation also because of its own special mechanism of action. With the continuous development of China's economy and society, people's living standards have greatly improved. Their value orientation and pursuit are thereby increasingly diversified, which is the basis for eligibility restriction to play its role as a new means of coercion. The reason the Supreme People's Court imposes restrictions on the eligibility of enforcee for extravagant spending is precisely because of the situation. For some people, in addition to meeting their own needs of life and development, extravagant spending also has the functions of demonstrating their social superiority and proving their social value. Especially in the society where hedonistic consumption continuous to increase, the significance of extravagant spending for the consumers is constantly strengthened. Therefore, restricting the eligibility of enforcee for extravagant spending may be a more effective means to guarantee the fulfillment of their obligations. Similarly, when choosing a means of implementing administrative enforcement against an obligated entity in the field of energy conservation and emission reduction, we should earnestly consider their concept of value and pursuit. If the means we choose has little or no impact on the obligated entity's concept of value and pursuit, the deterrent effect of the means may not be enough. Based on this, exploration can be made for application of the following types of qualification restrictions in the field of energy conservation and emission reduction.

First, consumption eligibility restrictions. Consumption eligibility restrictions mainly refers to restrictions on the consumption of the representative and the person directly responsible of a company or a public institution that has obligations of energy

---

[32] Yu Lingyun, *Administrative Law*, Tsinghua University Press, 2010, p. 320.

conservation and emission reduction but fails to meet the target during a statutorily defined period of time. In case that a company or public institution fails to fulfil the said obligations, the authors of this book think that the extravagant spending restrictions in the judicial field can be used as reference to restrict the consumption of its representative and the person directly responsible in the following aspects: (i) buying new immovable properties, or building, expanding or refurbishing high-end houses; (ii) extravagant spending in such places as star-rated hotels; (iii) choosing second-class or above cabins of airplanes, soft sleeper, or high-speed train in public transit rides; (iv) purchase vehicles that are not necessary for life and production; (v) travel and taking vacation; (vi) pay high premiums to purchase insurance wealth management products.

Second, credit eligibility restrictions. In a market economy, credit is an indispensable way for such market entities as companies to obtain funds for their operation and development. If a company lacks money for its operation and development, this will at least affect its normal operation. If the situation is serious, the company may go bankrupt. Therefore, market entities such as companies generally highlight establishing a close relationship with banks and other financial institutions. The purpose is to ensure an easy access to funds. In order to urge such entities as companies to perform their energy conservation and emission reduction obligations in time, credit qualification restrictions can be used as a means of implementing administrative enforcement. Of course, due to significant effects of credit eligibility restrictions, there should be restrictions on the use of the measure. First, the period during which credit eligibility of an entity is subject to restrictions should be clearly defined. Specific duration of the period can be determined with comprehensive consideration of such factors of the entity as its performance of the obligations of energy conservation and emission reduction (non-performance, partial performance, or improper performance, etc.), its operating conditions and other factors. In order to meeting the target of energy conservation and emission reduction, some local governments impose credit eligibility restrictions on an entity but the period during which credit eligibility of the entity is subject to the restrictions is not limited or not clearly defined. This should especially be prohibited. Second, there should be a clear division of restriction levels. Restriction level means it is not right to uniformly apply a certain restriction level or prohibition to credit eligibility of different companies indiscriminately. The restrictions should be classified into different levels through comprehensive consideration of such factors of the entity, which has the obligations of energy conservation and emission reduction, as its performance of the obligations (non-performance, partial performance, or improper performance, etc.) and its operating conditions. For example, if the entity failed to perform its obligations of energy conservation and emission reduction, the corresponding credit eligibility limitation should be M yuan; and if the entity only partially performed the obligations, the corresponding credit eligibility restriction should correspondingly be N yuan, and so on.

ii. **Improving the measure of publishing facts of a violation as a means of enforcement implementation**

Although publishing the facts of a violation, as a means of implementing enforcement, is clearly specified in the *Environmental Protection Law*, how on earth the measure is used in practice is not clear. In order to bring the role of the measure into full play, the following supportive actions need to be taken.

First, making the measure should be announced by a higher-level authority. According to organizational structure of the administrative organs of China, level of authoritativeness of acts of an administrative organ is closely related to its administrative level. Generally speaking, administrative acts of an administrative organ of a higher level are more authoritative, and are more likely to be recognized and cooperated by the public. In order to increase "deterrence" effect on companies and public institutions, an administrative organ of a higher level should be required to publish the facts of violations. For example, facts of a violation in a jurisdiction can be announced by the government of the jurisdiction instead of a certain department of the government. Facts of a cross-jurisdiction violation can be announced by a common administrative organ of the jurisdictions at a higher level. Announcing facts of a violation by an administrative organ at a higher level can increase the "deterrence" effect, and can also make information of the violation known by more people. Compared with an administrative organ at a certain level, an administrative organ at a higher level can make information of the violation geographically spread to a wider area and increase number of the audience that receives the information, which will further increase "deterrence" effect of the measure from another perspective.

Second, increase number of the platforms used to announce facts of a violation. From the perspective of communication, transmission speed and quality are highly correlated with the media used to transmit the information. Announcing facts of an illegal act is also an act of transmitting information essentially. In order to enhance actual impact of this measure on energy conservation and emission reduction, the issue of choosing what platform to announce the information cannot be neglected. Traditionally, administrative organs depend on website, newspaper, radio, and government gazette to announce information of illegal acts. However, with the development of society, these traditional ways of information transmission increasingly reveal their limitations whether in terms of audience or receiving efficiency (including retransmission efficiency). Therefore, aside from these ways, the government also needs to continuously make improvements about the platforms used to announce the facts of violations. New forms of media as WeChat, Weibo, blog could be used.

Third, improve feedback to announced information. The purpose of publishing facts of the violation of a company is not to simply transmit the information from the government to the public, but to help the public obtain information of the relevant company's violation through transmission of the information, and indirectly punish the company through acts that are against actual interests of the company (such as reducing purchase of the products of the company). In order to realize such a purpose, the feedback mechanism for announced facts of violations should be constantly improved so as to constantly understand the public's attitude and behavioral change and well improve of the work of publishing facts of violations.

3.3 Revising and Improving the Legal Provisions on Administrative Enforcement

China's administrative enforcement system for energy conservation and emission reduction needs to be improved. Relevant provisions of relevant laws need to be revised and adjusted timely, for example, the *Environmental Protection Law*, the *Law of the PRC on Energy Conservation, Law of the PRC on the Prevention and Control of Atmospheric Pollution, Law of the People's Republic of China on Prevention and Control of Water Pollution*, the *Cleaner Production Promotion Law*, and the *Law of the People's Republic of China on Promoting the Development of a recycling Economy*.

Typical types of administrative enforcement that are socially well-known or widely applicable have been listed in the *Administrative Coercion Law of the People's Republic of China*. This enumeration is a declaration and confirmation of the main types of administrative enforcement. In addition, the enumeration can also be used to guide the establishment of other separate laws in terms of the types of administrative enforcement. For types of administrative enforcement whose scopes of use are special, they are generally included in "other administrative enforcement measures" and "other means of administrative enforcement implementation". Such types are pertinently addressed by other separate laws in their respective fields. Therefore, in the field of energy conservation and emission reduction, in addition to the typical types of administrative enforcement specified in the *Administrative Coercion Law of the People's Republic of China*, specific types of administrative enforcement can also be set in relevant separate laws. The laws of China that involve energy conservation and emission reduction mainly include the *Environmental Protection Law*, the *Law of the PRC on the Prevention and Control of Atmospheric Pollution*, the *Cleaner Production Promotion Law*, the *Law of the PRC on Energy Conservation*, the *Law of the People's Republic of China on Promoting the Development of a recycling Economy*, and the *Law of the People's Republic of China on Prevention and Control of Water Pollution*, etc. In addition to the typical types enumerated in the *Administrative Coercion Law of the People's Republic of China*, practically effective types of administrative enforcement measures and administrative enforcement implementation in the special fields of such laws are needed to be established and used in the process of the amendment and adjustment of such laws.

According to the above analysis, the types of administrative enforcement that can be additionally established and used in the field of energy conservation and emission reduction include limiting the use of energy resources, mandatory security, restriction on the traffic of motor vehicles, mandatory relocation, and freezing funds; two indirect means of implementing administrative enforcement that can be additionally established and used include the enforcement penalty of non-property eligibility restrictions and the reputational enforcement penalty of publishing facts of violations. Some of the above-mentioned administrative enforcement measures and types of administrative enforcement implementation can be universally used in the field of energy conservation and emission reduction, and can be added to the above laws; some are only pertinent to limited scope, and need to be separately stipulated in individual laws. Such administrative enforcement measures and types of administrative enforcement implementation are separately described as follows:

(I) Types of Administrative Enforcement That Can Be Widely Used

The types of administrative enforcement measures that can be generally used in the field of energy conservation and emission reduction are: limiting the use of energy resources, freezing of funds with applicable scope expanded. As far as the basic factors that cause waste of energy resources and high carbon emissions are concerned, material-related factors are key and are caused by unreasonable development, production, use, etc. by the actors. Therefore, controlling material-related factors needs to be highlighted when it comes to reducing or controlling energy resource waste and high carbon emissions.

Energy resources and related equipment, products and processes are two most important forms of material-related factors that cause energy resource waste and high carbon emissions. Limiting the supply and use of energy resources can direct constrain energy resource waste and high carbon emissions. It is strongly pertinent and is widely used in local practice of managing energy conservation and emission reduction, and is practically effective. Therefore, it can be established as a new type of administrative enforcement measure in various relevant laws. It plays a mandatory role in conjunction with "sealing up premises, facilities or properties", "seizure of properties", and "freezing deposits and remittances".

Expanding the scope of application of freezing funds means funds involved in producing, purchasing, selling, using, and transferring of equipment and products that do not meet mandatory energy efficiency standards and seriously pollute the environment should be frozen so as to control such material related factors as equipment, products and processes. Therefore, this measure can be specified in various laws involving environmental protection and energy saving and emission reduction.

(II) Type of Administrative Enforcement Implementation That Can Be Generally Used

The types of administrative enforcement implementation that can be generally used in energy conservation and emission reduction include two indirect means of implementation, that is, enforcement penalty of non-property eligibility restrictions and reputational enforcement penalty of publishing facts of violations.

The reputational enforcement penalty of publishing facts of violations is an indirect means of administrative enforcement implementation that comes along with the development of modern society. As in the modern "credit" society, good social image and social reputation are an important indispensable soft power for citizens and companies. And the modern society is also an information society. Especially with continuous development of the Internet and communication technology, information transmission is more convenient and faster. Once some facts of an illegal act are announced by an administrative organ, they will be widely noticed by the society and social pressure will be formed. This will negatively influence the reputation of the individual or company, reducing his/its social reputation, and cause a crisis of confidence. Therefore, when announcing facts of an illegal act to the society, the mechanism of exercising social reputational pressure can be used to force the concerned party to perform the obligations stipulated by the administrative law as soon as possible. This indirectly brings the mandatory function of the enforcement penalty into display. Such a measure is simple and can be done easily. It can be widely used.

Enforcement penalty of non-property eligibility restriction develops from the traditional single-pattern property-based enforcement penalty. It can be found from the *Administrative Coercion Law of the People's Republic of China* and other relevant separate laws that property-based enforcement penalty is mainly reflected by "imposed fine" or "late fee". The function of enforcement penalties is presented by using "imposed fine" to promote the concerned party to fulfill its statutory obligations as soon as possible. However, "imposed fines" or "late fee" are only imposed against property, the deterrence effect is still limited, and choices of the implementation method are also limited. In addition, it is also stipulated in Article 45 of the *Administrative Compulsion Law* that "the amounts of the imposed fine or late fee shall not exceed the amount of the pecuniary payment obligation." Thus, enforcement penalties cannot be limited to traditional property penalty types, and objects other than property can also be included into the scope of enforcement penalties. Non-property enforcement penalties should be established to strengthen the effectiveness and extend application range of enforcement penalties. In the current rule of law-based society, eligibility-based rights are also important rights, and are, to some extent, more important than property rights. This is why eligibility restrictions often can have greater influence on interests of social members and bring more pressure on them. Therefore, non-property enforcement penalties based on eligibility restrictions can be established and be applied to practice. The rights brought by some important eligibility such as eligibility for credit, eligibility for consumption, free-travel eligibility can be used as objects of enforcement penalties. If concerned parties do not perform their legal obligations in time, such eligibility of them during a certain period of time can be restricted so as to force them to perform the obligations. Restrictions on the eligibility for credit can be implemented through financial institutions such as banks to stop credit loans; the *Certain Provisions of the Supreme People's Court on Restricting Extravagant Spending of Enforcees* can be referred to impose restrictions on the eligibility for consumption; restrictions on the eligibility for free travel can be imposed through the customs and the entry and exit administrations.

(III) Types of Administrative Enforcement That Can Be Independently Applied

Some administrative mandatory measures are only targeted at special subjects and are only suitable to be stipulated in separate laws. These measures are mainly restrictions on the traffic of motor vehicles, mandatory relocation, and mandatory security, etc.

i. The administrative enforcement measure of restricting the traffic of motor vehicles can be added to the *Law of the PRC on the Prevention and Control of Atmospheric Pollution*. Vehicles with high discharge or intensively used is one of the important sources of urban atmospheric pollution. This is proved by smog that frequently occur in many cities of China. However, there is a lack of administrative enforcement measures in the *Law of the PRC on the Prevention and Control of Atmospheric Pollution*. This makes the vehicles that cause heavy pollution and high emissions unable to be controlled as a type of important material-based factors as they should. Therefore, restricting the traffic of motor vehicle should be established as an applicable administrative enforcement measure in the *Law of the PRC on the Prevention and Control of Atmospheric Pollution* so that the mandatory measure can be used by relevant municipal governments according to the need of preventing and controlling air pollution and polluting conditions of motor vehicles in their administrative regions. The measure should be used based on the types, areas and times of restricted and prohibited motor vehicle traffic.
ii. The measure of mandatorily relocating polluting companies can be added in the *Law of the PRC on the Prevention and Control of Atmospheric Pollution* and *the Law of the People's Republic of China on Prevention and Control of Water Pollution*. Efforts must be made to govern relevant companies that heavily pollute the air and water. Mandatory relocation is one important measure for curbing pollution. For companies that are in an area that is densely populated, has a weak carrying capacity, and is close to water sources, the administrative organ should force the companies to move to places that are sparsely populated, have a strong carrying capacity, and are far away from water sources.
iii. The administrative enforcement measure of mandatory security can be added in the *Law of the People's Republic of China on Promoting the Development of a recycling Economy*. The legislative purpose of the law is to make the development of such market entities as companies sustainable so that their economic acts are less polluting and low resource consuming. According to the law, the obligations of a company in recycling economy mainly include reducing energy consumption, reducing the amount of waste generated and emitted and improving the level of reusing and recycling wastes. In order to ensure that companies perform their statutory obligations, the law stipulates such punishing mechanisms as administrative penalties. However, the mechanisms are just ex post punishments and cannot exercise the regulatory function of ex ante control. Therefore, the administrative enforcement measure of mandatory security can be added to force companies to provide corresponding property to guarantee their performance of statutory obligations. The property of a company will be

disposed by an administrative organ if the company fails to perform the obligations of reducing consumption of resources, reducing the generation of wastes and emissions, and improving the level of reusing and recycling wastes.

In order to give full play of the role of administrative enforcement in guaranteeing and regulating the activities of energy conservation and emission reduction, relevant prevailing laws should be adjusted and amended. In addition, there should be special provisions to regulate administrative enforcement in the field of energy conservation and emission in *The Act of the People's Republic of China Addressing Climate Change (The Draft Proposal)* that is currently drawn up by China. The special provisions should be an important part of the said law, and clearly specify the principles governing the application of administrative enforcement in the field of energy conservation and emission reduction, main types of the administrative enforcement, and implementation procedure of the administrative enforcement, etc. An administrative enforcement regulatory system that applies to low-carbon development should be formed and be made consistent with and closely linked with the provisions of the various prevailing separate laws about administrative enforcement. The special provisions should also provide guidance for promulgating separate laws and regulations involving addressing climate change in the future.

Chapter 10
Strengthening the Management of Carbon Information Disclosure

Carbon information is a basic element in the efforts of energy conservation and emission reduction, and the exchange and application of carbon information is an indispensable and important basic work. The government faces a new task of managing carbon information in the process of promoting energy conservation and emission reduction, which is a task not involved in traditional administrative activities. In carbon information management, carbon information disclosure is an important procedure. However, there is a lack of a complete carbon information disclosure system in China, thus this issue needs to be explored and studied.

1 Carbon Information Disclosure

1.1 Meaning of Carbon Information Disclosure

Currently, there is no definition of carbon information both in theory and in practice, let alone forming a clear legal concept of it. Broadly speaking, all information involving greenhouse gases that causing climate change can be said to be carbon information. The content of carbon information at least includes such ontological information of greenhouse gases as their connotation, constitution, and formation; information of the current status of greenhouse gases such as their discharge and the consequences of their influence; such information of the policies, decisions, measures and technologies for curbing the discharge of greenhouse gases. In terms of form, it includes information carriers in written form, image form, audio-visual form, electronic form and any other material form.

Carbon information disclosure is an activity that a particular entity discloses the carbon information possessed by it to the society or a particular object in a certain way. The function of carbon information disclosure is to break information closure so that the information is widely communicated and used and is made to display its due value.

S. Fang and B. Tan, *On the Administrative Law of China in Addressing Climate Change*,
https://doi.org/10.1007/978-981-19-7705-3_10

Carbon information disclosure does not mean that the body that possesses carbon information discloses all of the carbon information in its possession. The information that it should disclose is only a part of the carbon information in a broader sense. The information disclosed should have three characteristics: first, it's information that is not open to access, and cannot be obtained or is hard to obtain if not disclosed, and information that has been open to access and become known to people by book or by common sense does not need to be particularly disclosed anymore; second, information of a public nature, that is, if the information is not disclosed, public interest or the interests of others will be affected; third, information whose secrecy is not statutorily required, that is, the information is not national secret and trade secret that is statutorily required not to be disclosed.

1.2 Significance of Carbon Information Disclosure

For the government, the disclosure of necessary carbon information is an important condition for low-carbon administrative legislation. Fully, accurately and timely disclosing carbon information is a basis for the government to prepare relevant legislation and make decisions. By understanding and analyzing the carbon information disclosed by companies, the government can have an idea of the entire situation and the specific problems so that it can accurately put in place regulations and measures about energy conservation and emission reduction.

For a company, when it discloses carbon information with the content disclosed by it supervised by the social public, this will invisibly create external pressure on the company and effectively urge the company to actively perform its social duties of energy conservation and emission reduction. At the same time, in a more positive sense, for enterprises, carbon information disclosure is essentially an action to promote their competitiveness. Through carbon information disclosure, a company can understand the development prospects of the industry that it is in, know the strengths and weaknesses of itself and its products, learn from successful and effective peer experience in energy-conservation and emission reduction, and find the footholds and innovative angles for improving future development.

In addition, it is also stipulated in Article 53 of the newly revised *Environmental Protection Law* that citizens, legal persons, and other organizations legally have the right to obtain environmental information and participate in and supervise environmental protection. With regard to relevant carbon information of companies formed in their production and operational activities, timely publishing of the information is a guarantee of the right to know of citizens, legal persons, and other organizations. In addition, this can help to promote public participation in and supervision of environmental protection, and hence achieve their environmental rights and interests, investment interests in the companies, and consumer benefits of the products of the companies. Eventually, this is beneficial for leading a better life where energy resources are conserved and the ecological environment is protected.

It is just because of the aforesaid significance of carbon information disclosure, a government should include carbon information disclosure in its scope of administrative functions, and should provide necessary management of carbon information disclosure.

1.3 Two Basic Modes of Carbon Information Disclosure

Globally, there are two modes of carbon information disclosure management by the government, that is, voluntary disclosure and mandatory disclosure. Currently, these two modes have also been adopted by China, but the regulations of mandatory disclosure are not clear enough.

Autonomous disclosure of carbon information means a company, voluntarily discloses carbon information of its production and operational activities based on considerations of its social responsibilities, social ethics, and its interests and development. For example, a company faithfully discloses to the public density and total amount of its greenhouse gas emission, its measures and effects of curbing carbon emissions, its participation in trading of carbon information, its risks and opportunities, and its coping strategies and plans in curbing emissions, so as to accept supervision by the society. The feature of voluntary disclosure of carbon information is that it is not a statutory obligation. A company that does not voluntarily disclose its carbon information do not need to bear legal liability therefor. A company's motivation for voluntary disclosure of carbon information mainly comes from its intention to improve competitiveness, its awareness of its social responsibilities, and pressure from the social public and the media. The government's management of such a disclosure is mainly done through administrative guidance, administrative incentives, administrative contract, and other non-mandatory means to provide guidance.

Mandatory disclosure of carbon information is that an administrative entity takes necessary measures according to laws, and forces the person that possesses carbon information to fully, accurately, and timely disclose information or reach a state the same as having disclosed the said information. Mandatory disclosure of carbon information is generally a manifestation of rigid intervention by the government of carbon information disclosure. There are two ways of mandatory disclosure of carbon information. First, the competent government department collects and processes the carbon information of a carbon information possessor, and then translates the information into public information of the government, for example, carbon information that serves as a basis for the government to make decisions on promoting energy conservation and emission reduction, and then directly discloses the information to the society according to corresponding authorization. Since the disclosure does not need the consent of the possessor of the information as a prerequisite, the disclosure is mandatory. Second, a competent government department directly or indirectly forces the possessor of carbon information to disclose the carbon information to the society by itself, including ordering the possessor to disclose the carbon information, publicizing the information on behalf of the possessor (agency performance as a form of indirect enforcement), and imposing administrative penalties on the possessor if it refuses to disclose the information. The characteristic of mandatory disclosure is that it is a legal obligation that must be fulfilled. The state specifies that a company must disclose its carbon information through legislation. In addition, the state guarantees the disclosure through the compulsory power of law, that is, when a company fails to disclose its carbon information or fails to disclose its carbon information as required, the government can take mandatory measures to force it to disclose the same and hold it liable for failing to perform the obligation of disclosure.

China's *Environmental Protection Law*, the *Measures for the Publicity of Environmental Information* and other laws, regulations, and rules have certain provisions about the above-mentioned two modes of carbon information disclosure, but the provisions still mostly require voluntary disclosure. In case of mandatory disclosure, the government authorities collect and process the carbon information of a relevant company, and then publish the same to the public after the information having been transformed to public information of the government. Companies are not mandatorily required to directly disclose their carbon information to the society. Therefore, the disclosure made by the government can be said to be a form of informal mandatory disclosure.

2 Current Status of Carbon Information Disclosure Management in China

2.1 Provisions of the Current Legislation

Currently, no legislation in China specifically requires a company to disclose carbon information. The laws and regulations involving carbon information disclosure mainly include legislation requiring publication of government information, legislation requiring publication of environmental information and legislation about carbon trading.[1]

(I) **Relevant Provisions of the *Regulations of the People's Republic of China on the Disclosure of Government Information***

The *Regulations of the People's Republic of China on the Disclosure of Government Information* are mainly systematic provisions about the activities of publicizing government information. The provisions define the meaning of government information and specify the principles, scope, and procedures of publicizing government information and the measures to be taken to safeguard the publication.

The meaning of government information is defined in Article 2 of the *Regulations of the People's Republic of China on the Disclosure of Government Information.*

---

[1] See Liu Weimin, *Information Publication and China's Environmental Enforcement*, *Tian Fu New Idea*, no. 5 (2013).

Article 5 of the regulations stipulates the principles to be followed in publicizing government information. Articles 9, 10, 11, and 12 of the regulations list the information that should be voluntarily publicized by an administrative organ, and many of the provisions are closely related to the carbon information necessary for energy conservation and emission reduction. For example, "information that involves the vital interests of citizens, legal persons or other organizations", "information that needs to be extensively known or participated in by the general public", "national economic and social development plans, plans for special projects, regional plans and relevant policies", "statistics on national economic and social development", "catalogues and standards of the items for centralized government procurement, and the actual procurement", "bases, conditions, and procedures for granting administrative permission and for providing other services related to management of external affairs, and the results", "approval for construction of major projects and completion of such construction", "oversight and inspection with respect to environment protection, public health, work safety, food and drugs, and product quality", "important and major matters in urban and rural construction and management", "fiscal budgets and final accounts", and "other government information to be disclosed voluntarily, according to the provisions of laws, regulations, rules and relevant state regulations (including laws and regulations concerning energy conservation and protecting the ecological environment)". Article 14 of the *Regulations of the People's Republic of China on the Disclosure of Government Information* specifies the scope of the government information that should not be publicized. In addition, the regulations also specify the procedures, supervising and safeguarding measures, and relief system for information disclosure.

(II) Relevant Provisions of Legislation about Environmental Information Such As the *Environmental Protection Law*

Carbon information is a kind of environmental information in nature. According to Item 3 of Article 2 of the *Convention on Access to Information, Public Participation in Decision-making and Access to Justice in Environmental Matters* adopted in 1998, environmental information means any information in written, visual, aural, or any other material form on: first, the state of elements of the environment, such as air and atmosphere; second, factors affecting or likely to affect the elements of air or atmosphere, such as substances, energy, noise and radiation, and activities or measures, including administrative measures, environmental agreements, policies, legislation, plans and programs, and cost–benefit and other economic analyses and assumptions used in environmental decision-making. Article 2 of China's *Environmental Protection Law* clearly defines the meaning of environment. According to this, and based on the targets of carbon information, that is, air and atmosphere, and the specific content of carbon emission activities and governance, "carbon information is a part of environmental information."[2] Therefore, in case of disclosure of carbon information, relevant provisions about environmental information disclosure should be followed.

[2] Wang Zhiliang and Guo Linwei, *Survey of Carbon Disclosure Status of Chinese Companies and Improvement Suggestions*, *Communication of Finance and Accounting*, no. 16 (2015).

Currently, the laws of China related to environmental information disclosure mainly include the *Environmental Protection Law*, the *Cleaner Production Promotion Law*, the *Measures for the Publicity of Environmental Information (for Trial Implementation)*, the *Measures for the Publicity of Environmental Information by Enterprises and Public Institutions*, the *Measures for the Administration of Carbon Emissions Trading (for Trial Implementation)*, etc.

First, environmental information disclosure has been specially included in the *Environmental Protection Law* of China as an independent chapter (Chap. 5). It is stipulated in the second paragraph of Article 53 of the *Environmental Protection Law* that departments having the duties of environmental protection, supervision and management has the obligations of disclosing environmental information according to the law; the entities that have the obligation of disclosing environmental information are stipulated in Article 54 of the law.[3] The obligation of key pollution emission units of disclosing environmental information is stipulated in Article 55 of the law.[4] The obligation of project owners and government departments responsible for EIA review and approval of disclosing environmental information is stipulated in Article 56 of the law.[5]

Second, environmental information is classified into environmental information of companies and environmental information of the government in the *Measures for the Publicity of Environmental Information*. In addition, the corresponding scope, means and procedure for disclosing the different categories of environmental information are also stipulated. In terms of disclosing environmental information of the government, the scope of the environmental information to be disclosed by environmental protection authorities is stipulated in Article 11 of the measures.[6] In the meantime, it is stipulated in Article 12 of the measures that environmental protection authorities should establish and improve an environmental information release confidential review mechanism for disclosure of environmental information of the government, and improve the mechanism. The procedures and responsibilities for reviewing environmental information are also specified in the article. In terms of disclosure of environmental information of companies, it is pointed out in the measures that there are two types of environmental information for disclosure, that is, environmental information that is voluntarily disclosed and environmental information that is mandatorily disclosed.

The environmental information of companies that should be voluntarily disclosed is specified in Article 19 of the measures.[7] Of course, carbon information can be included in the said environmental information of companies that should be voluntarily disclosed. Since companies are encouraged to disclose environmental information, the more companies disclose various environmental information including carbon information the better. Therefore, companies are not constrained for

---

[3] See Article 54 of the *Environmental Protection Law*.

[4] See Article 55 of the *Environmental Protection Law*.

[5] See Article 56 of the *Environmental Protection Law*.

[6] See Article 11 of the *Measures for the Publicity of Environmental Information*.

[7] See Article 19 of the *Measures for the Publicity of Environmental Information*.

disclosing their carbon information. In this sense, relevant provisions of the *Measures for the Publicity of Environmental Information* can apply to voluntary disclosure of carbon information by companies. Mandatory disclosure of environmental information is also clearly specified in items 2 to 4 of Article 20 of the *Measures for the Publicity of Environmental Information.*[8] However, these provisions are not intended to force companies to disclose relevant carbon information, because the pollutants referred to thereunder are specific substances that pollute adjacent environmental spaces and do not include greenhouse gases that affect global climate change such as carbon dioxide. Four major pollutants are specified in the Twelfth Five-Year Plan of China, that is, chemical oxygen demand, ammonia nitride, nitrogen oxides, and sulfur dioxide, among which nitrogen oxides and sulfur dioxide are air pollutants. At the same time, according to the provisions of the *Integrated Emission Standard of Air Pollutants*, carbon dioxide is not included in the 33 air pollutants specified by the state, and it is even more difficult to assess the impact of the emissions of a company on global climate change. Therefore, the mandatory disclosure of environmental information set out in Article 20 of the *Measures for the Publicity of Environmental Information* does not apply to carbon information disclosure of companies.

Third, in terms of disclosure of environmental information of companies and public institutions, the provisions of the *Measures for the Publicity of Environmental Information by Enterprises and Public Institutions* are basically the same as the provisions of the *Measures for the Publicity of Environmental Information*, that is, the environmental information that is voluntarily disclosed by companies and public institutions can include carbon information. However, relevant carbon information will not be included if highlight of the disclosure is put on "major pollutants and their characteristics, names of pollutants, discharge mode, number and distribution of discharge outlets, emission concentration and total amount of discharge, exceedance of the discharge standards, pollutant discharge standard implemented, and verified total volume of discharge", "construction and operation conditions of the facilities used to prevent and control pollution", "evaluation of environmental impacts of construction projects and conditions of other environmental protection licenses", and "emergency plans of environmental emergencies", etc.

(III) Provisions of the *Measures for the Administration of Carbon Emissions Trading (for Trial Implementation)*

The *Measures for the Administration of Carbon Emissions Trading (for Trial Implementation)* does not specially require that companies and participants in carbon emissions trade should disclose carbon information, whether voluntarily or mandatorily. It is just stipulated in the *Measures for the Administration of Carbon Emissions Trading (for Trial Implementation)* that key pollution emission units must have discharge detection plans and file them with the carbon emission governing authority. The key pollution emission units should also prepare a greenhouse gas emission report for the preceding year and submit the report to relevant authorities. According to Article 25 of the *Measures for the Administration of Carbon Emissions Trading (for Trial*

[8] See Items 2–4 of Articles 20 of the *Measures for the Publicity of Environmental Information*.

Implementation), the key pollution emission units have an obligation of making a plan for detecting discharged pollutants.[9] According to Article 26 of the *Measures for the Administration of Carbon Emissions Trading (for Trial Implementation)*, the key pollution emission units have an obligation of preparing a report about their greenhouse gas emissions.[10]

In the meantime, the *Measures for the Administration of Carbon Emissions Trading (for Trial Implementation)* only require the government department responsible for EIA review should publish relevant information to the society, including some information of the key pollution emission units. Therefore, the carbon information of companies has been converted to public information of the government and is disclosed to the society. It is stipulated in Article 7 of the *Measures for the Administration of Carbon Emissions Trading (for Trial Implementation)* that a relevant government department of provincial level has the obligation of preparing a list of key pollution emission units and submitting the list to the relevant departments of the State Council. It is stipulated in Article of the *Measures for the Administration of Carbon Emissions Trading (for Trial Implementation)* that the State Council carbon emission governing department is obligated to prepare a list of key pollution emission units.

The provisions of the above-mentioned laws and regulations basically form the carbon information disclosure management system of China.

2.2 *Shortcomings of the Existing Carbon Information Disclosure Management System*

(I) **There Isn't a Mandatory Carbon Information Disclosure System for Companies Basically**

It can be found from the above analysis that currently there is a legal basis for the main entities of energy conservation and emission reduction such as companies to voluntarily disclose relevant carbon information. However, legally they are not mandatorily required to disclose carbon information to the society. Such a mandatory disclosure system has not been established yet.

At present, voluntary disclosure of carbon information by companies and public institutions has been covered in the system of voluntary disclosure of environmental information stipulated in the *Environmental Protection Law*, the *Measures for the Publicity of Environmental Information*, and the *Measures for the Publicity of Environmental Information by Enterprises and Public Institutions*. Only having voluntary disclosure available brings some defects as follows: (i) Disclosure not guaranteed, that is, carbon information can be disclosed or not disclosed which is autonomously

---

[9] See Article 25 of the *Measures for the Administration of Carbon Emissions Trading (for Trial Implementation)*.

[10] See Article 26 of the *Measures for the Administration of Carbon Emissions Trading (for Trial Implementation)*.

decided by possessor of the information. (ii) Completeness of disclosed carbon information not guaranteed. The person that discloses the information is entitled to fully disclose the information and can also only disclose some of the information. In this case, completeness of the disclose information cannot be guaranteed. (iii) Timely disclosure of relevant carbon information not guaranteed. Timeliness plays an important role in achieving the directing function of information. In voluntary disclosure of carbon information, the disclosure process is controlled by possessor of the information, so delayed disclosure may occur. It can be found from the practice that companies are not enthusiastic about voluntary disclosure of carbon information. Based on implementation conditions of the CDP2014 project in China, a majority of companies in China are still passive about environmental information disclosure.[11] Environmental information is mainly disclosed through mainstream financial reports, other compliance documents, and environmental information disclosure platforms of local governments. For companies, non-voluntary disclosure of environmental information will make them more passive to some extent. In 2014, totally 4,540 companies around the world disclosed climate change data to CDP. CDP sent questionnaires to the 100 largest Chinese companies by market value after investability weighting which were listed in the FTSE China A600 and FTSE All-World Asia Pacific (FTAW06) indices. Of the 100 invited Chinese companies, 45 (10 Chinese companies of them are Global 500) responded through Online Response System, only covering 10 sectors based on the Global Industry Classification Standard (GICS)34. Moreover, the questionnaire of CDP included four modules, 15 topics and involved more than 80 questions. The Chinese companies mainly answered the following questions: how to comprehensively manage multi-energy saving and emissions reduction targets; the business risks and opportunities that climate change presents; company reactions to current, proposed or expected regulations; long-term, profitable investments in GHG emissions reductions; and how climate change management can create a competitive advantage, etc. On the whole, the response rate of Management and Strategy and Risk and Opportunities were high while companies were conservative on emissions disclosure, with response rate below 20%. Companies willing to publicize the data were even less (only 3), and companies that disclosed and/or publicized the data were mainly low emissions companies. The main reason is that listed companies generally believe that specific emissions data is likely to influence the decision of investors, especially high emissions companies in industries such as Industrials, Energy and Materials with higher energy consumption and emissions data for industrial added value per unit, who have higher risks in energy cost, addressing climate change and energy saving and emissions reduction, therefor are more cautious when disclosing relevant data.

Based on in-depth analysis of the carbon information disclosure by the Chinese companies, there are several main reasons for low-level carbon information disclosure by the Chinese companies. First, the Chinese companies have not reached a consensus about "what is carbon information and why carbon information should be

[11] See *CDP China 100 Climate Change Report 2014*, accessed October 22nd, 2015, http://fs.tangongye.com/upload/files/2014/10/17/B2CBD442EFD54656.pdf.

disclosed" so they simply wait and see and passive attitude prevails. Second, there has been no unified calculation standard and framework for greenhouse gas emissions of companies. Third, many companies do not have a business department to cope with CDP survey. If a company does not have special employees to calculate emission data, it will be hard for the company to effectively complete the relevant work.[12] Four, currently, since they are not mandatorily required to disclose carbon information, companies are usually not willing to disclose their carbon information due to consideration of business interest. If they are mandatorily required to perform the obligation of disclosing carbon information, companies will not only face strong public pressure but will also face the economic pressure brought by carbon tax and carbon emission trade, etc.

Based on the above, the unitary system of voluntary disclosure of carbon information has defects. It is necessary to establish a mandatory disclosure mechanism for some carbon information that must be fully disclosed in time. With mandatory means used to guaranteed the implementation of the mandatory disclosure mechanism, shortcomings of the voluntary disclosure system can be overcome.

(II) Scope of Disclosure Stipulated by the *Measures for the Administration of Carbon Emissions Trading (for Trial Implementation)* and the *Trial Measures on Carbon Emission Administration* of Various Places is too Narrow

The *Measures for the Administration of Carbon Emissions Trading (for Trial Implementation)* and the *Trial Measures on Carbon Emission Administration* of various places are provisions specially targeted at carbon emission trading and carbon information disclosure. Especially, the *Measures for the Administration of Carbon Emissions Trading (for Trial Implementation)* is the first time to specify that carbon emission information should be publicized from the perspective of administrative law. However, it is obvious that the carbon emission information that is required to be disclosed according to the *Measures for the Administration of Carbon Emissions Trading (for Trial Implementation)* is too limited and not systematic, which can be found from the content of Article 34 thereof.[13] Take the *Trial Measures of Guangdong on Carbon Emission Administration* as an example which comparatively requires disclosure of more carbon emission information than the *Trial Measures on Carbon Emission Administration* of various places. The information that should be disclosed to the society only includes, among other things, total allowance issued in the province, measures for allocating allowance, name list of companies and entities with emission control, and reporting relevant credit information of a company about its performance conditions, carbon emission management, and carbon emission trading.[14] The information that is required to be disclosed is only a very limited

[12] See Xiang Miao, *Thoughts about Factors Affecting Carbon Information Disclosure by Chinese Companies*, *Research of Financial & Accounting*, no. 16 (2012).

[13] See Article 34 of the *Measures for the Administration of Carbon Emissions Trading (for Trial Implementation)* and the *Trial Measures on Carbon Emission Administration*.

[14] See Articles 11, 12, 29 and 32 of the *Trial Measures of Guangdong on Carbon Emission Administration*.

portion of carbon information and does not involve carbon information that is the most critical and closest to the core. In the administration of carbon emission trading of a company, the most critical information is its annual resource consumption, concentration and total volume of carbon dioxide directly or indirectly discharged by it, target of emission reduction, measures controlling carbon emission reduction, data related to monitoring and statistical data related to the monitoring of carbon emission amount, and surrendering of allowances, etc. This type of information is basic for the government to determine the allowances to be allocated to companies, and also quantitatively makes the public know how a company performs in reducing carbon emissions. The information can also reflect the basic work that is done by a company or entity to fulfill its carbon emission reduction obligations and is also basic information for judging whether the company or entity can fulfill such obligations of it. The information is especially important for investors. Failure to disclose the aforesaid key carbon information will make the portion of information that can be disclosed lose its value, because an information chain cannot be effectively created when there is only consequential information but there is no prerequisite information. In the meantime, the so-called relevant credit information of a company is only internally possessed by the government. Such information is not transparent and public and the degree of truthfulness is low. This is not good for investors to invest in the low-carbon sector.

(III) **Motivation of Companies not Fully Activated for Carbon Information Disclosure**

Currently, the legislation of China mainly encourages companies to disclose carbon information voluntarily. They are neither mandatorily required to disclose carbon information, nor motivated to do this from the perspective of inner demands. Their motivation is not fully activated. Companies are mainly motivated to disclose carbon information from two aspects: first, the external pressure brought by the mandatory obligation of disclosing carbon information imposed by relevant departments of the state and local government (for example, the Ministry of Ecology and Environment and local environmental protection departments); second, internally inspired to do so due to consideration of the interest of improving their competitiveness and attracting investors. The former is a hard constraint by the public power of the state, and the latter is a soft constraint imposed due to market regulation. However, the existing legislation does not make full use of these two mechanisms, so that enterprises won't take active actions on carbon information disclosure, and there is a long way to go for taking actions.

The Research Report on Corporate Social Responsibility of China (2014) issued by the Research Center for Corporate Social Responsibility, Economics Division, Chinese Academy of Social Sciences in 2014 shows that "from the perspective of the topics on responsibilities, state-owned companies and private companies tend to disclose financial data and compliance information and not fully disclose their environmental information. Nearly half of the foreign-funded companies are still at a wait-and-see stage. The situation of their disclosure of the information is less than optimistic."[15] It can be found that currently motivation of companies is not fully activated for carbon information disclosure.

3 Improvement of Carbon Information Disclosure System

3.1 Perfecting the Legislation for Carbon Information Disclosure System

Legislatively, the *Measures for the Publicity of Environmental Information* and the *Measures for the Publication of Environmental Information by Enterprises and Public Institutions* should be used as a reference to develop a specific *Measures for Carbon Emission Disclosure* to clearly define the concept of carbon information, application of carbon information disclosure, disclosing entities, means of disclosure, disclosing scope and standard, regulatory mechanism and legal responsibilities. This can solve the problem of poor operational scope of carbon disclosure. In addition, there should be corresponding provisions about supervisory responsibilities to ensure companies can better perform the obligation of disclosing carbon information.

The emphasis of the legislation should include:

(I) **Carbon Information Classification**

Carbon information classification helps different entities such as the government and companies to disclose their respective carbon information and correctly control the scope of the disclosure. First, carbon information should be divided into state public carbon information disclosed by the government and individualized corporate carbon information disclosed by companies. State public carbon information should be information that is like a macro policy providing overall guidance and management; individualized corporate carbon information should be particular and internal to the companies.

State public carbon information should be further divided into information that is directly developed and obtained by the government during the process of carbon management (for example, policies and regulations concerning disclosure of carbon emission information and environmental goals and plans) and public carbon information that is converted from the carbon information of relevant companies that has been collected and processed by competent departments of the government (for example, publishing the list of major companies that need to reduce emissions, the plan for allocating carbon emission allowances, the adjustment of the allowances allocated to key pollution emission units after such major changes as closure have occurred to such units).

---

[15] http://news.ifeng.com/a/20141113/42463862_0.shtml, See *The Research Report on Corporate Social Responsibility of China (2014)* issued by Chinese Academy of Social Sciences, accessed October 22nd, 2015, http://news.ifeng.com/a/20141113/42463862_0.shtml.

Individualized carbon information of companies mainly includes information of their carbon emissions and their carbon emission trading. Their carbon emission information refers to the information that is recorded and kept in a certain form and is related to the carbon emission and emission reduction activities occurring in their production and operational activities. Carbon emission information of companies includes their annual direct and indirect carbon emission volume, basic information of their carbon emission facilities, information of their carbon emission monitoring plans and activities, carbon emission reduction and control measures, implementation conditions of their carbon emission reduction measures. Carbon trading information of companies refers to the carbon information that is formed by enterprises in the process of participating in carbon emission trading. Carbon emission trading means a series of activities where key pollution emission units, institutions and individuals stipulated by trading rules buy and sell surplus allowances and voluntary emission reductions certified by the state through trading institutions. Such information as carbon emission allowances and their use, carbon emission trading volume, and carbon price will be formed in such activities.

(II) Clearly Stipulate Different Disclosing Entities, Disclosing Scope and Disclosing Means for State Public Carbon Information and Individualized Carbon Information of Companies

State public carbon information should be proactively disclosed by the government to the society or disclosed to the society subject to the application of the citizens. State public carbon information includes policies and regulations about disclosing carbon emission information, environmental goals and plans prepared, the list of key pollution emission entities, the plan of allocating carbon emission allowances, the adjustment of the allowances allocated to key pollution emission entities after such entities have had such major changes as closure.

Different disclosing entities, scope, and methods should be stipulated for individual carbon information of companies according to different conditions of the companies. As far as carbon emission information of a company is concerned, since its annual carbon emission volume, basic information of its carbon emission facilities, information of its carbon emission monitoring plans and activities, its carbon emission reduction and control measures, and implementation conditions of its carbon emission reduction measures are general information that all companies have, all companies can become disclosing entities of it and the general information can be disclosed by them to the society. However, such information should be disclosed by the following types of companies mandatorily: first, energy-intensive companies such as power plants, oil refineries, and chemical companies; second, entities whose carbon emission, energy production and energy consumption exceed specified limits; third, entities that participate in carbon trading including companies that apply for carbon trading; four, publicly listed companies. Other ordinary companies excluding the above-mentioned companies are encouraged to disclose carbon information to the society voluntarily. As for carbon trading information, all companies that participate in carbon trading should voluntarily disclose carbon trading information, and a mandatory disclosure system is implemented. This is done to protect the interest of the public and the interest of trading parties and investors.

(III) Specify the Relevant Procedures of Disclosing Carbon Information

i. Specifying the procedure of the government of disclosing state public carbon information

The procedure of proactive disclosure of information and the procedure of disclosing information according to an application that are specified in the *Regulations of the People's Republic of China on the Disclosure of Government Information* should be referred to when the above procedure is made clear. However, the particularity of carbon information disclosure should also be considered when following the procedures stipulated in the regulations. As some carbon information may involve business secrets of enterprises, government departments need to be careful about whether, how much and to whom the carbon information should be disclosed. Where necessary, certain communication should be made with the carbon discharging company, which should be secured by a special procedure. Notification, filing for an objection, and review should be included in the procedure. Notification means the government administration department should notify a carbon-emitting company of the content of its carbon information to be disclosed and the disclosing time before the government administration department discloses the carbon information of the carbon-emitting company to the society. The notification is intended to protect the legitimate rights and interests of the counterpart. This is intended, on the one hand, to protect the company's right to know and, on the other hand, to vest the company with the right to defense. When notified by the government administration department of disclosing its carbon information, the company can apply for objection to the disclosure within a specified period. If the company can fully prove that disclosure of the relevant information will lead to divulgence of its core trade secrets and cause such adverse consequences as an infringement on legitimate interests of the company or jeopardizing fair competition, the government administration department should accept the objection after having reviewed the application for objection. Then the corresponding adjustment should be made to, among other things, the content, object, and time of the disclosure of the carbon information of the company.

ii. Specifying the procedure of disclosing individual carbon information for companies

The procedure can be established by referring to relevant provisions of the Environmental Protection Law, the *Measures for the Publicity of Environmental Information (for Trial Implementation)* and the *Measures for the Publicity of Environmental Information by Enterprises and Public Institutions* concerning the procedure for companies to disclose environmental information. For a company whose carbon information can be voluntarily disclosed, the company can timely and correctly disclose its carbon information through websites, platforms for disclosing carbon information, carbon information disclosing columns, retrieval points for requested materials, electronic screens, radio, television, and local newspaper. For a company whose disclosure of carbon information is mandatory, the company should initiatively disclose its carbon information through the above-mentioned means within a statutory period starting from the day when the carbon information is formed or changes. Otherwise, the administrative organ can take the corresponding mandatory measures or impose an administrative penalty on the company so as to ensure the public to exercise the right to know and relevant rights. In the meantime, the companies of such a type shall not take keeping trade secrets confidential as excuse for refusing to disclose their carbon information. When citizens, legal persons and other organizations find a company does not disclose its carbon information according to laws or fails to disclose its carbon information within the specified period, the citizens, legal persons and other organizations are entitled to report the same to relevant authorities of the government. The relevant authorities of the government shall keep confidential relevant information of the reporting person and protect the legitimate rights and interests of the reporting person.

(IV) Establishing a Mechanism for Supervising Carbon Information Disclosure and Holding Violators Liable

With regard to a company's carbon information whose disclosure is voluntary, non-mandatory administrative actions can be done to urge the carbon-emitting entity to perform its social responsibilities. Non-mandatory administrative actions mainly include advocatory interest-induced administrative actions such as administrative incentives and administrative guidance. Non-mandatory administrative actions are not highlights of this chapter so they are not further explained in this chapter.

Companies should duly and honestly disclose to the society their carbon information whose disclosure is mandatory. This should be made a statutory obligation of companies. When companies fail to perform their statutory obligations, environmental authorities can take such measures as administrative penalties or administrative enforcement implementation according to laws. As far as administrative enforcement is concerned, many means of implementing administrative enforcement are stipulated in the *Administrative Compulsion Law of the People's Republic of China* among which additional imposition of fines or late fees are indirect ways of implementing administrative enforcement, that is, enforcing authorities externally impose pressure on a counterpart to force the counterpart to perform its obligations under the Administrative Law. The remaining means are direct means of implementing administrative enforcement, that is, enforcing authorities directly force a counterpart to perform its obligations. According to the characteristics of a company's administrative obligation of disclosing carbon information, the following means of implementing administrative enforcement can be adopted.

First, getting negative acts recorded in credit history. Getting a negative act recorded in credit history means when a company fails to disclose its carbon information in a specified period or fails to disclose its carbon information according to a specified procedure, an administrative organ can record the negative act in its credit history to lower its credit rating. In modern society, the credit information of a social subject is usually shared with financial institutions such as banks. It is hard for a company or individual that has bad credit history to engage in financing. This can force a counterpart that fails to perform its carbon information disclosure obligation as required to perform the obligations automatically by pressuring the counterpart in terms of social reputation and financing activities.

Second, performing the obligations of security. The following are approximately the situations where security can be applied for carbon information disclosure. First, the relevant executors of some projects, especially projects that have environmental impacts, need to perform certain security obligations for carbon information disclosure to administrative authorities before the commencement of the projects. If the obligor of a project discloses necessary carbon information at the risk assessment stage of the project and at every stage of the project from commencement of the project to completion of it, the corresponding administrative organ may return the corresponding deposit and interest or other material incentives after the end of a certain stage to restrain and encourage the obligor to legally perform its obligations under the administrative law. Second, an obligor that is indeed unable to disclose relevant carbon information due to objective conditions may choose to provide the corresponding administrative organ with a guarantor or a deposit to delay the disclosure date to some extent. If conditions permit and after the obligation is fulfilled, the administration organ can rescind the security. This can urge the obligor to perform the obligation and also through this the actual conditions of the obligor are given into consideration. These are only two of the situations where security obligations can be used. There are many situations where this mandatory performance is applicable in real life. As long as conditions permit, efforts can be made to explore the applicability of the security obligations to constrain the corresponding obligor and urge the obligor to perform its obligations.

3.2 *Fully Motivating the Enterprises to Disclose Carbon Information*

The real source of power for a company to disclose carbon information is its need for development and attracting investment. Therefore, the government should strengthen its basic work when managing carbon information disclosure. The government should proactively take actions to fundamentally mobilize such internal source of power of companies. In this regard, references can be made to the operation of the Carbon Disclosure Project (CDP). CDP is an independent not-for-profit organization. It has sent carbon information disclosure requests to thousands of companies around the world on behalf of institutional investors, purchasing groups, and government bodies since its establishment in 2000.[16] Currently, it is the repository of corporate information on climate change in the world. It has created a relatively perfect basic framework for carbon information disclosure, providing relatively complete carbon information

[16] See carbon information disclosure project, accessed December 14th, 2015, http://www.syntao.com/Themes/Theme_Menu_CN.asp?Menu_ID=42.

to capital market stakeholders. And now it is the benchmark of carbon information disclosure and the main source of corporate carbon information in the world. *CDP China 100 Climate Change Report 2014* shows that more and more companies have realized that they will pay a high price for carbon emissions. This will push them to obviously and significantly change their operation mode because assessment, transparency and accountability in information disclosure will push the business community and investment community for active changes.[17] The cooperating experience between CDP and 4,500 companies suggest that disclosing carbon information can bring many benefits to companies for their survival and development. First, when a company discloses its carbon information, this can fully demonstrate to the society that it is actively performing its social responsibilities of energy conservation and emission reduction. This can also show the goals, measures and effectiveness of its work in the field of energy conservation and emission reduction, which helps to build a good social image and improve its competitiveness. Second, through comparing the carbon information disclosed by different companies, one can have an idea of the prospects for development of an industry, and learn from and refer to the successful and effective practices of other excellent companies in the field of energy conservation and emission reduction. Third, the problems revealed in a company's carbon information disclosure can drive it to make a technological transformation in energy conservation, innovate its operation management, and take effective measures to reduce energy consumption and carbon emissions.

The government should pay attention to playing an active role in three aspects to internally mobilize companies. First, more efforts should be made in publicity and education to make companies know that their disclosing of carbon information is of positive significance to them, and hence help the companies increase their awareness of the responsibility of disclosing carbon and their awareness of the benefits of disclosing carbon information. Second, the government should help and support companies to disclose their carbon information through a variety of means. For example, funds are earmarked for them to establish a team specializing in carbon information disclosure and public services such as professional guidance and training are provided to relevant workers of companies. Third, relevant government bodies should praise those companies that proactively save energy and reduce emissions and disclose carbon information timely and accurately. The relevant government bodies should give priority to such companies when providing funds earmarked for energy conservation and emission reduction, and when recommending pilot low-carbon production programs or other preferential policies of finance, tax, and price, etc.

At the same time, the government should also realize that investors are the main stakeholders of companies, so investors are also an important force for driving companies to proactively disclose carbon information. Li Rusong, CDP China Director, ever made known his analysis, "Carbon information reporting is driven via the market in the West, such as the influence of investors and buyers, while the influence of policy

[17] http://www.cdpchina.net/media/cdp/file/appendix.pdf, See *CDP China 100 Climate Change Report 2014*, accessed December 13rd, 2015, http://news.hexun.com/2013-12-03/160227577.html.

is relatively big in China."[18] This is enlightening, that is, it is not enough to only using administrative means to force companies to disclose carbon information. The market forces such as investors and purchasers should also be mobilized to change the way how corporate carbon information disclosure is managed. The CDP is, in fact, the biggest joint action of investor in the world. Since 2002, it has sent a questionnaire to thousands of big companies around the world, inviting them to participate in a survey on carbon information disclosure. The information and data disclosed by the companies in the survey are critical for investors to refer to from the perspective of impacts of climate change on their current and future investments and become one of the important bases for the investors to refer to in decision making.[19] Market shapers who are mainly investors will value a company's environmental performance, safety, proceeds, and trend of future development. In the long run, if a company does not disclose its carbon information or discloses fake carbon information, its investors will lose faith in it and will change their decision-making on investments. This is an important force that can drive companies to timely and accurately disclose their carbon information. In view of this, the government should fully mobilize market forces to promote companies to disclose their carbon information. For example, the government should remind and instruct investors, through various means, to pay attention to investigating into and assessing the development direction and the conditions of energy conservation and emission reduction of the industry in which they invest. The government should make companies able to share results and proceeds of the work of energy conservation and emission reduction with their investors through certain tax policies, etc. The government should take appropriate incentives to make more domestic investors participate in carbon information disclosure projects and use survey results of the projects to make investors play an incentivizing role in proactive disclosure of carbon information.

[18] See *CDP2013 China Report: Companies not Ready for Carbon Trading*, accessed December 13rd, 2015, http://news.hexun.com/2013-12-03/160227577.html.

[19] Anonymous author, *Why is the Carbon Information Disclosure Project (CDP) a Dismal Failure in China*, accessed December 13rd, 2015, http://blog.sina.com.cn/s/blog_63f0dbd60100kubu.html.

Chapter 11
Low-Carbon Administrative Liability and Construction of Its Investigation Mechanism

In order to address climate change, the administrative law needs to be improved in terms of basic principles, administrative entities, administrative acts, and administrative procedures. Aside from this, the establishment of new administrative responsibilities for maintaining a legal order for low-carbon development is also called for. Administrative liability is important for ensuring the effective implementation of the administrative law system. Administrative liability in the sense of administrative law usually refer to the negative, adverse, and punitive political and legal consequences that administrative entities should assume due to violation of relevant administrative laws and regulations. In the current institutional framework of China, administrative liability can be assumed through two mechanisms. First, investigating liability through bureaucracy in the administrative system, which mainly refers to performance assessment and administrative accountability system. Second, investigating liability outside of the administrative system, which mainly includes administrative review and administrative litigation system. These two mechanisms form a complete system for assuming administrative liability. The following explores how to assume administrative liability internally and externally.

1 Construction of Internal Administrative Liability Investigation Mechanism

In the *Decision of the CCCPC on Some Major Issues Concerning Comprehensively Deepening the Reform*, a strategic arrangement,[1] has been made about creating a mechanism for the ecological sector of China for internally realizing administrative

[1] It is clearly pointed out in the *Decision of the CCCPC on Some Major Issues Concerning Comprehensively Deepening the Reform* that "In order to promote ecological progress, we must establish complete and integrated institutions and systems, implement the strictest source protection system, damage compensation system and accountability system. We will also improve environment treatment and ecological restoration systems, and use set rules to protect the ecological environment.".

S. Fang and B. Tan, *On the Administrative Law of China in Addressing Climate Change*,
https://doi.org/10.1007/978-981-19-7705-3_11

liability and for improving the mechanism. It is emphasized that "we will establish a lifelong accountability system for ecological and environmental damage." Since the beginning of the twenty-first century, we have been brought to face increasingly severe ecological and environmental issues. A batch of laws and policies about investigating administrative liability related to low-carbon developments and environmental protection have been successively promulgated by authorities ranging from the central government to local governments. As far as the central government is concerned, *Interim Regulations on Giving Punishments for Illegal Acts and Disciplinary Offences in Environmental Protection* were jointly promulgated by the Ministry of Supervision and the Ministry of Ecology and Environment. As far as local governments are concerned, *Interim Regulations on Giving Administrative Punishments for Violating Environmental Protection Laws and Regulations* were introduced by Hubei Province and Chongqing City, etc. *Interim Regulations of Shanxi Province on Giving Punishments for Illegal Acts and Disciplinary Offences in Environmental Protection* and *Interim Regulations of Harbin on Giving Punishments for Illegal Acts, Disciplinary Offences, and Order Disobeying Acts of Workers in Environmental Protection System,* etc. were promulgated by Shanxi Province and Harbin City, etc. These specialized laws and policies play a certain role in low-carbon and environmental protection administration. However, from the perspective of the entire system used to internally realize administrative liability, the existing mechanisms of China for realizing administrative liability in the field of low-carbon development and environmental protection have many shortcomings and still need to be further improved.

1.1 Shortcomings of Internal Administrative Liability Investigation Mechanism

(I) **Lack of Reasonable Consistency Between Administrative Duties and Administrative Liability in the Field of Low-carbon Management**

Legally, administrative duties are the primary obligations specifying what duties and obligations an administrative entity and its civil servants should perform and what should be done by them. Administrative liability is the secondary obligations specifying what negative comments and adverse consequences an administrative entity and its civil servants must be held liable for if they fail to perform the administrative duties specified by laws. The relationship between administrative duties and administrative liability is: the former is a prerequisite for the latter. If there are no administrative duties, there won't be corresponding administrative liability. Administrative liability guarantees that the effectiveness of administrative duties can be realized. Without the constraints of administrative liability, the legal provisions concerning the performance of administrative duties may become a dead letter. Administrative duties should reasonably correspond to administrative liability and they should be like "Die juktimklausel". In legislation, administrative liability must be comprehensively stipulated. Administrative duties and administrative liability must be seamlessly linked to ensure power comes with liability. However, it can be found from the legal provisions in the field of low-carbon development and environmental protection that the administrative duties are discordant with the administrative liability. On the one hand, this is reflected by relatively less specified administrative duties. On the other hand, there is a lack of necessary administrative liability and accountability systems to press for the performance of the existing administrative duties. Take the *Law of the PRC on the Prevention and Control of Atmospheric Pollution* as an example. Chapter 2 of the law ("Supervision and Management of Atmospheric Pollution Prevention and Control") is a chapter about administrative duties, however, its provisions are mostly about the obligations of the administrative counterparts of preventing and controlling atmospheric pollution. Only Article 17 and Article 20[2] are about the supervision and management duties of the administrative entities. This is unproportionate between duties and liability due to a lack of provisions about administrative duties to be performed. In addition, although there are administrative duties of administrative entities for environmental governance in these two articles, there are no corresponding administrative liability for acts or omissions in the chapter of "Legal liability".

(II) Weak Regulatory Force of the Legal Provisions about Low-carbon Administrative Liability

According to the principles of legislative science, when setting a legal liability norm, the structure norm of "behavioral pattern—legal consequences" or "assumption–handling" should be followed. "In addition, such elements as the main bodies (main bodies investigating accountability and main bodies held accountable), acts (illegal acts and their severity), and consequences (liability and forms of the liability) should be available. The expression should be definitive, clear, specific, and operable."[3] When the legal provisions of existing legislation about low-carbon administrative liability are inspected, it can be found that the number of regulations is generally scarce. In addition, the content of the provisions themselves also shows a deficiency in regulatory force or in liability. This is reflected in three aspects. First, a lot of legal provisions are highly generalized, are about principles or are citations, and the description of behavioral patterns and legal consequences (assumption and handling) is too abstract and general. Second, there is no defining for illegal acts for which administrative liability should be investigated. For example, such formatted expressions as "abuse of power, neglect of duty and play favoritism and commit irregularities" that have broad connotations are used in most of the legal provisions about the administrative liability in the field of low-carbon development and environmental protection. In addition, provisions of the legislation in various fields are

[2] See Articles 17 and 20 of the *Law of the PRC on the Prevention and Control of Atmospheric Pollution*.

[3] Liu Zhijian, *Incapability of Fulfilling Administrative liability for Environmental Supervision and Regulation and Analysis of the Reasons*, *Journal of Political Science and Law*, no. 5 (2013).

highly similar and there is a suspicion of plagiarism between different legislation. For example, it is uniformly stipulated in the parts concerning legal liability in the *Law of the PRC on the Prevention and Control of Atmospheric Pollution* and the *Forest Law* that "if a relevant worker should abuse their power, neglect their duties, or playing favoritism and committing irregularities, such workers shall be given administrative sanctions if the offenses do not yet constitute crimes, and shall be held criminally liable if such offenses constitute crimes." Third, the counterparts for which administrative accountability is investigated are only limited to state workers that belong to an administrative entity and do not include the administrative body itself. There is a legal gap about the administrative liability of administrative entities that are institution legal persons and entities under organization laws.

(III) **Unitary Form of Liability**

Currently, the form of administrative liability that a regulator should assume in the field of low-carbon development and environmental protection is unitary. There are few legal provisions about the administrative liability of administrative entities, and how the civil servants belonging to the administrative organs are held liable are almost only limited to "administrative penalties", only one way of assuming administrative liability. This may be due to the fact that administrative penalties are the main means for internal administrative accountability as stipulated in exiting general laws and regulations in this field such as the *Civil Servant Law of the People's Republic of China*, the *Law of the People's Republic of China on Administrative Supervision*, and the *Regulations on the Punishment of Civil Servants of Administrative Organs*. Undoubtedly, investigating administrative liability of a regulator needs to follow the provisions of these general legislation. However, the types of administrative liability stipulated in such general legislation as the *Civil Servant Law of the People's Republic of China* are general and principled, and they are programmatic norms of the administrative accountability assumed in all fields. This determines that it is impossible to establish liability targeted at different administrative entities and their civil servants in such legislation and also not possible to list more diversified types of liability. Due to peculiarities of the administrative management in different fields and departments, other special legislation is needed so that more pertinent and operable types of liability can be established according to the serious problems and actual conditions that exist in the process of administrative management of a field. Administrative management in different fields involves different legal duties, environment for the performance of duties, requirements for the performance of duties and consequences of misconducts. In addition, administrative liability should be determined with a combination of leniency and punishment, and based on a differentiation of their different types and also on the severity of the illegal acts, subjective faults, and severity of the consequences.

(IV) **Unclear Principles of Liability**

"Principles of liability are the criteria that should be followed to identify and measure liability and determine who is accountable. They are a generic term for the legal norms on which a subject of liability uses to assume liability."[4] The types of the principles of liability mainly include equitable liability principle, the principle of fault liability, and strict liability principles. It can be found from the entire legal system of China that there have been many provisions about investigating administrative liability for illegal acts in the field of low-carbon development and environmental protection. However, the principles for investigating administrative liability in the low-carbon field are not expounded based on the classification of the principles. This may make it difficult for sharing the burden of proof and judging who is accountable in case of investigating accountability.

1.2 Thoughts on Perfecting the Internal Administrative Liability Investigation Mechanism

Currently, the mechanism of internal administrative liability for administrative management in the field of low-carbon development and environmental protection has many shortcomings. Because of this, it is necessary to improve the mechanism according to the characteristics and actual conditions of administrative management in the field of low-carbon development and environmental protection. The complicated and systematic mechanism investigating administrative liability in the field of low-carbon development involves a wide range of aspects. The following are preliminary thoughts about the cause for liability investigation, counterparts of liability investigation, form of liability investigation, and principles of liability.

(I) **Causes for Liability Investigation**

According to the practical needs of building a low-carbon society, the causes for liability investigation must be related to the major problems in building a low-carbon society and management in ecological and environmental protection. The causes must be more pertinent thereto. With regard to this, it is believed in this book that at least the following types of circumstances can be used as typical causes for investigating an administrative liability in low-carbon field: (i) omissions in the field of low-carbon regulation. The building of a low-carbon society requires that administrative entities actively do their duties and externally fulfilling their regulating and guiding functions. If an administrative entity and its civil servants do not perform or are remiss in performing their statutory duties, this should be a cause for administrative liability investigation. (ii) Administrative abuse. The building of a low-carbon society requires that the government actively perform its duties, but there are some acts that the government cannot do or should not do. Such acts are statutorily forbidden. Once an administrative entity and its civil servants conduct such acts, they will be held accountable therefor. For example, cancellation of an ecological function

[4] Jiang Min, *On the Principle of Liability of Chief Executive Accountability System——Enlightenment from the Practice of Chief Executive Accountability in Chongqing, Political Science and Law*, no. 10 (2009).

zone without authorization or adjusting or changing the nature, scope, boundaries, functional division of an ecological function zone without authorization; exceeding bottom lines for environmental quality, maximum limits on using resources, red lines for ecological protection such as ecological function baselines without authorization. (iii) Wrong administrative decision-making about the environment. "Administrative decision making about the environment means an administrative organ's act to eventually make decisions after having analyzed and judged the environmental damage, possible environmental risks and the costs of various acts of making use of the environment."[5] Making major administrative decisions about the environment involves such public issues as ecological and environmental protection and extracting natural resources concerns environmental interests of the people and sustainable development of the state and the nation. With regard to this type of issues that are involved in administrative decision making, the government has a duty of care, so the government must reasonably make decisions based on scientific assessment of the ecological and environmental risks. In the past, environmental protection work has not received widespread attention, and decisions in the field of environmental ecology are not administrative accountable. Such a consequence is that blind decisions are made regardless of resources and ecological environment, and even serious consequences are generally not held accountable. Obviously, a thorough change needs to be made to such a situation. In case that an administrative organ blindly makes decisions without considering resources and the ecological environment in the future, we should timely call for the accountability system to hold the relevant administrative entity and its civil servants liable for the decisions made. (iv) Serious waste of resources and energy by administrative activities. Rigid requirements of administrative activities have been raised by state regulations and regulations and laws of the party such as the *Energy Conservation Regulation for State-funded Institutions* and the *Regulations on Rigorous Enforcement of Economy and Anti-Waste for the Party and Government Organs*. If administrative entities and their civil servants are extravagant and luxurious and cause waste of state resources and energy, they should assume administrative liability therefor (including being held liable in the party). (v) Below targets in the evaluation of the performance in energy conservation and emission reduction. In order to effectively respond to climate change, the Chinese government has put forth a series of restraining indicators.[6] In 2015, it was further emphasized in the

---

[5] Wang Jin, *Environmental Law*, Peking University Press, 2006, p.283.

[6] *The Written Reply of the State Council on Allocated Target of Reducing Energy Consumption per Unit GDP at Provincial Level during the Eleventh Five-Year Plan Period* was issued in 2006. In the reply, the indicators of energy conservation and emission reduction were decomposed among the provinces. It was clearly required in the reply that "various provinces (regions and cities) should incorporate the targets in the comprehensive assessment of their economic and social development, performance evaluation and political performance evaluation, and the targets should be decomposed to various cities (regions), counties and relevant industries and major companies." See "The Written Reply of the State Council on Allocated Target of Reducing Energy Consumption per Unit GDP at Provincial Level during the Eleventh Five-Year Plan Period," *the Legislative Affairs of the State Council*, accessed January 13, 2015, http://www.chinalaw.gov.cn/article/fgkd/xfg/fgxwj/201003/20100300250922.shtml. In 2007, the *Notice of the State Council on Approving and Forwarding the Implementation Plan and Measures for the Statistical Monitoring and Evaluation on Energy*

Guidelines of the CPC Central Committee and the State Council on Accelerating Ecological Civilization "to improve the system of evaluation and accountability of the target liability for energy conservation and emission reduction". This signified that the Chinese government had established a target responsibility system for energy conservation and emission reduction in policy. In a hierarchical performance evaluation system, the government at a certain level or a certain functional department of the government that fails to reach the target of energy conservation and emission reduction set by the government at a higher level will be correspondingly held liable for the failure administratively.

(II) **Counterparts of Liability Investigation**

From the perspective of individual civil servants, the counterparts that are held liable for low-carbon administrative liability may include: (i) chief executives. Chief executives not only include the leaders of the governments at various levels but also include the leaders of the Party committees at various levels, including both the chief leaders and the deputy leaders. This applies to the practical operation of the public power in China. It was emphasized many times in the decision-making arrangement of the central government for constructing ecological civilization that the heads of the party committees and the governments at various levels are generally responsible for their local ecological civilization. This means the heads of the governments and the Party committees at various levels play a leading role in low-carbon administrative management, so they are the targets that may be held liable for low-carbon administrative liability. (ii) Law enforcement officers. Law enforcement officers are people that engage in low-carbon administrative management and are the first persons responsible for low-carbon administrative management. In case of illegal administrative acts and they have faults, they should be investigated for low-carbon administrative liability. This is also an appropriate way to respond to social and public pressure.

In terms of its actual needs and practices, low-carbon administrative management should adopt a "dual punishment system", that is, not only individual civil servants but civil servants of administrative organs and administrative entities (or the government at a certain level) should be investigated for administrative liability due to the following reasons. First, from the perspective of the principle of legally prescribed administration, only administrative entities are subjects with abstract personalities that are able to do administrative acts in their own names and independently assume legal responsibilities. Second, administrative entities, their organizations and administrative organs are also important sources of energy resource consumption and entities that produce carbon emission. Investigating them for administrative liability is in line with the objective reality of building a low-carbon society and ecological and environmental protection. Third, investigating administrative entities (organs and

Saving and Emission Reduction was also issued. The operation methods for energy conservation statistics, monitoring and appraisal were specifically stipulated in the notice.

units) for administrative liability and making them liable for adverse legal consequences can warn and deter their civil servants and urge them to actively and effectively perform the administrative duties of low-carbon emission and environmental protection supervision.

(III) **Forms of Accountability Investigation**

Currently, some governments do not perform their duties and fail to fully perform their duties. This has become an important barrier that obstructs environmental and low-carbon regulation. For example, when it inspected 126 industrial parks in 11 provinces, autonomous regions and municipalities directly under the central government, the Ministry of Ecology and Environment of the PRC found that 110 of them held illegal environmental acts, that is 87% of them.[7] The acts included committing illegal review and approval, carrying out review and approval by exceeding their authorities and failing to meet the "three simultaneous" requirement. The targets of energy conservation and emission reduction set by the state almost became a dead letter due to loose implementation by some local governments. The difficulty in "supervising environmental supervisors" that practically exists indirectly shows that ordinary administrative penalties in the current accountability system have been unable to fully work. Therefore, it is necessary to add forms of accountability investigation to administrative penalties to internally improve the mechanism for investigating low-carbon administrative liability.

For individual civil servants, different forms of accountability investigation can be used according to their different statuses and the different situations. In this part, the highlight will be put on the ways of investigating the liability of leaders and cadres. For leaders and cadres that have ordinary misconducts in the administrative management of low-carbon emission and environmental protection, they can be held liable therefor by ordering them to present a written review at a standing meeting of the Party committee (government) or transferring them from core positions; For leaders and cadres that fail to reach pre-defined targets in performance assessment for energy conservation and emission reduction and ecological construction, one ballot veto can be used in their promotion. This has been stipulated in the *Opinions of the State Council on Strengthening Major Environmental Protection Work*.[8]

Currently, there is no mechanism for investigating the accountability of administrative entities in low-carbon field. The state's deployment of policies and peculiarities in the administrative management of low-carbon development and environmental protection need to be combined to establish such a mechanism. The authors of this book believe that it is appropriate to investigate accountability of administrative entities in low-carbon field through such means that are similar to behavior sanctions,

---

[7] See Gu Ruizhen, *90% Industrial Parks in 11 Provinces Have Illegal Environment Acts and Local Governments are Blamed for Ingratiating themselves with Merchants*, accessed May 18th, 2015, http://env.people.com.cn/GB/6064812.htm.

[8] *The Opinions of the State Council on Strengthening Major Environmental Protection Work, The Chinese Central Government's Official Web Portal*, accessed January 13rd, 2015, http://www.gov.cn/zwgk/2011-10/20/content_1974306.htm.

that is, providing a behavior wedge to carbon emission and resource use of relevant administrative entities that have illegal administrative acts to make up for the loss caused to the ecological environment and the waste of energy resources. For example, a local government that fails to reach the predefined targets of energy conservation and emission reduction and environmental protection or causes ecological environment degradation due to controllable factors can be made to be liable therefor through limiting the approval of its projects; or proportionately reducing its financial appropriations and transfer payments until the ecological environment has been improved; or through correspondingly holding it liable if it fails to duly implement low-carbon environmental protection regulations and its supervision or regulation is ineffective.

(IV) **About the Principle of Liability**

Since adverse consequences in low-carbon regulation and environmental supervision and regulation are easy to get criticism in the society, the main principle of liability adopted in investigating administrative liability therefor is the principle of strict liability, that is, as long as major environmental accidents occur or an administrative organ fails to reach its predefined ecological targets in its performance assessment, it will nevertheless be held accountable no matter it has subjective faults or not.

2 External Administrative Liability Investigation Mechanism: Taking Administrative Litigation as an Example

In a broad sense, external administration liability investigation mechanisms include administrative litigation and administrative review. In view that administrative review and administrative legislation are very similar in principle and mechanism, an exploration is made only about administrative litigation in this section.

With acceleration of the trend of global warming and the frequent occurrence of such harmful environmental consequences as smog, citizens gradually become more aware about the risks of climate change and also require more effective climate change governance by administrative organs. It is expected that administrative disputes caused by climate change governance will constantly occur shortly. For example, a citizen in Shijiazhuang initiated an administrative lawsuit against Shijiazhuang Ecology and Environment Bureau in February 2014 due to the serious smog blanketing in North China, demanding Shijiazhuang Ecology and Environment Bureau to fulfill its regulatory duties to curb extreme weather events and additionally pay ten thousand yuan as administrative compensation. The lawsuit marked the first time a prosecutor had sued an administrative entity due to climate change in China. It was torturous to get the case accepted.[9] The prosecutor successively brought the case to the Higher People's Court of Hebei Province and Shijiazhuang Intermediate

[9] Smog is mainly composed of sulfur dioxide, nitrogen oxides and inhalable particulate matter. Among them, sulfur dioxide and nitrogen oxides are greenhouse gases. In addition, smog and climate

People's Court on February 19th but was not accepted. On February 20th, Shijiazhuang Yuhua District People's Court accepted his litigation materials and indicated that it would give him a reply after a preliminary review of the materials. Until now, it is still unknown whether the case was eventually accepted or not.[10] In order to address climate change, the central and local legislature of China has issued several special legal documents. The Standing Committee of the National People's Congress passed a Resolution on Making Active Responses to Climate Change in 2009. The state entrusted the Chinese Academy of Social Sciences to draw up *The Act of the People's Republic of China Addressing Climate Change* and publicly solicit opinions on the document in 2012. In 2014, 9 government bodies including the National Development and Reform Commission, the Ministry of Finance, and the Ministry of Agriculture and Rural Affairs jointly issued the *National Strategy for Climate Change Adaptation*. At the local level, the provinces of Qinghai, Shanxi, Anhui, Fujian have successively promulgated the *Measures of Responding to Climate Change in Qinghai Province*, the *Measures of Responding to Climate Change in Shanxi Province*, the *Measures of Responding to Climate Change in Anhui Province* and the *Measures of Responding to Climate Change in Fujian Province*, etc. Unfortunately, as far as addressing climate change is concerned, there are no mechanisms for providing administrative relief and solving such disputes in these legal documents. When we turn our eyes to foreign countries, we could say that "the situation there is beyond compare". There have been many lawsuits about climate change in countries and districts with a developed level of nomocracy such as the United States, Canada, Australia, New Zealand, Germany,[11] and the EU. This shows that the administrative litigation system in China needs to be improved.

Addressing climate change has put forth many new requirements of the basic principles, administrative entities, administrative acts and administrative procedures of the administrative law. Further, the establishment of an order ruled by low-carbon administrative law is called for. Administrative litigation is an important means to guarantee the legitimate rights and interests of administrative counterparts and to realize the public interest. It also has the functions of supervising and regulating the use of administrative power and supervising whether the purposes of the activities of administrative organs are legal. To this end, it is urgent to establish and improve low-carbon administrative legislation to guarantee and maintain a new order ruled by low-carbon administrative law.

---

change are caused by the same reason, i.e., mainly caused by fossil fuel combustion. In addition, it is also stipulated in Article 2 of the *Law* of the People's Republic of China on the *Prevention and Control of Atmospheric Pollution (Draft Revision)* issued by the Standing Committee of the National People's Congress "... to conduct cooperative control of atmospheric pollutants and greenhouse gas such as particles, sulfur dioxide, nitrogen oxide, and volatile organic, etc. Therefore, smog and climate change are one same topic.

[10] Ma Tianyun & Wu Hao, *Shijiazhuang: Hard to Bear Smog, A Citizen Sued the Environmental Protection Bureau and Sought 10,000 Yuan in Compensation*, *Xinhua Daily Telegraph* (February 27th, 2014).

[11] See Shen Yaodong, *Judicial Check of Political Tug of War in Climate Change*, Science *of Law*, no.6 (2014).

2.1 Foreign Case: Analysis on the First Case of Climate Change Administrative Litigation in America

(I) Significance of Reviewing Climate Change Litigation in the United States

China and the United States are the world's two largest emitters of greenhouse gases, both with petrochemical energy as the basis of their economic structure. Compared with other countries in the world, China and the United States are the most similar in addressing climate change and developing low-carbon economy. At the APEC Summit in 2014, China and the United States jointly released the *China-U.S. Joint Statement Addressing the Climate Crisis*,[12] and for the first time reached a political consensus about climate change based on the principle of "common but differentiated responsibilities". They expanded the field of pragmatic cooperation, making their relationship closer in addressing climate change. There is more convergence in their relevant legal systems. On the other hand, the United States has repeatedly pressed China to fulfill the obligation of compulsory energy conservation and emission reduction in international negotiations. When there is no low-carbon administrative relief in China, studying and analyzing the relevant judicial practice of the United States can provide enlightenment for China to explore climate change administrative litigation. This can also help China to compete against and cooperate with the United States in the judicial field on the basis of knowing each other.

As of February 2014, there have been 635 lawsuits against climate change in the United States, including many administrative lawsuits where administrative organs are defendants.[13] Among the lawsuits, "*Massachusetts V. EPA*" (hereinafter referred to as the "Massachusetts Case") is a landmark case. The case is known as the first US landmark climate change litigation case and is a typical administrative litigation. In the Massachusetts Case, the Supreme Court of the United States determined greenhouse gases are air pollutants under the *Clean Air Act* and can be regulated by the Environmental Protection Agency, and the Environmental Protection Agency must proactively fulfill this duty. The Massachusetts Case has had a profound impact on the laws and policies of the United States addressing climate change and various industries dependent on various types of fossil energy. The following is an analysis of this.

(II) Review of the Case

The case began with a group of 19 private organizations (including the International Center for. Technology Assessment) that petitioned the Environmental Protection Agency (EPA), on October 20, 1999, to regulate the increasing concentration of greenhouse gases caused by motor vehicle emissions based on section 202 of the

---

[12] Full text of *China-U.S. Joint Statement Addressing the Climate Crisis*, *China Daily* (November 12th, 2014).

[13] Cf. the databases published by the Center of Climate Change Law at Columbia Law School on both US and non-US litigation, accessed January 29th, 2015, http://web.law.columbia.edu/climaete-change/resources/us-climate-change-litigaion-chart.

Clean Air Act.[14] After years of struggle, the Environmental Protection Agency ultimately denied the petition, reasoning that greenhouse gases are not air pollutants under the *Clean Air Act* so the Environmental Protection Agency does not have authority to regulate greenhouse gases; and, even if it did have authority, it would be unwise to regulate the emission of greenhouse gases according to George W Bush's policy of reducing emissions voluntarily to address climate change. Therefore, temporarily the Environmental Protection Agency would not take regulatory measures.[15]

After the petition was denied, the petitioners joined by 12 states (including Massachusetts), 4 cities (including New York), and 13 environmental organizations such as Friends of the Earth sought review in the D.C. Circuit, demanding that the Supreme Court of the United States judge that the Environmental Protection Agency should set administrative rules according the *Clean Air Act* to administratively regulate the emissions of greenhouse gases by motor vehicles. On July 15th, 2005, the D.C. Circuit ruled 2–1, denying the request of the petitioners. Judges Randolph and Sentelle were in the majority. They pointed out that the denial was mainly based on three reasons. First, EPA has authority to regulate greenhouse gases as air pollutants according to the *Clean Air Act*, which should be respected by the court; second, regulating emissions of greenhouse gases will hamper the United States to persuade China and other developing countries to reduce greenhouse gas emissions and hence affect the implementation of the President's foreign policy; third, the plaintiffs did not have standing to sue. Judge Sentelle cited the ruling of *Lujan v. Defenders of Wild-Life* and pointed out he believed petitioners failed to demonstrate the element of injury necessary to establish standing. In his view, they had alleged that climate change is ecologically harmful to humanity at large, but could not allege particularized injuries to themselves. Judge Tatel was in the minority. He dissented. He believed that EPA's failure to curb greenhouse gas emissions contributed to the sea level changes that threatened the coastal safety and property of Massachusetts and other coastal states. Massachusetts had satisfied the elements of standing.[16]

The petitioners were not satisfied with the court decision in the first instance and appealed to the Supreme Court of the United States in June 2006. In the trial, the Supreme Court of the United States showed great compassion to and eventually ruled in favor of the environmental protection organizations on April 2nd, 2007 by a vote of 5:4. The case was a landmark environmental case in the United States. The following are main points of the ruling. (i) Petitioners have standing to challenge the EPA's denial of their rule-making petition. (ii) Greenhouse gases fit well within the Act's definition of air pollutants. EPA's administrative interpretations that do not include greenhouse gases in air pollutants are unavailing. Hence, EPA has statutory

[14] 127 S. C.t 1438, 1449 (2007).

[15] 127 S. C.t 1438, 1450 (2007).

[16] *Massachusetts v. EPA*, 415 F. 3d 50, 58 -59 (D.C. Cir. 2005).

authority to regulate emissions of such gases from motor vehicles. (iii) EPA's incidental reason—according to the foreign strategy of the president, even if EPA has the authority of regulating emissions of greenhouse gases, it would be unwise to regulate the same now due to violation of the legislative purpose of the *Clean Air Act*. (iv) if the defendant cannot prove that there is no legal causal relationship between loss of health and property and emissions of greenhouse gases from motor vehicles, the defendant must implement rule-making.[17] The dissenting minority was represented by Chief Justice Roberts. Although he also thinks that climate change may be the most pressing environmental problem of our time and he acknowledges the governments have done too little to address it, he still pointed out the petitioners lacked three necessary elements for establishing standing (injury in fact, causation, and redressability). First, for the element of injury, climate change is a global problem. The injury suffered by the petitioners is not unique and particularized. Second, for causation, the greenhouse gases from motor vehicles referred to by the petitioners contribute a very small portion of global greenhouse gas emissions and are not a sufficient and necessary cause of loss of coastal land and public health. Third, for redressability, the injuries alleged by the petitioners are caused by the global emission of greenhouse gases. Aside from the United States, other countries are also discharging greenhouse gases substantially. Only requiring EPA to regulate greenhouse gas emissions contributes very little to redress injuries of the petitioners. The passive response of other countries such as China and India are likely to overwhelm any decreases that the United States tries to achieve.[18]

(III) **Analysis of Legal Issues**

The legal issues involved throughout the evolution of the Massachusetts Case from denial of the D.C. Circuit to the supportive ruling of the Supreme Court of the United States can be generalized as follows:

i. **Whether the petitions have standing to sue**

The plaintiff's standing to sue is the prerequisite for a court to conduct a substantive review. In the common law of the United States, the doctrine of standing to sue in an environment litigation (including administrative environmental litigation and environmental infringement litigation) was formed in *Lujan v. Defenders of Wild-Life* in 1992. In general, standing to sue includes three necessary elements, that is, injury in fact, causation, and redressability.[19] The denial of the D.C. Circuit was mainly based on a lack of the element of injury. The element of injury requires the occurrence of an injury that is "real, imminent" and "particularized". The D.C. Circuit thought that on the one hand, the harmful consequences of climate change are still not certain scientifically and even today some scientists still have doubt about the existence of climate change. On the other hand, the petitions alleged that refusal

[17] *Massachusetts v. EPA*, 127 S. Ct. 1438 (2007).

[18] Roberts, C. J., dissenting, 549 U.S. (2007).

[19] *Lujan versus Defenders of Wildlife*, 504 U.S. 555 (1992).

by the defendant to regulating the emission of greenhouse gases would jeopardize the welfare of the public. The D.C. Circuit thought this is a generalized grievance common to all members of the public,[20] hence this can not meet the "particularized" standard of injury.

When the case was reviewed in 2006, the Supreme Court of the United States did not rigidly apply the elements of standing to suit determined in *Lujan v. Defenders of Wild-Life*. The Supreme Court of the United States used a circuitous judicial strategy to support standing of the petitions. First, for injury in fact, the Supreme Court of the United States avoided the legal factors that were not favorable to the petitioners. The majority represented by Chief Justice Scalia affirmatively pointed out that "A well-documented rise in global temperatures has coincided with a significant increase in the concentration of carbon dioxide in the atmosphere. Respected scientists believe the two trends are related."[21] The Supreme Court of the United States intentionally neglected the political fact that the United States Senate unanimously vetoed the ratification of the Kyoto Protocol and the technical fact that there are scientific disputes about climate change.[22] Then, the Supreme Court of the United States must face an issue related to standing to sue, that is, whether climate change had caused particularized harm that was not generalized to the plaintiff that consisted of 12 states, 4 cities and 13 environmental states. With regard to this, the Supreme Court of the United States adopted a loose way of handling this, that is, only one of the 29 petitioners needed to have standing to authorize review.[23] The Supreme Court found a breakthrough in standing to sue in the Massachusetts Case. Then the Supreme Court analogized the special position and quasi-sovereign interests of Massachusetts to the special position and quasi-sovereign interests of the state in *Georgia v. Tennessee Cooper Co.*[24] The so-called quasi-sovereign interest is a historical concept and stemmed from royal prerogative in ancient times, that is, the monarch, as the guardian of his subjects, has the obligation of protecting the interest of his people that cannot protect themselves. Since modern times, royal prerogative has gradually evolved into parens patriae standing——as long as the well-being of the people of a sovereign nation is jeopardized, the owner of the sovereign nation is entitled to initiate an action. To some extent, the tradition of parens patriae standing has been inherited in the common law of the United States. According to the political framework and the spirit of the constitution on which the United States of America was founded, the various states joined the federation as independent political entities. Although the federal government exercises sovereignty rights on behalf of the nation, the states still retain some "Residual Powers" that have not been specifically authorized to the federal government. These residual powers are sovereignty powers in nature and hence become the foundation of quasi-sovereign interests. Based on

---

[20] *Massachusetts v. EPA*, 415 F. 3d 50, 60 (D.C. Cir. 2005).

[21] See Shen Yuedong, *Judicial Check of Political Tug of War in Climate Change*, Science *of Law*, no.6 (2014).

[22] *Massachusetts v. EPA*, 549 U.S. 497, 505 (2007).

[23] *Massachusetts v. EPA*, 549 U.S. 497, 520 (2007).

[24] *Georgia v. Tennessee Cooper Company*, 206 U.S. 230 (1907).

quasi-sovereign interests, the various states should protect the health, safety, and other public welfare that the citizens are unable to fully protect, including environmental pollution and public nuisance. According to sovereign interests, suits initiated by public agencies should be exempt from the standing limitations that apply to citizen suits, by analogy to the implied exemption from standing requirements in *Lujan v. Defenders of Wild-Life* for criminal prosecutions filed by a state.[25] On the contrary, the plaintiff only needs to prove property or interest of the state is harmed and the state government is capable of participating in the litigation on behalf of the harmed citizens.[26] Based on this, the Supreme Court thought by analogy that the failure of EPA to regulate greenhouse gases jeopardized the safety and relevant property interests of coastal Massachusetts, the state government has parens patriae standing to initiate a public interest action for public interest similar to one based on quasi-sovereign interests.[27]

ii. **Whether greenhouse gases are air pollutants**

When the United States had no litigation about climate change yet, the main law on which the Massachusetts Case was based was *Clean Air Act*. Judging whether greenhouse gases are air pollutants under *Clean Air Act* was the basis and prerequisite of the entire case. Otherwise, EPA would not have regulating authority. The request of the plaintiff would have no object and fail. Therefore, the plaintiff, the defendant, and the judges of the Supreme Court had a fierce tug of war over the nature of greenhouse gases.

The plaintiff thought that greenhouse gases are air pollutants under the *Clean Air Act*, while EPA argued greenhouse gases are not air pollutants under section 302 (g) of the *Clean Air Act*.[28] Air pollution causes air to be impure or unclean while greenhouse gases themselves are components of the air and do not comply with the definition of air pollution. Therefore, it is not under the statutory authority of EPA to promulgate rules that regulate motor vehicle GHG emissions.[29]

The majority of the judges of the penal of the Supreme Court did not agree with what EPA said. They denied the argument of EPA based on interpretation of the statutory text, teleological restriction and cited precedents, and ruled that greenhouse gases are air pollutants. Specifically: (i) From the perspective of the statutory text, air pollutants are broadly defined in the *Clean Air Act*, and greenhouse gases are not

---

[25] See Thomas W. Merrill, *Global Warming as a Public Nuisance*, 30 Colum. J. Envtl. L. 293, 304. at 305 (2005).

[26] See Ma Cunli, *Analysis of a Plaintiff's Standing in Administrative Litigation in the Situation of Global Warming*, *Peking University Law Journal*, no. 4 (2008).

[27] *Massachusetts v. EPA*, 549 U.S. 497, 520 (2007).

[28] See Wang Hui, *Administrative Interpretation and Judicial Review in Climate Change Litigation——Analysis of the First Case of the Supreme Court of the United States Related to Climate Change*, *Journal of East China University of Political Science and Law*, no. 2 (2012). The term "air pollutant", as defined in this section, means any air pollution agent or combination of such agents, or other harmful physical, chemical, biological, radioactive matter which is emitted into the ambient air.

[29] Colin H. Cassedy, *Massachusetts v. EPA: The Causes and Effects Creating Comprehensive Climate Change Regulations*, 7 J. Int'l Bus. & L. 145, 149.

specifically excluded. At the same time, according to section 202 (a) (1) of the *Clean Air Act*, newly added air pollutants may endanger public health or well-being and EPA should promulgate corresponding emission standards and get involved in the regulation. According to section 302 (h) of the *Clean Air Act*, the expression "well-being" includes weather change and climate change. (ii) From the perspective of the legislative purpose, when the Congress promulgated the *Clean Air Act* and revised section 202 of it in 1977, the topic of climate change was not highlighted. Therefore, it was promulgated by the Congress, this does not mean that it was originally intended by the Congress to avoid or repel regulation of greenhouse gas emissions. (iii) From the perspective of precedents, a majority of the judges in the panel thought that application of the precedent (*FDA v. Brown & Williamson Tobacco Corp.*) by EPA was not appropriate,[30] because the regulatory acts of FDA in the precedent would prohibit the sales of tobaccos, while the regulatory acts of EPA in this case do not involve prohibition the use of motor vehicles but involve improving emission standard. The consequences to these two regulatory policies cannot be lumped together.[31]

The minority judges represented by Chief Justice Scalia dissented. In their opinion, greenhouse gases are not air pollutants in a strict sense mainly because of the following two reasons: first, from the perspective of air composition, greenhouse gases cannot be classified as unclean or harmful air in nature yet; second, they affect the composition of the atmosphere of the Earth and are not "air" in daily life within the meaning of the *Clean Air Act*.[32]

iii. **Can administrative discretion be a reason for the defendant to refuse to regulate the emission of greenhouse gases?**

If greenhouse gases are judged to be air pollutants, this means EPA has authority to regulate their emissions. Then the question follows: is this administrative regulatory authority statutory duty or administrative discretion? If it is the former, EPA's refusal to regulate the emissions is no doubt an illegal omission; if it is the latter, EPA can decide whether or not to implement administrative regulation based on its own judgment. In this case, the plaintiff would lose.

EPA claimed even if it has authority to regulate greenhouse gases, it is discretionary and EPA is entitled to decide whether or not to exercise the authority out of appropriate consideration. Specifically, according to section 202 (a) (1) of the *Clean Air Act*, "If new motor vehicles or engines cause an increase of air pollutants, EPA can promulgate administrative regulations about the air pollutants that endanger public health or social well-being, and use regulatory actions applicable to them based on its own judgment." However, the problem is, EPA thinks this gives it broad discretion.

---

[30] See *FDA v. Brown & Williamson Tobacco Corp.*, 529 U.S. 120 (2000). In the case, the U.S. Food and Drug Administration was not entitled to regulate tobaccos according to the *Federal Food, Drug, and Cosmetic Act* based on the opinions of the majority of the panel of the Supreme Court of the United States.

[31] *Massachusetts v. EPA*, 549 U.S. 497, 531 (2007).

[32] See Wang Hui, *Administrative Interpretation and Judicial Review in Climate Change Litigation——Analysis of the First Case of the Supreme Court of the United States Related to Climate Change*, *Journal of East China University of Political Science and Law*, no. 2 (2012).

Given the scientific uncertainty of climate change, it is reasonable and lawful for EPA to be cautious and temporarily does not regulate.[33]

The majority of the judges of the Supreme Court viewed this differently. To a great extent, they viewed the argument of EPA as an excuse for its passive performance of the duty. First, as far as the authority is concerned, the original intent that the *Clean Air Act* authorized EPA to "judge" the hazards of newly added air pollutants was to increase the adaptability of administrative regulation to constantly changing environmental governance through the flexibility of administrative discretion and is not a pretext for its passive performance on the regulatory duty. Second, due to uncertainty of climate change, the majority of the judges seemed adopted the precautionary principle. They claimed unless EPA had sufficient scientific evidence to prove that there was no causal link between greenhouse gas emissions and climate change and harms of the plaintiff, the uncertainty of climate change could not be used as a lawful reason for refusing the regulation.[34]

Chief Justice Scalia reserved his opposing opinions. Based on his usual textualist interpretation position and Chevron deference,[35] he put forth two causes for the opposition: first, the opinions of the majority of the judges had no solid basis of statutory text and, in the meantime, were not supported by precedents; second, the *Clean Air Act* has vested big administrative discretion in EPA. No matter how severe climate conditions are, courts should not interfere too much and replace the judgment of the administrative organs with their own.[36] Obviously, Chief Justice Scalia worried the court might be reduced to an administrative law court due to too much interference of entity policies.

iv. **Whether consideration of foreign policy become a reason for refusing regulating greenhouse gas emissions**

Another important point of dispute in Massachusetts v. Environmental Protection Agency was whether the foreign policy of the president could be used as a cause of EPA for refusing to regulate greenhouse gas emissions. EPA claimed unilaterally implementation of domestic regulation when major developing countries having not promised to mandatorily reduce emissions, might, on the one hand, make the emission reduction efforts overwhelmed by the increase of unrestrained carbon emission of developing countries, and, on the other hand, conflict with the President's foreign policy on climate change and hamper the government's ability to bargain with other nations over greenhouse gases. Therefore, the conclusion of EPA was it did not think its decision of not regulating greenhouse gases was, in any way, unreasonable.[37]

---

[33] See Michael Sugar, *Massachusetts v. Environmental Protection Agency, 31 Harvard Environmental Law Review*, 535.

[34] *Massachusetts v. EPA*, 549 U.S. 497, 532–534 (2007).

[35] Chevron U. S. A., *Inc. v. Natural Resources Defense Council*, Inc. 467 U. S. 837, 843 (1984).

[36] See Colin H. Cassedy, *Massachusetts v. EPA: The Causes and Effects Creating Comprehensive Climate Change Regulations*, 7 J. Int'l Bus.& L. 145, 153.

[37] See Colin H. Cassedy, *Massachusetts v. EPA: The Causes and Effects Creating Comprehensive Climate Change Regulations*, 7 J. Int'l Bus.& L. 145, 147.

The majority of the judges of the Supreme Court refuted the claim of EPA. They preferred to believe EPA could not and should not consider the factor of national foreign policy when taking regulating measures because it had no corresponding legal authority to do so. That is to say, whether it was reasonable or not for EPA to regulate greenhouse gas emissions from motor vehicles had nothing to do with the foreign policy of President George W. Bush. EPA's consideration of such a factor as a reason for withholding regulation was irrelevant.[38] With regard to this, Chief Justice Scalia once again represented the minority of the judges of the court and uttered an opposing opinion. He identified with EPA's argument, that is, domestic regulation of greenhouse gases would make the President lose an important bargaining chip in negotiations with foreign nations and become passive in the negotiations.[39]

(IV) **Enlightenment for China**

A comprehensive review of the US lawsuits on climate change can at least bring the following enlightenment:

i. **Incorporating interpretation of policies addressing climate change into regulatory interpretation in judicial review.** It can be found through the Massachusetts Case that the Supreme Court of the United States always had its own policy stance, that is, it acknowledged the petitions of the environmental groups and sympathized them. It preferred that measures should be taken to address and regulate climate change. However, when judicial rights are used, this must be based on the use of legal regulations. This requires that a court must incorporate its policy consideration into its explanation and inference of existing legal regulations and systems. For example, when the Supreme Court determined the injury in fact caused by climate change, the Supreme Court of the United States intentionally used judicial interpretation to avoid the legal factors that were not favorable to the plaintiff—scientific uncertainty of climate change. Compared with the United States, China is a socialist country, which requires that the people's court should have more functions of "creating public policies".[40] However, implementation of public policies on climate change cannot be realized only through the general slogan upholding "consistency between legal effect and social effect." It must be based on law and needs the people's court to explore and interpret existing administrative laws and regulations with political wisdom and make them effectively facilitate fulfillment of the purpose of providing low-carbon relief.
ii. **Appropriately relaxing standing requirements for administrative lawsuits.** It can be easily found through the Massachusetts Case that the Supreme Court

[38] Michael Sugar, *Massachusetts v. Environmental Protection Agency, 31 Harvard Environmental Law Review* 539.

[39] See Andrew P. Morriss, *Litigation to Regulate: Massachusetts v. Environmental Protection Agency*, 2007 Cato Sup. Ct. Rev. 193, 201–202 (2006–2007).

[40] Zhang Youlian, *Why Courts Need to Create Public Policy—Analysis from the Perspective of Jurisprudence, Zhejiang Academic Journal*, no.1 (2009).

of the United States preserved standing of the plaintiff by using the state government's "quasi-sovereign interests" and, in fact, challenged the necessary elements of standing established in *Lujan v. Defenders of Wild-Life* in 1992. Due to scientific uncertainty of climate change and obscurity of the harms of climate change in real life, if standing requirements of a plaintiff are the same as those required in a traditional administrative lawsuit, this will greatly influence the provision of low-carbon administrative remedies and availability of the channels through which the remedies can be provided to the plaintiff. In this regard, the Supreme Court in the Massachusetts Case bypassed the standing review in *Lujan v. Defenders of Wild-Life*. This practice is worthy of being referred to in China. According to the provisions of the *Administrative Litigation Law of the People's Republic of China*, new rights such as environmental rights and carbon emission rights are not included in a people's court's acceptable scope of administrative lawsuits. With regard to this, the legislative bodies and adjudicative bodies must consider how to relax standing requirements in administrative suits through the corresponding promulgation of laws and judicial interpretation.

iii. **Judicially force the government to effectively exercise its functions of addressing climate change.** In the Massachusetts Case, one thing that is worth ruminating is the inciting of a tug of war by the supreme court against the administrative power and even the legislative power in the field of climate change. According to EPA, one of the factors considered by it for refusing regulation of greenhouse gases was implementing President George W Bush's foreign policy of pressing developing countries. However, the Supreme Court took diplomacy to euphemistically fight back against the federal government represented by EPA due to the conscience of addressing climate change and protecting the public environment. The majority of the panel of judges of the Supreme Court denied EPA's political stance since the *Clean Air Act* did not authorize EPA to consider the factor of foreign policy when taking regulatory measures. China, as a responsible power, always adheres to the principle of "common but differentiated responsibilities". The leaders of the central government such as Wen Jiabao voluntarily undertook to reduce the emission of greenhouse gases in many international negotiations. However, since it is the local government's concept of development that only GDP is of their paramount concern, the problem that "political regulations stay in Zhongnanhai" is prominent in the field of addressing climate change and protecting the ecological environment. Sometimes some local governments passively respond to climate change and even sacrifices the interests of ecological environment to pursue short-term economic interests. Courts are a reason-based public platform and are the last defense of social justice. The practice that the Supreme Court of the United States forces the government to respond to climate change through environmental lawsuits is enlightening for the Chinese courts when the Chinese courts restrain the potential motivation of local governments of responding to climate change passively. This is especially true when the reform of the Chinese judicial system continues to go deeper so that the institutional design that personnel and finance-related issues of local courts are centralized at the provincial level makes courts at the basic level gradually get rid of the shackles of local governments. Institutionally, the ability of enforcing administrative power to address climate change will be improved. Looking into the future, it is a historic mission for the people's courts of China to counter and correct the passive attitude of some local governments through judicial activism and legal interpretation to actively push for active response to the public policy of the Central Government to address climate change.

2.2 Thoughts on Establishing China's Low-Carbon Administrative Litigation System

The climate change related lawsuits of the United States provide us important experience and enlightenment from the perspective of judicial strategy and reviewing technology, etc. However, the differences between China and the United States in politics, culture, economy, and legal background determine that we cannot simply copy the US system. On the contrary, we must be fully grounded in actual conditions and the existing legal framework of China, and fully make use of existing institutional resources to explore a low-carbon administrative litigation system with Chinese characteristics that suits the national conditions of China.

(I) **Gaps in Existing Administrative Litigation System in Terms of Low-carbon Regulation and Administrative Accountability**

Although low-carbon remedies are required due to the severe situation of climate change, there are some gaps in the administrative litigation system of China in terms of low-carbon regulation and judicial investigation of administrative accountabilities, which are mainly shown in the following three aspects:

i. **Unable to include administrative disputes related to climate change in the existing scope of accepted administrative litigation**

From the perspective of the scope of acceptable suits, currently, China's scope of acceptable administrative litigation is still only limited to concrete administrative acts and abstract administrative acts are not accepted. Although a "supplementary review system" is stipulated in Article 53 of the *Administrative Litigation Law of the People's Republic of China* revised in 2014,[41] such supplementary review is only limited to other regulatory documents of the government that are of a level that is lower than rules. Therefore, in case that an actual administrative dispute is similar to the dispute involved in the Massachusetts Case and is caused by asking an administrative organ to promulgate administrative legislation addressing climate change, or refusing to accept an administrative organ's certain abstract administrative

[41] See Article 53 of the new *Administrative Litigation Law*.

decision and administrative planning that are intended to address climate change, the case will be unable to be heard due to the administrative acts being sued are abstract. In terms of specific administrative acts, the new *Administrative Litigation Law* expands the scope of administrative cases that can be accepted by a people's court and includes some disputes about administrative requisition and expropriation and administrative contracts in the scope of administrative cases acceptable by a people's court based on the *Interpretation on Several Issues concerning the Application of the Administrative Litigation Law of the People's Republic of China.*[42] However currently, we are afraid that there are still institutional barriers affecting acceptance by a people's court of administrative disputes involving impacts of administrative acts on environmental rights and carbon emission rights. The above-mentioned case in which a citizen of Shijiazhuang sued Shijiazhuang Ecology and Environment Bureau for its failure to perform the duty of curbing smog was not accepted, which reflects, to a great extent, the difficulty in having a climate change related case to be heard by a people's court.

ii. **Hard for a litigant to have the qualification required by prevailing laws to support standing to sue**

Whether there is an interest relationship between a plaintiff and an administrative act is an important basis for use to judge whether the plaintiff has standing to sue. From the perspective of ensuring completeness of the concept and the practice of judicial trials, such a factor has three essential elements according to the provisions of the *Interpretation on Several Issues concerning the Application of the Administrative Litigation Law of the People's Republic of China*: (i) the plaintiff has the lawful rights and interests stipulated by positive laws in and to the specific administrative act; (ii) the lawful rights and interests of the plaintiff has been derogated; (iii) the derogation is directly correlative to the specific administrative act.[43] Since climate change is a public issue and poses risks for a wide range of people, it is hard for the plaintiff in a low-carbon administrative lawsuit to have all of the three essential elements for standing to sue (excluding, of course, traditional administrative acts directly targeted at specific administrative counterparts as mentioned above). Specifically, first, the plaintiff has not had the lawful rights and interests under positive laws to specific administrative acts. As is known to all, the rights at issue in a low-carbon administrative lawsuit are mainly environment rights and carbon emission rights. As far as exiting legislation of China is concerned, no stipulation of such rights of individual citizens either in the *Environmental Protection Law*, a basic law in the field of ecological civilization, or other climate change-related laws. In the meantime, the government's obligation of protecting citizens' environmental rights and carbon emission rights is not rigidly stipulated in existing legislation, while the guaranteeing obligation of the government is another form of public law rights in existence.[44]

---

[42] See Item 11 of Article 12 of the new *Administrative Litigation Law*.

[43] See Shen Kui, *Standing in Administrative Litigation: Space of and Limits on Judicial Discretion*, *Peking University Law Journal*, no. 2, (2004); Si jinjin, *Standing in Administrative Litigation: A study of the "important elements of legal interest"*, *Public Law Research*, no. 2, (2005).

[44] This legislative condition will not be dealt with here and will be further elaborated in the following text.

Second, it is hard for a plaintiff to prove derogation or eminent derogation of his/her lawful rights and interests. As mentioned above, the risks of climate change are counterfactual and uncertain and the harmful effects of climate change can only be shown after a certain historical period. This determines that the impacts of low-carbon administrative acts addressing climate change on the lawful rights and interests of the plaintiff must be indirect and potential and it is hard to find concrete evidence to prove the impacts. Third, the impacts of low-carbon administrative acts on the lawful rights and interests of a plaintiff are probable and in general, it is hard to find a direct causal link between the two. Scientifically, due to the uncertainty and complexity of climate change, the causation between climate change and relevant negative environmental effects often shows a vague pattern of "single cause-multiple effect" or "multiple cause-single effect". It is hard to establish the clear and definite causation pattern of one cause-one effect that is required by existing legislation. For example, although authoritative medical experts have pointed out that "smog is linked to lung cancers" and "whenever there is a smog day, the number of outpatients increases by 10% to 15%." However, it still needs time to draw a conclusion about these issues.[45] Therefore, if a litigant claim there is a legal correlation between the harm to his health and the administrative act (or omission) of the government of failing to effectively control smog, it will be hard to gain support from the court. In fact, the requirements of standing to sue established in *Lujan v. Defenders of Wild-Life* in 1992 are the same as the requirements of standing of a plaintiff in an administrative suit, that is, the plaintiff must prove that he/she has suffered from a specific, particularized, real or imminent harm and there is a causation relationship between the harm and behaviors of the defendant. While in the Massachusetts Case, the Supreme Court of the United States bypassed the standing requirements established in *Lujan v. Defenders of Wild-Life*, and took the trouble to resort to quasi-sovereignty interests based parens patriae standing in precedents of more than one hundred years. This fully proves that due to strict standing requirements of plaintiffs in modern administrative suits, it is hard to have standing to initiate an administrative suit even if having exhausted judicial interpretation and judicial review methods.

In addition, four interest relationships are supplementarily listed in Article 13 of the *Interpretation on Several Issues concerning the Application of the Administrative Litigation Law of the People's Republic of China*, that is, "the administrative action against which a complaint is filed involves the contiguous right, or the right of fair competition, of the citizen, legal person, or other organization"; "the citizen, legal person, or other organization is added as a third party in administrative review, or otherwise with an interest in the administrative action"; "the citizen, legal person, or other organization requires the administrative agency to hold the author of an injury legally liable by the law"; "the revocation or modification of an administrative action involves interest relationship with the citizen, legal person, or other organization."[46]

[45] Ma Li, *Zhong Nanshan: Smog is Correlated to Lung Cancer*, *The Beijing News*, March 11, 2015.

[46] *The Interpretation on Several Issues concerning the Application of the Administrative Litigation Law of the People's Republic of China*, the website of Renmin University of China, accessed January 20th, 2015, http://www.npc.gov.cn/npc/lfzt/2014/2013-12/20/content_1817962.htm.

However, even by using such judicial techniques as expanded interpretation or purposive presumptions, it is difficult for these provisions to fully cover the scenarios in the practice of low-carbon administrative litigation.

iii. **There is no low-carbon administrative litigation system for public interest yet**

Generally speaking, when the party involved in an administrative dispute has no standing to sue and the interest relationship required by law, other entities that are not "competent" can obtain remedies by making use of administrative public interest litigation according to special legal provisions. Hence, administrative public interest litigation that is done through an "interest representative model"[47] can be used to obtain universal remedies. Although standing to sue has been further expanded by the *Interpretation on Several Issues concerning the Application of the Administrative Litigation Law of the People's Republic of China* and the new *Administrative Litigation Law of the People's Republic of China* promulgated in 2014, it is a pity these two documents still blindly emphasize competence of the plaintiff and the old concept of subjective administrative litigation still has a grip on these two documents. As early as in 2005, the State Council highlighted the efforts to "push for administrative public interest litigation".[48] Administrative public interest litigation obviously includes the environmental public interest litigation mentioned here. Environment-related public interest litigation system was initially established through Article 55 of the *Civil Procedure Law of the People's Republic of China* revised in 2013.[49] However, up till now, administrative public interest litigation is still not added to the *Administrative Litigation Law* revised in 2014. Therefore, current low-carbon administrative disputes cannot be solved through administrative public interest litigation.

To sum up, because of the absence of low-carbon remedies in the current administrative litigation system of China and the urgent need of solving administrative disputes involving climate change, it is necessary to explore and establish a low-carbon administrative litigation system with Chinese characteristics. When analyzed macroscopically, establishing low-carbon administrative litigation mainly involves litigation mode (including standing to sue and scope of acceptable cases), governance rules, review methods and form of judgment, and other important issues. Such issues will be further discussed separately in the following text.

---

[47] With regard to the "interest representative model" in administrative law and judicial review, see Richard B. Stewart, *The Reformation of American Administrative Law*, trans. Shen Kui (The Commercial Press, 2011), 184–187.

[48] The State Council pointed out in the then adopted *Decision on Implementing the Scientific Concept on Development and Strengthening Environmental Protection* that "social supervision should be intensified …The function of civil societies should be full exerted to encourage the reporting and disclosure of all types of environmental law-breaking activities so as to promote the lodging of lawsuit in environmental public interest.".

[49] See Article 55 of the *Civil Procedure Law of the People's Republic of China*.

(II) Establishing a Two-model Low-carbon Administrative Litigation System

i. Establishing a dual-track-model low-carbon administrative litigation system including subjective litigation and objective litigation

Establishing models of litigation concerns such prerequisite issues as who initiates low-carbon administrative litigation and how to initiate low-carbon administrative litigation. According to classic classification of procedural law theory of mainland China, administrative litigation can be divided into two models: subjective litigation and objective litigation. Subjective litigation is a type of administrative litigation initiated to obtain remedies for one's own subjective public rights, for example, revocation litigation and payment are both subjective litigation, that is, one can request a court to provide remedies only when one's own lawful rights and interests suffer from particular harm. Objective litigation is also called public interest litigation. It is not initiated purely for one's own personal benefits, but for maintaining objective order of law and is based on public interest, for example, taxpayer lawsuits in the United States and popular actions in Japan.[50] It can be found from the Massachusetts Case that as far as climate change administrative litigation is concerned, the court only accepts subjective litigation and objective litigation is expelled. This originated from the standing requirements established in *Lujan v. Defenders of Wild-Life* in 1992. It requires that there should be particular harm brought by climate change to individual interests of the plaintiff. The authors of this book think that in combination with the actual conditions of China, both subjective litigation and objective litigation should be used for obtaining low-carbon administrative remedies in China. This is because, on the one hand, climate change provides citizens some new public law rights (for example, carbon emission rights and environmental rights). Rights come with remedies. Citizens are entitled to initiate subjective litigation based on these rights, which belongs to the topics of low-carbon administrative remedies. On the other hand, the same applies to low-carbon administrative litigation. Addressing climate change needs that the citizens widely participate in supervising the performance of the government of its administrative duties of developing a low-carbon economy and building a low-carbon society. However, climate change affects many aspects of social life, it is hard to realize such a purpose of supervision only depending on subjective litigation. With regard to this, it is pointed out in *China's National Climate Change Programme* issued by the State Council that "participating role of companies and supervising role of the public should be played ... to promote the people and all sectors of the society to participate in the program of slowing down climate change." When it specifically comes to administrative litigation, with the help of participation by the public, objective litigation can play an important supplementary role in supervising the performance of administrative organs of their low-carbon duties. Currently, some developing countries have initially formed a climate change

[50] See *Administrative Law*, ed. Yang Jianshun, China Renmin University Press, 2012, 326.

related objective litigation system in some fields. The courts of India and Brazil have adopted a *Convention on Economy, Social and Cultural Rights* and provide expanded interpretation of the right to food and the right to life in their constitutions, allowing private non-government organizations to initiate public interest litigation about failure of the government to effectively address food crisis caused by climate change, demanding the government to perform the statutory obligation of guaranteeing food supply. For example, India was hit by a severe drought in 2001 due to climate change, causing famine in many places. With regard to this, the People's Union for Civil Liberties, a national non-governmental organization, initiated public interest litigation against the central government of India, demanding governments at various levels to create social welfare programs and properly perform the obligation of supplying and distributing food.[51]

ii. **Building a low-carbon related subjective administrative litigation system**

Subjective administration litigation is a basic model of administrative litigation in China. The scope of the remedies available for subjective litigation is the widest and the litigation threshold is low, so building such a system should be first considered. As is known to all, the core of subjective litigation is how to define "interest of litigation", only the person that has interests in litigation has standing to initiate a subjective suit.[52] According to the theory of administrative litigation of the civil law system, there are two essential elements for interests of litigation: first, there is a relationship of interest between the concerned party and an administrative act; second, interests of the concerned party are subjective public rights specially protected by administrative regulations. The former is embodied by Article 12 of the *Interpretation on Several Issues concerning the Application of the Administrative Litigation Law of the People's Republic of China*.[53] The latter is embodied by Article 2 of the new *Administrative Litigation Law*.[54] Although the *Administrative Litigation Law of the People's Republic of China* was revised in 2014, the specific administrative acts that are covered in the scope of acceptance are still listed.

The element of legal interest relationship is required in the *Administrative Litigation Law Interpretation on Several Issues concerning the Application of the Administrative Litigation Law of the People's Republic of China*.[55] It is reasonable to require

51 See Yang Xing, *Legal Choice of Rising Developing Countries to Address Climate Change—Access from Citizens' Right to Food, Law Review*, no. 5 (2014).

52 Mitsuo Kobayakawa, *Analysis of the Construction of Administrative Litigation*, trans. Wang Tianhua, China University of Political Science and Law Press, 2014, 240–272.

53 It is stipulated under Article 12 of the *Interpretation on Several Issues concerning the Application of the Administrative Litigation Law of the People's Republic of China* that "when a citizen, legal persons or other organization that has interests in a specific administrative act is not satisfied with such an administrative act, he or it may initiate an administrative suit according to the law.".

54 It is stipulated in Article 2 of the new *Administrative Litigation Law* that "If a citizen, a legal person or any other organization considers that his or its lawful rights and interests have been infringed upon by a specific administrative act of an administrative organ or its personnel, he or it shall have the right to bring a suit before a people's court in accordance with this law.".

55 The *Interpretation on Several Issues concerning the Application of the Administrative Litigation Law of the People's Republic of China* requires that there are actual and particular impacts on the

such a necessary element of the plaintiff's standing to initiate an ordinary subjective administrative suit due to consideration of preventing abuse of lawsuits and prioritize the allocation of legal resources. However, the relationship between climate change and the interests of individual citizens is complicated, subtle, and also scientifically uncertain. It will undoubtedly block the channel through which a concerned person can obtain administrative remedies if too strictly requiring the concerned person to strictly prove the consequences of climate change such as smog concern interests of the person. Therefore, the litigation threshold for the element of interest relationship involved in subjective low-carbon administrative litigation should be appropriately lowered with the help of judicial interpretation. Specifically, the notion of particularized injury in *Lujan v. Defenders of Wild-Life* should be referred to,[56] that is, as long as a citizen can prove that the injury sustained by him is particularized and not shared by the general public, it can be presumed that legally there is an interest relationship. However, there shouldn't be too higher a requirement of such kind of particularized injury. For example, in an environmental suit in the United States, an Alaska citizen liked polar bears and spoke of the "great pleasure" that the animals bring to the people who saw them. Based on this, he claimed that climate change had caused a particularized injury, aesthetic injury, to him because climate change seriously endangered the survival of polar bears.[57] In the above-mentioned case where a Shijiazhuang citizen sued Shijiazhuang Ecology and Environment Bureau, as long as the citizen could prove that smog caused particularized health hazards to him, for example, catching respiratory diseases, blocked his outdoor workout. It can be deemed that the element of interest relationship was available.

About subjective public rights. Although the Administrative Litigation Law of the People's Republic of China was revised in 2014, the administrative acts covered by administrative cases that are acceptable by a people's court are listed in the law. The acts only involve the personal rights, property rights, and right to social security. The problem whether new environmental rights related to climate change can be protected in a subjective lawsuit as rights under public laws is still not thoroughly solved. The above-mentioned case was an example where the citizen sued the Ecology and Environment Bureau for its omission on grounds that his environmental rights and right to health were jeopardized. With regard to such a problem, the solution to the problem should be sought by resorting to defining subjective public rights. In order

rights and obligations of the plaintiff and lists four special circumstances, that is, "the administrative action against which a complaint is filed involves the contiguous right, or the right of fair competition, of the citizen, legal person, or other organization"; "the citizen, legal person, or other organization is added as a third party in administrative review, or otherwise with an interest in the administrative action"; "the citizen, legal person, or other organization requires the administrative agency to hold the author of an injury legally liable in accordance with the law"; " the revocation or modification of an administrative action involves interest relationship with the citizen, legal person, or other organization. "For more information, refer to *Interpretation on Several Issues concerning the Application of the Administrative Litigation Law of the People's Republic of China*, the website of Renmin University of China, accessed January 20th, 2015, http://www.npc.gov.cn/npc/lfzt/2014/2013-12/20/content_1817962.htm.

56 *Lujan versus Defenders of Wildlife*, 504 U.S. 555, 575, n.1 (1992).

57 *Animal Legal Def. Fund v. Glickman*, 154 F. 3d 426, 432–33 (D.C Cir. 1998).

to integrate subjective public rights and administrative litigation, German scholar Buehler defined subjective public rights which later becomes a classic definition that is widely accepted, "public rights define a subject's status in relative to the state. They are constraining regulations prepared for protecting legal acts or individual interests of citizens and can be cited by subjects against administrative organs. They determine what subjects can request from the state or can do for the state."[58] The definition includes three essential elements of subjective public rights. First, protecting private interests, that is, they are legally defined to protect the private interests of citizens instead of public interest. Second, constraining obligations, that is, legal provisions impose the obligation of doing certain acts by administrative organs. Third, applicability, that is, it is legally stipulated that citizens can use or claim them according to law. Therefore, in order to expand the content of subjective public rights and the scope of remedies that can be obtained through subjective administrative litigation, work should be done from the following two aspects: (i) it is stipulated in Article 12 (12) of the prevailing *Administrative Litigation Law of the People's Republic of China*, a basic provision about subjective public rights of citizens, that "where it is felt that an administrative organ has violated rights in person or property, or other lawful rights and interests." This, in fact, expels the possibility of obtaining remedies for other types of rights and is a constraint on other rights and interests. In order to remove the limit on the right to the person and property, the item should be replaced with "where it is felt that an administrative organ has violated other statutory rights" to remove the limit on the public rights covered by subjective litigation, and hence make it possible to include new environmental rights related to climate change. (ii) Although a lot of environmental protection laws and regulations have been promulgated in China, it is still not clear whether citizens have independent environmental rights. Generally, citizens' low-carbon and environmental protection obligations are stipulated under prevailing environmental laws, but it is rare that citizens should have environmental rights and administrative organs should have corresponding obligations. For example, it is only stipulated in the *Environmental Protection Law* promulgated in 2014 that "Citizens shall raise their awareness of environmental protection, adopt low-carbon and economical lifestyles, and conscientiously fulfill their obligation to protect the environment." Improvement needs to be made in this regard. In order to solidify environmental rights and make them become subjective public rights and hence be covered by the remedies provided by subjective litigation, relevant laws and regulations that are closely related to climate change such as the *Environmental Protection Law*, the *Law of the PRC on the Prevention and Control of Atmospheric Pollution* and the *Law of the People's Republic of China on Prevention and Control of Water Pollution* should be revised so that it is stipulated that citizen should enjoy such environmental rights as the right to clean air, right to clean water, and right to aesthetic appreciation of environments. In this regard, local Chinese legislation in the field of carbon trading management has included carbon emission right of the entities whose carbon emission is controlled into the scope of acceptance of

---

[58] Mitsuo Kobayakawa, *Analysis of the Construction of Administrative Litigation*, trans. Wang Tianhua, China University of Political Science and Law Press, 2014, p. 66.

administrative litigation as a subjective public right. For example, Article 44 of the *Interim Measures for Managing Carbon Emissions Trading.*[59] (Of course, whether local governments can supplementarily specify the scope of administrative cases acceptable to a people's court by promulgating rules, this is a question of which the legality still needs to be discussed.)

iii. **Building a low-carbon objective administrative litigation system**

With regard to such external issues as climate change, it is not enough to only allow administrative counterparts to initiate subjective litigation against administrative acts of the government addressing climate change. There are two reasons for this. First, many low-carbon administrative acts are abstract and are not targeted at particular subjects, which objectively creates a barrier in terms of standing to initiate subjective litigation. Second, relevant administrative acts are public and professional. Individual administrative counterparts are not motivated to sue due to their interests are not directly affected by such acts, or they hope to sue but they do not have the corresponding ability to sue. Therefore, low-carbon administrative remedies require that an objective litigation system is established to make up for the shortcomings of subjective litigation. Compared with subjective litigation, objective litigation is a special form of administrative litigation, so the customary practice of countries around the world is to specially regulate objective litigation through a special law. A subjective suit about an administrative act can be initiated if it is not prohibited by the law. On the other hand, an objective suit about an administrative act cannot be initiated if it is not stipulated by the law to be one acceptable by a people's court. From the perspective of institutional design, at least the following questions involved in low-carbon objective litigation need to be specially stipulated through legislation.

(i) **Restrictions on standing to sue**

Objective administrative litigation involves maintaining public interest, so standing of the plaintiff in an objective administrative suit should be more carefully required than standing of the plaintiff in a subjective administrative suit. In the meantime, the judicial resource of a nation is limited, after all, meaningless abusive litigation needs to be avoided. Therefore, standing to initiate objective litigation must be restricted to avoid populism in litigation. Theoretically, standing to sue is defined based on the following three models of objective administrative litigation. First, administrative public prosecution, that is, state procuratorate, initiates objective administrative litigation as the only qualified plaintiff. Administrative prosecution can be initiated through two ways, that is, directly initiated by a procuratorate according to its duty or

[59] It is stipulated in Article 44 of the *Interim Measures for Managing and Trading Emissions Allowances in the City of Shenzhen*, "if the body responsible for management and control disagrees with carbon check result, the body can apply to the competent body for review. The competent body should provide a decision of the review within ten business days after its acceptance of the application of review. If the body responsible for management and control disagrees with the decision of the competent body of the review, the body responsible for management and control can apply for administrative review or initiate an administrative action.".

initiated upon application of citizens. It was proposed in the decision adopted at The Fourth Plenary Session of the 18th Communist Party of China Central Committee that "the system of instituting public interest litigation by the prosecutors shall be actively explored and established." Second, group litigation, that is, other social groups other than prosecutors also have standing to initiate objective litigation according to certain conditions.[60] Third, popular litigation. Popular litigation is also a model of litigation that exists most widely. From procuratorial organs and social groups, standing to initiate objective litigation further extends to individual citizens and the scope of the bodies that have standing to sue is maximally expanded.[61] The authors of this book think currently, the models of objective administrative litigation in low-carbon field should not blindly extend to popular litigation, and temporarily should mainly be constrained to administrative public prosecution and group litigation because of the following reasons. First, low-carbon objective administrative litigation usually involves important and complicated environmental cases while individual citizens have limited money and energy. It is doubtful whether they have sufficient standing to sue. Second, when they are not satisfied with the administrative acts of administrative organs to address climate change, individual citizens can solve the issue through subjective litigation and do not need to occupy judicial resources available for objective litigation. Third, low-carbon objective administrative litigation involves complicated entanglement of interest, and there may be a conflict of interest between different groups. In this regard, prosecutors and such social groups as environmental protection groups are more broadly representative than individual citizens. However, two things need to be noticed in the institutional design of administrative public prosecution and group litigation. Administrative public prosecution should mainly be initiated via the application of citizens and be supplemented by the initiation of such proceedings ex officio to avoid too much interference of prosecutorial power with administrative power and maintain a reasonable balance of power. The environmental protection organization that initiates group litigation should be a public-benefit non-for-profit organization that has been legally registered with a civil administration body and have standing to sue to prevent some illegal organization to make a profit through abusive litigation.

(ii) **Clarifying scope of cases that can be accepted by the people's courts**

The scope of low-carbon objective administrative litigation acceptable by the people's courts can be discussed from three perspectives: First, whether abstract administrative acts can be included in the scope. It can be found from the above analysis of the Massachusetts Case that the US climate change litigation was aimed at formulating regulatory standards (administrative regulations) by the administrative agency, thereby indirectly requiring it to implement low-carbon regulations, that is to say,

---

[60] This is a model that is very customary in civil law system, for example, the *German Federal Environmental Law* clearly stipulates that environmental public interest litigation should be initiated by sentimental organization that have the irreducible constitutional minimum of standing.

[61] See Lin Lihong & Ma Liqun, *Administrative Public Interest Litigation as Objective Litigation, Administrative Law Review*, no. 4 (2011).

abstract administrative acts could be included in the scope of acceptable cases in the United States. Although it has been stipulated in the *Administrative Litigation Law* of China revised in 2014 that the people's courts can, in conjunction with other things, review the legality of the administrative regulations on which administrative acts are based, currently, the people's courts can first be authorized to examine the non-low-carbon and environmental protection related regulations on which administrative acts are based in objective administrative litigation. When conditions are ripe in the future, omissions in administrative legislation can be included in the scope of cases accepted by the people's courts through revision or judicial interpretation. Second, whether the actual occurrence of environmental damage is required. The condition for a people's court to accept subjective litigation is that the corresponding subjective public rights have been infringed, that is, injury in fact has occurred. However, low-carbon related objective administrative litigation usually involves significant environmental benefits. Once harmful consequences are brought about, it is difficult to reverse them or costly to treat the negative effects. Therefore, certain prevention is needed. Administrative acts that pose significant ecological and environmental risks should be included in the scope of cases that can be accepted by the people's courts. There have been precedents in practice. In 2009, All-China Environment Federation sued the Land and Resources Management Bureau of Qingzhen Town, Guizhou Province. The plaintiff initiated the case due to the defendant failed to perform its administrative duty of taking back land and hence caused potential risks to the ecological environment of Baihua Lake Scenic Spot.[62] The case was intended to prevent risks. Third, administrative acts for which low-carbon-related objective administrative litigation can be initiated. In practice, the administrative acts of administrative organs that involve climate change are complicated. It is hard to list them all. Generally, they can be classified into the following: (i) an administrative organ slacks in its performance of low-carbon administrative duties which threatens the ecological environment, or the administrative organ fails to disclose information concerning environmental and carbon emission monitoring and refuses to reply within a specified period. (ii) Acts of administrative organs are illegal or inappropriate, which may significantly affect the ecological environment and climate change adversely. For example, starting a project without having assessed its environmental impacts, or factors related to low-carbon development and environmental protection are not considered in administrative planning for extracting and making use of natural resources. (iii) An administrative organ itself uses materials that do not meet the standard of low-carbon and environmental protection.[63] With regard to this, it can be stipulated in legislation that social groups and the public prosecutor can initiate low-carbon objective administrative litigation to sue the administrative organ

---

[62] Qie Jianrong, *The First Environmental Public Interest Administrative Case Initiated by a Social Group Accepted*, *Legal Daily*, July 29th, 2009.

[63] *China's Energy Conservation Regulations for State-funded Institutions* require that efforts should be made "to promote energy conservation in state-funded institutions, improve their energy efficiency and give play to their model role in the energy conservation of the whole country". Specific requirements for energy conservation and emission reduction are also put forth from the perspective of office building operation and the use of government vehicles and office supplies.

for its internal high energy consuming and heavy pollutant emitting administrative acts.

(iii) **Setting acceptance procedure**

Some scholars proposed "setting administrative review to be a procedure preceding to environmental administrative public interest litigation",[64] that is, a concerned party must apply for administrative review before initiating administrative public interest litigation. Only when the concerned party's application for administrative review is not replied to within a specified period or is rejected can administrative litigation be initiated. The authors of this book think that this proposal is worth considering in low-carbon objective administrative litigation due to the following reasons: First, low-carbon administrative acts addressing climate change are new for administrative management. Administrative review provides administrative organs with a chance to correct their own mistakes. Second, addressing administrative disputes related to climate change needs professional and scientific knowledge. Administrative review organs are more institutionally capable than courts and have an advantage over courts in terms of knowledge. Third, preceding administrative litigation with administrative review can filter some low-carbon disputes, which can prevent courts from being too heavily burdened and reasonably reroute administrative disputes.

(iv) **Establishing litigation incentives**

Low-carbon objective administrative litigation is altruist. The concerned person (excluding procuratorates) usually digs into his own pocket to pay for the litigation. Therefore, it is necessary to provide necessary incentives to him through reasonable institutional design. First, low-carbon objective administrative litigation is intended to safeguard the public interest of society. This amounts to a special sacrifice made by the concerned person (excluding procuratorates) for the country. It is necessary for the country to provide compensation, appropriately reduce litigation costs or stipulate that the costs of low-carbon objective administrative litigation should be borne by the defendant. For example, the *Measures for Paying Litigation Costs* can be modified to include low-carbon-related objective administrative litigation into the scope of litigation whose costs can be exempted; in addition, the government can, at its own cost, provide free legal assistance and legal services to the concerned person so that his burden in the litigation can be reduced from professional and economic perspectives. Second, with regard to the plaintiff that has won low-carbon-related objective administrative litigation, certain material, and spiritual incentives can be given to the plaintiff to encourage him to contribute to low-carbon development and environmental protection undertaking.

---

[64] Cao Heping & Shang Yongxin, *Obstacles of and Countermeasures for China to Build an Environmental Administrative Public Interest Litigation System*, *Social Sciences in Nanjing*, no. 7 (2009).

(II) Clarifying Jurisdiction Rules of Low-carbon Administrative Litigation

i. Limitation of existing jurisdiction rules of administrative litigation

Influenced by civil litigation, the basic rule to be followed for the territorial jurisdiction of administrative litigation is the principle of "the plaintiff accommodating the defendant". In general, the first instance court of an administrative case is the basic people's court in the place where the administrative act of an administrative organ was originally done. This is mainly intended to facilitate the litigation and cutting down the expenditure, however the principle of "the plaintiff accommodating the defendant" is not appropriate for low-carbon administrative litigation. Such inappropriateness is mainly shown in the following aspects: (i) While the GDP-only performance evaluation system has not been radically changed, there is a considerable tension between tackling climate change, protecting the ecological environment and local governments' pursuit of economic development, which is difficult to eliminate in the short term. Currently, local governments belittle environmental benefits and even sacrifice the ecological environment to develop the economy. Such a condition is serious. For example, some local governments tend to be partial to environmental violators and even interfere in enforcing environmental protection laws.[65] In this situation, it is inevitable for basic courts that "have no financial power and sharp swords" to be improperly interfered in by local governments in the acceptance and trial of low-carbon administrative cases, such as "interceding" and "passing a message". Although China is exploring judicial system reform in which personnel and finance-related issues of local courts are centralized at the provincial level, "in local political ecology, it is very easy for courts, the Party committees, and governments to form a tacit agreement: courts, in general, will not touch the bottom line of local Party committees and governments.[66] Therefore, it is not optimistic to expect that centralization at the provincial level can solve local administrative interference in low-carbon administrative litigation." (ii) Climate change and other environmental problems are often cross-regional, which means that addressing climate change needs administrative organs in different administrative regions to cooperate with each other. For example, Chen Tian, Director General of Beijing Municipal Environmental Protection Bureau, said that Beijing, Tianjin, and Hebei need to cooperate to prevent and control air pollution at the National People's Congress (NPC) and the Chinese People's Political Consultative Conference (CPPCC) in Beijing in 2015.[67] That is to say, low-carbon administrative litigation may involve administrative acts of administrative organs in different regions or administrative acts of administrative organs at a level higher than that of basic courts. In such a situation, it is hard to apply the principle of "the plaintiff accommodating the defendant". (iii) Addressing

[65] See Wang Shuguang, *Why Local Governments Lack Motivation to Protect the Environment*, *China Environment News*, April, 17, 2013.

[66] Sang Benqian & Zhao Yaotong, *Pour Cold Water on Judicial Independence*, accessed February 3rd, 2015, http://www.cwzg.cn/html/2014/china_0527/2947.html.

[67] See Li Dandan & Huang Danlu, *Many Provinces will Coordinate to Curb Smog*, *The Beijing News*, January 30th, 2015.

climate change is not only highly professional but involves complicated political and economic factors, which puts forward high requirements for the trial of low-carbon administrative litigation. The judges need to have rich professional knowledge, a great deal of political wisdom, and superb judicial technology. Currently, the judges of most basic courts fall down on the job.

ii. **Tentative plan of jurisdiction rules for low-carbon administrative litigation**

It can be found from the above analysis that it is not appropriate to apply the principle of "the plaintiff accommodating the defendant" to the jurisdiction of low-carbon administrative litigation, and it is not appropriate to put low-carbon administrative litigation under the jurisdiction of basic people's courts. Special rules of jurisdiction that suit the characteristic of low-carbon administrative litigation should be established. The following measures should be considered within the existing legal framework. **(i) Increasing the levels of access to justice.** Due to the complexity of the problems involved in low-carbon administrative litigation and the consideration of avoiding improper local interference, improving such litigation's levels of access to justice should be considered. For this, the US experience in handling climate change-related litigation can be referred to. For example, the court first taking jurisdiction of the Massachusetts Case was not a state court or a common court but the Court of Appeals for the District of Columbia Circuit. In Chinese legal system, the court taking jurisdiction of low-carbon administrative litigation should be a court of a higher administrative level than that of the sued administrative organ, and the court should at least be an intermediate people's court. According to the *Administrative Litigation Law*, the cases whose levels of access to justice can be increased should be "significant and complicated administrative cases in the concerned jurisdiction to be heard at first instance". Therefore, when specifically handling such special jurisdiction in practice, it should be made clear what administrative suits are complicated and significant. It is not realistic and scientific to separately list them all. Taking in consideration of the features of environmental issues, the following indicators can be used to judge whether a case meeting the requirement of being "significant and complicated" and whose level of access to justice can be increased. First, administrative acts that involve the low-carbon and environmental protection interests of unspecified groups of people; Second, an administrative act that is jointly decided on by more than one administrative organ; Third, an administrative act of a government at above-county level; Fourth, low-carbon-related objective litigation is involved; Fifth, administrative acts that involve disputes related to global climate change. **(ii) Special jurisdiction.** In recent years, environmental incidents and conflicts have frequently occurred and the number of environmental administrative disputes has been growing year by year.[68] In such a situation, an attempt can be made to establish

[68] From 2002 to 2011, courts across China accepted 118,779 various types of criminals, civil and administrative environment cases of first instance relating to environment and concluded 116,687 cases, of which 15,749 were administrative environmental cases of first instance and 15,722 were concluded. See Yuan Chunxiang, *Aanalysis of environmental Cases heard by Courts across the country from 2002 to 2011*, *Legal Information*, no. 12 (2012).

circuit environmental courts or establish special environmental tribunals in people's courts above-intermediate level to specially take jurisdiction of low-carbon administrative litigation in a certain area (also including relevant civil litigation and criminal litigation). In the existing legal system, there is sufficient legal basis to do so. It is stipulated in Article 2 of the *Organization law of the people's Court of the People's Republic of China* (hereinafter the *Organization law of the people's Court*) that "military courts and other special people's courts" can be established to exercise judicial power. The word "other" undoubtedly provides room of authority for establishing special courts. Due to the pressing need for trialing an increasing number of environmental cases, the state can establish special environment courts through the statutory procedure.[69] And now a batch of basic courts have implemented pilot programs of establishing environmental tribunals according to the provisions of Article 19 of the *Organization law of the people's Court.*[70] **(iii) Centralized jurisdiction.** A system for relatively centralizing jurisdiction of administrative cases should be established with judicial control and administrative control over one same area separated. The purpose is to avoid various judicial interference and increase the impartiality and credibility of trials. Although there is a tendency of gradual increase of administrative disputes in the field of low-carbon development and environmental protection, environmental administrative suits are not evenly distributed in different places due to different economic structures and social conditions. Some courts have no case to hear. Some courts are too busy to hear cases. Such a situation will become more and more obvious when it comes to administrative litigation related to low-carbon development and the environment. The allocation of judicial resources can be optimized if some courts that have many environmental cases to hear and have rich experience in trials are appointed to take centralized jurisdiction of environment-related administrative cases.

(IV) Selection of Review Methods in Low-carbon Administrative Litigation

After the types of litigation and jurisdiction rules have been made clear, investigation of a sued administrative act depends on the application of the specific review method. Review method is a general term for the judicial principles and technologies on which a people's court conducts judicial review of an administrative act. Applicable review methods such as review of legality, rationality review, and preventive review should be selected in low-carbon administrative litigation.

i. Review of legality

Review of legality is a basic review method in administrative litigation. In a broad sense, review of legality includes: (i) as far as an ordinary administrative act is

---

[69] See Article 19 of the *Organization law of the people's Court of the People's Republic of China.*

[70] Cai Shouqiu, *Conception of Establishing Environmental Courts, Oriental Law*, no. 5 (2009). For example, Shakou District People's Court established a circuit tribunal for environmental protection (in Environmental Protection Sub-bureau of Shahekou District) in Dalian, Liaoning Province in 2004; Chiping County People' Court established a circuit court for environmental protection in Liaocheng, Shandong Province in 2006; Jianye District people's court in Nanjing established a circuit court (in Jianye District Environmental Protection Bureau) in 2008.

concerned, the legality of the administrative entity, whether the act is ultra vires, whether the statutory procedure is followed, and whether the content is legal should be reviewed. (ii) as far as an administrative omission is involved, whether the statutory obligation of acting is breached should be reviewed; (iii) as far as administrative discretion is concerned, whether the scope of the discretionary power is exceeded should be reviewed.[71] In this paragraph, the meaning of law as contained in the term legality includes laws, administrative regulations, and local regulations and rules. Other regulatory documents can become applicable for a people's court only when they do not contradict the legislation of upper levels.

Specifically, review of legality can apply to the following circumstances in low-carbon administrative litigation: **(i) a low-carbon-related procedural illegal act.** When legislation requires that a certain administrative procedure of an administrative organ should be low-carbon and convenient for the people, the administrative organ should try to choose such a convenient and fast procedure to reduce carbon emission by the administrative entity and administrative counterparts in the administrative procedure. Otherwise, the statutory procedure related to low-carbon development shall be deemed to have been breached. **(ii) Low-carbon related content violation.** low-carbon-related content violation means the content of an administrative act fails to meet the low-carbon criteria stipulated in existing legislation. It is stipulated in Article 18 of the *Energy Conservation Regulations for State-funded Institutions* that a government act of procurement,[72] if not in compliance with the state catalog of energy-efficient products, is a content violation. **(iii) Low-carbon related administrative omission.** The low-carbon related omission refers to the administrative organ's inaction in fulfilling or not fully fulfilling the low-carbon duty stipulated in the legislation. Currently there are at least two categories of acts are administrative omission. The first category of acts are acts of failing to fulfill the obligation of disclosing environmental information. For example, the *Measures for the Publicity of Environmental Information (for Trial Implementation)* issued by the Ministry of Environmental Protection require that the government should proactively disclose 17 types of environmental information such as environmental quality status and environmental protection planning. A violation of such an obligation is a low-carbon-related violation that concerns administrative omission. The second category of acts are acts of failing to fulfill regulating obligation. For example, it is stipulated in Article 91 of the *Regulations of Beijing Municipality on Atmospheric Pollution Prevention and Control* that the competent administrative body of environmental protection and other relevant competent administrative body should be held liable legally if they "fail to investigate and punish according to law after receiving reports from citizens about acts that pollute the atmospheric environment".

---

[71] See Xie Zhiyong, *On Standard of Review for Administrative Litigation*, doctoral thesis, China University of Political Science and Law, 2003.

[72] See Article 18 of the *Energy Conservation Regulations for State-funded Institutions*.

ii. **Rationality review**

Since climate change is a professional issue that is regulated by policies. It is impossible to stipulate every detail of the administrative acts addressing climate change through legislation. It is often the case that there are gaps in the regulations and room for discretion for which decisions need to be made by administrative organs based on their professional judgment. In such a situation, the need to examine administrative acts addressing climate change cannot be fully met only depending on legality examination. Therefore, it is necessary to introduce a rationality review taking in consideration the characteristics of low-carbon administration litigation. In the *Administrative Litigation Law* passed in 1989, courts can only examine the rationality of the discretionary power in inflicting administrative penalties. It was stipulated in Article 70 of the *Administrative Litigation Law* adopted in 2014 that courts can examine "obviously improper" acts and hence expanded the scope of rationality review to ordinary administrative discretion, which provides a normative basis for examining the rationality of administrative acts in the field of low-carbon development and environmental protection. However, detailed criteria are still needed to be set to assess what is "obviously inappropriate" in combination with the characteristics of low-carbon-related administrative litigation. For example, in the case of using discretionary power in imposing administrative penalties, "obvious inappropriateness" is shown by two situations that is, obvious unfairness and abuse of power. The following methods can be considered to examine the rationality of an administrative act in low-carbon-related administrative litigation.

(i) Fit-for-legal-purpose review. This means when there are no clear legal provisions about the result of a relevant administrative discretionary act, the result of the relevant administrative discretionary act should be consistent with the value orientation of low-carbon development and environmental protection, including reducing energy consumption as much as possible, reducing environmental pollution, reducing the emission of greenhouse gases and other low-carbon purposes, and should at least not contradict with the purpose of low-carbon development and environmental protection. Otherwise, the relevant administrative discretionary act will be presumed to be unreasonable or inappropriate. Fit-for-legal-purpose review is a review method that applies to any sued administrative discretionary act in low-carbon administrative litigation. In the Massachusetts Case, the Supreme Court of the United States reviewed whether EPA could use administrative discretion as the reason for its refusal to regulating greenhouse gas emissions, this, to some extent, was a fit for purpose review. The court thought that EPA had authority under the *Clean Air Act* to judge the harmful consequences of newly added air pollutants. The court also thought the discretion power of EPA was originally intended to make its enforcement of the law more flexibly and hence the purpose of promulgating the law could be better realized, that is, improving air quality and improving public health. However, EPA used the discretionary power as the reason for its failure to regulate the emission of greenhouse emissions, which was obviously against the original intention of granting it such power. Therefore, the discretionary act of EPA was not reasonable. Further, administrative licensing can also be used as an example to analyze the applicability of the criterion of fitting for legal purpose. In addition, the criterion of fitting for legal purpose also requires that administrative acts in low-carbon field and environmental protection should not consider irrelevant factors. In the Massachusetts Case, EPA did not take regulating measures due to consideration of the President's foreign policy. The Supreme Court thought that such a factor was an irrelevant factor and consideration of such a factor was not in line with the legislative purpose of the *Clean Air Act*. Taking the aforesaid case as an example where a Shijiazhuang citizen sued the Ecology and Environment Bureau. If the Ecology and Environment Bureau decided not to curb greenhouse gas emissions due to consideration of the only purpose of protecting local economic development. The consideration of such a factor was also consideration of an irrelevant factor. Such administrative act was also not fit-for-the-legal-purpose of low-carbon development and environmental protection.

(ii) Proportionality review. In some cases, aside from the orientated value of low-carbon development and environmental protection, an administrative act may also be oriented at a multiple of other values. The values may be conflicting and competing. For example, when making administrative planning, a government needs to consider environmental protection and also needs to consider that rapid socio-economic development should be guaranteed. The many values of an administrative act are also its important aims. When reviewing the rationality of the administrative act, one should not only use the aforesaid criterion of low-carbon development and environmental protection. Instead, one needs to measure the benefits of the different values, that is, the different aims, and reasonably balance the relationship between the different values. One shouldn't emphasize other aims and sacrifice the value of low-carbon development and environmental protection, or partially pursue low-carbon development and environmental protection and neglect the protection of other important values. A balance of interests does not mean equally treating different administrative aims or values indiscriminately, but reasonably choose some values and abandon other values. This will cause a situation where certain benefits and aims are highlighted and emphasized and other benefits and aims also considered. Generally speaking, when this proportionality criterion is used, the principle of proportionality stricto sensu should be used as the bottom line, that is, judged from the well-being of society as a whole, the derogation of other benefits brought by the balance of interest should be much less than the benefit brought to low-carbon development and environmental protection. Therefore, generally, this helps to maximize social benefit. However, it must be emphasized that such a trade-off can only reduce particular benefits to some extent and cannot, in fact, form a non-balanced result with a certain benefit sacrificed or deprived.

Take a specific case as an example to show the use of the criterion of proportionality.

Case 1: there have been many administrative disputes about choosing the locations of waste incinerators or waste-to-energy plants in many places in recent years. Worrying about being harmed by dioxin and other harmful chemical substances generated by burning wastes, residents near potential locations of waste incinerators object to the building of such waste incinerators in their neighborhoods. This is called Not In My Backyard Theory (NIMBY).[73] Choosing the location of a waste incinerator is an act of environmental administrative planning. If the residents that have interests in the act initiate low-carbon administrative litigation before a court, the court can use the criterion of proportionality to examine whether the selection of the location is reasonable. It is not difficult to find that the act has two purposes. The first is protecting the environment. Currently, the ability of cities to carry wastes is overwhelmed. Using waste incineration technology is inevitable in treating urban environment pollution. If waste incineration is used to generate power, this can reduce waste volume by 95% and can also increase energy supply.[74] The second purpose is public health. Dioxin, fly ashes, malodorous gases, and other harmful substances (including malodorous substances) that may be generated by waste incineration threaten public health and peace of life, and secondary air pollutants are also generated.[75] Therefore, when the government chooses a place to build waste incinerators and waste-to-energy plants, impacts on the health of the surrounding residents must also be considered. Choosing a location for waste incineration, on the one hand, can address the situation of "waste siege", which concerns low-carbon environmental benefits, and, on the other hand, concerns the health of surrounding residents. Brought to face the dual purposes of the choice, the administrative organ should properly balance the associated benefits in its administrative planning. Otherwise, the choice will be unreasonable. Specifically, the court should analyze whether the benefits brought by the building of the waste incinerator, that is, taking away of wastes and generating power, far exceed the health hazards and other property loss of surrounding citizens caused by this (for example, the building of the waste incinerator may cause a falling of their house prices of the surrounding residents), which can be endured by a normal person and has been provided proper administrative compensation. Otherwise, the administrative act is unreasonable.

Case 2: Since 2013, the regulating measure of restricting road traffic of private cars has been implemented in many large and medium-sized cities to curb the haze that blanketed the whole country. However, as estimated by environmental scholars, the environmental benefits brought by restricting the road traffic of private cars are only worth RMB 57 million in China while the extra costs that need to be borne by citizens are as high as 4 billion Chinese yuan.[76] In such a case, if consumers or car owners initiate an administrative action against the government for its measure to restrict road traffic of private cars, the court should carefully consider the case. The government demands the people to bear billions of economic costs for the sake of

---

[73] Refer to Wen Jing, *Most of the Locations Chosen for Garbage Disposal Incinerators are Alleged to be Unreasonable*, *Beijing Times*, June 9th, 2011.

[74] Wang Kezhen & DI Wu Yan Yan, *Realize Energy Conservation and Emission Reduction through Promoting Waste-to-Energy Plant*, *Shenzhen Special Zone Daily*, November 4th, 2008.

[75] See Mao Da, *Open Air Waste Incineration is Harmful*, *Environment and Life*, no. 6 (2012).

[76] Zhou Wei, *Foreign Less Proves Restricting Traffic of Cars is Useless for Controlling Smog*, Netease, accessed January 27th, 2015, http://news.163.com/14/1201/10/ACCELHN60014JHT.html.

just thousands of millions of environmental benefits. Has the sued administrative act properly balanced the relationship between the value of low-carbon environmental protection and private property interest in such a situation?

iii. **Preventive review**

Preventive review is also called hazard review. It was raised by Professor Xie Zhiyong earlier in China.[77] Preventive review fits well the characteristics of low-carbon administrative litigation because the hazards brought by climate change and environmental pollution are not certain and some harmful consequences are irreversible, which requires that the state take preventive measures and shift the boundaries of interventions. In low-carbon administrative litigation, at least there are two types of preventive review:

(i) Preventive review of common administrative acts. Preventive review of common administrative acts mainly applies to administrative acts that are used to address potential climate change and risks of environmental pollution. It is a review system similar to temporary right protection, which is manifested in the form of ruling to suspend the implementation of the sued administrative acts. In low-carbon litigation, what is protected by preventive review is not limited to the environmental rights of a natural person, and the ecological environment system itself is also included. The biggest difference between preventive review and the above-mentioned legality review and reasonableness review is that legality review and reasonableness review are final legal comments on administrative acts and the aim is to stop disputes, and preventive review is a legal comment on a process and is intended to prevent significant environmental harm that is hard to reverse from occurring in the course of litigation before the ruling of administrative litigation is made or takes effect. For example, in the case related to "the Third Phase Development Zone of the Central Taiwan Science Park" in Taiwan province of China in 2011, Taibei "High Administrative Court" ruled that implementation of the administrative permit granted to the Central Taiwan Science Park should be stopped on the grounds that background value of health hazard to the people was not estimated and local environment had been polluted due to absence of second-stage environmental impact assessment in granting of the permit by the "Environmental Protection Administration". The preventive review method used in low-carbon administrative litigation was reflected in the ruling

[77] Preventive review means "a court orders an administrative organ to temporarily delay the performance of certain administrative acts before the acts are done or order the administrative organ to perform it statutory obligations if the administrative organ fails (or its refusal or omission) to perform its statutory obligations, and at the same time, review the administrative organ's administrative act. This is done according to the power of the court or based on the application of an administrative counterpart. The purpose is to prevent significant or irreparable harm." See Xie Zhiyong, *On Standard of Review for Administrative Litigation*, doctoral thesis, China University of Political Science and Law, 2003, p. 81.

to some extent.[78] Specifically, the following are the steps involved in a preventive review. First, reviewing whether the low-carbon risks of an administrative act that is being sued are irreversible. Some consequences are irreversible and may lead to permanent loss of the ecosystem. If the low-carbon risks of an administrative act that is being sued are irreversible, implementation of the sued administrative act should be stopped before the court's decision is made. By doing this can the court's decision have a chance to be effectively implemented. Second, reviewing whether the risk consequences of the sued administrative act are obvious and eminent. Although the low-carbon risk consequences caused by some administrative acts are irreversible, the court still needs proof to prove their urgency before they can be decided to be stopped during the litigation process instead of being granted remedies after the end of the litigation process. That is to say, there should be poof to prove that such risk consequences are obvious and eminent, and if the administrative acts are not stopped in time, the effective opportunity available for granting remedies will have been lost when the court's decisions are made about the administrative acts.

(ii) Preventive review of administrative omissions. Since there are scientific disputes and uncertainty about climate change and environmental pollution, some administrative organs refuse to regulate climate change and environmental pollution on the grounds of a lack of sufficient factual basis. This is also one of the core legal issues in the Massachusetts Case. Therefore, it is necessary for the court to examine whether the acts or omissions of a sued administrative organ have significant risks of causing climate change and environmental pollution. If the acts or omissions of the sued administrative organ indeed have significant risks of causing climate change and environmental pollution, the court will rule that the administrative organ loses the case and order it to take corresponding preventive measures. In terms of specific operation, the following standards can be used in a preventive review related to omissions of an administrative organ. (i) severity standard. That is, climate change and environmental pollution caused by omissions of administrative organs involve major public interests and are serious. Currently, China is in a period when the incidence of environmental accidents is high, but the resources available for enforcing laws by administrative organs are limited. It is undoubtedly inefficient to require preventive regulating measures to be taken against low-carbon risks that are even trivial. In order to optimize the allocation of law enforcement resources, a preventive review can only require administrative organs to regulate climate change risks that involve major public interest and have serious consequences, for example, smog. (ii) Causation standard. Unless the administrative organ that is being sued has sufficient scientific evidence to prove that its omissions cannot cause relevant climate change and environmental pollution otherwise, the administrative organ has not violated the law. (ii) Efficiency standard. That is, the court should judge whether the administrative organ can effectively prevent the relevant climate change and environmental

[78] See Lin Yumei, *High Administrative Court 's Mode of Reviewing the Protection of Temporary Rights—Comment on the Relevant Ruling Ordering Suspension of the Implementation and Development of Central Taiwan Science Park's Phase 3 Development Zone, The Law Monthly*, no. 10 (2010).

pollution risk by adopting the corresponding administrative regulation act. If the administrative regulation act plays a substantial positive effect on the prevention of climate change and environmental pollution risk, the administrative omission is illegal.

(V) Application of Adjudication Forms of Low-carbon Administrative Litigation

The effectiveness of the remedies of low-carbon administrative litigation is eventually realized through administrative adjudication. It is stipulated in the *Administrative Litigation Law* adopted in 2014 that the forms of first instance judgment of administrative litigation include rejecting the plaintiff's claims, canceling administrative acts, performing statutory duties within a specified period, changing administrative acts that confirm the amounts, providing administrative compensation and confirming an administrative act to be illegal or ineffective and other forms of judgment addition. Aside from administrative judgments, the court can also make corresponding judicial recommendations to supplement and support the judgments. Such suggestions can also be deemed as a type of flexible judgement. The core of low-carbon litigation is providing effective remedies and solving disputes, which determines that the effect of the forms of judgment that simply confirming violations or ineffectiveness is not good because no actual response is given to the plaintiff's claims. Changing a judgment only applies to an administrative act that wrongly confirms an amount, so such a form of judgment is also not consistent with the goal of low-carbon administrative litigation. From the perspective of the remedial function of low-carbon administrative litigation, emphasis should be put on the following forms of judgment.

i. Cancellation of a judgment

Based on the application of the aforesaid reviewing methods, the decision of canceling a judgment can be made in low-carbon administrative litigation at least in the following circumstances. First, an administrative act fails to meet low-carbon and environmental protection requirement that is required to meet according to the law. For example, according to Article 7 of the *Law of the People's Republic of China on Environmental Impact Assessments*, local governments should, in the process of working out the relevant programs concerning the use of land and the programs for construction, development and utilization, conduct environmental impact assessments. If relevant administrative programs are worked out without appropriate environmental impact assessments, the court can decide to cancel the programs based thereon. Second, an administrative act is obviously against the goal of administrative management related to low-carbon development and environmental protection. For example, a local government neglected the requirement of environmental protection and the health of the residents and launched a heavy polluting project due to the consideration of developing the local economy. Even if such an act is not prohibited in legislation, the court can also decide to cancel the project based on fit-for-legal-purpose review. Third, an administrative act fails to appropriately balance the low-carbon interests and other interests. For example, in the above-mentioned case concerning choosing where to build a waste incinerator, although the government's original intention of building a waste incinerator is consistent with the low-carbon environmental protection purpose, the administrative act will be unreasonable due to inappropriate balancing of the interests if the incinerator seriously jeopardizes the health of nearby residents due to its location or no appropriate compensation is paid to nearby residents for the harm brought to them.

ii. **Execution of judgement**

Execution of judgement mainly applies to omissions of a defendant to regulate climate change and environmental pollution. However, we should realize that administrative regulating of climate change and environmental pollution has the nature of a public policy and involves complicated entanglement of political and economic interests, and reasonable decisions need to be made only by administrative organs based on their professional judgement. In such a case, undoubtedly a court needs to be very cautious to enter a judgment that orders an administrative organ to perform the regulating obligation within a specified period. Generally, only when an administrative organ fails to perform its duties related to low-carbon development and environmental protection that are stipulated by laws can a court enter a judgment order the administrative organ to perform the duties. For example, an administrative organ fails to perform the statutory obligation of disclosing environmental information and fails to perform the duty of administrative enforcement of environmental law. With regard to other administrative omissions of an administrative organ that do not have a clear legal basis, the court before which the case is brought should exercise restraint and respond to the claims of the plaintiff through making judicial recommendations to the administrative organ that is being sued.

iii. **Judicial recommendations**

Based on the theoretical categorization of judicial recommendations by scholars, judicial recommendations can be categorized into four types[79]: judicial recommendations that guide adjudication, judicial recommendations that are supplemental to adjudication, judicial recommendations that prevent conflict, and judicial recommendations that implement adjudication. In low-carbon administrative litigation, the use of recommendations that are supplemental to adjudication could be focused on. The recommendations refer to the ones that should be proposed by a court to an administrative organ as a beneficial supplement to the content of an administrative judgment. With regard to the issues that are not appropriate to be mandatorily required through an administrative judgment but are closely related to the point at issue, the court can enter a judgment and at the same time make such recommendations. Specifically, a court can make judicial suggestions, which are supplemental to the judgment, to the administrate organ in a low-carbon and environmental protection administrative litigation in the following circumstances. (i) The plaintiff also requires the court to examine whether the regulatory document an administrative act meets low-carbon and environmental protection standard, or demands the administrative

[79] See Zhang Zhiyuan, *Study on Judicial Recommendation System of China's Administrative litigation*, *Studies in Law and Business*, no. 2 (2011).

organ to promulgate administrative legislation about climate change and environmental pollution. Such abstract administrative act often involves complicated public interests. In principle, the court needs to respect the legislative choice of the administrative organ. However, as a response to the plaintiff's claims, if the court thinks that relevant regulatory document contradicts with the policy of the state related to climate change and environmental protection, or particular climate change and environmental pollution make it necessary to promulgate administrative legislation, the court can still raise judicial recommendations of abolishing or modifying the relevant regulatory document and studying and preparing relevant administrative legislation to the defendant and the governing body of the defendant at a higher level. (ii) If, in a legality review, the court finds that the act of a sued administrative organ is against low-carbon standard in terms of procedure and content (for example, the administrative organ adopts a procedure that is too complicated and causes a public disturbance, or the administrative organ fails to follow state laws about saving energy by public institutions), but it is meaningless to order the administrative organ to cancel or do the act since the administrative act has already been done, the court may suggest the administrative organ making rectification, demand it to follow the low-carbon standard stipulated by laws, and send a copy of the suggestion to the competent governing body of the administrative organ, suggesting the governing body of the administrative organ deciding whether or not to start accountability investigation. (iii) The plaintiff demands the defendant to implement regulating measures about climate change and environmental protection. However, the relevant administrative act involves professional knowledge and policy consideration and it is not appropriate for the court to replace the political judgment with a judicial judgment. In this case, the court itself may make suggestions to the administrative organ. For example, in the above-mentioned case where a citizen in Shijiazhuang sued the local Ecology and Environment Bureau for its failure to perform the duty of regulating smog, it was not appropriate for the court to utter opinions about treating such cross-region environmental pollution due to its scope of practice. However, the court could urge the local environmental protection bureau to actively perform its duties and enhance law enforcement by making judicial suggestions to the local environmental protection bureau.

iv. **Administrative compensation or indemnity**

In some low-carbon administrative suits where administrative organs are demanded to perform their environmental duties, the eventual realization of the remedies of the plaintiff depends on addressing climate change and effective treatment of environmental pollution. However, this is a long process where actions of the administrative organs are needed and cannot be accomplished at one stroke. In such a situation, the court can't rule that the administrative organs should treat environmental pollution or perform their duties within a specified period. In fact, this cannot be accomplished. However, in the meantime, the environmental harm sustained by the plaintiff and other groups of people vulnerable to climate change is real. Let's take the increasingly severe smog as an example, the people are direct victims and can be harmed in any aspect, such as their property rights, right to health, and environmental rights.

For example, in terms of property rights, restrictions on the traffic of cars are implemented in many big cities due to smog. This undoubtedly is a legal restriction on people's right to use their private property; in terms of the right to health, the harm caused by outdoor air pollution to the people is obvious[80]; in terms of environmental rights, smog derogates the right of many citizens to breathe clean air and do outdoor exercise, and, to some extent, and cause aesthetic injury to them for making them unable to appreciate the beauty of nature. With regard to such types of injuries that have been suffered by the plaintiff and relevant vulnerable groups thereto but are not attributable to a certain polluter, the state as the representative of sovereignty should assume guaranteed and supplementary legal responsibilities. In this kind of situation when the court is unable to specify a period for the performance of duties, the court can decide on certain administrative compensation or indemnity to appropriately respond to the plaintiff's claims for remedies. For example, in low-carbon administrative litigation related to smog control, the court can enter a judgment that requires the government to issue anti-smog masks to citizens and lessen the cost of air purifiers with a subsidy to compensate the public for the environmental harm sustained by them during the period of smog control. These types of judgments, on the one hand, reasonably make up for the loss of interest suffered by the plaintiff and other groups that are vulnerable to climate change, and, on the other hand, play a beneficial role in externally pressuring administrative organs to actively perform their regulating obligation and improve the regulating effect.

[80] It is pointed out in *The Global Burden of Disease (GBD) 2010* that "public health risks caused by outdoor air pollution cause more than 3.2 million people around the world die prematurely every year, killing more than 76 million people." Cited from anonymous author, *A study of Tsinghua University Show 3.2 million People Die Prematurely from Air Pollution Every Year*, *China Business News*, April 2nd, 2013.

References

Chinese Literature

1. X. Guodong, *Interpretation of Basic Principles of Civil Law—Overcoming the Limitations of Statutory Law* (China University of Political Science and Law Press, 1992)
2. Z. Youyong, *A Study of the Basic Principles of Administrative Law* (Wuhan University Press, 2005)
3. J. Chen, *Metatheory of Basic Principles of Administrative Law* (Intellectual Property Publishing House, 2009)
4. L. Haocai, B. Honghai (eds.), *New Perspectives on Administrative Law* (The Commercial Press, 2011)
5. D. Chen, *Monograph of Environmental Law's Principle* (Law Press China, 2008)
6. D. Guo, *Research on the Legal System Responding to Climate Change* (Law Press China, 2010)
7. X. Yang (ed.), *Study on the Relationship between Sustainable Development and Administrative Law* (Law Press China, 2008)
8. G. Liu (compiled), *Risk Regulation: Theory and Practice in Germany* (Law Press China, 2012)
9. R. Cao (ed.), *The Global Warming: Economics, Politics and Moral of Climate Change* (Social Science Academic Press, 2010)
10. W. Wang, *Addressing the Climate Change: the EU Experience* (China Environmental Science Press, 2011)
11. W. Wang, G. Zheng (eds.), *Green Book of Climate Change: annual Report on Actions to Address Climate Change (2013)* (Social Sciences Academic Press, 2013)
12. B. Lin (ed.), *Urban Carbon Management Toolkits* (Science Press, 2011)
13. H. Zhou, *Low-carbon Economics* (China Machine Press, 2012)
14. J. Zhang et al., *Selected US Environment Law Enforcement Cases* (China Environmental Science Press, 2013)
15. S. Breyer, *Breaking the Vicious Circle: Toward Effective Risk Regulation*, translated by Song Hualin (Law Press China, U.S., 2009)
16. M. Olson, *The Logic of Collective Action*, translated by Chen Yu et al., (Truth & Wisdom Press, Joint Publishing, Shanghai Renmin Press, U.S., 2011)
17. A. Giddens, *The Politics of Climate Change*, Translated by Cao Rongxiang (Social Sciences Academic Press, UK, 2009)
18. D.J.C. Shearman, J.W. Smith, *The Climate Change Challenge and the Failure of Democracy (Politics and the Environment)*, translated by Wu Xishen and Li Nan (Social Sciences Academic Press, Australia, 2009)

S. Fang and B. Tan, *On the Administrative Law of China in Addressing Climate Change*,
https://doi.org/10.1007/978-981-19-7705-3

19. C. Azar, *Solving the Climate Challenge*, translated by Du Heng and Du Ke (Social Sciences Academic Press, Sweden, 2012)
20. N. Stern, *The Global Deal: climate Change and the Creation of a New Era of Progress and Prosperity* translated by Wu Xishen (Social Sciences Academic Press, UK, 2011)
21. Garnaut, *Garnaut Climate Change Review*, translated by Zhang Zheng (Social Sciences Academic Press, Australia, 2009)
22. Erhan Si Harald Vail et al., *Renditions Future Climate Crisis: the Social Reality of Climate Change and Ultimate Concern* (Chinese Edition), translated by Jin Haimin (Central Compilation & Translation Press, Germany, 2013)
23. Georg Nolte, *General Principles of German and European Administrative Law—A Comparison in Historical Perspective*, translated by Yu'An, *Administrative Law Review*, vol. 2 (Germany, 1994)
24. C. Zhongmo, *Principle of Legal Reservation*, *The Taiwan Law Review*, vol. 98 (2003)
25. L. Zhongmei, *Roadmap for Law Construction of China's Ecological Rule, Social Sciences in China*, vol. 5 (2013)
26. Y. Li, W. Cao, *Breaking the Deadlock: A New Interpretation of "Common but Differentiated Responsibilities, Journal of Renmin University of China"*, vol. 2 (2013)
27. K. Jian, *The Evolution of the Polluter-Pays Principle, Law Review*, vol. 6 (2010)
28. H. Aibao, *Innovation of Ecological Administration and Construction of Low-Carbon Government, Social Science Research*, vol. 5 (2010)
29. H. Wang, *Administrative Interpretation and Judicial Review in Climate Change Litigation, Journal of East China University of Political Science and Law*, vol. 2 (2012)

Foreign Literature

1. B. Schwarts, H.W.R. Wade, *Legal Control of Government: Administrative Law in Britain and the United States* (Clarendon Press, 1972)
2. J. Schwartz, *European Administrative Law* (Sweet& Maxwell, 1992)
3. F. Yamin, J. Depledge, *The International Climate Change Regime: a Guide to Rules, Institutions and Procedures* (Cambridge University Press, 2004)
4. J. Balkan. *The Corporation, The Pathological Pursuit of Power and Profit* (Constable & Robinson Ltd, 2004)
5. A. Bradbrook, R. Lyster, R.L. Ottinger, X. Wang (eds.), *The Law of Energy for Sustainable Development* (Cambridge University Press, 2005)
6. C.R. Sunstein, *Law of Fear* (Cambridge University Press, 2005)
7. M. Peeters, K. Deketelaere (ed.), *EU Climate Change Policy* (Edward Elgar Publishing Inc., 2006)
8. R. Lyster, A. Bradbrook, *Energy Law and the Environment* (Cambridge University Press, 2006)
9. Bonyhady, P. Christoff, *Climate Law in Australia* (The Federation Press, 2007)
10. J. Robinson, J. Barton, C. Doswell, *Climate Change Law: emissions Trading in the EU and the UK* (Cameron May, 2007)
11. T.L. Friedman, *Hot, Flat and Crowed—Why We Need a Green Revolution and How It Can Renew America, Farrar* (Straus and Giroux, 2008)
12. German Advisory Council of Global Change, *World in Transition: Climate Change as a Security Risk* (Earthscan Publications Ltd., 2008)
13. C. Wold, D. Hunter, M. Powers, *Climate Change and the Law* (Matthew Bender & Co, 2009)
14. H. Selin, S.D., VanDeveer (eds.), *Changing Climates in North American Politics Institutions, Policymaking, and Multilevel Governance* (The MIT Press, 2009)

Postscript

This book is revised on the basis of the final results of the key project of the National Social Science Fund "Research on Issues of Administrative Law in Response to Climate Change" (Project Approval No.: 11AFX011).

It has become an international consensus to positively cope with the global climate change crisis impacting the future survival of human beings. While the government plays an irreplaceable role of leadership and organization in the process, and it has become a new administrative function of the contemporary government to lead the whole society in realizing the low-carbon economic transition and the low-carbon society construction. As an important department law to adjust and regulate the functions & responsibilities and administrative acts of administrative organs, the administrative law shall change and develop to adapt to the requirements of the times. Currently, the humanities and social sciences disciplines including politics, sociology, public administration, economics and environmental law have made extensively research on this problem, while the administrative jurisprudence are obviously lagging. The research purpose of this book is to explore and answer the vital role of the administrative law in coping with climate changes as well as the development of theories and systems of the administrative law, so as to comply with the new requirements proposed on the government administration in the low-carbon era.

I conducted the overall design of the research ideas, contents, structures and main viewpoints in this book, and wrote this book together with Tan Binglin who is also the main author after we made a research and discussion. In the process of writing and revision, Teng Xinyao, deputy secretary-general of the Standing Committee of Hubei Provincial People's Congress, provided important opinions and shared a lot of information. My doctoral and postgraduate students also participated in the task. Ge Wei assisted in revising the part of Introduction; Sun Caihua wrote the first draft of partial contents of the first chapter; Xu Wei wrote the first draft of the fifth chapter; Zhu Maolei wrote the first draft of the tenth chapter; Yi Wei wrote the first draft of partial contents of the seventh chapter; and Yu Xiaoxu wrote the first draft of partial contents of the eleventh chapter. Yang Ru, Chen Meng and Liu Yaping et al. made great efforts in collating and proofreading the manuscript. Finally, I finalized the manuscript after revision in a unified manner.

S. Fang and B. Tan, *On the Administrative Law of China in Addressing Climate Change*,
https://doi.org/10.1007/978-981-19-7705-3

It is a pioneering research in the administrative jurisprudence and a very meaningful task to construct the theories and systems of the administrative law adapting to the climate changes. We hope that the exploration of this book can be beneficial to the development of the theories of the administrative law as well as the construction of related systems. As the research on the role of the administrative law in coping with climate changes is only at the preliminary stage in the whole circle of administrative jurisprudence, the academic achievements available for reference are rare, and this topic involves a wide range of aspects, complex problems and broad contents. This book only selects some key problems to elaborate and doesn't cover the whole field of the administrative law. At the same time, our research is only preliminary, and the demonstration of some contents is not in-depth, and could have been more precise, which needs to be improved in the subsequent further research work. Criticism and suggestions are welcome for this book.

Shirong Fang
March 2016
By the South Lake of Wuhan

The manufacturer's authorised representative in the EU is Springer Nature Customer Service Centre GmbH, Europaplatz 3, 69115 Heidelberg, Germany. If you have any concerns regarding our products, please contact ProductSafety@springernature.com

Printed and bound by CPI Group (UK) Ltd, Croydon, CR0 4YY
30/09/2026
02225244-0010